Orangeism; its origin and history

Ogle Robert Gowan

ORANGEISM;

ITS

ORIGIN AND HISTORY.

By OGLE ROBERT GOWAN, Esquire,

LATE LIEUT. COLONEL COMMANDING THE "QUEEN'S ROYAL BORDERERS," AND MEMBER
OF THE LEGISLATIVE ASSEMBLY OF CANADA.

TORONTO:

PRINTED BY LOVELL AND GIBSON, YONGE STREET.

1859.

TO THE

HONORABLE JOHN HILLYARD CAMERON, Q.C.,

Most Worshipful Grand Master of British America,

AND

SOVEREIGN OF THE ROYAL SCARLET,

FORMERLY

M.P FOR THE CITY OF TORONTO, AND MEMBER OF THE EXECUTIVE COUNCIL OF CANADA,
ETC. ETC. ETC.

MY DEAR SIR AND BROTHER,

It is known to you that I have, for some time, contemplated writing the History of our Loyal and Protestant Order—its origin—the circumstances which gave it birth—its introduction into the various Countries to which it has extended—when, and by whom, introduced—the chief events in which its members have taken a part—a defence of the principles by which they have been governed—and an exposition of the present state and extent of the Society throughout the Empire

I purpose, this day, placing the manuscript of the first number in the Printer's hands; and in doing so, I am not aware that I can perform a duty more agreeable to my own feelings, or more acceptable to the Brethren at large, than that of dedicating the work to one, who has been so recently elevated by them, to the high and most honorable post of Grand Master and Sovereign of the Order, on the Continent of America

Be pleased then, my dear Sir, to accept this tribute of respect, not less as being due to the elevated office you have been called upon to fill, than to the acknowledged ability as a Statesman, and the private integrity as a Citizen, which you are known to possess

That Orangemen, united in Brotherly affection, and following in the footsteps of the honored Sires from whom they have descended, may long continue to guard our Anglo-Canadian Institutions, and to hand down Religious and Civil Liberty unimpaired to posterity, is the ardent prayer of,

My dear Sir and Brother,

Yours faithfully,

OGLE R. GOWAN.

NEBO LODGE, TORONTO,
13th July, 1859

ORANGEISM:

ITS

ORIGIN AND HISTORY.

CHAPTER I

The Carbonari, Thugs and Ribbonmen—Orangemen alone have no Written History—Diversity of opinion as to the Origin of Orangeism—Necessity of tracing it to its Source—Man's Natural State as distinguished from his Civilized—Introduction of Christianity—Its effects upon the Human Mind—Ecclesiastical Intolerance—Clerical "Money Changers"—Sacerdotal Imposture and its Effects—Persecution of the early Christian Reformers—Their Hiding Places.

SHOULD an Italian be asked for information as to the origin, the nature, or the extent of the *Carbonari*, he could refer the inquirer to the history of that Society, for the information he sought   Should a native of Bengal or Benares, be questioned about the *Thugs* of India, he could turn to some one of the numerous descriptions that have been given of them by tourists, elementary writers, and others.   Should an Irishman be interrogated relative to the *Ribbon* Society of his native land, he might supply a "History of Captain Rock," to satisfy the thirst for information which the inquiry indicated.   There are few Societies, — however brief their existence, or limited their numbers, or vile their objects,—that have not had their history placed before the world . some in volumes of ponderous size; some in the reviews, magazines, and periodicals of the day . and others through the less durable and more transient literature of the newspaper press.   The Orange Institution is, perhaps, the only organized body that can lay claim to the same importance—that can count within its ranks the same number of members—or that has existed for a period so lengthened—or extended over fields so wide and varied, of which no history has ever been given   The question being once put to a number of Orangemen,—" When and where did your Society originate, and what

was the immediate cause of its origin ?" Out of fourteen respectable and
intelligent members present, only four ventured to offer a reply. The
first said,—"It was brought over to Ireland by King William, who
planted it at the Boyne, on the first day of July (O.S), 1690." The
second alleged,—"It was formed at the Battle of the Diamond, in the
County of Armagh, Ireland, about the year 1795 " The third would give
all the honor to the "Bandon True Blues," into whose good town—

> "Turk, Jew, or Atheist
> Might enter—but not a Papist "

While the fourth claimed the credit for the renowned " 'Prentice Boys,"
who closed the gates of the far-famed "Maiden City" against the armies
of King James If Orangemen were thus puzzled to account for the origin
of their Society, and if such varieties in opinion existed, even amongst the
initiated, how must the outward world be lost in amazement, when they
seek some annals—some historical information—touching the origin, the
progress, or the extent of an Association so extensively known, yet so little
understood ? To supply a defect so glaring, is the object of the present
work

It has been said by Lord Bolingbroke, that the erring nature of man,
and the constant state of affairs in this mutable world, often preclude
the reception of materials from tradition, and even sometimes from history, but such as are generally uncertain in the one case, and perhaps
greatly altered from the original in the other   Where the early ages of
a Society may be enveloped in some obscurity, though curiosity may prompt
to trace it through many of its intricate and diversified meanderings, yet
the abilities of the author will be misspent, and the time of the reader
wasted, who may rely on such recitations as upon authentic history
Though it is true that tradition may be often fabulous, and even history
occasionally uncertain, yet good ore may be sometimes dug out of the
traditions of mankind , and the writings of uncertain authors, when
patiently sifted, may oftentimes produce pure mineral   It is an old maxim
with philosophers, that it is difficult to understand things thoroughly, unless their origin can be traced, and their principles of action clearly defined.
The closer, then, that the beginning of the Orange Society can be investigated, and the great and momentous circumstances out of which it
grew understood, the more must the mind be informed, the reader gratified,
and the work itself rendered complete

Man, in his savage or natural state, is but an animal, endowed with a
higher order of intelligence than any other created being. Improve his
intellect by draughts from the fountains of knowledge, divested of all sense
of religion—of all ideas of a Creator and a Saviour—and the savage
nature is but imbued with a keener appetite for natural propensities, and

with greater facilities for indulging in them. Improve the intellectual tastes, and, with the improvement, combine a knowledge of the Redeemer, and inculcate the precepts which are taught by Christianity, and man, as he advances in literary and scientific knowledge, will also advance in civilization, and be restored to a state of social and moral goodness, which was forfeited by the fall of his first parents. The religion which the meek and lowly Saviour planted upon earth, was not a system of persecution, but of love. it was not designed to embitter the mind of man by the clouds of bigotry, but to enlighten and chasten it by the sunshine of liberality. As religion extended, and men cast aside their pagan gods to follow Him who proclaimed "Peace on earth and goodwill to men," many who professed not only to be His disciples, but the special ambassadors deputed by Him to dispense His religion and its ordinances to others, lost sight of the humility of the Master, in the pride and ambition of the Minister The meekness and charity which the Saviour inculcated by His words and exemplified in His life, soon gave place to the pride of ecclesiastical power , and the precepts of Him, who declared His kingdom was "not of this world," were soon set aside by the Clerical "money changers," who sold "Indulgencies" for lucre, and who granted "Dispensations" for value received ! The inventions of "Purgatorial" fires to purify from sin, and the necessity of "Masses" to give relief to suffering souls from such fires, soon filled the Clerical exchequers, by drafts from the purses of relatives and friends of deceased persons, who could by such means only enlist the sympathies of the Priesthood, and secure the continued repetition of "Masses !" Nor was the ecclesiastical influence extended to the regions of "Purgatory" alone, for even in this material world, the mind of man was brought into subjection to Clerical domination, and "Auricular Confession," with "Pecuniary Atonement" placed in the scale, to balance the "Holy Oil" of "Priestly absolution !" The teachings of Christ were set aside, and the teachings of the Church set up as the standard of Faith It mattered little what the written word of the Redeemer might have inculcated , it was only what the Church promulgated that could be received. Christ was only allowed to speak through an "Infallible Church;" and His "Vicar on earth," as "the only head" of that Church, pronounced ex cathedra, all dogmas of faith, all rules of practice, and all other things necessary to salvation

Had this system of sacerdotal imposture and clerical tyranny, been confined to the affirmative qualities of religion alone, it might have been borne by some and laughed at by the remainder of mankind ; but when it assumed the garb of negative authority, and forbid men, under penalties in this life as well as in the next, from reading and expounding God's Word, except as read and expounded by the Church—when it denied the right of private judgment, and bound all men to pin their opinions upon clerical sleeves—when, instead of elevating man, it sought to reduce him to the level of the ass or the ox, by compelling him to do the bidding of his Ecclesiastical masters, then, indeed, was the cord drawn too tight, and the intelligence it sought to enthral revolted at the deceptions, and rebelled against the tyrants who were enriched by the frauds.

Ecclesiastical authority had, however, become firmly seated , and as protests upon protests were sent forth against the sacerdotal impositions, martyrdom upon martyrdom followed, till the Tiber and the Po, the Danube and the Rhine, the Seine and the Rhone, ran red with the blood of the bold men who would not submit to such tyranny ; and the Alps and the Apennines, the Carpathians and the Pyrenees, wafted their cries, from their loftiest peaks to the fair fields, which spread carpets of beauty and loveliness at their feet.   To detail the sufferings of the martyrs to religious freedom, would be to fill volumes.   Scarcely a kingdom or a state, from the sands watered by the Euxine in the east, to the rocks washed by the Atlantic in the west, in which the dogma was not enforced, that Christ died only for one creed, and that to promulgate any other was a heresy—meriting death in this life, and eternal punishment in the life to come.

The mind of man, not being the gift of man, but of a higher Power,—no terrors threatened, no pains imposed, and no manacles framed, could bind the conscience or fetter the understanding   Hypocrites might be made by thousands, and whole hecatombs sent to the dungeons of an "Inquisition," or to the tortures of a rack, a gibbet, or a stake , still the mind would find an outlet—still would the rays of light and freedom pour their refulgence upon the mental body, and draw forth that expression of spring-like resuscitation and life which alarmed the icy hand of the clerical executioner, and forced those who dreaded his vengeance to the forests of Bohemia, Moravia, and France ; to the caves of the Alps and the Apennines, and the secluded spots of the Western Isles.

CHAPTER II.

The first Secret Association of Christians and its Sign—Claims set up by Odd Fellows and by Freemasons—Bayle's Statement—The first Password of the early associated Protestants—How divided and given—The Martyrs' Dells— The "Smithfield Fires" in England—The "Forty-one Massacre" in Ireland —Henry the Eighth—Edward the Sixth—"Bloody Queen Mary"—"Glorious Queen Bess"—James the First and the "Gunpowder Plot"—National Prayer and Humiliation—Romish Hopes and Romish Plots, to favor Mary Queen of Scots

THE earliest record of the formation of a Secret Christian Association for mutual protection and defence against physical danger, runs back as far as the reign of the Emperor Nero, A.D. 55. When that cruel tyrant —whose name will be held in execration while the world lasts—ruled at Rome, the early Christians formed themselves into an Association for mutual encouragement. They called themselves "FELLOW CITIZENS;" and it is said, they recognized one another by putting the open hand upon the mouth, as emblematic of their condition, which was to be *silent*. Some publications of recent date, to wit, the "*Odd Fellow*," and the "*Odd Fellows' Record*," claim this Association as the origin of the Odd Fellows' Society; and they add that, twenty-four years afterwards, namely, in the year 79, the Emperor Titus presented the members with a warrant of the Imperial protection, engraven on a plate of gold, accompanied by a number of the emblems in use at the present day. The Society of Freemasons goes farther back than the Christian era, and assert their existence, as a body, as ancient as the days of Solomon's Temple But with what justice either association can lay claim—the one to the Emperor Titus or the other to King Hiram—is a mystery not less profound to the initiated, than to the outward world

Bayle, who, both as a philosopher and a historian, was able and learned, has left on record, that the early associated Protestants of Germany were in the habit of making use of the fourth verse of the 68th Psalm, as a *password* to recognize each other. The words are,—"Sing unto God, sing praises to His name extol Him that rideth upon the heavens by His name JAH, and rejoice before Him" That persons suffering the persecutions of the early Protestants, should find "secret signs and passwords" a powerful means of protection and security, is natural to suppose. Secret tokens of mutual recognition are not only serviceable for the purposes of friendly intercourse and recommendation, but are a *sine qua non* to the security of parties encompassed by enemies. To this day, no army is left without its outposts and piquets, and no citadel without guards and sentries, nor is a piquet sent, or a sentry posted, without a "watchword" or "countersign." What the "watchword" was and is to the army, the "password" was and is, to persecuted Protestants.

The early history of the European Reformers—the men who carried the freedom, truths, and beauties of the Christian religion triumphant—who, with a singleness of purpose and nobleness of resolution, which nought but conscious rectitude could inspire, failed not to bear witness against the usurpations and corruptions of Rome—show that they were but small armies, often reduced by the unrelenting tyranny of the foe to mere piquets and sentinels. In such a state, they surely needed to keep "watch and ward;" to have their "watchword" and its "countersign"—their "sign and pass."

German tradition hands down the statement that the "password" mentioned by Bayle was thus given : When one of the persecuted met a stranger, his first exclamation was *Jo !* (J.) which was then used as an expression of surprise. If the person addressed was not a Protestant, he would make the response usual in the country to such a salutation ; but if a Protestor against the corruptions of Rome, he would reply *eh !* (A.) as if he did not understand, or had not heard the word first spoken. To such a response the first interrogator would close with the words, "*Each* (H) *of us understand*" These three letters, J, A, H, it will be seen, is not only taken from the fourth verse of the 68th Psalm, as mentioned by the historian, but, when united, form the very name therein given to Him, to whom they are commanded to "sing praises" and to "extol." When the words, "Each of us understand," were uttered, the whole "password" would be pronounced, and both would then join in the words of the Psalm, as in a song of praise and thanksgiving, thus

First person—"Sing unto God,
Second ditto—"Sing praises to His name,
First ditto —"Extol Him that rideth upon the heavens,
Second ditto—"By His name JAH,
First ditto —"And rejoice before Him."

This ended the whole ceremony of introduction, password and recognition : and, it will be seen, was clearly scriptural in its origin, full of gratitude in its expression, and intended for mutual protection and security in its design and purpose.

To these causes, and to this period, is clearly traceable the origin of secret signs and passwords If they had prior existence, no traces of them remain of record ; but, at this early date, they evidently were in use.

This occurred as already mentioned, on the Continent of Europe. There indeed the first lights of the Protestant Reformation dawned, and there the first of the "noble army of martyrs" left their witness against Rome, written in the testimony of their blood To that "noble army," then, is to be ascribed the honour of the "secret sign and pass," and to the country that gave them birth, and to the secluded but sacred dells, and caves, and forests, which afforded them shelter and hiding places "from the face of their enemies," is to be given the credit of originating that mysterious system, which, in every age down to the present, has been used by christian men, as tokens of mutual recognition and friendship, to foster brotherhood and fraternity on the one hand, and to guard against wickedness and imposture on the other.

While the proceedings already alluded to were passing on the Continent of Europe · while all Germany and Italy. from the Carpathians to the Alps, were convulsed by the cries of the early Reformers, the British Isles were not silent.   There, too, were to be found many "good men and true," to stand up for the rights of conscience, and to deny that Christ's atonement was for a mere creed, or a party, or a faction, but freely offered, "without money and without price," for the Jew and the Gentile world.   Nor was the example of the Continental "signs and passwords," as used by the first Christian Reformers, lost upon their Island brethren.   The latter like the former, had to pass through the "fiery ordeal" of persecution, they were destined to have their "Smithfield fires" in England, their "Forty-one massacres" in Ireland, and to surrender their lives, in every form of torture and cruelty, for the Truth   Like causes produced like results, and similar persecutions pointed to similar precautions.

In England, however, the church having cast off the yoke of Rome under the authority of the State, and the Eighth Henry having placed himself at its head, there was, during the remainder of his reign, full freedom given to the Reformers. He was called to the throne in the year 1509, and ended his reign in 1547, being succeeded by Edward the Sixth, who died very young, in the year 1553   The successor of Edward was Mary, usually called "Bloody Queen Mary " Her reign commenced in 1553, and ended in 1558   It was relentless and cruel, stained with every barbarity, and to this day is remembered by all Protestants as "the bloody reign." Mary was succeeded in 1558 by her half-sister, Elizabeth, usually styled "Glorious Queen Bess " During her reign, the reformation of the church of England, its full separation from the see of Rome, the purity of its doctrines, and the moral and exemplary conduct of its ministers were encouraged,—Protestantism was fostered,—the great "Spanish Armada" was defeated,—"Trinity College," Dublin, (the famous Irish University,) was founded,—the great "East India Company," that now rules our empire from the Coast of Coromandel to the Himmaleh Mountains, and from the crags of Afghanistan to the swamps of Birmah, was established,—in truth, her reign was

"Great, glorious, and free."

Elizabeth was followed in the year 1603 by James the First, who also favored the Protestant reformation. It was on the fifth of November, in the year 1605, and during the reign of this monarch that the famous "Gunpowder Plot" occurred

As a solemn "Form of Prayer and Thanksgiving" has been appointed by the church and nation, "to be used yearly upon the fifth of November, " for the happy deliverance of King James the First, and the three estates " of England, from the most traitorous and blood-intended massacre by " gunpowder, and also for the happy arrival of His Majesty King William " upon that day, for the deliverance of the church and nation,"—and as every minister is commanded by the church, by the laws of the realm, and in the Book of Common Prayer "to give warning to his parishioners, pub- " licly in the church, at Morning Prayer, the Sunday before, for the due " observance of the said day,—and after Morning Prayer or Preaching, " upon the said fifth of November, to read publicly, distinctly and plainly, " the Act of Parliament made in the third year of the reign of King James " the First, for the observance of it," it may be proper to take a hasty glance at the said "bloody-intended massacre by gunpowder."

The present generation cannot better answer the occasion of remembrance and gratitude, than by looking back on the train of that horrid "conspiracy," and tracing the footsteps of a good Providence in the discovery and disap- pointment of it Matters of fact are the best lessons of instruction , and, at this time particularly, the public especially need the recollection of the past in order the better to discern the present and to prepare for the future.

In the beginning of Queen Elizabeth's reign, the Romish interest in England was much propped up by the prospect of Mary Queen of Scots, who was a Roman Catholic, succeeding to the throne They saw a single life only between them and the regal power, and patience and connivance were resorted to as the most effectual to secure Mary's succession But when, by the flight of Mary from Scotland, they were deprived of all hope of relief from that quarter, they became impatient of delay, and from thenceforth every year was distinguished by some new design to transfer the crown to a Romish possessor A few of the most prominent of these "plots" may be here enumerated

First Mary Queen of Scots, came into England in the tenth year of the reign of Elizabeth, that is to say, in May, 1568 In that year, two "plots" were discovered one to marry Mary, as the next heir to the throne, to the Romish Duke of Norfolk

Second. The second was carried on by Robert Ridolph, a Florentine, employed by the Pope as a factor in London, to animate the Roman Catholics of England to an insurrection.

Third In the following year (1569,) there were three "plots" discovered : one against Cecil, Queen Elizabeth's Prime Minister

Fourth Murray's conspiracy with Norfolk.

Fifth The Rebellion in the North.

Sixth. The next ensuing year (1570,) developed three other Romish "plots" The most important of these, as exercising the most extensive influence, as laying a base for all future conspiracies, and to which, as Sir Edward Coke stated in his celebrated speech, they may be all imputed, was the bull of Pope *Pius Quintus* against the Queen to deprive her of her dominions.

Seventh. The rebellion attempted in Norfolk.

Eighth. The rebellion in Ireland

Ninth. The year 1571 ushered in two "plots". one, the conspiracy of the Duke of Norfolk, to set at liberty Mary Queen of Scots, and

Tenth Dr John Story's, to encourage the Popish and cruel Duke of Alva to invade England

Eleventh. The next year brought with it two other Romish "plots". one, the conspiracy of Barns and Mather to kill certain Lords of the Council, and deliver Norfolk out of the tower ; and, the other, the

Twelfth. The rebellion in Connaught, in Ireland

.hirteenth The year 1573 brought the "plot" of the Bishop of Ross, and also great commotions with the Romanists of Ireland.

Fourteenth. 1574 exhibited the negotiations of Sir Francis Englefield for the Popish interest in the court of Spain.

Fifteenth The year 1575 was distinguished by the Border tumults, and the Scots invasion

Sixteenth. The next year (1576,) ushered in the secret tampering of Meredith, a Romish priest of Lancashire, and also great tumults in Ireland

Seventeenth 1577 disclosed the "plot," to marry Mary Queen of Scots to Don John of Austria, as also the Treason of the Rev Cuthbert Maine, a Romish Priest.

Eighteenth. In 1578 was the design of the Pope and the Spaniard to invade England ; and also the English fugitive, Stukely's expedition

Nineteenth. The year 1579 brought out the Rebellion in Ireland, raised by the Pope and the Spaniard

Twentieth. The year 1580 was distinguished by the arrival in England of Father Parsons and Campian, with Bulls from the Pope

Twenty-first In the following year, 1581, several Jesuits and Priests were executed for Treason

Twenty-second In 1582 there were several other Romish Priests and Jesuits executed for Treason

Twenty-third The year 1583 brought with it the " plot " of Somerville to murder the Queen.

Twenty-fourth The next year introduced the Treason of Thockmorton, &c., and of Mendoza, the Spanish Ambassador

Twenty-fifth. 1585 brought out the " plot " of William Parry against the life of the Queen

Twenty-sixth. In the year 1586 was the "plot" of John Savage to kill the Queen ; also the " plot " of Ballard, &c , and also of Babington, &c , upon which was the trial and death of Mary Queen of Scots

So long then as it was expected that Mary Queen of Scots would shortly come to the Throne, so long were the Roman Catholic subjects of Elizabeth quiet and reserved , but so soon as the hope of Mary faded away, so soon did their " plots " burst forth, and not a single year passed over without dragging some of them to light   The multitude of the " plots " at length created a necessity for more stringent legislation in order to do justice to the safety of the nation and the preservation of its Monarch and established institutions

---

CHAPTER III.

Romish intrigues to catch James the First—Romish opinions upon Fidelity to Protestant Governments—Rome the true source of the " Gunpowder Plot"—Atrocity of the Scheme—Charles the First—Oliver and Richard Cromwell—Charles the Second—James the Second—Views of Tillotson and Locke.

James the First, after his mother's death, was continually solicited to change his religion and become a Roman Catholic , and numerous indications were made to him, that his right of succession depended upon his conforming to the Romish Church   When he refused compliance with the suggestions made to him, his hereditary right was declared void for heresy To set up a Pretender, Father Parsons wrote his " *Doleman,*" or Conference about the next succession to the Crown of England , to exclude the Scots title, and assert that of the Spanish Infanta   Cardinal Farnese was also encouraged by him to set up his pretensions to the English Crown, as appears clearly from the letters of Cardinal D'Ossat to the French Court. *Vide* fol. 1620, pages 545, 546, and 552.   The Jesuits wrote books against the O⸺ ⸺ ⸺ ⸺ ⸺ ⸺ the Pope himself sent over his mandates to inhibit the admission of any successor who would not swear to defend the Roman Church and Faith. On this declaration of the Pope, as "the Vicar of Christ upon earth," Catesby, the great projector of "the Gunpowder Plot," openly declared, that he thought the will of His Holiness to be sufficiently signified in these Bulls; for if it were by them lawful to refuse or repel an Heretical Prince, it was just as lawful to cast one out. Garnett, who was the chief manager of the "Plot," stated in effect the same thing. In 1601 Pope Clement the Eighth sent over to Garnett, Provincial of the Jesuits in England, two Briefs or Bulls, one to the Clergy, *Dilectis Filiis Archipresbytero and Religio Clero Anglicano.* The other to the Nobility, *Dilectis Filiis Principibus and Nobilibus Catholicis Anglicanis Et quandocunque contigerit misseram illam fœminam ex hac vita excedere—non admitterent quantumcunque Propinquitate Sanguinis niterentur, nisi ejusmodi essent, qui fidem Catholicam non modo tolerarent, sed omni ope ac Studio promoverent, and more majorum jurejurando se id præstituros suscperent.* The full import of these important documents may be judged correctly by reading Sir Edward Coke's speech at the trial of the "Gunpowder" traitors. In Cardinal D'Ossat's letter to Henry the Fourth of France, dated at Rome the 26th of November, 1601, after an account of the Pope's setting up two Pretenders to the Crown of England, the *Duke of Parma,* and his brother, *Cardinal Farnese,* who should marry the Lady Arabella, he tells his Majesty, that His Holiness has lately sent to his Nuncio in the Low Countries, three Briefs to keep in his own hands, till he should know the Queen of England was dead, and then to send them into England; one to the Ecclesiastics, another to the Nobility, and the other to the Third Estate; by which the Three Estates of the Realm of England were admonished and exhorted by His Holiness to unite together in order to receive a Catholic King, whom His Holiness should name to them, for the restoration of the Catholic Religion, &c &c. The same Cardinal D'Ossat, in a letter to Monsieur Villeroy, dated at Rome the 30th of Dec., 1602, declared it to be the resolution of that Court, that the King of Scotland should succeed in England if he would turn Catholic, otherwise it must be some other person. And Father Watson, in his "*Quodlibets,*" imprinted in 1602, confesses that the Jesuit Parsons made the observation, that they would all follow and prosecute the King of Scot's title if he would become a Catholic; but if he would not they would all die, one after another, against him, (*Vide,* page 150.) It will easily be seen, then, that the true source of the "Gunpowder Plot" was at Rome—that the Head of the Church sanctioned the bloody design—that fanatical zeal for that Church urged on the preperators—and that the merciful decrees of an overruling Providence alone saved the nation from the meditated destruction. Whatever noise, therefore, may be now made by a party, or by partizans, about loyalty to Hereditary Right, it is plain that the end and aim of all their movements is the good of the Church and obedience to the will of its Ecclesiastical rulers   The Roman Catholic Church never yet asserted the right of a Protestant Heir to any empire or kingdom where Popery obtained a footing.   That Church has ever acted upon the one invariable principle, that every ruler should be for their cause and of their Church.   If this were not so, how could any Church or people hesitate an instant to discountenance a project so infamous as the "Gunpowder Treason ?"

An attempt to murder secretly, even though it was only a private person, and no matter what the pretence for it, is abominated by all mankind. To assassinate a public magistrate is held to be still more horrible ; and justly so, because the latter crime not only includes the former, but also adds to the guilt of taking away human life, contempt for the office and position of the party slain.   Here then is not only the guilt of an attempt at individual murder and individual public and private wrong, but here was a "Plot" of destruction, by treachery and surprise, of the King, the Queen, the Members of the Royal Family, the Nobility, and the whole Commons of England,—in fact, it may be said, the whole nation, so far as it could be struck off by one blow.   Nor can this horrible crime be placed to the account of a few inconsiderate zealots only.   The heads of Orders in the Romish Church were consulted upon, and decreed the lawfulness of it, and there appears every just reason for believing, that it not only received the approbation, but even the benediction of the Pope himself

Charles the First succeeded his Son, James the First, in the year 1625 He entertained the most unconstitutional notions of the Royal Prerogative, and a fierce Civil War set in   Charles being defeated by his Parliament, was taken prisoner, and beheaded in the year 1649.

Oliver Cromwell, or as he was usually called, "the Lord Protector," rose from the lowest estate, to the highest office in the realm.   He reduced Ireland to obedience—zealously supported the Protestant Reformation— caused the English name to be feared and respected abroad—and triumphed over all opposition.   He was said to be "a zealous hypocrite," and in one of his addresses to his Army, originated the somewhat remarkable saying, to this day so common, "put your trust in God my Boys, but keep your "powder dry !"

Richard Cromwell, succeeded his Father, Oliver, in September, 1658 · but in two years, gave way to Charles the Second , who ascended the Throne in 1661.   Like the whole race of the Stuarts, he was an absolute and capricious Monarch   It was during his reign, that Algernon Sydney and Lord William Russell suffered

James the Second, succeeded his Brother, Charles the Second, in 1685. This bigoted and absolute Monarch, was openly reconciled to the Pope . he determined to abolish the Protestant Religion ; and to substitute his own Will for the Constitutional Liberties of the people. LORD MACAULAY says, the Judges were his tools, the Corporations were filled with his creatures, and that his pride rose so high, that he was not the same man. It is impossible to deny, says the same historian, that Roman Catholic casuists of great eminence, wrote in defence of equivocation, of mental reservation, of perjury, and even of assassination. Nor had the writings of this odious school of sophists, been barren of results. The massacre of St. Bartholomew, the murder of the first William of Orange, the murder of Henry the Third of France, the numerous conspiracies which had been formed against the life of Queen Elizabeth, and above all, the "Gunpowder Treason," might be cited, as instances of the undeniably close connection between vicious theory and vicious practice. Everard Digby was a scholar and a gentleman, admitted to have been upright in all ordinary dealings, and strongly impressed with a sense of duty to God , yet was he, with many others of the first Roman Catholics in the Kingdom, deeply concerned in the "Plot," to blow up the King, Lords and Commons In the letters, written in lemon juice, from the Tower to his Wife, and when he was on the brink of eternity, he declared it was incomprehensible to him, how any Roman Catholic could think such a design (the "Gunpowder Plot,") sinful. In fact evidence upon evidence, in every shape and form poured in daily, to show that with the King, James the Second, and his adherents, however fair his and their general character might have been, there was no excess of fraud and cruelty, of which they were not capable, when the supposed safety or honor of the Romish Church were at stake Indeed to such extremes did James push his horrid duplicity and tyranny, and such were the frightful doctrines inculcated by his Romish adherents, that Archbishop Tillotson, whose extreme toleration and liberalism brought down reproach upon himself, declared, in his Sermon before the House of Commons, fifth of November, 1678, that it was the duty of Parliament, to make effectual provison against the propagation of a religion, more mischievous than irreligion itself—a religion which demanded from its followers, services directly opposed to the first principles of morality He added, that Pagans, who had never heard the name of Christ, and who were guided only by the light of nature, were more trustworthy members of civil society, than men who had been formed in the schools of Popish casuists. The celebrated John Locke too, whose judgment and temper, in favor of the utmost stretch of liberality, will not be questioned, was so impressed with the cruelty of the King, and the infamous teaching of his adherents, that in his first letter on Toleration, while he laboured to show, that even the grossest forms of idolatory, ought not to be prohibited under penal restrictions ; yet, that the Church which taught men not to keep faith with those she regarded as Heretics, had no claim to toleration

CHAPTER IV.

*James' ingratitude to the Protestants of England—Louis the Fourteenth of France
—Revocation of the Edict of Nantes—Inhuman Treatment of the Huguenots—
Their Dispersion—Their Settlements in the British Isles—Mr. Crommelin of
Carradore—Description of Lisburn (formerly Lisnegarvey)—Effect of the
Huguenot Persecutions upon the Protestant Mind of Europe—James the Second,
his Deceptions and Cruelty—Summary of his acts of Despotism in England.*

When James attempted to promote the interests of his Church, by
violating the fundamental Laws of his Kingdom, and the solemn promises
he had made in the face of the whole world, it could hardly be doubted,
that the charges which were then brought against the Roman Catholic
religion, would be considered by all Protestants, as fully established.   For
if ever a member of the Romish Church could be expected to keep faith
with Heretics, James the Second might have been expected to have kept
faith with the Clergy of the Established Church   To them he owed his
Crown.   But to their steady opposition to the Bill of Exclusion, he would
never have been the Sovereign of England.   He had over and over again,
and in terms the most solemn and emphatic, acknowledged his deep and
lasting obligations to them, and had vowed, in every form of language, to
maintain to them their just and legal rights.   If he could not be bound by
ties like these, no tie of gratitude, no obligation of honor, no bond of duty,
could bind him   And if the Sovereign of the Nation, under such circumstances, could not be trusted, what subject of the Romish Church could?
James was not supposed to be habitually or constitutionally, of a treacherous
disposition   Indeed he was called by his eulogists, "James the Just."
Not then to the natural characteristics of the man, but to the religious
principles which had been inculcated in him, by his Romish instructors,
are to be attributed the dissembling, the promise-breaking, and the cruel
propensities, by which he was distinguished.

While James was dismissing the Protestant Lord President of his Council, Lord Halifax, struggling to set aside the Test Acts, and openly
violating the Laws, by the organization of new Regiments, officered by
Roman Catholics, Louis the Fourteenth, of France, was busily engaged in
similar struggles of treachery and despotism against his Protestant subjects   The Edict of Nantes was revoked, and then followed innumerable
decrees against the Huguenots.   History records the facts that boys and

girls were torn from their parents, and sent to be educated in Convents—all Protestant Ministers were commanded, either to abjure their religion, or to quit their country within a fortnight—the other professors of the Reformed Faith were forbidden to leave the kingdom, and, in order to prevent them making their escape, the outposts and frontiers were strictly guarded. It was thought that the Flocks, thus separated from the evil Shepherds, would speedily return to the true fold. But in spite of all the vigilance of the Military Police, there was a vast emigration from France. It was calculated that not less than fifty thousand families quitted the kingdom forever. Nor were the Protestant refugees such as a country could well spare. They were generally persons of intelligent minds, of industrious habits, and of austere morals. In the sad catalogue were to be found names eminent in war, in science, in literature, and in art. Some of these Protestant exiles offered their swords to William of Orange, and distinguished themselves by the fury with which they fought against their persecutor. Others avenged themselves by weapons still more formidable, and by means of the Presses of Holland, England, and Germany, inflamed the public mind of Europe against the French Government. A more peaceful class erected Silk Manufactories in the eastern suburb of London. One detachment of emigrants taught the Saxons to make the stuffs and hats of which France, till then, had enjoyed a monopoly. Another, planted the first vines in the neighbourhood of the Cape of Good Hope, and many of them settled in small colonies in various Counties of Ireland, where their descendants remain to this day. Referring to one of those Colonies, the Rev. J. B. Finlay, LL.D., at page 10 of his "IRELAND THE CRADLE OF EUROPEAN LITERATURE," thus speaks: Among the Settlements made by the HUGUENOTS in Ireland, was one at Lisburn, (County of Antrim,) where they commenced the Linen trade, to which they had been brought up. It has ever since been successfully carried on by the inhabitants of that Town, and of Ulster generally; until Irish Linens, by their superior finish, have obtained a world-wide celebrity, being used in all civilized countries. Nearly all the Crowned Heads of Europe are supplied with the produce of the diaper and damask manufactories of Lisburn. The armorial and other devices of each, whether emblematic of rank, or of achievements, are tastefully drawn in the pattern of the work, so that family traditions are handed down to posterity in a style hitherto unknown and unattempted. This flourishing trade is the due result of wise forethought on the part of the British Government, when it received the *Huguenot* exiles who had been driven from their native land by the power of Ecclesiastical ignorance and fanaticism, in 1685. They were given a Patent for conducting the Linen manufacture according to the customs of their own country, and not only that, but the Pastor, whom they brought with them, was supported by an annual grant of £60 a year from the

Treasury, though he did not belong to the Established Church. The virtuous conduct and civilized manners of those worthy people were of great
advantage to the place. Their skill and industry set an example to those
who were engaged in the same business, which soon had the effect of raising the quality of their manufacture to a degree of excellence till then
unknown. The Rev. Samourez Dubourdien was the name of their Pastor,
whose descendants yet remain at Lisburn. Nicholas De Lacherois Crommelin, Esq , of Carradore Castle, (a very old and intimate acquaintance of
the writer,) who had been for nearly thirty years Grand Master of the
Orangemen of the County of Down, is the immediate descendant of Monsier Louis Crommelin, to whom the original Patent was granted by the
British Government. The Town of Lisburn stands on the River Lagan,
on the Mail road from Dublin to Belfast. It is about six miles from the
latter, and about seventy-three from the former. The environs are the most
lovely in "the north country"—indeed the whole surrounding neighbourhood is at once beautiful, ornate, and brilliant. From Lisburn to Belfast
may be said to be one continued chain of plantation beauty. The place
was originally called Linsley Garvin, probably from its founder ; and it
continued to bear that name, in the corrupted form of Lisnegarvey, till
1641. "The battle of Lisnegarvey," is the name of a celebrated Irish air,
well known through all parts of the north of the kingdom. The proprietor
of Linsley Garvin was an O'Neill, of the family of Tyrone. After the forfeiture of the estate, a grant of it was made by Charles the First to Lord
Conway, ancestor to the Marquis of Hertford. It still continues invested
in the same noble family. The tenantry upon the Hertford estates, in the
County of Antrim, are amongst the most prosperous, loyal, and contented
in Ireland

A cry of grief and rage arose from the whole Protestants of Europe at
the treachery and cruelty of the French King, who had broken every tie of
honor and good faith, and turned a savage and licentious soldiery loose
upon an unoffending people, and those people his own subjects

The tidings of the revocation of the Edict of Nantes reached England
about a week before the day to which the Parliament stood adjourned. It
was clear then, to the whole nation, that the spirit of Gardiner and of
Alva was still the spirit of the Romish Church Louis of France was not
inferior to James of England, in generosity and humanity, and was certainly far superior to him in all the abilities and acquirements of a statesman. Louis had, like James, frequently promised to respect the privileges
of his Protestant subjects , yet Louis soon became the persecutor, even to
death, of the Reformed Religion What reason was there then to doubt
that James only waited for an opportunity to follow the example ? He
was already forming, in defiance of the Law, a Military Force, officered
chiefly by Roman Catholics. Was there anything unreasonable in the

apprehension that this newly levied force might be employed to do in England what the French Dragoons had already done in France?

It may not be proper, probably, that this History should be incumbered by detailing the numerous acts of illegal assumption, multiplied duplicity, persecution and cruelty, by which the latter years (from 1685 to 1688,) of the reign of James were distinguished. A brief recital of a few of the most prominent must suffice.

Lord Halifax, his chief and most eloquent Minister, was summarily dismissed, because he would not yield to his Popish designs—In his Speech to both Houses of Parliament, on the 9th of November, James openly announced his determination, to double the Army, and to officer it with men, who were not eligible by law—He openly received an Ambassador and a Nuncio from the Pope, a Dominican Friar named Leyburn, who had just been consecrated by Pope Innocent, as Bishop of *Andrumetum* and Vicar Apostolic in Great Britain, and Ferdinand, Count of Adda, an Italian—Kirke and Jeffreys committed the most cruel butcheries with the Royal sanction—James sullenly reprimanded the House of Commons for their Address—John Coke, Member for Derby, was sent to the Tower, because he uttered the following words in his place in Parliament, " I hope that we are all Englishmen, and that we shall not be frightened from our duty by a few high words," (meaning the King's Speech)—He violently and hastily dismissed Parliament, only allowing ten days for its Session—Charles Fox, Son of Sir Stephen Fox, was dismissed from the Paymaster-ship of the Forces, and Captain James Kendall from the Army, because they dared to vote independently in the House of Commons—Dr. Henry Compton, Bishop of London, and Son of the Earl of Northampton, was deprived of the Deanry of the Chapel Royal, and struck from the list of Privy Councillors, because he declared, in his place in the House of Lords, that in his opinion, the Civil and Ecclesiastical Constitution of the Country, were in danger—Thomas Grey, Earl of Stamford, one of the most illustrious Noblemen of England, was sent to the Tower—Charles Gerard, Lord Gerard of Brandon, eldest Son of the Earl of Macclesfield ; John Hampden, Grand-Son of the great Leader of "the Long Parliament ," and Henry Booth, Lord Delamere, were likewise seized and cast into prison—James took Father Edward Petre, a Jesuit, for his Confessor and Chief Adviser—He sent Richard Palmer, Earl of Castlemaine, (a low degraded Papist, who purchased his title by his wife's dishonor,) on an ostentatious embassy to Rome—A small volume, published on the Continent by John Claude, one of the most eminent of the persecuted Huguenots, describing the sufferings of his co-religionists in France, though written in a foreign tongue, printed at a foreign press, and relating entirely to transactions which had occurred in a foreign country, was, by James' order, seized and burned by the common hangman, before the Royal Exchange—The Archbishop of Canterbury

was notified, that the Clergy of the Established Church, should not presume to preach upon the sufferings of the French Protestants—The voluntary subscriptions raised throughout England, for the relief of the suffering
Huguenots, would not be permitted to be dispensed out to them, unless :
they received the sacrament according to the Church of England ritual— ;
Chief Justice Jones of the Common Pleas, Chief Baron Montague of the ;
Exchequer, and Judges Neville and Charlton, were deprived of their offices,
because they would not override the Law, to meet the King's will—Mr.
Finch, the Solicitor General, first, and afterwards Mr. Sawyer, the Attor
ney General, were both dismissed from office, for the like offence—James
dispensed with the Law, and appointed four Roman Catholics, . Lords .
Powis, Bellasyse, Arundel, and Dover, to his Privy Council—In like manner he issued his Warrants of dispensation in favor of Popish Ecclesiastics,
to fill Protestant Benefices ; Edward Sclater who had two livings, administered the Sacrament to his Parishioners according to the Rites of the
Church of Englad, on Palm Sunday, 1686, and on Easter Sunday, only
seven days after, he was at Mass ! The Royal Dispensation authorised
him to retain his Benefices and their emoluments—Obadiah Walker, an
aged Minister of the Church, and Master of University College, Oxford,
well known at that eminent Seminary, as a man of great learning, threw
off the disguise of Protestantism, and, with some Fellows and Under
Graduates, openly joined Popery ; James issued Warrants of Dispensation,
authorising Walker, and his Apostate Fellows, to hold their offices—The
Rites of the Roman Catholic Church were publicly performed in University
College, Oxford, and a Jesuit quartered there as Chaplain—A Press was
also established in the same College, and under the Royal sanction for the
printing of works favourable to the Romish view of Religion—John Massey,
a Popish Priest, was appointed Dean of Christ's Church, and an Altar was
decked in the same establishment, in which Mass was daily celebrated—
James, in direct defiance of two Acts of Parliament, placed the whole
government of the Church in the hands of seven Commissioners , and if
any one, from the Primate down to the humblest Curate, did, or said
anything distasteful to the Government, he was immediately accused before
this irresponsible pack, interrogated by them, and if contumacious, might
be excommunicated, deprived of all civil rights, and imprisoned for life—
The Rev. Samuel Johnson, for opposing the King's arbitrary proceedings
was imprisoned, and afterwards publicly whipped.

Can the Protestants of England ever forget the " *Glorious and Immortal Memory*" of the man who, under God, relieved their Church and
nation from such a state of vassalage and suffering ?

Thus were matters at this time proceeding in England, when James and
his Jesuit advisers, turned their attention to Scotland.

CHAPTER V

How matters were conducted in Scotland.—A view of the state of things in Ireland —Removal of the Duke of Ormond and appointment of Lord Tyrconnell— Dismissal of Protestants and arming of the Romish peasantry—Lists prepared by the Roman Catholic Priesthood—Removal from office of Lords Clarendon and Rochester—General panic throughout the Protestant Settlements of Ireland, and dreadful persecutions against the " Sassanaghs"—All minds turned to a Deliverer.

In that portion of the Empire called North Britain, William Douglas, Duke of Queensberry, Lord Treasurer of Scotland, was stripped of all his offices, and ordered to remain in Edinburgh, because he would not give way to James' will in Parliament. The Bishop of Dunkeld, who as a Lord of Parliament, had opposed the wishes of the Court, was arbitrarily ejected from his See, and a more pliant successor appointed. All elections of Magistrates and of Town Councils were prohibited, and the King assumed to himself the right of filling up the chief Municipal offices. Royal instructions were issued to the Judges, to treat all the Laws against Papists, as null and void. And as the Representatives for Towns, were found not to yield to the King's pleasure in the Scottish Parliament, he determined to make a revolution in every Burgh in the Kingdom, by a simple mandate from the Crown.

Have not then the Scotch, as well as the English people, reason to bless and praise God, for sending to the shores of Britain, the " *Glorious, Pious and Immortal*" Deliverer of their Nation, from Popish thraldom and Arbitrary power ?

It may be proper now, to cast an eye across the Channel, and to take a glance at the state of affairs at this time in Ireland And here, as has been well remarked by Lord Macaulay, when the historian of this troubled reign turns to Ireland, his task becomes peculiarly difficult and delicate. His steps are on the crust of ashes, beneath which the lava is still glowing At this period, the Roman Catholic of Ireland may be said to have stood upon an equal footing with his Protestant fellow-subject There were no rigorous laws against Popery, as in England and Scotland The Irish Statute Book then contained no enactments, imposing penalties upon Roman Catholics as such Jesuits might walk the streets of Dublin in security, and the Oath of Supremacy not being an essential qualification to office, no person was excluded from office or employment, whom the

Government wished to promote—the Sacramental Test and the Declaration against Transubstantation were unknown ; and both Houses of Parliament were open to persons of any and of every religious denomination

Under such circumstances it was, that James determined to become the aggressor He openly avowed his resolve, of again confiscating, and of again portioning out the soil of half the Island ; and by giving to the aboriginal inhabitants the whole kingdom, then use them as instruments, to assist him in setting up arbitrary government in England. The Duke of Ormond, the greatest in wealth, in rank, and in influence in the kingdom, was removed from the Vice-royalty. Richard Talbot, Earl of Tyrconnel, a Papist, and a most inhuman butcher also, was appointed to the Commandership in Chief of the Troops ; and subsequently as Lord Deputy of the Kingdom Roman Catholics were sworn of the Privy Council, and appointed to all offices, Civil and Military, under the Crown. Royal Orders were issued for their admission into all Chief Municipal offices. Protestant Officers were arbitrarily deprived of their commissions, and Roman Catholics appointed in their stead. Orders were sent from England for arming and drilling the whole native (Roman Catholic) population of the Kingdom ; and every Romish Priest received instructions, to prepare an exact list of all his male parishioners capable of bearing arms, and to forward it to his Bishop. In June, 1686, Tyrconnel passed over to Ireland with enlarged powers from King James, and the day after his arrival at the Castle of Dublin, he announced, that most of the Chief Protestant officers must be dismissed, to make way for Roman Catholics ; and orders were immediately issued to the new officers, that no more men of the Protestant religion, were to be suffered to enlist. Clarendon was dismissed in Ireland, and Rochester in England, (both the brothers-in-law of James) simply because they were Protestants. Fifteen hundred Protestant families fled from the persecutions in Ireland, in the course of a few days. A general panic ran throughout the whole kingdom, and the work of exterminating the whole Protestant population went bravely on. Almost every Privy Councillor, Sheriff, Mayor, Alderman, and Justice of the Peace, was a Celt and a Roman Catholic. The Protestant Lords became a prey and a laughing-stock to their own menials. The houses of the English and Scotch Colonists were burned, and their cattle and other property taken with impunity. The newly-raised rabble, called soldiers, roamed through the country, pillaging, insulting ravishing, maiming , tossing one *"Sassenagh"* (Saxon,) in a blanket, tying up another by the hair and scourging him , and so harassing the English and Protestant population, that in a short period, the whole Island must be in the hands of its Celtic and Romish inhabitants.

Such is a very brief summary of the state of things as they really were in Ireland in 1688 ; and surely that Irish Protestant heart must be cold indeed, that will not remember with grateful pride and admiration the services of that great and good man, who, on the first day of July (O S), 1690, crossed the Boyne, to relieve the nation from a yoke so galling, so oppressive, so cruel, and so sanguinary

It is remarked by Lord Macaulay, (*Vol II page* 125,) that the dismission of the two Brothers, (Lords Clarendon and Rochester,) was a great epoch in the reign of James From that time it was clear, that what he really wanted, was not liberty of conscience for Roman Catholics, but liberty for them to persecute the members of all other Churches. Pretending to abhor Tests, he had himself imposed a Test. He thought it hard, that able and loyal men should be excluded from office because they were Roman Catholics; yet he had turned out of office his own Brothers-in-law, the Viceroy of Ireland (Lord Clarendon), and the Lord Treasurer of England, (Lord Rochester,) whom he admitted to be both able and loyal, solely for being Protestants Upon this point he made no disguise. The cry of the nation soon became general, that the proscription of the whole Protestant population was at hand—that every public functionary must make up his mind, to lose his soul or to lose his place,—that Ireland was on the eve of a second "Forty-one Massacre," and England and Scotland to be visited by a second "St. Bartholomew." Who indeed could hope to stand, where the Hydes (Clarendon and Rochester) had fallen ? They were the Brothers-in-law of the King, the Uncles and natural guardians of his children, his friends from early youth, his steady adherents in adversity and peril, and his obsequious servants since he had been on the Throne. Their sole crime was their religion, and for it alone they had been discarded. In great perturbation men began to look round for help, and soon all eyes were fixed on one, whom a rare concurrence, both of personal qualities and of fortuitous circumstances, pointed out as their "GREAT DELIVERER."

This "GREAT DELIVERER" was William Henry, Prince of Orange and Nassau, afterwards William the Third, King of England, of "*Pious, Glorious and Immortal Memory*" The place which this great man occupied, not only in the history of Great Britain and Ireland, of Holland, France, and Germany, but of mankind at large , and the fact of the great Association, the history of which is being traced in these pages, being called by his name, and the members thereof professing to adhere to his principles and to hold up his example to the world, for the guide and imitation of its inhabitants, justly call for more than a passing glance at the origin of his family, and at the eventful history of his own glorious life and actions.

CHAPTER VI.

William Prince of Orange—His Family, Name and Descent—His Age and Personal Appearance—His Character—His personal Tastes and personal Courage—His Delicate Constitution and strong Impulses—Bentinck and William.

HIS FAMILY, NAME AND DESCENT.

Julius Cæsar, in his first book of Commentaries (De bello Gallico,) says, "one Nasuam (Nassau) with his brother Cimberius, led a body of Germans out of Swabia, and settled with them upon the banks of the Rhine, near Treves." This is as far back in antiquity as we choose to go, to trace the origin of the family of Nassau. For although many legends represent several achievments, as being performed by members of this illustrious Family, at dates still more antiquated; we desire not to occupy our time in relating, or the readers in studying, matters as historical, which rest upon authorities obscure and uncertain, and which, to say the least of them, are of doubtful authenticity.

Upon the very spot of ground mentioned by Cæsar, there is an estate which to this day appertains to the Nassauian Family. The most impartial historians admit, that for over ten centuries this distinguished House has had an uninterrupted succession of the highest dignitaries; and more than six hundred years ago, it had the honor to be graced with the Imperial dignity in the person of Adolphus of Nassau, Emperor of Germany. So that the "*immortal*" hero, whose "*glorious*" achievements fill the pages of many histories, is descended from a long line of illustrious ancestors, whose origin is lost in the most remote antiquity.

William Henry, the third Prince of Orange and Nassau, was the posthumous son of William the second, Prince of Orange, by the Princess Mary, eldest daughter of Charles the First, King of England. He was born on the 4th of November (O S) 1650, but a few days after the death of his father. His early education devolved upon his mother, the Princess Dowager, who died in the month of December, 1660; when the guardianship of the young Prince devolved upon his grandmother, the Princess Emelia de Solms, daughter of John Albert, Count of Solms, one of the most amiable and most accomplished women at that period in Europe. In the month of June, 1670, the young Prince was first introduced to the Council of the States of Holland; and in the month of October following he made his first journey to England, on the 30th of which month he arrived at

Whitehall, where he was most graciously received by His Britannic Majesty. On the 10th of November in that year the Lord Mayor and Sheriffs of London gave a splendid entertainment at Drapers' Hall in honor of the young Prince's visit ; upon which occasion he was presented with the freedom of the City in a gold box The University of Oxford conferred upon him the honorary degree of Doctor of Laws, and the highest honors were paid him by all classes in the kingdom.

Holland was at this period threatened by a most powerful league ; and it was thought that the danger impending must end in her utter ruin The States saw the great storm ready to burst upon them, and from the great promise of the young Prince, invited him—then only in his twenty-second year—to take the command of all their forces by sea and land The Prince, though a youth and possessing a very delicate constitution, was remarkable for sagacity, deep thought, unassuming manners, and a quiet, silent and retiring disposition. He accepted the important command offered him, and immediately joined the army, then encamped near Nieukop. Such was the prudence, discretion, and bravery of the young Prince in this critical campaign, that he not only maintained his ground with inferior numbers, but he compelled the French forces, commanded by the King in person, to retire with great loss, and to abandon the strong works of which he had been in the possession The discretion and valor of the youthful hero shone so conspicuously in this campaign, that his conduct became the theme of admiration of both friends and foes, and immediately after (in 1672) the Prince was publicly proclaimed by the Magistrates, in the Common Hall of Dort, *Stadtholder, Captain General,* and *Admiral* of all their forces by land and sea All the Cities of Holland and Zealand, grateful for their delivery, and thoroughly satisfied of the high promise of bravery and discretion with which he had inspired the public mind, hastened to follow the example of Dort, and the Grand Assembly of all the States presented his Highness with a public instrument, confirming him in the Stadtholdership, with all the dignities and privileges, which his ancestors of glorious memory had enjoyed.

HIS AGE AND PERSONAL APPEARANCE

At the period of the English Revolution (1688), undertaken, and happily, under Providence, carried out, by William Henry, Prince of Orange and Nassau, His Highness was thirty-seven years of age. He acted, however, with as much wisdom and discretion as if he were four score. The skill he displayed in planning, the vigor he exhibited in fitting out, the tact he evinced in the selection of officers, the indomitable personal courage which in every moment of danger marked his career in the execution of his expedition to England, clearly proved the capacity, the vigor, and the serenity of his mind. Difficulties that would have appalled other hearts, and shattered other minds, were borne by him with as much composure as if they were trifles, not sufficient to cast a gloom over or to raise a smile upon the countenance,—they were met with the philosophy of a stoic, the firmness of adamant. · In height, William was about five feet nine inches; a thin slender frame, a weak and sickly constitution, pale cheeks, bearing the furrows of care and sickness, a curved aquiline nose, small keen piercing eyes; thin lips; sullen brow; and a full ample forehead. His whole exterior appeared to be that of a pensive, thoughtful man, one who was not to be over elevated by success, nor daunted or turned from his purposes by reverses and disappointments.

HIS CHARACTER.

Lord Macaulay, the great English historian, says (*Vol. 2, page 126,*) that nature had largely endowed William with the qualities of a great Ruler, and education had developed those qualities in no common degree. With strong natural sense, and rare force of will, he found himself, when first his mind began to open, a fatherless and motherless child; the Chief of a great but depressed and disheartened party, and the Heir to vast and indefinite pretensions, which excited the dread and aversion of the Oligarchy, then supreme in the United Provinces, (Holland) The common people, fondly attached through a century, to his House, indicated whenever they saw him, in a manner not to be mistaken, that they regarded him, as their rightful Head. The able and experienced Ministers of the Republic, mortal enemies of his name, came every day to pay their feigned civilities to him, and to observe the progress of his mind. The first movements of his ambition were carefully watched, every unguarded word uttered by him, was carefully noted down; nor had he near him an Adviser, on whose judgment reliance might be placed He was scarcely fifteen years old, when all the domestics who were attached to his interest, or who enjoyed any share of his confidence, were removed from under his roof by the jealous Government He remonstrated with energy beyond his years; but in vain Vigilant observers saw tears more than once, arise in the eyes of the young State Prisoner. His health, naturally delicate, sank for a time, under the emotions which his desolate situation had produced. Such situations bewilder and unnerve the weak, but call forth all the strength of the strong Surrounded by snares, in which an ordinary youth would have perished, William learned to tread warily and firmly. Long before he reached manhood, he knew how to keep secrets, how to baffle curiosity by dry and guarded answers, how to conceal all passions under the same show of grave tranquility Meanwhile, he made little proficiency in fashionable or literary accomplishments. The manners of the Dutch Nobility of that age, wanted the grace, which was found in the highest perfection, among the gentlemen of France, and which, in an inferior degree, embellished the Court of England ; and his manners were altogether Dutch. Even his countrymen thought him blunt   To foreigners he often seemed churlish. In his intercourse with the world in general, he appeared ignorant, or negligent, of those arts which double the value of a favor; and take away the sting of a refusal.   He was little interested in letters or science The discoveries of Newton and Leibnitz, the poems of Dryden and Boileau, were unknown to him. "Dramatic performances tired him ; and he was glad to turn away from the Stage, and to talk about public affairs, while Orestes was raving, or while Tartuffe was pressing Elvira's hand.   He had indeed some talent for sarcasm , and not seldom employed, quite unconsciously, a natural rhetoric, quaint indeed, but vigorous and original He did not however, in the least affect the character of a wit, or of an orator.   His attention had been confined to those studies, which form strenuous and sagacious men of business.   From a child, he listened with interest, when high questions of alliance, finance, and war, were discussed.   Of geometry, he learned as much as was necessary for the construction of a ravelin, or a hornwork.   Of languages, by the help of a memory singularly powerful, he learned as much as was necessary to enable him to comprehend and answer, without assistance, every thing that was said to him, and every letter which he received.   The Dutch was his own tongue.   He understood Latin, Italian, and Spanish He spoke and wrote French, English, and German, inelegantly, it is true, and inexactly, but fluently and intelligibly. No qualification could be more important to a man, whose life was to be passed in organizing great alliances, and in commanding armies assembled from different countries.

One class of philosophical questions had been forced upon his attention by circumstances, and seems to have interested him more than might have been expected, from his general character.   Among the Protestants of the United Provinces, as amongst the Protestants of the British Isles, there were two great Religious parties, which almost exactly coincided with two great Political parties.   The Chiefs of the Municipal Oligarchy, were Armenians, and were commonly regarded by the multitude, as little better than Papists.   The Princes of the House of Orange, had generally been the patrons of the Calvinistic divinity, and owed no small share of their popularity, to their zeal for the doctrines of election and final perseverance, a zeal not always enlightened by knowledge, or tempered by humanity. William had been carefully instructed from a child, in the theological system to which his Family had been attached, and regarded that system with even more than the partiality, which men generally feel for a hereditary Faith.   He had ruminated on the great enigmas which had been discussed in the Synod of Dort, and had found in the austere and inflexible logic of the Genevese school, something which suited his intellect and his temper. That example of intolerance, indeed, which some of his predecessors had set, he never imitated. For all persecution he felt a fixed aversion, which he avowed, not only where the avowal was obviously politic, but on occasions when it seemed that his interest would have been promoted by dissimulation, or by silence. His theological opinions, however, were even more decided than those of his ancestors The tenet of predestination was the key-stone of his religion. He even declared that if he were to abandon that tenet, he must abandon with it all belief in a Superintending Providence, and must become a mere Epicurean Except in this single instance, all the sap of his vigorous mind, was early drawn away from the speculative to the practical The faculties which are necessary for the conduct of great affairs, ripened in him at a time of life when they have scarcely begun to blossom in ordinary men Since Octavius, the world has seen no such instance of precocious statesmanship. Skilful diplomatists were surprised to hear the weighty observations, which, at seventeen, the Prince made on public affairs; and still more surprised to see the lad, in situations in which he might be expected to betray strong passion, preserve a composure as imperturble as their own At eighteen, he sate among the Fathers of the Commonwealth, grave, discreet and judicious as the oldest among them. At twenty-one, in a day of gloom and terror, he was placed at the Head of the Administration. At twenty-three, he was renowned throughout Europe, as a soldier and a politician. He had put domestic factions under his feet, he was the soul of a mighty Coalition; and he had contended with honor in the field, against some of the greatest Generals of the age.

His personal tastes were those rather of a warrior than of a statesman; but he, like his great grandfather, the silent Prince, who founded the Batavian Commonwealth, occupies a far higher place among statesmen than among warriors The event of battles, indeed, is not an unfailing test of the abilities of a Commander; and it would be peculiarly unjust to apply this test to William, for it was his fortune to be almost always opposed to Captains who were consummate masters of their art, and to troops far superior in discipline to his own If his battles were not those of a great tactician, they enabled him to be called a great man. No disaster could, for one moment, deprive him of his firmness, or of the entire possession of all his faculties His defeats were repaired with such marvellous celerity, that before his enemies had sung the *Te Deum* he was again ready for the conflict; nor did his adverse fortune ever deprive him of the respect and confidence of his soldiers That respect and confidence he owed in no small measure to his personal courage Courage, in the degree which is necessary to carry a soldier, without disgrace, through a campaign, is possessed, or might, under proper training, be acquired by the great majority of men. But courage like that of William is rare indeed. He was proved by every test , by war ; by wounds ; by painful and depressing maladies ; by raging seas , by the imminent and constant risk of assassination—a risk which has shaken very strong nerves—a risk which severely tried even the adamantine fortitude of Cromwell. Yet none could ever discover what that thing was which the Prince of Orange feared. His advisers could with difficulty induce him to take any precaution against the pistols and daggers of conspirators. Old sailors were amazed at the composure which he preserved, amidst roaring breakers, on a perilous coast. In battle his bravery made him conspicuous, even among tens of thousands of brave warriors ; drew forth the generous applause of hostile armies, and was never questioned, even by the injustice of hostile factions. During his first campaigns he exposed himself like a man who sought for death , was always foremost in the charge, and last in the retreat ; fought, sword in hand, in the thickest press, and, with a musket ball in his arm, and the blood streaming over his cuirass, still stood his ground, and waved his hat under the hottest fire. His friends adjured him to take more care of a life invaluable to his country ; and his most illustrious antagonist, the great Condé, remarked, after the bloody day of Seneff, that the Prince of Orange had, in all things, borne himself like an old General, except in exposing himself like a young Soldier. William denied that he was guilty of temerity. It was, he said, from a sense of duty, and on a cool calculation of what the public interest required, that he was always at the post of danger The troops which he commanded had been little used to war, and shrank from a close encounter with the veteran soldiery of France. It was necessary their leader should show them how battles were to be won. And, in truth, more than one day which had seemed hopelessly lost, was retrieved by the hardihood with which he rallied his broken battalions, and cut down, with his own hand, the cowards who set the example of flight. Sometimes, however, it seemed he had a strange pleasure in venturing his person It was remarked his spirits were never so high, and his manners never so gracious and easy, as amidst the tumult and carnage of a battle Even in his pastime he liked the excitement of danger. Cards, Chess, and Bil-liards, gave him no pleasure The Chase was his favorite recreation , and he loved it most when it was most hazardous His leaps were sometimes such, that his nearest friends dare not like to follow him. He seems even to have thought the most hardy field sports of England effeminate, and to have pined, in the great Park of Windsor, for the game which he had been used to drive to bay in the forests of Guelders—Wolves and Wild Boars, and huge Stags, with sixteen antlers.

The audacity of his spirit was the more remarkable, because his physical organization was unusually delicate. From a child he had been weak and sickly. In the prime of manhood his complaints had been aggravated by a severe attack of small pox. He was asthmatic and consumptive. His slender frame was shaken by a constant hoarse cough. · · He could not sleep unless his head was propped by several pillows, and could scarcely draw his breath in any but the purest air   Cruel headaches frequently tortured him . Exertion soon fatigued him   · The physicians constantly kept up the hopes of his enemies, by fixing some date beyond which, if there were anything certain in · medical science, it was impossible his broken constitution could hold out   Yet, through a life which was one long disease, the force of his mind never failed, on any great occasion, to bear up his suffering and languid body.

He was born with violent passions and strong sensibilities , but their strength was not suspected by the world.   From the multitude his .joy · and his grief were hidden by a phlegmatic serenity.   Those who brought · him good news could seldom detect any sign of pleasure.   Those . who saw · him after a defeat, looked in vain for any trace of vexation.   He praised and reprimanded, rewarded and punished with the stern tranquillity of a Mohawk Chief.   But those who knew him well and saw him near, were aware, that under this ice, a fierce fire was constantly burning   It was seldom that anger deprived him of power over himself.   But when he was really enraged, the first outbreak of his passion was terrible   It was indeed scarcely safe to approach him   On these rare occasions, however, as soon as he regained his self-command, he made such ample reparation to those whom he had wronged, as tempted them to wish, that he would go into a fury again.

His affection was as impetuous as his wrath.   Where he loved, he loved with the whole energy of his strong mind   When death separated him from what he loved, the few who witnessed his agonies, trembled for his reason and his life.   To a very small circle of intimate friends, on whose fidelity and secrecy he could absolutely depend, he was a · different man from the reserved and stoical William, whom the multitude supposed to be destitute of human feelings   He was kind, cordial, · open, even convivial and jocose ; would sit at table many hours, and would bear his full share in festive conversation.   Highest in his favour, stood a gentleman of his Household named Bentinck, sprung from a noble Batavian race, and destined to be the founder of one of the great patrician Houses of England. The fidelity of Bentinck had been tried by no common test   It was while the United Provinces were struggling for existence against the French power, that the young Prince, on whom all their hopes were fixed, was seized by the small pox.   The disease had been fatal to many members of his family, and at first, wore in his case, a peculiarly malignant aspect. The public consternation was great.   The streets of the · Hague were crowded from daybreak to sunset, by persons anxiously asking how his Highness was.   At length his complaint took a favourable turn. ' His escape was attributed, partly to his own singular equanimity, and partly to the intrepid and indefatigable friendship of Bentinck From the hands of Bentinck alone, William took food and medicine. By Bentinck alone, William was lifted from his bed and laid down in it. "Whether Bentinck slept or not while I was ill," said William to Temple, with great tenderness, "I know not. But this I know, that through sixteen days and nights, I never once called for anything, but that Bentinck was instantly at my side" Before the faithful servant had entirely performed his task, he had himself caught the contagion. Still, however, he bore up against drowsiness and fever, till his master was pronounced convalescent. Then, at length, Bentinck asked leave to go home. It was time, for his limbs would no longer support him He was in great danger, but recovered, and, as soon as he left his bed, hastened to the Army, where, during many sharp campaigns, he was ever found, as he had been in peril of a different kind, close to William's side.

CHAPTER VII.

Marks of William's affection for Bentinck,—his hatred of English factions, and his attachment to the Dutch—his settled dislike of the French, and his constant efforts to thwart them—his designs to unite the rest of Europe against France.

Such was the origin of a friendship as warm and pure as any ancient or modern history records The descendants of Bentinck, (Dukes of Portland,) still preserve many letters written by William to their Ancestor; and it is not too much to say that, no person who has not studied those letters can form an opinion of the Prince's character He, whom even his admirers generally accounted the most distant and frigid of men, here forgets all distinctions of rank, and pours out all his feelings with the ingenuousness of a school-boy. He imparts without reserve, secrets of the highest moment He explains with perfect simplicity, vast designs, affecting all the Governments of Europe Mingled with his communications on such subjects, are other communications of a very different, but perhaps not of a less interesting kind All his adventures, all his personal feelings, his long runs after enormous stags, his carousals on St Hubert's day, the growth of his plantations, the failure of his melons, the state of his stud, his wish to procure an easy pad nag for his wife, his vexation at learning that one of his Household, after ruining a girl of good family, refused to marry her, his fits of sea sickness, his coughs, his headaches, his devotional moods, his gratitude for the Divine protection after a great escape, his struggles to submit himself to the divine will after a disaster, are described with an amiable garrulity hardly to have been expected from the most discreet and sedate statesman of the age.   Still more remarkable is the careless effusion of his tenderness, and the brotherly interest which he takes in his friend's domestic felicity.   When an heir is born to Bentinck, "He will live, I hope," says William, "to be as good a fellow as you are ; and if I should have a son, our children will love each other, I hope, as we have done."   The original letter, in the Prince's own handwriting, from which the foregoing is an extract, bears date the 3rd of March, 1679.   Through life, he continues to regard the little Bentincks with paternal kindness. He calls them by endearing diminutives ; he takes charge of them in their father's absence, and though vexed at being forced to refuse them any pleasure, will not suffer them to go on a hunting party, where there would be risk of a push from a stag's horn ; or to sit up late at a riotous supper. When their mother is taken ill during her husband's absence, William, in the midst of business of the highest moment, finds time to send off several expresses in one day, with short notes, containing intelligence of her state.   On one occasion, when she is pronounced out of danger, after a severe attack, the Prince breaks out into fervent expressions of gratitude to God.   "I write," he says, "with tears of joy in my eyes."   There is a singular charm in such letters, penned by a man whose irresistible energy and inflexible firmness, extorted the respect of his enemies ; whose cold and ungracious demeanour, repelled the attachment of nearly all his partizans, and whose mind was occupied by gigantic schemes, which have changed the face of the world.

William long observed the contest between the English factions attentively ; but without feeling a strong predilection for either side.   Nor in truth did he ever become, to the end of his life, either Whig or Tory. He wanted that which is the common groundwork of both characters, for he never became an Englishman.   He saved England, it is true, but he never loved her, and he never obtained her love.   To him, she was always a land of exile, visited with reluctance, and quitted with delight.   Even when he rendered to her those services which, at this day, the happy effects are felt, her welfare was not his chief object.   Whatever patriotic feelings he had, was for his native Holland.   There was the stately tomb, where slept the great politician whose blood, whose name, whose temperament, and whose genius, he had inherited.   There the very sound of his title was a spell, which had, through three generations, called forth the affectionate enthusiasm of "boors" (*farmers*) and artizans.   The Dutch language was the language of his nursery.   Among the Dutch gentry he had chosen his early friends.   The amusements, the architecture, the landscape of his native country had taken hold on his heart.   To her he turned with constant fondness from a prouder and fairer rival.   In the gallery of White-

Hall, he pined for the familiar house in the wood, at the Hague ; and never was so happy, as when he could quit the magnificence of Windsor, for his far humbler seat at Loo · During his splendid banishment, it was his consolation to create round him, by building, planting, and digging, a scene which reminded him of the formal piles of red brick, of the long canals, and of the symmetrical flower-beds, amidst which his early life had been passed Yet even his affection for the land of his birth, was subordinate to another feeling, which early became supreme in his soul, which mixed itself with all his passions ; which impelled him to marvellous enterprises ; which supported him when sinking under mortification, pain, sickness and sorrow, which towards the close of his career, seemed during a short time to languish, but which soon broke forth again fiercer than ever, and continued to animate him, even while the prayer for the departing was read at his bedside. That feeling was enmity to France

It is not difficult to trace the progress of the sentiment which gradually possessed itself of William's whole soul When he was little more than a boy his country had been attacked by France, whose King, (Louis,) in ostentatious defiance of justice and public law, had overrun it, had desolated it, had given it up to every excess of rapacity, licentiousness and cruelty. The Dutch had, in dismay, humbled themselves before the Conqueror, and had implored mercy They had been told in reply, that if they desired peace, they must resign their independence, and do annual homage to the House of Bourbon The injured nation, driven to despair, had opened its dykes, and had called in the sea as an ally against the French tyranny It was in the agony of that conflict, when peasants were flying in terror before the invaders, when hundreds of fair gardens and pleasure houses were buried beneath the waves, when the deliberations of the States were interrupted by the fainting and the loud weeping of ancient Senators, who could not bear the thought of surviving the freedom and glory of their native land, that William had been called to the head of affairs For a time it seemed to him that resistance was hopeless He looked round for succor, and looked in vain. Spain was unnerved, Germany distracted, England corrupted. Nothing seemed left to the young Stadtholder but to perish sword in hand, or to be the Æneas of a great emigration, and to create another Holland in countries beyond the reach of the tyranny of France. No obstacle would then remain to check the progress of the House of Bourbon. A few years, and that house might add to its dominions Lorraine and Flanders, Castile and Aragon, Naples and Milan, Mexico and Peru. Louis might wear the Imperial Crown ; might place a Prince of his Family on the Throne of Poland ; might be sole master of Europe, from the Scythian deserts to the Atlantic Ocean ; and of America, from regions north of the Tropic of Cancer to regions south of the Tropic of Capricorn. Such was the prospect which lay before William when first he entered on public life, and which never ceased to haunt him till his latest day. The French Monarchy was to him what the Roman Republic was to Hannibal ; what the Ottoman power was to Scanderbeg ; what the southern domination was to Wallace. Religion gave her sanction to that intense and unquenchable animosity. Hundreds of Calvinistic preachers proclaimed that the same person which had set apart Samson, from the womb, to be the scourge of the Philistine, and which had called Gideon from the threshing floor to smite the Midianite, had raised up William of Orange to be the Champion of all Free Nations, and of all Pure Churches. Nor was this notion without influence in his own mind. To the confidence which the heroic fatalist placed in his high destiny, and in his sacred cause, is to be partly attributed his singular indifference to danger. He had a great work to do, and till it was done nothing could harm him Therefore it was that, in spite of the prognostications of physicians, he recovered from maladies which seemed hopeless—that bands of assassins conspired in vain against his life—that the open skiff to which he trusted himself on a starless night, on a raging ocean, and near a treacherous shore, brought him safe to land —and that on twenty fields of battle the cannon balls passed by him right and left. The ardour and perseverance with which he devoted himself to his mission, have scarcely any parallel in history. Three great coalitions, three long and bloody wars, in which all Europe, from the Vistula to the Western Ocean, was in arms, are to be ascribed to his unconquerable energy. When, in 1678, the States General, disheartened, were desirous of repose, his voice was still against sheathing the sword. If peace was made, it was made only because he could not breathe into other men a spirit as fierce and determined as his own. At the very last moment, in the hope of breaking off the negotiation, which he knew to be all but concluded, he fought one of the most bloody and obstinate battles of that age

The feeling with which William regarded France, explains the whole of his policy towards England His public spirit was a European public spirit. The chief object of his care was not the British Isles, not even his native Holland, which he loved so much, but the great community of Nations, threatened with subjugation by one too powerful member. Those who commit the error of considering him as an English Statesman, must necessarily see his whole life in a false light, and will be unable to discover any principle, good or bad, Whig or Tory, to which his most important acts can be referred But, when considered as a man, whose especial task it was to join a crowd of feeble, divided, and dispirited states, in a firm and energetic union against a common enemy—when he is considered as a man in whose eyes England was important, chiefly because, without her, the great coalition which he projected must be incomplete, then all must be forced to admit that no long career recorded in history has been more uni-

uniform, from the beginning to the close, than that of this great Prince

All this is said of the character of this illustrious and lion-hearted man by Lord Macaulay, the greatest and most eloqent of modern Historians, who gives a summary of his life, compiled from information more varied and authentic than had been previously submitted to the public eye There was another *trait* in the character of William, which it may be necessary here to notice. It has been said, and it is even at this day said, by many, that the great Prince of Orange was uncompromising in his hostility to Papists. His memory is often invoked by zealous bigots of the Protestant faith, to bear testimony against all those Orangemen who evince a Christian, and, therefore, a tolerant, spirit towards their Romish fellow subjects. How unjustly the great hero is dragged from his grave to bear testimony against the true-hearted but moderate Orangemen, the world should know. If the intolerant and unreflecting Bigots who so abuse his great name and illustrious example will only turn to Macaulay's second volume, page 323, they will find that, while " the Glorious and Immortal" Prince was meditating a descent upon the English Coast , that while he was about to peril his own life, and the lives of his most intimate Friends, to secure "the Protestant Religion and the Liberties of England," he was not only strengthening his alliance with Romish Austria and Popish Spain, but actually in league with " the Scarlet Lady" herself !

In the expedition which he meditated he could succeed only by appealing to the Protestant feeling of England, and by stimulating that feeling till it became, for a while, the dominant and almost supreme sentiment of the nation. This would, indeed, have been a very simple course, (says the Historian,) had the end of all his politics been to effect a revolution in England and to reign there But he had in view an ulterior end, which could be obtained only by the help of Princes sincerely attached to the Church of Rome He was desirous to unite the Empire (Austria), the Catholic King (Spain), and the Holy See (Rome), with (Protestant) England and Holland, in a league against the French. It was therefore necessary, that while striking the greatest blow ever struck in defence of Protestantism, he should yet continue not to lose the good-will of governments which regarded Protestantism as a deadly heresy.

CHAPTER VIII.

Difficulties to be surmounted—upon what grounds William appealed for Union—
his liberality towards Roman Catholics, and devotion to Protestantism—" tri-
bute' to his memory—his farewell address to the States of Holland—his prepa-
rations to deliver England, and his landing in that country—description of
Torbay, where William landed, and of the " Princess Mary," the ship in which
he sailed.

Such were the complicated difficulties of this great undertaking. Continental Statesmen saw a part of those difficulties ; British Statesmen another part   One capacious and powerful mind alone, took them all in at
one view, and determined to surmount them all.   It was no easy thing to
subvert the English Government by means of a foreign army, without
galling the National pride of Englishmen.   It was no easy thing to obtain
from the Batavian faction, which regarded France with partiality, and the
House of Orange with aversion, a decision in favour of an expedition,
which would confound all the schemes of France, and raise the House of
Orange to the height of greatness   It was no easy thing to lead enthusiastic Protestants on a crusade against Popery, with the good wishes of
almost all Popish Governments, and of the Pope himself.   Yet, all these
things William effected. The whole history of ancient and of modern times,
records no such triumph of statesmanship   Upon this subject, Lord Macaulay further remarks, at page 341, that William saw with stern delight,
his adversaries toiling to clear away obstacle after obstacle from his path.
While they raised against themselves the enmity of all Sects, he laboured
to conciliate all   The great design which he meditated, he with exquisite
skill presented to different Governments in different lights.   And, it must
be added that, though those lights were different, none of them was false.
He called on the (Protestant) Princes of Northern Germany, to rally
around him in defence of the common cause of all Reformed Churches.
He set before the two Heads of the (Popish) House of Austria, the danger
with which they were threatened by French ambition, and the necessity of
rescuing England from vassalage, and of uniting her to the European confederacy   He disclaimed and with truth, all bigotry.   He declared that
the real enemy of the British Roman Catholics, was the short-sighted and
headstrong Monarch, who, when he might easily have obtained for them a
legal toleration, had trampled on law, liberty, property, in order to raise

them to an odious and precarious ascendancy If the misgovernment of James was suffered to continue, it must produce, at no remote time, a po-pular outbreak, which might be followed by a barbarous persecution of the Papists. The Prince declared, that to avert the horrors of such a perse-cution was one of his chief objects. If, he said, he succeeded in his design, he would use the power which he would then possess, as head of the Pro-testant interest, to protect the members of the Church of Rome. Perhaps the passions excited by the tyranny of James, might make it impossible to efface the Penal Laws (against Popery) from the English Statute-Book ; but those Laws, he declared, should be mitigated by a lenient administra-tion.

Nor was the "Glorious, Pious and Immortal" Prince, when he did suc-ceed, unmindful of his declarations, but scrupulously adhered to them After he became King of England, no Monarch could show more lenity to his Roman Catholic subjects. Every office and post which the Law qua-lified them to fill, was freely given to them—the Penal disabilities were leniently enforced—and security and respect vouchsafed to their religion, their persons and their property. Even before William was safely fixed on the Throne, and while the Roman Catholics of Ireland were in open rebel-lion against him, his toleration extended to the English Roman Catholics was marked and decisive Lord Macaulay states, page 464, that in a very few days the confusion which the invasion, the insurrection, the flight of James, and the suspension of all regular government had produced was at an end, and the Kingdom wore again its accustomed aspect There was a general sense of security. Even the classes which were most obnoxious to public hatred, and which had most reason to apprehend a persecution, were protected by the politic clemency of the Conqueror. No body of men had so much reason to feel grateful to William, as the Roman Ca-tholics. It would not have been safe to rescind formally the severe resolu-tions which the Peers had passed against the professors of a Religion generally abhorred by the Nation , but by the prudence and humanity of the Prince, those resolutions were practically annulled On his line of march from Torbay to London, he had given orders, that no outrage should be committed on the persons or dwellings of Papists. In London he re-newed these orders, and directed Burnett to see that they were strictly obeyed. He listened kindly to the complaints of the Roman Catholics , procured passports for those who wished to go beyond sea, and went him-self to Newgate, to visit the Romish Prelates who were imprisoned there. He ordered them to be removed to a more commodious apartment, and supplied with every indulgence. He solemnly assured them, that not a hair of their head should be touched, and that as soon as he could venture to act as he wished, they should be set at liberty. The Spanish Minister reported to his Government, and through his Government to the Pope, that no Catholic need feel any scruple of conscience, on account of the late revolution in England ; that for the danger to which the members of the true Church were exposed, James alone was responsible , and that William alone had saved them from a sanguinary persecution.

To this might be added, the testimony of the great Whig Nobleman, the late Lord Holland, and of Mr Hallam, who possessed, probably, one of the greatest minds that ever adorned the jurisprudence of England, or expounded the constitutional liberties of Englishmen   Mr Grimblot, too, one of the most eloquent and impartial of French writers, confirms the judgment of Mr. Hallam, and adds his own testimony to the great merits of this great Prince.   In the *"Preface"* to his Letters on the *"Domestic and Foreign Politics of England,"* from the Peace of Ryswick to the accession of Philip the Fifth of Spain, he says, (*Vol.* 1. *page* 13) : " William the Third was not a man of one Nation more than another— " he was the representative of a Principle   Frenchman though I am, I " look upon William the Third as one of the greatest characters in history ; " and I willingly say with Mr. Hallam, that '*a high regard for the* " ' *Memory of William the Third, may justly be reckoned one of the Tests* " ' *by which genuine Whigism, as opposed both to Tory and Republican* " ' *principles, has always been recognized.*'   Throughout his whole life, " William never thought of himself   If he desired elevation, it was to " raise the cause to which he was devoted   '*It must ever,*' says Mr. " '*Hallam, 'be an honor to the English Crown, that it has been worn by* " ' *so great a man ·*' and to this sentiment I cordially respond "

It would be useless to quote further, relative to the liberal and tolerant views of this Great Prince.   All authorities admit, what his own conduct amply demonstrated, and what his private despatches most fully proved, that to Religious bigotry he was a stranger, and that Religious intolerance and exclusion he curbed and reprobated   That he loved the Protestant Religion is true—that upon many occasions he perilled his life in its defence is equally true—and that he was, under God, "the Saviour and Deliverer of the Church and Nation from Popish thraldom and Arbitary power," is declared in the Book of Common Prayer, and embodied in the Statutes of the Realm ; but while the records of Britain and the annals of Europe, will carry down his great and glorious name to the latest posterity, with thanks and gratitude , it is but just to his memory, that it should be purged from the stain of intolerance, which violent and unreflecting partizans would fain cast upon it ; but which every act and word of his eventful and glorious life repudiate and condemn.   Let this description of the character of "the Glorious, Pious and Immortal Prince" close, with the following tribute to his memory :

He was, but is no more—
The head, hand, and heart, of the Confederacy!
The asserter of Liberty!
The deliverer of Nations!
The support of the Empire!
The bulwark of Holland and Flanders',
The preserver of Britain!
The saviour of Ireland! and—
The terror of France!
His thoughts were, wise and sacred;
His words few and faithful,
His actions many and heroic;
His government without tyranny,
His justice without rigor, and—
His religion without bigotry
He was—
Great without pride;
Valiant without violence;
Victorious without triumph;
Active without weariness;
Cautious without fear, and—
Meritorious without recompense.
King, Queen, or Potentate, I never saw,
So just, wise, honest, valiant, as Nassau.
He was!—but words are wanting to say what·
Say all that's GREAT AND GOOD, and he was that.

Born November the fourth, 1650, died March the eighth, 1702.

Having given the character of the great Prince, whose name the Orange Society bears, and whose "Immortal Memory" its members hold in reverence; it would occupy too much space to dwell in detail, upon the many incidents, connected with his expedition to England, and his assumption of the Regal dignity in that Kingdom   There are, however, a few particulers that cannot be passed over

On the 16th of October, 1688, William Prince of Orange, attended a solemn sitting of the States of Holland   He came, he said, to bid them farewell. He expressed his gratitude to them, for the care with which they had watched over him, when he was left an Orphan Child; for the confidence they had reposed in him while he administered the Government, and for the aid they had rendered him, at the momentous crisis in which he was then placed   He besought them to consider, that he had no interest at heart, but the prosperity and interest of his Country   He was now quitting them, he added, perhaps never to return; and if he should fall in defence of the Protestant Religion, and of the safety and independence of Europe, he commended his dearly beloved Wife to their especial protection   The Grand Pensionary of the States replied, in proper and feeling language; but overcome with emotion, his voice faltered, and he, as well as the whole assembly of grave senators, were melted to tears.   All the Deputies from every Town, accompanied the Prince to his Yacht, and

Prayers were offered up for his safety in all the Churches of the Hague. Arrived at Helvoetsluys on the evening of the same day, he immediately went on board the *"Brill"* Frigate, (afterwards called the *"Princess Mary,"*) displaying at the mast-head, the Arms of Nassau, quartered with those of England   The motto of the House of Orange was *"I will maintain"*   It was in an elliptical device, and the ellipsis was now filled up with the words, *"the Protestant Religion and the Liberties of England."* So that the whole being inscribed in letters, at least three feet long, read thus · *"THE PROTESTANT RELIGION AND THE LIBERTIES OF ENGLAND, I WILL MAINTAIN"*   After encountering adverse winds and much danger, William landed at Torbay, in Devonshire, England, on Monday, the 5th of November, 1688 · As this was the first spot on British soil, honored by the landing of the *"*Great Deliverer,*"* it may be necessary to give some slight description of it.

Torbay is a highly picturesque and commodious Bay on the coast of Devon, five miles north east of Dartmouth, and containing Tor-quay, a beautiful watering place, with Brixham and Paignton.   It is about twelve miles round, and is formed by two capes, about four miles apart—that on the east called Bob's-nose, and that on the west Berry-head   This almost semicircular recess is a secure and general rendezvous for vessels in westerly winds   In the limestone chain, forming the coast land of this Bay, and about a mile from Torquay, is Kent's Cavern, so justly celebrated for the fossil bones which it contains   The floor of this cave was first broken in 1824, by Thomas Northmore, Esq , of Exeter, who investigated it for the purpose of establishing its character as a Druidical temple.   Mr Northmore found it to contain the baptismal lake of pellucid water, the creeping path of stone purification, the oven mouth, and the mystic gate of obstacle—the essential elements if they may be so called, of a Mithratic temple , and is satisfied, from these and other circumstances, that this cave was once employed in the celebration of the Helio-Arkite mysteries.   This opinion is, in some measure, confirmed by the British remains—such as flint knives—which have been discovered in the stalagmite.   The bones which have been discovered are principally those of the Rhinoceros, Hippopotamus, Elephant, Hyena, Cavern Bear, Elk, Tiger, Ox, Horse, Wolf, Rat, &c   The length of Kent's Cavern, is about 650 feet, the breadth varies from 2 to 71 feet ; the height does not exceed 18   It was at this place, the great Prince of Orange made his first landing on English soil, to " deliver our Church and Nation from Popish thraldom and Arbitrary power "

Alluding to Torbay, the landing-place of William, it may not be out of place to observe, that the *Art Journal* for July, 1852, contains an admirable picture descriptive of this memorable event.   It is termed *"The Landing of the Prince of Orange, at Torbay ;"* and is designed from the picture of J. M. W. Turner, Esq , R A , in the Vernon Gallery.   A de-

,scription is given of this picture in a recent newspaper article, which may be here safely copied.   In it the reader may behold a faithful represen-tation of the Deliverer of the British Empire, first landing on the coast of Devon, to secure the liberties of England   The group of vessels of all sizes, takes a triangular form, the largest ship, from which the Prince is supposed to have disembarked, occupying the centre, its main-top forming the apex of the angle : the balance on either side of this vessel is pre-scred in a most masterly style, by the several introductory features, all subordinate, however, to the principal.   But the whole are thrown into distance, and assume a secondary importance, by the State Barge, which, mounted on the crest of a broad rolling wave, approaches the spectator. The fishing-boats are on the left, and occupy the gap between the Dutch Fleet and the Royal Barge.

As every incident connected with this memorable event, is deserving of perpetual record ; the reader will readily excuse a brief diversion, to notice the Vessel which conveyed the "Immortal William," to the shores of England

This celebrated ship was built on the Thames in the earlier part of the 17th century, and was afterwards purchased by the Prince, or by his adhe-rents, as an addition to the fleet which was destined to effect the Revolu-tion.   The Prince expressly selected this vessel to convey himself and suite to England, and he bestowed on her the name of the *Princess Mary*, in honor of his illustrious consort, the daughter of James II   With the suc-cess of her noble freight, the fame of the *Princess Mary* correspondingly rose.   During the whole of William's reign she held a place of honour as one of the Royal yachts, and was afterwards regularly used as the pleasure yacht of Queen Anne   By this time, however, her original build was much interfered with from the numerous and extensive repairs she had from time to time undergone.   On the death of the Queen she came into the posses-sion of his Majesty George I , by whose order she ceased to form part of the Royal establishment, and became the property of one of the noblemen connected with the court.   The vessel seems to have again got into the hands of the government, by whom it was eventually sold to the Messrs. Walters of London, and was by them re-christened the *Betsey Cairns* in honour of some lady connected with the West Indies, to which the now venerable vessel traded.   She was next sold to Messrs Carlens of London, as a collier , and conveyed many a cargo of black diamonds from the Tyne to London.   Notwithstanding the grimy appearance which the aged ship had assumed, she was looked upon with veneration by the sailors.   The ship seems to have been again restored, and was purchased by Mr G W. Wilson of South Shields, and under the charge of Henry Wilson, traded as merchantman to various ports ; at length, while on a voyage from Shields to Hamburg, the brave old ship, which had rode triumphantly through so many gales, was caught in a storm, too strong for her weather-beaten ribs to withstand. A heavy snow was falling, and the wind, blowing a perfect hurricane, lashed the ocean to a pitch of fury. In this fearful state of things, the old ship became quite unmanageable, and was driven on to a dangerous reef of rocks, near Tynemouth Castle, called the Black Middens. The crew were saved by the life-boat, which put off to their assistance.

In length, the *Betsey Cairns* was 80 ft. 3 in., by 23 ft. broad. She had two decks, the height between which was 6 feet 6 inches.—She was carvel-built, was without galleries, square sterned, and devoid of figure head.— She had two masts, and was square-rigged, with standing bowsprit. The remnant of her original timbering, though but scanty, was extremely fine. There was a profusion of rich and elaborate carvings, the colour of the wood, from age and exposure, closely resembling that of ebony. As soon as the news of her wreck became known throughout the country, the people of Shields were inundated with applications for portions of her remains. Snuffboxes and souvenirs of various kinds were made in large numbers, and brought exorbitant prices. Each of the members of the then corporation of Newcastle was presented with one of these boxes, which exhibit, in a marked degree, the durability and immitable qualities of the British oak. The carved figures, part of the nightheads, are, we believe, now in the possession of the Brethren of the Trinity House at Newcastle, and a beam, with mouldings covered with gilding, and forming a part of the principal cabin, is the property of Mr. Rippon, Waterfield, North Shields.

CHAPTER IX

Advance of the Prince of Orange from Torbay—Description of his Army, and of his entry into Exeter—Duke Schomberg—Bishop Burnett—Several persons of distinction join the Prince—His Public Reception of them—Sir Edward Seymour —Formation of the Orange Association in the Cathedral of Exeter—Mr. Rogers' Account of this Event—The English Statute, 6th and 7th of William III, chap. 27—Closing Speech of King William to his Parliament—Mr. Giffard's Account—Lord Macaulay's—Bishop Burnet's—Monsieur de Thoyras' —Continental Associations—THE FIRST PASSWORD!

Immediately after landing, the Prince, accompanied by Duke Schomberg, proceeded to examine the country, and on Tuesday the 6th of November, he advanced some Regiments of his Army as far as Newton Abbot, taking up his own residence at Ford, a seat of the ancient and noble Family of Courtenay, where he remained for two days. On the 8th of November, he advanced to the City of Exeter. The entrance of the Prince into that

City, is thus described by the historian   The people of Devonshire, altogether unused to the splendour of well ordered Camps, were overwhelmed with delight and awe   The Dutch Army (fifteen thousand strong,) being composed of men who had been born in various climates, and had served under various standards, presented an aspect at once grotesque, gorgeous, and terrible to Islanders who had, in general, a very indistinct notion of Foreign Countries. · First rode the Earl of Macclesfield at the head of two hundred Gentlemen, mostly of English blood, glittering in helmets and cuirasses, and mounted on Flemish war horses.   Each was attended by a Negro, brought from the sugar plantations on the coast of Guiana.   The citizens of Exeter, who had never seen so many specimens of the African race, gazed with wonder on those black faces, set off by embroidered turbans and white feathers.   Then with drawn broad swords, came a squadron of Swedish Horsemen, in black armour and fur cloaks. They were regarded with a strange interest , for it was rumoured that they were natives of a land where the Ocean was frozen, and where the night lasted for half the year, and that they had themselves slain the huge Bears, whose skins they wore.   Next, surrounded by a goodly company of Gentlemen and Pages, was borne aloft the Prince's banner   On its broad fold, the crowds which covered the roofs and filled the windows, read with delight the memorable inscription, "*THE PROTESTANT RELIGION AND THE LIBERTIES OF ENGLAND, I WILL MAINTAIN.* But the acclamations redoubled when, attended by forty running Footmen, the Prince himself appeared, armed on back and breast, wearing a White Plume, and mounted on a White Charger   With how martial an air he curbed his horse ; how thoughtful and commanding was the expression of his ample forehead and falcon eye, may·still be seen on the canvass of Kneller   Next to the Prince was one, who divided with him, the gaze of the multitude.   That, men said, was the great Count Schomberg, the first Soldier in Europe, since Turenne and Condé were gone.   The man whose genius and valor, had saved the Portuguese Monarchy on the field of Montes Claros ; the man who had earned a still higher glory, by resigning the truncheon of a Marshal of France, for the sake of his Religion.   It was not forgotten, that the two Heroes who, indissolubly united ,by their common Protestantism, were entering Exeter together, had twelve years before, been opposed to each other under the walls of Maestricht, and that the energy of the young Prince, had not been found a match for the cool science of the Veteran, who now rode in friendship by his side   Then came a long column of the whiskered Infantry of Switzerland, distinguished in all the Continental Wars of two centuries by pre-eminent valor and discipline, but never till that week, seen on English ground.   And then marched a succession of Bands designated, as was the fashion of that age, after their Leaders, Bentinck, Solmes, and Ginkell, Talmash, and Mackay.

With peculiar pleasure, Englishmen might look on one gallant Brigade, which still bore the name of the honored and lamented Ossory .The effect of the spectacle was heightened, by the recollection of the renowned events, in which many of the Warriors, now pouring through the west gate, had borne a share. Some of them had repelled the fiery onset of 'the French on the field of Seneff ; and others had crossed swords with the Infidels, in the cause of Christendom, on that great day when the siege of Vienna was raised The very senses of the multitude, says the historian, "were fooled by imagination "

On Sunday, the eleventh of November, Dr Burnet, afterwards Bishop of Salisbury, preached before the Prince, in the Cathedral of Exeter, and dwelt at great length, upon 'the singular Providence vouchsafed by God, to the English Church and Nation, in the person and success of the Prince William waited several days, before any Gentlemen of consequence, had joined his Army. On Wednesday, the 12th of November, Mr Burrington, a gentleman of some standing and property, resident in the neighborhood of Crediton, joined the Orange Standard, and several other Gentlemen, his neighbours, soon followed his example Lord Lovelace, a distinguished Whig Nobleman, with seventy followers, set out to join the Orange Standard, but they were intercepted at Cirencester, by the Militia under Lord Beaufort, by whom they were defeated, and Lovelace was made prisoner, and sent to Gloucester Castle On the same day that Lovelace was defeated at Cirencester, the Prince received vast accessions of strength from other quarters , amongst those was Lord Colchester, Son to the Earl of Rivers, accompanied by over sixty troopers At the same time with Lord Colchester, came the daring and somewhat noted Thomas Wharton. A few hours later, arrived Edward Russell, Son of the Earl of Bedford ; and immediately after, James Bertie, Earl of Abingdon. On the 14th of November, Edward Hyde, Viscount Cornbury, Son of the Earl of Clarendon, and a Colonel in the Royal Army of James, passed over to the Prince. Trelawney, Bishop of Bristol, was one of the seven Bishops, who had been imprisoned by James His brother, Colonel Charles Trelawney, commanded one of those fiery and hot headed Corps, called the Tangier Regiments, now known as the Fourth Regiment of Foot. The Colonel had signified his readiness, at any moment, to draw his sword for the Protestant Religion , and the Regiment (the Fourth,) he commanded, was afterwards considered William's favourite Corps No sooner had the news spread, that the Earl of Clarendon's son had joined the Prince of Orange, than hundreds poured in to the same standard Amongst the earliest and most noted were Sir William Portman of Bryanstone, and Sir Francis Warre of Hestercombe The most important of all, however, was Sir Edward Seymour, whose great dignity, parliamentary abilities, and extensive influence, gave to his adhesion to the Orange cause, an importance it had not before acquired. The following anecdote, characteristic of Sir Edward's sense of his own dignity, is related of his first interview with William. "I think Sir Edward," said the Prince, intending to be very civil, "that you are of the Family of the Duke of Somerset" "Pardon me Sir," said Sir Edward, who never forgot that he was the head of the elder branch of the Seymours, "the Duke of Somerset is of my Family" This story, which is related by several writers, bears a close resemblance to what is told of the Manriquez Family, who, it is said, took for their device, the words "*Nos no descendemos de los Reyes, sino los Reyes, descienden de nos.*"

Over sixty Noblemen and Gentlemen of the highest standing in England, had now attached themselves to the Prince s standard ; and it was deemed desirable that he should give them a public reception. This *MEMORABLE EVENT* took place at Exeter, on Wednesday, the 21st of November, 1688 It was under those circumstances, and at this meeting, that the Society called *ORANGE* was first instituted Mr Edward Rogers, a member of the Grand Committee of the Grand Lodge of Ireland, at page 18 of his little book, entitled, "THE RISE AND PROGRESS OF THE LOYAL ORANGE INSTITUTION OF IRELAND," printed by John Thompson, at "*The Guardian*" Office, Armagh , describes this event in the following words.

" In order to redress these grievances, the Prince said, he came over to England
" with an armed force, and that he had no other design, than to procure the full
" and lasting settlement of the Protestant Religion and the Laws of England   An
" Association was immediately formed by the direction of the Prince of Orange
" after his landing, to be signed by all who wished to adhere to his cause , for, said
" he, till we have that accomplished, we are as a rope of sand   Men may leave
" us when they please, and we have them under no tie , whereas, if they affixed
" their signatures to an Association, they would consider themselves bound to
" stick to us.   According to his wishes, the matter was arranged forthwith   A
" Declaration was drawn up by Bishop Burnet, engrossed on parchment, and
" signed by all his followers, to the intent, that they would support and defend
" William Prince of Orange, in upholding the Laws and Protestant Religion, and
" that if any attempt should be made on his person, it should be revenged on all,
" by whom, or from whom, any such attempt should be made.   This combination,
" at the time denominated ' *THE ORANGE CONFEDERATION*,' had the
" desired effect   The Nobility and Gentry, with one accord flocked to the Protes-
" tant standard."

In a letter published by the same author in the course of the last year, (1858,) he describes the origin of the Society somewhat more fully, though substantially the same, in the following language

" History informs us that, although the Prince of Orange had landed without obstruction and proceeded without opposition, yet for several days he was not without perplexities and difficulties.   Though the people were ready enough to show their joy and good wishes, they were extremely fearful of offering their services and persons. The memory of the severities against the Duke of Monmouth s adherents was yet so recent that every one feared to engage in a like enterprise. The Clergy and Magistrates had not made up their minds, and the Bishop and Dean ran off to King James. He was made to believe that all the Gentlemen of the west would join with him upon his first landing, but, for a length of time, scarce any person of note had come in to him, and he began to think of returning and publishing the invitation he had received from those lords, as a justification for having come at all. He found that the Mayor and Aldermen of the city of Exeter came to visit him rather out of fear than affection, being busied in dubious consultations among themselves. He found that as his recruits increased he wanted money to pay off his men as well as the countenance of great persons ; and indeed he began so far to doubt the success of his expedition, that, in a council of war held at Exeter, he suffered it to be proposed to him to re embark for Holland   We find also, that, in his reply to some persons from Somersetshire and Devonshire, he complained of the way in which he was treated,—' We expected that you who dwelt so near the place of our landing would have joined us sooner. Let the whole world now judge if our pretensions are not just, generous, and sincere, and above price, since we might have even a bridge of gold to return back,' &c.

These gentlemen having given in their adhesion were soon followed by several others of greater note   After their arrival at Exeter, Sir Edward Seymour sent for Dr. Burnet and asked him ' Why they had not got an association, without which they were only a rope of sand, and none would think themselves bound to stick to them ?'

The Doctor told him, ' It was for want of a man of his authority and credit to support such an advice'   He then proposed it to the Prince, who, with the Earl of Shrewsbury, and all present, approved the motion.   Accordingly the Doctor drew up an association, which was laid on the table in the Prince's lodgings, in the deanery, where the lords and gentlemen of his court, and others signed it

It is recorded as an undoubted fact, that from this time the face of the Prince's affairs was entirely changed.   Every day persons distinguished by birth, estates, or employments offered him their services

The powerful effect which this combination of Protestants had upon the country, and especially on the King, may be seen from the following extract from a letter which James wrote to the Earl of Feversham upon his departure from England :

' I hope you will keep yourselves (officers and soldiers) free from associations and such pernicious things.'

This important admission from the unfortunate James—the last of the Stuarts—proves how much he dreaded the effects of the Orange Association.

William being now safely placed on the throne, and peace being established in England, we turn our attention to Ireland, where Tyrconnell had turned the Protestants out of all employment and supplied their places with Papists, who had been rebels in the massacre of 1641, or their descendants.   The Protestants of Ireland looked upon themselves thus at the mercy of an unprincipled government, and were struck with terror to see a man of Tyrconnell's temper and principles in full possession of the sword. Remembering the miseries of 1641, they determined to unite for their mutual defence, and they did so effectually as evidenced by their bravery at Enniskillen and Londonderry The objects of this association, which had spread over several counties are fully described, for self-defence, and for securing 'he Protestant religion, their lives, liberties and properties, and the peace of the kingdom, disturbed by Popish and illegal counsellors and their abettors, resolving to adhere to the laws, to the Protestant religion, to act in subordination to the government of England, declaring also, that if they were forced to take up arms it would be contrary to their inclination, and should be only defensive, not in the least to invade the lives, liberties and estates of their fellow subjects, no not of the Popish persuasion whilst they demeaned themselves peaceably,' &c That they would admit none but Protestants into this association, yet that they would protect even Papists from violence, while they remained peaceable and quiet, and doubted not but all good Protestants would in their several stations join with them in the same public defence, and that God would bless their just, innocent, and necessary undertaking for their lives, laws and religion.' It is not necessary to state that Lords Mount Alexander, Blaney, Kingston, with Chidley Coote and the noble Walker and the defenders of Londonderry, were members of this band of union.

The eventful battles of the Boyne, Aughrim, &c , decided the fate of James and gave peace to the Irish Protestants.

This confederation embraced the members of the House of Commons, who presented their determination to their king in a body with their request,—' That he would order both that and all other associations by the Commons of England to be lodged among the records in the Tower, to remain as a perpetual memorial of their loyalty and affection to his Majesty ' Whereupon the King told them that, ' As they had freely *associated* themselves for his and the common safety, *he did heartily enter into the same association*, and would be always ready with them to venture his life against all who should endeavour to subvert the religion, laws, and liberties of England,' and promised ' that this, and all other associations should be lodged among the records in the Tower.'

The next day the Commons

Resolved—'That whoever should by word or writing, affirm that the association was illegal, should be deemed a promoter of the designs of the late King James, and an enemy to the laws and liberties of the kingdom.'—7 and 8 *Wm. III cap.* 27.

The Lords also resolved on forming an association. In fact, the entire population of England freely entered into combination for the defence of the Protestant religion, their lives and properties.

These associations occasioned, among others, two small medals. First, on the face is represented Saul surrounded with his guards, casting a halbert at David, playing on a harp, which is the emblem of Ireland, denotes King William, and by Saul and his guards are meant King James. The reverse contains a cockade or knot of ribands, on each bow of which is represented a crown, and on the cockade are these words interwoven in English, 'Tri-national association for King William III.'

The other medal relates to the disappointment of the conspirators The face represents William's bust. On the reverse stands a column (like our society now), against which arrows, swords, and flames spend themselves without doing the least injury.

Harris informs us that the parliament of Ireland met on the 27th of June, but that no business was transacted except signing the Orange association, conformable to that in England, which was done by every member except the representative for the county of Cavan, who was expelled the house for his refusal.

In closing the session of parliament of 1698, King William made the following observations (July 5):

'That he could not take leave of so good a parliament without acknowledging his sense of the great things they had done for his safety and honour. The happy uniting of us in an association for mutual defence, the making such provisions for our common security, &c., are such things as will give a lasting reputation to this parliament, and will also be a subject of emulation to those who shall come after,' &c.

Matters being thus settled to the satisfaction of Protestants in these countries, they enjoyed peace and prosperity for many years, until in Ireland from 1757 the most fearful atrocities were committed by bodies of Romanists on the poor Protestants of the north of Ireland These outlaws, not mentioning the Jacobites of 1745, assumed at different times the appellation of ' Hearts of Steel,' 'Hearts of Oak,' 'Defenders,' 'Peep of-day Boys,' 'United Irishmen,' "Shanavist,' 'Caravats,' 'Threshers,' 'Carders,' Ribbonmen,' 'Whiteboys,' and in later days, 'Young Irelanders,' who kept Ulster in a state of anarchy and rebellion until the formation or re organisation of the Orange association, which spread rapidly over the country, bringing with it peace and determined loyalty to the British crown. In 1688 the Protestants united together to stick firm to the Protestant cause, to William, and to one another; and never to depart from doing so until their religion, laws, and liberties, were so far secured to them that they should no more be in danger of falling under popery and slavery.' This was a noble resolution on the part of our illustrious forefathers, and a mighty foundation laid, upon which it was by Heaven ordained that their posterity should construct a temple.

Two centuries have almost passed away, and we find ourselves surrounded with conspiracies and disaffection to a Protestant government—living in time fraught with danger to our religion, laws, and all that is dear to us as Protestants. In associating themselves together, our forefathers laid down a good example, and true to the letter, their sons have availed themselves of the many advantages arising therefrom Affiliated branches of the parent society have been established in every clime and in every land where a British Protestant has set his foot. Alike in all its details to the original confederation, is constituted the Orange association of the present day, having for its object the maintenance of the Protestant religion, *Protestant succession to the throne*, civil and religious liberty, and mutual protection in times of persecution. Had such an institution existed in 1640, the awful massacre of Protestants which then occurred would have been impossible. Universal vigilance, immediate communication, preparation and devoted union on the part of the Protestants would have rendered such a catastrophe as that which merciless Rome then inflicted, even beyond the hope of malignant and murderous superstition.

· We have proved that Orange associations have rendered effective service to Protestants, and especially to the House of Brunswick, · in placing them upon the throne of England. Its efficiency has been recognised *during the storm* on many occasions, but no sooner is quiet restored, by means of · its taking a stand on the side of loyalty and order, than an ungrateful government once more surrenders to the factious clamour of Popish adventurers, who know full well that so long as our Institution is in activity they could not successfully carry out their traitorous designs against the constitution. However, extreme oppression always produces an impetuous tide of resistance, and so it is with respect to Chancellor Brady's *ukase* So far from the Grand Orange Lodge acceding to the demand of place-hunters, they have adopted the cry of the apprentice boys of Derry—No Surrender ! and as a sedative to the Lord Lieutenant, there has been an increase to the ranks of the society, in three counties, of upwards of five hundred within one month.—Esto Perpetua. Edmund Rogers, G.S., Armagh."

As Mr Rogers alludes so particularly to the Act of the 6th and 7th of William the Third, chapter 27, it is deemed most satisfactory to quote at length all such parts of the Statute, as refer to the matters now under consideration We copy from the Journals as preserved in the Library of the Commons of Canada. The Statute is intituled,

"AN ACT FOR THE BETTER SECURITY OF HIS MAJESTY'S ROYAL PERSON AND GOVERNMENT " (*6th and 7th of William the Third, chap. 27*)

WHEREAS the welfare and safety of this kingdom, and of the Reformed Religion, do, next under God, entirely depend upon the preservation of His Majesty's Royal Person and Government, which, by the merciful Providence of God, of late have been delivered from the bloody and barbarous attempts of traitors, and others, His Majesty's enemies, who, there is just reason to believe, have in a great measure, been encouraged to undertake and prosecute such, their wicked designs, partly by His Majesty's great and undeserved clemency towards them, and partly by the want of a sufficient provision in the law, for the securing of offices and places of trust, to such as are well affected to His Majesty's Government, and for the repressing and punishing such as are known to be disaffected to the same. For remedy whereof, it is hereby enacted by the King's most excellent Majesty, by and with the advice and consent of the Lords, Spiritual and Temporal, and Commons, in this present Parliament assembled, and by the authority of the same.

Sections 1 and 2, then go on to enact, that all persons refusing to take the Oaths prescribed by the 1st of William and Mary, Session 1, chapter 8, shall be liable to the penalties inflicted on Popish Recusants.

Section 3. " And whereas for the better preservation of His Majesty's Royal Person and Government, against the aforesaid wicked and traitorous designs, upon a full discovery thereof, great numbers of His Majesty's good subjects have entered into and subscribed AN ASSOCIATION, in the words following, viz.: ' *Whereas* '*there has been a horrible and detestable conspiracy, formed and carried on by* ' *Papists, and other wicked and traitorous persons, for assassinating His Majesty's* ' *Royal Person, in order to encourage an Invasion from France, to subvert our* ' *Religion, Laws and Liberties*   *We whose names are hereunto subscribed, do* ' *heartily, sincerely, and solemnly, profess, testify, and declare, that his present* ' *Majesty, King WILLIAM, is rightful and lawful King of these Realms.*   *And* ' *we do further mutually promise and engage to stand by and assist each other to* ' *the utmost of our power, in the support and defence of His Majesty's most sacred* ' *Person and Government, against the late King JAMES and all his adherents.* ' *And, in case His Majesty come to any violent or untimely death (which God for-* ' *bid !) we do hereby further freely and unanimously pledge ourselves to unite,* ' *associate, and stand by each other, in revenging the same upon his enemies and* ' *their adherents, and in supporting and defending the succession to the Crown,* ' *according to an Act made in the first year of the reign of King William and Queen* ' *Mary, intituled,* An Act declaring the rights and liberties of the Subject, and ' settling the Succession of the Crown '"

Sections 4, 5, 6, 7, 8, 9, 10 *and* 11 declare THE ASSOCIATION to remain good and lawful—that Commissioners of accounts, and Officers under the King, &c , within thirty miles of London, shall, in Easter term, subscribe the ASSOCIATION, or do so before the 1st of August, at the Quarter Sessions—that all persons admitted into office, must join the said Association—that persons neglecting or refusing to sub-scribe the Association, shall be declared incapable of holding office—and that a penalty shall be inflicted upon all persons executing office after neglect or refusal to join the Association.

Sections 12, 13 *and* 14, enact sundry provisions relative to Quakers—to servants in the Royal employment—to persons on board the fleet, or in service beyond seas.

Section 15 provides that the King may pardon penalties for not taking the Oaths.

Sections 16, 17 *and* 18, after reciting the 3rd and 4th of William and Mary, chapter 13, provides that, after this Parliament, all members must subscribe the Association, or be disabled from sitting, and that if any member of the House shall refuse or neglect to join the Association, a writ shall issue for a new election in lieu of such member.

Section 19 enacts provisions for persons refusing to take the Oaths prescribed by the 1st of William and Mary, the 1st Session, chapter 18—and that they are not permitted to vote as electors.

Section 20 authorizes the detention in custody, of persons accused upon oath of High Treason

Section 21 continues in force all Commissions for six months after the demise of the Crown.

Section 22 declares the Act does not make void any office of inheritance, if a Deputy thereto should be appointed, who will join the Association. and who shall be approved of by His Majesty.

Particular reference having been also made to the Speech with which His Majesty closed the Parliament in 1698, we have here inserted it entire. The copy is taken from the *Lord's Journals, vol.* 16, *page* 344

CLOSING SPEECH OF KING WILLIAM III, TO THE PARLIAMENT OF ENGLAND, 5TH JULY, 1698

"MY LORDS AND GENTLEMEN:

"I cannot take leave of so good a Parliament, without publicly acknowledging the sense I have of the great things you have done for my safety and honor, and for the support and welfare of my People

"Every one of your Sessions hath made good this character. The happy uniting of us in an Association for our mutual defence—the remedying of the corruption, of the Coin, which had been so long growing on the Nation—the restoring of credit —the giving Supplies in such a manner for carrying on the War, as did, by God's blessing, produce an honorable peace—and, after that, the making of such pro vision for our common security, and towards satisfying the debts contracted in so long a war, with as little burthen to the Kingdom as possible, are such things as will give a lasting reputation to this Parliament, and will be a subject of emula- tion to those who shall come after.

"Besides all this, I think myself personaly obliged to return my thanks to you Gentlemen of the House of Commons, for the regard you have had to my honor, by the establishment of my Revenue.

"MY LORD'S AND GENTLEMEN

"There is nothing I value so much as the esteem and love of my People ; and, as for their sakes, I avoided no hazards during the war, so my whole study and care shall be, to improve and continue to them, the advantages and blessings of peace.

"And I earnestly desire you all, in your several stations, to be vigilant in pre- serving peace and good order, and in a due and regular execution of the laws, especially those against Profaneness and Irreligion "

In the year 1813, a pamphlet was published by James Charles, Printer and Bookseller, May Street, Dublin, said to be from the pen of John Giffard, Esq., High Sheriff of that City, and Deputy Grand Master of Ireland. At page 6 of this pamphlet, the following passage occurs "The "enlarged Institution was copied from one, which, since the Revolution, "has existed in the Fourth Foot, a regiment raised by the King William, "into which Orange Lodge, several Princes of the House of Hanover, "have not thought it beneath them to be initiated We believe the King "(George III,) was. We know that the Prince of Wales, (George IV,) and "Prince Frederick, (the Duke of York,) were made Orangemen." The following account of the memorable meeting at Exeter is given by Lord Macaulay, volume ii page 396 : "It was now thought desirable that the Prince should give a public reception to the whole body of noblemen and gentlemen who had assembled at Exeter. He addressed them in a short, but dignified and well considered speech. He was not, he said, acquainted with the faces of all he saw ; but he had a list of their names, and knew how highly they stood in the estimation of their country. He gently chid their tardiness, but expressed a confident hope that it was not yet too late to save the kingdom. Therefore, said he, Gentlemen, Friends, and Fellow Protestants, we bid you, and all your followers, most heartily welcome to our court and camp. Seymour, (Sir Edward,) a keen politician, long accustomed to the tactics of faction, saw in a moment that the party which had begun to rally around the Prince stood in need of organization. It was as yet, he said, a mere rope of sand ; no common object had been publicly and formally avowed ; nobody was pledged to any thing As soon as the assembly at the Deanery broke up, he sent for Burnet and suggested that an Association should be formed, and that all the English adherents of the Prince, should put their hands to an instrument, binding them to be true to their leader and to each other Burnet carried the suggestion to the Prince and to (the Earl of) Shrewsbury, by both of whom it was approved. A meeting was held in the Cathedral A short paper, drawn up by Burnet, was produced, approved, and eagerly signed " The following description of these events are taken from the words of the Bishop himself :—

" While the Prince (of Orange) was staying at Exeter, the rabble of the people came into him in great numbers; so that he could have raised many regiments of foot, if there had been any occasion for them. But what he understood of the temper of the King's (James') army was in, made him judge it was not necessary to arm greater numbers. After he had stayed eight days at Exeter, Seymour (Sir Edward,) came in with several other gentlemen of quality and estate. As soon as he had been with the Prince, he sent to seek for me. When I came to him he asked me why we had not an Association signed by all that came to us, since, till we had that done, we were as a rope of sand ; men might leave us when they pleased, and we had them under no tie, whereas, if they signed an Association, they would reckon themselves bound to stick to us. I answered, it was because we had no man of his authority and credit to offer and support such an advice, I went from him to the Prince, who approved of the motion, as did also the Earl of Shrewsbury, and all that were with us. So I was ordered to draw it. It was in a few words, an engagement to stick together in pursuing the ends of the Prince's Declaration, and that if any attempt should be made on his person, it should be revenged on all by whom, or from whom, any such attempt should be made. This was agreed to by all about the Prince. So it was engrossed in parchment, and signed by all those that came in to him "— *Vide Bishop Burnet's " History of his own Time " London. William Smith,* 113 *Fleet Street,* 1840. *Vol 2, page* 502.

" The Prince went from Hungerford to Newbury, and from thence to Abingdon resolving to have gone to Oxford, to receive the compliments of the University, and to meet the Princess Anne, who was coming thither. At Abingdon he was surprised with the news of the strange catastrophe of affairs now at London, the King's (James') desertion, and the disorders which the city and neighbourhood of

London were falling into   One came from London and brought him the news, which he knew not well how to believe, till he had an express sent him from the Lords, who had been with him from the King. Upon this the Prince saw how necessary it was to make all possible haste to London: So he sent to Oxford to excuse his not coming thither, and to offer the Association to them which was signed by almost all the heads, and the chief men of the University."—*Ibid, p* 506

" " After a warm debate, it was carried in both Houses, that an Association should be laid on the table, and that it might be signed by all such as were willing of their own accord to sign it. This was signed by both Houses, excepting only four score in the House of Commons, and fifteen in the House of Lords. The Association was carried from the Houses of Parliament over all England, and was signed by all sorts of people, a very few only excepted Soon after this, a Bill was brought into the House of Commons, declaring all men incapable of public trust or to serve in Parliament, who did not join the Association. This passed with no considerable opposition, for those who had signed it of their own accord, were not unwilling to have it made general ; and such as had refused it when it was voluntary, were resolved to sign it as soon as the law should be made for it. At the same time an order passed in Council, for reviewing all the Commissions in England, and for turning out of them, all those who had not signed the Association while it was voluntary ; since this seemed to be such a declaration of their principles and affections, that it was not thought reasonable that such persons should be any longer either Justices of the Peace or Deputy Lieutenants "—*Ibid, pages* 624 *and* 625.

To the preceding authorities may be added the following, taken from the writings of a French Roman Catholic author, de Thoyras.

" The Prince (of Orange) remained nine days at Exeter, without being joined by any person of distinction. It is even pretended that in a Council of War, held at Exeter, he suffered it to be proposed to him to re-embark for Holland. But on the tenth day some of the principal gentlemen of the country joined him. Among these was Sir Edward Seymour, by whose advice an Association was drawn, and joined by all persons there with the Prince, or who afterwards repaired to him. It soon spread through other parts of the Kingdom and was joined by great numbers,"— *Vide History of England, written in French by* Rapin de Thoyras. *Translated into English, with additional notes, by the* Rev N. Tindel, M. A., *Vicar of Great Waltham, in Essex. Second Edition, Printed for James, John and Paul Knapton, at the Crown in Ludgate Street, near the west end of St. Paul's.* 1733. *Vol.* 2, *Book* 24, *page* 777.

" Meanwhile, as it was absolutely necessary to put an end to the present anarchy, the Prince of Orange assembled the Lords, Spiritual and Temporal, in London, to the number of about three score, and made this short speech to them · '*My Lords, I have desired to meet you here to advise the best manner how to pursue the ends of my declaration in calling a Free Parliament, for the preservation of the Protestant Religion, the restoring the Rights and Liberties of the Kingdom, and the cause so that they may not be in danger of being again subverted*' Upon speaking these

words, he withdrew, and left them to consult together His declaration was read
and the Lords voted him their particular thanks.   Then they resolved to assemble
every day in their old house at Westminster, and named five of the most eminent
Lawyers to assist them in the room of the Judges, who were most of them absent.
It was further proposed that the whole assembly should join the Association subscribed by the Nobility and Gentry at Exeter.   To this all agreed except the
Duke of Somerset, the Earl of Nottingham, the Lord Wharton, and all the Bishops
but that of London."—*Ibid, pages* 782 *and* 783.

It has been already mentioned, upon the authority of Bayle, the historian, that the early associated Protestants of Germany had their secret
organizations, and the very *Passwords* then in use are given in a preceding
portion of this work   Doubtless many of the Protestants who accompanied William's expedition to England, were members of the Continental
Associations, and assisted at the formation of the one organized at the
Cathedral in the City of Exeter, on the 21st of November, 1688   If
Bayle's statement is correct—and it has never yet been questioned—
the presumption is, that nearly all, if not all William's army were members
of the secret societies formed on the European Continent   Those Societies
were organized by the early Protestants of Germany, to guard against
intrusion and surprise , to help and succour the persecuted, and to render
more binding and fraternal the common feelings by which they were animated.   Had the force which accompanied William to England, been
drawn from one Kingdom, or from one State alone, there might be some
opening for doubt, as to their prior knowledge of the secret associations
referred to by the Historian before quoted.   But when it is remembered
that the Prince's army was drawn from the Protestant people of all the
States of the Continent ; that it included Swedes and Danes ; Dutch and
Hanoverians ; Flemish and French ; Hungarians and Moravians , Poles
and Prussians ; Swiss and Tyrolese ; and that all these Protestant refugees
had enlisted under the banners of a Leader, whose devotion to the Reformed Religion, friends and foes alike admitted , then no room remains
for the admission of a doubt, as to the prior knowledge they must necessarily have had, of the existence and working of the secret Associations
of the Continent   Be that, however, as it may ! Tradition as well as
History, gives to the Society then formed at Exeter, the name of the
" *ORANGE CONFEDERATION,*" and its Password was *Seymour,* '(the
name of the first most important personage who joined the Orange ranks,
after the landing of the Prince in England)   The word was thus ordered
to be given   If in conversation with a stranger, and it was desirable to
discover, whether the stranger was a member of the Confederation or not,
some sentence that might fall from him, would be feigned not to be heard,
or not to be understood, and he would be asked, " What did you say ?"
(*S ») To which (if a member) he would reply, "nothing more (mour)

The word would then be pronounced "*Sey-mour*," and an immediate re-cognition would take place. Report says, that this simple system was introduced into the First Tangier Regiment, (the Fourth of the Line,) by its Commanding Officer, Colonel Charles Trelawney ; that all his Officers, and nearly all his men, were members of the "CONFEDERATION ," and that this simple system of a single *password* so continued, till it was super-seded by the introduction of a more enlarged and comprehensive system in the year 1793

CHAPTER X.

Colonel Trelawney—Original Declaration of the Orange Confederation—Names of the first Subscribers—The present Orange Declaration contrasted with the Original—Exeter, (the City where the Society was first formed) its Description and History—Reminiscences which bind Holland and Britain—The Prince of Orange's advance upon London—Declaration of the Lords and Commons of England—William and Mary, Prince and Princess of Orange, declared King and Queen of England—Description of the Ceremony—Consummation of the "Glorious Revolution."

Lord Macaulay, at page 287 of his second volume, alludes to the Tre-lawney family, and especially to this Colonel Trelawney's brother, men-tioned in the preceding chapter, who was then Bishop of Bristol, and who was one of the seven Bishops sent to the Tower by James the Second The people of Cornwall, says the Historian, a fierce, bold, and athletic race, among whom there was a stronger provincial feeling, than in any other part of the realm, were greatly moved by the danger of Trelawney, whom they honored less as a ruler of the Church, than as the Head of an honorable House, and the Heir, through twenty descents, of ancestors who had been of great note before the Normans had set foot on English ground All over the Country was sung a song, of which the burden is still remem-bered.

> "And shall Trelawney die, and shall Trelawney die ?
> Then thirty thousand Cornish Boys, will know the reason why ! "

The "DECLARATION," drawn up by the Rev Dr Gilbert Burnet, do-mestic Chaplain to the Prince, and approved by His Highness, immediately before his setting out with his army from Exeter to Axminster, on the 21st of November, 1688, is the origin of the "GENERAL DECLARATION," which, to this day, precedes the "OBLIGATION ," the "CONSTITUTION AND LAWS ," the "OPENING AND CLOSING PRAYERS ," and the "FORMS AND RITUALS ," in all the Books of the "ORANGE INSTITUTION " The sole

difference in the "DECLARATION" now used, from that originally drawn
by Dr. Burnet, Bishop of Salisbury, in the Cathedral Church at Exeter,
and approved by the Prince, has reference only to the altered circumstances of the times.   The following is a copy of the Bishop's manuscript,
approved by the Prince of Orange (with whom, at the time, was the Earl
of Shrewsbury, Sir Edward Seymour, and Mr. Sidney,) as handed down
in the archives of some of the early Fathers of Orangeism.

"We do hereby associate ourselves, to the utmost of our power, to support and defend our Great Deliverer, His Highness the Prince of Orange,
in his present enterprise for the delivery of the English Church and Nation
from Popery and Arbitrary Power , and for the maintenance of the Protestant Religion, and the establishment of a Free Parliament   for the
protection of His Highness' person, and the settlement of Law and Order
on a lasting foundation in these Kingdoms   We further declare, that we
are exclusively a Protestant Association , yet, detesting as we do, any
intolerant spirit, we solemly pledge ourselves to each other, that we will
not persecute any person, on account of his Religious opinions, provided
the same be not hostile to the State , but that we will, on the contrary,
be aiding and assisting to every Loyal subject, of every Religious description, in protecting him from violence and oppression."   This "DECLA-
RATION " (written in cipher by Bishop Burnet,) was signed by upwards
of six hundred of the Nobility and Gentry of England, and other adherents
of the Prince of Orange, at Exeter and Axminster, on the 21st of November, and five following days   Amongst the names originally attached, were
those of the following distinguished characters :—

>   The Earl of Shrewsbury,
>   The Earl of Devonshire,
>   The Earl of Danby,
>   Lord Lumley,
>   Henry Comptom, Bishop of London,
>   Edward Russell,
>   Henry Sidney,
>   Sir Edward Seymour,
>   Gilbert Burnet, D D ,
>   The Earl of Macclesfield,
>   Admiral Herbert,
>   The Earl of Abingdon,
>   Frederic, Count Schomberg,
>   Thomas Wharton, M.P., Buckingham,
>   Archchibald Campbell, Duke of Argyle,
>   Charles Paulet, Marquis of Winchester,
>   Mr. Ogle,

Peregrine Osborne, Lord Dumblane,
Mr Burington, of Crediton,
The Earl of Manchester,
The Earl of Stamford,
The Earl of Rutland,
The Earl of Chesterfield,
General Bentinck,
General Solmes,
General Rede de Ginkell,
Lord Mordaunt,
Fletcher of Saltoun,
Sir Patrick Hume, Bart,
Mr Wildman,
General Talmash,
Mr. Courtney, of Ford,
Richard Savage, Lord Colchester,
Edward Hyde, Viscount Cornbury,
Sir William Portman, Bart ,
Sir Francis Warre, Bart.,
The Earl of Bath,
Lord Delemere,
Lord Cholmondley,
Lord Grey de Ruthyn.

In order that the reader may, at one view, discover the difference between the "Orange Confederation," as originally formed in the Cathedral Church of Exeter, on the 21st of November, 1688, and the "Orange Institution" as now established in British America, there is here transcribed a copy of the "General Declaration" of the last named body, as now in use

"LOYAL ORANGE INSTITUTION.

"Thou shalt teach men ordinances and laws, and shalt show them the way wherein they must walk, and the work they must do , moreover, thou shalt provide out of all the people, able men, such as fear God, men of truth, hating covetousness, and place them to be rulers of thousands, and rulers of hundreds, and rulers of tens.'—*Exodus, c.* xviii , *vs* 20, 21.

" GENERAL DECLARATION.

" At all times nothing can be more natural, and at this time nothing can be more reasonable, than that those who have common rights to protect, and common interests to defend, should act together and know each other. It is by division, that the benevolent objects of true patriots are frustrated, and their best and noblest efforts for the public good, defeated. In these distant but important appendages of our Great Empire, it must be obvious to every loyal and reflecting mind, that a union of intelligence, an increase of means, and a knowledge of each other are essential.

"The LOYAL ORANGE INSTITUTION is formed by persons desirous of supporting, to the utmost of their power, the principles and practice of the CHRIST-IAN RELIGION, to maintain the LAWS AND CONSTITUTION of the County, afford ASSISTANCE TO DISTRESSED MEMBERS of the Order, and otherwise promote such laudable and benevolent purposes, as many tend to the due ordering of *Religion* and *Christian Charity*, and the supremacy of LAW, ORDER, and CONSTITUTIONAL FREEDOM.

" Its Members associate in honor of *King William the* III, *Prince of Orange*, whose name they bear, and whose immortal memory they hold in reverence, tending as he did, under Divine Providence, to the overthrow of the most oppres-ive bigory, and to the restoration of pure Religion and Liberty. They reverve the Memory of that immortal Prince, not only as a Patriot, a Constitutional Monarch and a Hero, but also as a true Christian, and hope in the adoption of his name, to emulate his virtues, by maintaining RELIGION, without persecution, or trenchnig upon the rights of any.

' The Orange Society lays no claim to exclusive Loyalty or exclusive Protest-antism, but it admits no man within its pale, whose principles are not Loyal, and whose creed is not Protestant

Disclaiming an intoleiant spirit, the Society demands as an indispensable qualification, without which the greatest and the wealthiest may seek admission in vain, that the candidate shall be believed to be incapable of persecuting or injuring any one, on account of his Religious opinions The duty of every Orangeman being, to aid and defend ALL LOYAL SUBJECTS, of every Religious persuasion, in the enjoyment of their constitutional rights.

" The Rules of the Society are open, not only to Members of the Institution, but to the whole community, there is no reserve, except the signs and symbols whereby Orangemen know each other, and these mysteries are essential to the proper qualification of the brotherhood, to the recognition of the Members, and the prevention of intrusion and imposture from strangers and enemies. The Association is general, not confined to any particular place, person or nation, but extends itself wherever a Loyal Protestant Briton is to be found, to the remotest corners of the Globe, for the establishment of Protestant Faith and British Liberty, to the latest ages of posterity. The whole Institution is one neighborhood, within which every Orangeman is at home, in the farthest parts of the world, and such is the mechanism of the Association, that while its operations are thus extended, its every movement is alike felt and answered in every part

" The Orange Institution, like a glorious moral luminary, is intended to pour its refulgence, not on one part only of the ample circumference of the British dominions, but simultaneously on every portion, equally enlightening the whole periphery

" The Institution in these Colonies, can never be suppressed, but by means which would subvert the Constitution, and annihilate the connection with the Mother Country

"In many quarters, where the true nature of the Orange Institution is not properly known, its designs and objects have, by some, been misunderstood, and by others, misrepresented. From the name it bears,—being connected in every one's mind with the history of parties in Ireland,—some are apt to suppose that its sphere is necessarily confined; not reflecting that an instrument, which has been chiefly used in the country of its birth to suppress rebellion, repel invasion, and secure domestic tranquillity, may be found equally efficacious to loyal men of all countries, in protecting their lives, liberties, and properties, in these Colonies. The Society is constituted upon the broadest principles of National Freedom *It takes its stand upon the glorious principles of the Revolution of* 1688, it lays its foundation in the field of British Liberty, it disdains the badge of faction, and knows no emblem save the "*Altar and the Throne*"

"As the Prince of Orange was invited to England by a Coalition of Parties, who were united by a common sense of their sacred duty, to preserve their Religion and Liberties, so the Orange Society, named after that Immortal Prince, invites a similar combination, and calls upon the sons of Britain, to lay aside political feuds, and, like their illustrious ancestors, who signed and sealed the Great Covenant of Freedom, to sacrifice every private consideration, and establish a centralization of Freedom, upon such a comprehensive basis, as will enable every limb and fibre to receive vitality and nourishment from the parent stem."

Mr. Grimblot, in his "*Domestic and Foreign Politics of England,*" in a note, at page 25, speaks of the "*Illustrious seven who signed the celebrated ASSOCIATION in June* 1688" This "celebrated Association," was undoubtedly the germ of the Orange, and the "Illustrious seven" spoken of were the Earl of Shrewsbury, the Earl of Devonshire, the Earl of Danby, Lord Lumley, Compton, Bishop of London, Mr Edward Russell, and Mr. Henry Sidney As these seven illustrious men were the first heroes of the "glorious Resolution"—were "the seven Conspirators" who first invited William to England, and the first seven signers to the "Celebrated Association" at Exeter, it may be proper here to give a short discription of them.

No 1. Charles Talbot, twelfth Earl and first Duke of Shrewsbury, of one of the most Illustrious Families of England, was born in 1660, and succeeded to the first title at a very early age, his father having been killed in a duel with the Duke of Buckingham The Duke seduced the Countess of Shrewsbury, her Lord challenged his Grace, and he fell Some said that the abandoned woman witnessed the combat in man's attire; and others, that she clasped her victorious lover to her bosom, while his shirt was still dripping with the blood of her husband. The Talbot family was at the time Roman Catholic, but the young Earl embraced the Protestant faith in the year 1679, under the instruction of that Reverend and able Divine, Dr. Tillotson Having embraced the doctrines of Protestantism from thorough conviction and after long and careful examination, he soon gave proof of the sincerity of his conversion in prefering, after the accession of James the Second, to incur his displeasure, rather than to reconcile himself to the Church of his Fathers.   The same conviction led him to oppose the measures of that Monach for the re-establishment of the Roman Catholic worship, and he was among the foremost of those who invited the Prince of Orange   As early as May 1687, we find a letter of his, conveying professions of his zeal for the Prince   And Monsier Grimblot states that, "he was likewise one of the illustrious seven, who signed the celedrated Association in June 1688," (*Vol 1 page 25*) Lord Macaulay states also, (*vol 2. page 319,*) that he was one of the seven Chiefs of the Conspiracy," who signed the invitation to the Prince, to invade England.   Convinced of the necessity of an immediate Revolution, he even mortaged his Estates, and repaired to Holland, offered his purse and his sword to the Prince of Orange. He accompanied William to England, and while the Prince remained in suspense at Exeter, Lord Shrewsbury was one of the Nobles in whom he chiefly trusted, and by whose advice he drew up the famous Declaration. Immediately on the establishment of William and Mary on the Throne, he was nominated one of the Privy Council, appointed Secretary of State, intrusted with the Lord Lieutenancy of three Counties, and raised soon after to a Dukedom.   The services of the Duke of Shrewsbury, his amiable character and his talants for business, endeared him to William; and so polished, engaging and conciliatory were his manners, as to make him loved and trusted by all parties   King William used to call him "THE KING OF HEARTS," and Lord Bolingbroke, who was his enemy, says of him, "I never knew a man so formed to please and to gain upon the affections"   The Church of England welcomed the illustrious convert with delight · his popularity was great, and it became greater when it was known, that Royal solicitations and promises, hadbeen vainly employed to seduce him back to the superstition he had abjured.   For this he was deprived by James, of the Lord Lieutenancy of Staffordshire, and the Colonelency of his Regiment   Such was the character of the great man, whose name stood at the head of the list of the "Illustrious seven."   For more full particulars of his life and character, reference may be had to *Grimblot,* and *Macaulay,* (already quoted,) and to Coxe's "*Shrewsbury Correspondence,*" "*Life of Charles Duke of Shrewsbury;*" *Birch's Life of Tillotson,*" "*Burnet's History of his own Times,* "and "*Mackay's Memoirs.*"

No 2 Is the Earl of Devonshire This Nobleman, William Cavendish, Earl of Devonshire, was second to no man in England in wealth and influence.   Macauley states that, the general voice of the Nation designated him as the finest gentleman of his times.   His magnificence, his taste, his talents, his classical learning, his high spirit, the grace and urbanity of his manners, were admitted by his enemies   Though an enemy to Popery and Arbitrary Power, he was averse to extreme courses, and had never been concerned in the illegal and imprudent schemes, which had brought discredit on the Whig party   But though regretting part of the conduct of his political friends, he had not, on that account, deserted his party, or failed to perform the perilous duties of friendship   He stood near Russel at the bar, had parted with him on the sad morning of the execution with close embraces and with many bitter tears ; nay, had offered to manage an escape at the hazard of his own life.   For a more full portrait of this great Nobleman, see the "*Funeral Sermon of the Duke of Devonshire*," preached by Kennet in 1708. *Burnet,* Vol 1, page 560   *Macaulay,* Vol. 2, pages 24–5, and *Cosmo* the Third's "*Travels in England.*"

No. 3, is the Earl of Danby.   This Nobleman—in early life, Sir Thomas Osborne—was made Treasurer of the Navy in 1671, and in the following year advanced to the Privy Council   In 1673 he was constituted Lord High Treasurer of England ; and created in a few months after Baron of Kiverton, and Viscount Latimer.   The year following, he was advanced to the dignity of Earl of Danby.   He was a Yorkshire gentleman, whom Burnet describes as a very plausible speaker, but too copious   He had been one of the high Cavaliers ; got into the confidence of King Charles, and long retained it   In 1675, he was bitterly attacked by the House of Commons ; but having in vain struggled to bring off the King from the French interest, he was greatly instrumental in bringing about the marriage between the Princess Mary and the Prince of Orange.   In the following year, he was impeached for High Treason , but in 1679, a new Parliament was convened, and Danby retired from the Treasury   To the new House, he presented a Pardon from under the Great Seal, notwithstanding this, the Commons persisted ; a Bill of Attainder was brought in, Danby delivered himself up, was sent to the Tower, and remained there for five years. He was very active in bringing about "the glorious Revolution"   He it was who galloped up to the Militia at York, raised the cry of "*No Popery,*" "*the Protestant Religion,*" "*a Free Parliament,*" and succeeded in carrying the ancient City and Shire of York, for the Prince of Orange   He was created Marquis of Carmarthen, and made President of the Council by King William.   In May, 1694, he was advanced to the dignity and title of Duke of Leeds   For a more full account of the Earl of Danby's life and transactions, reference may be had to *Mr. Grimblot's* work, before referred to, Vol. 1, page 229 ; and also to *Macaulay* and *Burnet,* particularly the last named author.

No 4, is Lord Lumley.   This gentlemen, Richard Lumley-Saunderson, was the owner of large estates both in England and Ireland.   His chief seats were at Lumley Castle, in the County of Durham, and at Sandbeck Park in Yorkshire.   He had been enobled in the Irish Peerage so long back as the year 1628, by Charles the First ; and, singular enough, his Patent of Nobility bears date *the 12th of July* in that year.   In early life,

Lord Lumley had been a strict Roman Catholic ; but like the great Earl of Shrewsbury, he had renounced the faith of the Church of Rome, and conformed to the Protestant religion.   He had served the Court of James the Second with distinguished valor and untarnished loyalty ; but in spite of the eminent service he had performed at the period of the western insurrection ; he was detested by James and his adherents, not only as a heretic but as a renegade also.   He was the fourth name in the list of the "illustrious seven," who invited the Prince to England.   In the early part of the year 1690, and immediately before setting out from England, to the relief of the Irish Protestants, William advanced Lord Lumley to the Earldom of Scarborough in the Peerage of England

No. 5, is the Bishop of London   Henry Compton, Bishop of London, was son of the second Earl of Northampton, who had fought fiercely for Charles the First, and when surrounded by the Parliamentary Soldiers, had fallen, sword in hand, refusing to give or take quarter.   The Bishop himself, before he was ordained, had borne arms in the Life Guards, and though he afterwards became grave and serious, yet, to the last, some flashes of the military spirit would occasionally break forth.   He was the Religious Tutor of the two Princesses, Mary and Anne, whose minds he had well grounded in the Protestant faith.   In the great debate which took place in the House of Lords in November, 1685, Bishop Compton took an active part against the Court, and declared that he was empowered to speak the sense of his Brethren of the Episcopal Bench, and that in their opinion and in his own, the whole Ecclesiastical and Civil Constitution of the Realm was in danger The Bishop was suspended from all his spiritual functions by James' new and illegal Court, called the Court of High Commission, and the charge of his great Diocese was committed to his corrupt Judges Sprat and Crewe. Bishop Compton was a sound Protestant, a man possessed of a strong mind and clear judgment, but not eloquent or commanding in debate.   Fuller particulars of the life of this eminent Prelate, may be seen in Gooch's " *Funeral Sermon on Bishop Compton.*"

No 6 Edward Russell, Esq.   The sixth name on the list of the " Conspirators," is Edward Russell, commonly called Lord Edward.   He was the Nephew of the Earl of Bedford, and was a gentleman of undoubted courage and capacity, but of loose principles and turbulent temper   He had been a sailor, and distinguished himself in his profession, and had held an office in the Royal Palace under Charles the Second   But all the ties which bound him to the Stuart Dynasty, had been severed by the death of his cousin, Lord William Russell   The daring spirit of Edward Russell was impatient of restraint, and he longed for the moment of the Prince of Orange's arrival, that he might be enabled to draw his sword against the Tyrant James, on the first day in which it could be drawn with reasonable hope of success.   *Vide Macauley's England*, Vol 2, pages 196-7.

No. 7 Henry Sidney, Esq. Last on the list of the "Illustrious Seven," stands the name of Henry Sidney. He was the younger son of Robert, Earl of Leicester, and younger brother of the celebrated Algernon Sidney. He was created Baron of Milton and Viscount Sidney in 1689, and raised to the dignity of Earl of Romney in 1694. It is remarkable that both Edward Russell and Henry Sidney had been in the household of James the Second ; that both had, partly on public, and partly on private grounds, become the enemies of that Monarch ; and that both had to avenge the blood of near kinsmen, who had, in the same year, fallen victims to James' implacable severity. Here the resemblance between these two remarkable men ends. Russell, with considerable abilities, was proud, acrimonious, restless and violent. Sidney, with a sweet temper, and winning manners, seemed to be dificient in capacity and knowledge, and to be sunk in voluptuousness and indolence. His face and form were eminently handsome. In his youth, he had been the terror of husbands, and even at fifty, he was the favourite of women, and the envy of younger men. He had formerly resided at the Hague in a public character, and had then succeeded in gaining a large share of William's confidence. Sidney, though ignorant and dissipated as he seemed to be ; understood well, with whom to be reserved, and with whom he might safely venture to be communicative The consequences was, that he did what Lord Mordaunt, with all his vivacity and invention, or Bishop Burnet, with all his multifarious knowledge and fluent elocution, never could have done. He filled successively the office of Secretary of State, Lord Lieutenant of Ireland, and Master of the Ordnance. Further particulars connected with the life of Mr Sidney, may be seen upon referring to *Count Tallard's Letters to Louis the Fourteenth,* dated "London, April 16th, 1698," and a note attached, on page 381, in the 1st Vol of *Mr. Grimblot's* work. Also to *Burnet's History,* Vol. I., page 763, *Mackay's Memoirs,* with Swift's note ; and *Sidney's Diary,* as edited by Mr. Blencowe.

The above closes a slight sketch of the personal history, of each of the "illustrious seven," who signed the "celebrated Association" in 1688. Lord Macaulay says, (Vol 2, page 319,) that the paper was signed in cipher by the seven Chiefs of the Conspiracy, Shrewsbury, Devonshire, Danby, Lumley, Compton, Russell, and Sidney : and Herbert was their messenger to the Prince

There are three other names so closely allied with the "illustrious seven," that it is but proper they should be here briefly alluded to. These are Dr. Burnet, Sir Edward Seymour, and Admiral Herbert. By the first, the "Orange Confederation" was written—the name of the second, was the first Password of the Association—and the latter, was the messenger of the "illustrious seven," to the Prince.

Gilbert Burnet, D.D., was a native of Scotland He possessed high

animal spirits, his parts were quick, his industry unwearied, and his reading various and extensive He was at once a historian, an antiquary, a
theologian, a preacher, a pamphleteer, a debater, and an active political
leader , and in every one of these characters, made himself conspicuous
among able competitors The many spirited tracts which he wrote on
passing events, are now only known to the curious ; but his " History of
his own Times,"—his " History of the Reformation,"—his ;" Exposition of
the Articles"—his " Discourse on Pastoral Care,"—his " Life of Hale,"—and
his " Life of Wilmot,"—all prove his research, his industry, his capacity,
and his great and varied abilities As Lord Macaulay most justly remarks :
a writer whose voluminous works, in several branches of literature, find
numerous readers a hundred and fifty years after his death, must have
possessed great merits In the pulpit, he was always clear, often lively, and
sometimes rose to solemn and fervid eloquence. The effect of his discourses,
which were delivered without note, was heightened by a noble figure, and
by pathetic action His enemies—and he had many—often attacked him
about his amorous propensities , but 'tis certain he was emphatically an
honest man, possessed of great excellence, and raised high above the influence of cupidity or fear His nature was kind, generous, and forgiving,
and his religious zeal, though ardent, was restrained by steady respect for
the rights of conscience. Further particulars touching the character of
Bishop Burnet, may be seen upon reference to Speaker Onslow's " *Note
on Burnet*," Vol 1, page, 596 . Johnson's " *Life of Sprat*," and Macaulay's
" *History of England*," Vol 2, pages 136-7-8.

Sir Edward Seymour, was a man of high birth, being the head of the
older branch of the Seymour family, and graceful, bold, and quick. He
was the most assuming Speaker that ever sat in the Chair of the British
Commons. He knew the House and every Member in it so well, that by
looking about him, he could tell the fate of any question, and made his
arrangements accordingly. Lord Macaulay expressly states in his second
volume, page 485, that Sir Edward Seymour, " Though a tory, had, in the
last Parliament, headed with conspicuous ability and courage, the opposition to Popery and Arbitary Power He was among the first gentlemen,
who repaired to the Dutch head-quarters at Exeter, and he was the author
of the Association, by which the Prince's adherents bound themselves to
stand or fall together "

Bishop Burnet, upon what ground is not stated, alleges that he was a
very corrupt man, and received large sums of money from the King That
he was able, bold and eloquent, and a thorough Protestant, is admitted by
all. See *Grimblot's Letters* Vol. 1, page 353, and *Macaulay*, Vol. 2, page
485.

Arthur Herbert, was brother to the Lord Chief Justice of England,
Member for Dover, Master of the Robes, and a Rear Admiral of England.

He was greatly beloved by the sailors, and was reputed to be one of the best of the aristocratical class of Naval Officers. It had been generally supposed that he would yield a ready compliance to the wishes of James II, for he was believed to be one of his most devoted adherents. When, however, he was brought to the test, and personally asked by the King to vote for a repeal of the Test Act, he told his Majesty that his honor and conscience would not permit him to give such a pledge "Nobody doubts your honor," said the King "but a man who lives as you do (alluding to his reputed attachment to the fair sex,) ought not to talk of his conscience." To this reproach Herbert manfully replied, "I have my faults, Sire, but I could name people who talk much more about conscience than I am in the habit of doing, and yet lead lives as loose as mine." He was dismissed from all his places under the Government of James. Herbert was a true Protestant, but somewhat loose in his morals; he was a brave and skilful seaman, and an attached subject of Constitutional Monarchy He occupies a large space in the history of all the contemporary writers of his times

As the City of Exeter had the honor of giving birth to the original Association, formed directly under the auspicies of the Immortal Prince himself, as it was also the first City in England in which he established his Head Quarters, and which he made the general rendezvous for the Protestants who flocked to his standard, some more particular description of it may be required.

Exeter is a City and County of itself, the seat of the see of Exeter, and the capital of the County of Devon. It is 173 miles from London The situation of the place is commanding and picturesque It stands on a flat ridge rising about 150 feet above high-water level of the river Exe, and on the south-west and north west rather precipitous. Around the south-western side of the City flows the Exe, over which at the western entrance to the City, a little above the site of the original ancient bridge, built in 1250—an elegant stone bridge of three arches was erected in 1776–8, at the expense of £20,000, after many unsuccessful attempts, owing to the rapidity of the stream The general character of the surrounding scenery is that of a succession of small undulations, increasing in height as they recede from the City, and eventually lost in the eminences which bound the horizon, excepting to the south-east, where the estuary of the Exe opens to the English Channel On the north are the Whitestone Hills, rising to the height of 740 feet. The stoke range connects those with the Woodbury Hills to the eastward On the south-west is Halden Hill, exceeding 800 feet in altitude: and beyond that is the lofty ridge of Dartmoor, whose mean height is 1792 feet. The Exe, immediately below the City walls, is 120 feet in bredth, by 9 in average depth. The place has all the appearance of an ancient City The remains of its wall, and many of its streets and buildings, still invest it with the features of antiquity Eighty years after the glorious Prince of Orange entered Exeter, Leland thus describes the City. "The town is a good mile and more in compass, and is right strongly walled and maintained. There i e divers fare towers in the town wall betwixt the south and west

E

gate There be four gates in the town by name of east, west, north and south.
The east and west gates be now the fairest, and of one fashion of building; the
south gate has been the strongest." None of these gates now exist. Exeter is of
antiquity so remote that its origin cannot be distinctly ascertained. There can
be no doubt that it was a settlement of the Britons long previous to the Roman
Invasion. From the number of coins, small bronze statutes—evidently household
gods or penates—tesselated pavements, and other Roman antiquities, which have
been discovered near its walls, and in the vicinity of the City, it must have been
an important station. The earliest event relating to Exeter, mentioned by any of
our historians, is its having been besieged by Vespasian It has been its fate to
sustain several severe seiges, but the greatest calamities it ever, sustained, were
inflicted by the Danes, who in the reign of Alfred, in 876, in violation of a solemn
treaty, suprised Exeter Alfred afterwards invested the City, and having defeated the Danish fleet, which was coming to the assistance of their countrymen, the
latter were compelled to evacuate the City At the Norman Conquest, Exeter
withstood the authority of William the First, who besieged and took it. It was
subsequently exposed to hostilities in the reigns of Stephen and Edward the Fourth.
The last siege sustained by the City, was in the reign of Edward the Sixth, when
the proposed changes in religious worship occasioned an alarming insurrection of
the inhabitants of Cornwall and Devonshire. The insurgents encompassed the City
for five and thirty days, and the inhabitants were reduced to great extremities.
Their loyalty and bravery on this occasion obtained for them a grant of the entire
manor of Exe Island. During the Parliamentary war, Exeter at first espoused the
Royal cause, but the City soon fell into the hands of the Parliamentarians. It was
subsequently taken by Prince Maurice and Sir John Berkely, the latter of whom
was appointed Governor, and it became the head quarters of the Royalists in the
west of England. Charles' Queen made it her residence, and her daughter, the
Duchess of Orleans, was born there. In 1646, it surrendered to General Fairfax,
after a blockade of two months. Since that period its history records no very important events, if we except those connected with the great Prince of Orange,
whose entry into it has been already described.

And now that we have seen this great Association transplanted from Holland
to England—now that we have seen the German origin—and the British graft—
permit a few sentences to be recorded—a few thoughts to be traced upon paper—
touching the reminiscences which bind the Countries, and the affinities which unite
their Peoples, in bonds of sympathy and affectionate remembrance

Mr Davies remarks in his "History of Holland and the Dutch Nation," Vol. 1,
pages 1, 2, 4, 354, and 359 That links the brightest and strongest, ties the most
holy, woven by patriotism and hallowed by time, bind Britain and Holland together
as two great and enlightened nations From England, the light of the Christian
Religion first shone on Holland;—from Holland, England imbibed her first ideas
of Civil Liberty and Commerce—with the Netherlands she made her first Commercial Treaty—side by side they have fought for all the dearest rights of mankind
—side by side they have struggled against the tyranny of Spain; against the
bigotry of the Stuarts, against the grasping ambition of the most powerful Monarch
of France—Louis the Fourteenth—when the clouds of despotism and superstition

hung dark and lowering over England, it was in William of Holland she hailed her deliverer—and when Holland writhed under the lash of Alva and the cruel Popish Inquisition, it was to England she looked as her trust and consolation. If there be yet left among us one Patriot, in the old and true sense of the word—one who loves his Country, not for the wealth and honors she can bestow, but because she herself is great and free—who can sympathize with his fellow men striving to obtain for their fatherland those blessings which his own enjoys, surely the blood of such an one must beat warm within him, as he contemplates the struggle made by the brave and noble Dutch in defence of their Religion and Liberties against the bigoted tyranny of Spain—a struggle unparalleled, unrivalled, perhaps, in the annals of ancient or modern history—protracted through forty years of suffering, under which the stoicism of Greece would have sunk—of deeds at which the heroism of Rome would have trembled—maintained, too, by a people whose spot of earth is so small as scarcely to deserve a place on the map of Europe, against a nation of boundless extent, of gigantic power, whose heart was strong with the blood of her chivalrous Nobility, and into whose bosom the riches of the new world were pouring If such a Patriot there is, a throb of joy will respond in his breast when he beholds the issue of that contest, defy all human calculation, mock all human foresight For once the righteous and feeble cause triumphed , the haughty foe of Holland shrank cowering before her.

If Saxony was the nursing mother of the Reformation in its infancy, Holland was the guardian and defender of its maturer growth

In 1522, John Baker, a Priest of Woerden, was accused of holding heretical (Protestant) opinions, was tried at the Hague, condemned to death, impaled and burnt. He was the first Martyr to the Reformed Church. He perished in silence and obscurity, but his blood was not shed in vain ; from it sprung a "noble army of Martyrs," who presented their undaunted breasts as a rampart to defend the struggling faith. This John Baker—this early Dutch Martyr—was but the forerunner of those Protestant Britons, whose lives were immolated by the fires of Smithfield—of those struggling but noble-hearted Irish Protestants, whose blood, in 1641, dyed the Blackwater and the Bann—of those devoted and unyielding spirits, whose cries reached to Heaven in 1798, from Vinegar Hill ; whose blood crimsoned the Slaney from the Bridge of Wexford ; and for whose destruction the fires of Smithfield were re-lit at the Barn of Scullabogue, in the same memorable year.

To trace the numerous incidents which followed the career of the Prince of Orange from the City of Exeter to the City of London, and to pursue that career till he ascended the British Throne, would be, perhaps, foreign to the object of this work. The following summary of the Declaration of the Lords and Commons of England, in Convention assembled, must suffice upon that head. The Declaration began, says the Historian, by recapitulating the crimes and errors which had made a Revolution necessary. James had invaded the province of the Legislature—had treated modest petitioning as a crime—had oppressed the Church by means of an illegal tribunal—had, without the consent of Parliament, levied taxes, and maintained a standing army in time of peace—had violated the freedom of election, and perverted the course of justice—proceedings which could lawfully be questioned only in Parliament, had been made the subjects of prosecution in the King's Bench—partial and corrupt Juries had been returned—excessive bail had been required from prisoners—excessive fines had been imposed—barbarous and unusual punishments had been inflicted —the estates of accused persons had been granted away before conviction —he by whose authority these things had been done, had abdicated the Government—the Prince of Orange, whom God had made the gracious instrument of delivering the Nation from superstition and tyranny, had invited the Estates of the Realm to meet, and to take counsel together, for the securing of religion, of law, and of freedom—the Lords and the Commons having deliberated, had resolved that they would first, after the example of their ancestors, assert the ancient rights and liberties of England—it was then declared that the dispensing power, lately assumed and exercised, had no legal existence—that without grant of Parliament no money could be exacted by the Sovereign from the subject—that without consent of Parliament, no standing Army could be kept in time of peace— the right of subjects to petition ; the right of Electors to choose Representatives freely , the right of Parliament to freedom of debate; and the right of the Nation to a pure and merciful administration of justice, according to the spirit of its own mild laws, were solemnly affirmed   All these things the Convention claimed, in the name of the whole Nation, as the undoubted inheritance of Englishmen.   Having thus vindicated the principles of the Constitution, the Lords and Commons, in the entire confidence that the Deliverer would hold sacred the Laws and Liberties which he had saved, resolved that William and Mary, Prince and Princess of Orange, should be declared King and Queen of England, for their joint and separate lives , and that during their joint lives the administration of the Government should be in the Prince alone.   After them, the Crown was settled on the posterity of Mary ; then on Anne and her posterity ; and then on the posterity of William   Thus was William, Prince of Orange Nassau, called to the British Throne   The following account of the ceremony attending his inauguration, is taken from Macaulay, page 512 ·

On the morning of Wednesday, the 13th of February, 1689, the Court of Whitehall, and all the neighbouring streets, were filled with gazers.   The magnificent Banquetting House, the master-piece of Inigo, embellished by master-pieces of Rubens, had been prepared for a great ceremony.   The walls were lined with the Yeomen of the Guard   Near the southern door, on the right hand, a large number of Peers had assembled   On the left were the Commons with their Speaker, attended by the Mace.   The northern door opened, and the Prince and Princess of Orange, side by side, entered, and took their place under the canopy of State.   Both Houses approached bowing low William and Mary advanced a few steps. The Marquis of Halifax, (Speaker of the Lords,) on the right, and Mr. Powle (Speaker of the Commons,) on the left, stood forth ; and Halifax spoke The Convention, he said, had agreed to a resolution, which he prayed their Highnesses to hear. They signified their assent ; and the Clerk of the House of Lords read, in a loud voice, the Declaration of Right When he had concluded, Halifax, in the name of all the Estates of the Realm, requested the Prince and Princess to accept the Crown.

William in his own name, and in that of his wife, answered, that the Crown was, in their estimation, the more valuable because it was presented to them as a token of the confidence of the Nation. " We thankfully accept," he said, " what you have offered to us " Then, for himself, he assured them, that the Laws of England, which he had once already vindicated, should be the rules of his own conduct , that it should be his study to promote the welfare of the kingdom ; and, that, as to the means of doing so, he should constantly recur to the advice of the Houses, and should be disposed to trust their judgment rather than his own These words were received with a shout of joy, which was heard in the streets below, and was instantly answered by huzzas from many thousands of voices The Lords and Commons then reverently retired from the Banquetting House and went in procession to the great gate of Whitehall, where the Heralds and Pursuivants were waiting in their gorgeous tabards All the space as far as Charing Cross, was one sea of heads The kettle drums struck up ; the trumpets pealed , and Garter King at Arms, in a loud voice, proclaimed the Prince and Princess of Orange, King and Queen of England , charged all Englishmen to pay from that moment, faith and true allegiance to the new Sovereigns, and besought God, who had already wrought so signal a deliverance for the Church and Nation, to bless William and Mary with a long and happy reign.

Thus was consummated the ENGLISH REVOLUTION And when it is compared with those Revolutions which have overthrown so many ancient governments, all must be struck by its peculiar character

> Then Britons come, the chorus join,
> For each to each is Brother ,
> One REVOLUTION to defend,
> We will oppose another

Having pourtrayed the character of the Great Prince, by whose auspices, under God, the Revolution of 1688 was accomplished : and seeing that memorable event itself happily consummated, by which the Church and Nation were delivered from Popery and Arbitary Power, and the Laws and Liberties of England placed upon the surest and best foundations, it may be proper now to leave England, and turn to the Sister Island

CHAPTER XI.

*Ireland, its state National, Religious and Social—Its " Chiefs of other days "—
tenacity of the aboriginal inhabitants to their Religious customs—Social distinc-
tion between them and the Protestant Colonists—Richard Talbot, Earl of
Tyrconnell, his perfidy and cruelty—The " Sassenach" persecutions in Ireland—
The Protestant inhabitants associate for mutual protection—The " Antrim.
Association," its Leaders and Password—Description and History of Antrim
—The Password used at the battle of Lisnaskea*

From the earliest plantations of British Colonists in Ireland, that portion
of the Empire had been subjected to one continued series of deeds of vice
—no crime in the whole catalogue of guilt was too vile for perpetration—
no sex was too delicate—no place too sacred—no day too public—no age too
feeble—and no torture too barbarous, to screen the doomed victims. The
horrible state of society in Ireland may be traced to a variety of causes.
Those causes were in part National, in part Religious, and in part Social.

Ireland, prior to the English conquest, was ruled by its own Chieftains.
Each Feudal Prince commanded his own territory, and received the fealty
of his own clan. Though a nominal Sovereign of the Island ruled at Tara,
each of the provinces of Leinster, Ulster, Munster, and Connaught, had
its separate Monarch. Nor were the Rulers of Ireland confined to the four
Provinces into which the Kingdom was divided ; for almost every County,
from Meath to Tyrone, had its King ; and almost every Barony, from the
lands of the O'Tool's of Wicklow, to those of the O'Donnel's of Donegal ;
and from those of the McGowan's of Dalradia, to those of the McCarthy's of
Desmond, had its Prince or Chieftain. As the English Colonists attempted
to effect settlements in the Country, the lands of the native Princes were
encroached upon, and their clansmen and retainers driven back It was
galling to the pride of a McMahon or a McQuillan, an O'Connor or an
O'More, to be driven from the rude independence of the Chieftain to the
more humble lot of the Subject ; but still more humiliating the torture
which tore their families from the native possessions of their fathers, and
beheld them bestowed upon the "Sassenah" and the stranger, as the reward of victory and conquest To this day, the title deeds of millions of
acres, in various parts of Ireland, are retained as a precious inheritance
by the descendants of former Princes and Rulers And these descendants
are now, in many instances, the poor, miserable " hewers of wood and
drawers of water," to the ennobled offspring of the fortunate soldiers who
received free grants of the " forfeited estates" of the "Chiefs of other
days T. that cause may be traced out of the chief sources of discord

and jealousy by which the two classes in the Island have been divided. To this may be added the religious difficulty. The faith of the aboriginal Irish was chiefly the Romish. Though many of the most ancient and honorable Families in the kingdom, such as the O'Neill's of Shane's Castle, the O'Brien's of Rostellan and Dromoland, the O'Kavanagh's of Borris, the O'Whelan's of Rath, the O'More's of Kinnegad, the O'Molloy's of Clare, the O'Callaghan's of Cork, the McGowan's of Dalradia, the McMahon's of Dartry, and the McCarthy's of Desmond, &c , &c., &c , have long since renounced all allegiance to the See of Rome ; yet, it must be acknowledged, that the great bulk of the aboriginal Irish have clung to the Romish worship, with a tenacity unexampled in other parts of Europe The religious element, uniting so cordially with the national, added fuel to the flame of discord, and gave to the conflict a peculiarity of hate and bitterness unknown in other countries To these combined causes, may be added Social distinctions. The greater portion of the nobles and gentry of Ireland who were the chief proprietors of the soil, were Protestants, and attached to the British Government. On the other hand, the greater portion of the peasantry were Roman Catholics, tenants and servants of the landed proprietors, and hostile to every badge indicative of British rule. These three causes combined, gave to Irish bickerings and to Irish bloodshed a keenness of atrocity to which the inhabitants of other lands were strangers ; and which, even to this day, carry with them into the souls of Irishmen resident in other lands, a settled hate, and a fixed and rooted malignity against every thing Protestant and British, which time seems inadequate to efface, and distance, generosity and kindness ineffectual to subdue.

When "the glorious revolution of 1688" was consummated, and William and Mary proclaimed King and Queen of England and Ireland, Richard Talbot, Earl of Tyrconnel, was the Viceroy of the latter kingdom He was a bigoted Roman Catholic, a devoted adherent of the exiled Monarch, James the Second, and a relentless, cruel, and evil-minded man. No crime was too foul to be committed under his sanction, and no atrocity too severe to visit upon his enemies The sufferings of the Protestant Colonists were cruel in the extreme The entire Romish population of the kingdom, (then in a semi-barbarous state,) were enrolled and armed , and no encouragements were withheld to fall upon their "*Sassenach*" or "*Saxon*" fellow-subjects, to destroy their properties, and to commit the grossest outrages of all kinds upon their persons Houses were burned , cattle were houghed , property of every kind was destroyed , the chastity of females was violated , and men were waylaid and murdered, in the most barbarous manner, on the public highways, as they returned from the fairs and markets of the country This state of things led to the organization of the Protestant population into small bands or parties, for mutual help and protection. In the more remote Districts of the Island the scattered

Protestant settlers met each night by appointment, at a place of rendezvous, where they kept "watch and ward" during the hours of darkness.
And when proceeding to, and returning from, fairs, markets, trading
villages, and other places of public resort, they usually proceeded together
in small parties, armed and united for self-preservation. In the north
east of the province of Ulster they organized in the year 1688 a more
general confederation, which they called "THE ANTRIM ASSOCIATION," at
the head of which stood the names of two distinguished noblemen of irre-
proachable character, and of large landed possessions, the Earl of Massarene
and the Earl of Mount Alexander It is said in the traditions of the Antrim,
Derry and Tyrone Protestants, that " the Antrim Association " adopted a
Password for mutual recognition, which word was *Oxford*, and was thus
given If a member of the Association met a stranger he would salute him
thus : " Did you happen to see a stray *Ox* to day ?" Or, " Did you happen to meet an *Ox* on the road ?" Or some similar interrogatory, in which
the word *Ox* would occur If the person addressed was not a member, he
would simply reply either in the affirmative, or in the negative, as the case
might be ; when the enquirer would rejoin, by passing off the conversation
in the easiest and best manner that might occur to him at the moment
Sometimes he would say, " probably I shall not find him." Or, " I have
been looking for one that has gone astray." Or, "he may have got into
some of the fields," &c , &c If the person interrogated was a member of
the Association, he would reply—" Yes, I saw one at the last *ford* " Both
parties would then recognize each other, and pronounce the word " OX-
FORD "

As the "Antrim Association" is admitted by Graham and other authors
to have had precedence of the Orange organization in Ireland, some description of the County in which it originated may be expected

Antrim is a maratime county in the extreme north east of the province of
Ulster. It is bounded on the north by the Atlantic, on the east by the
north channel, on the south and south east by the County of Down, and on
the west by the counties of Tyrone and Derry The county is nearly insulated between a sweep of the sea, and an alternate chain of fresh water,
consisting of Belfast Lough, the River Lagan, Lough Neagh, Lough Beg and
the River Bann. The greatest length, say from Bengore Head on the north
to Spencer's bridge on the south, is over 40 miles And its greatest breadth,
say from the Gobbins on the east, to Island Reagh Troone on the west, is
about 24 miles Along the summit line, and athwart nearly all the seaward
declivity of this county, the mountains are quite a picture gallery of landscape ; they combine in the rarest proportions, power, grandeur, romance
and beauty Here also is the far famed " Giants' Causeway," the theme of
the wonder and delight of tourists and others. Many and many a visit has
I   ...d to this bold, noble and enchanting coast, by the writer—often

has he drank out of the "Giants' Well" on the "Causeway Hill," and often too, has he partaken of the rough, but kind attention shown him by the members of Kane's Lodge, on this same "Causeway Hill" Here too, has he often visited the deserted ruins of the old military Castle of Dunluce, and the more modern but inhabited Shane's Castle, the residence of the late Right Honorable Charles Henry St John, Earl O'Neill, for several years the Grand Master of Ireland, and the lineal descendant, in a direct line of the Great Hy Nial, and other Monarchs of the North The whole district of Antrim was originally the kingdom of Dalriada. It is now divided into several large estates, upon which there is planted a number of independent country gentlemen, and a large population of industrious, thrifty and prosperous yeomen The chief proprietors are the Earl O'Neill, the Marquis of Donegal, the Marquis of Hertford, the Earl of Antrim, Lord Massarene Sir Edward Packenham, Mr Macartney, and Mr Leslie Sir Robert Savage at the head of a small party of English, is said to have slain 3,000 of the Irish in one day, near the town of Antrim. In 1649, the town was burned by General Munroe , and in fact from the year 1600, till near the close of the last rebellion, it was the scene of a doleful series of burnings, murders and battles The last action occurred on the 7th of June 1798, when the rebels were defeated by a small body of troops, assisted by Orange volunteers, under General Nugent The insurgents were driven off, after a loss of nearly 200 men, to Donnegar Hill, and the force of the rebellion in the north entirely broken Earl O'Neill and about 30 of the Loyalists were killed in the engagement

It would appear that the word *Oxford*, already alluded to, was not only in use amongst the Protestants united in "the Antrim Association," but had also extended in a few months afterwards to those of Down, Cavan and Fermanagh The Revd. John Graham A M , Rector of Magilligan, in the Diocese of Derry, thus alludes to this word in his "History of the Siege of Londonderry, and defence of Enniskillen," page 140. The "Enniskilleners, under the command of Lieutenant Colonel Berry, marched on the first day of July, (1689,) from Lisnaskea, towards the enemy, who lay about six miles from them. They had not proceeded more than two miles when the scouts discovered, at Donagh, a considerable body of horse and foot coming towards them, upon which they fell back to the main body, and all retreated towards the post they had moved from in the morning ; the enemy still advancing towards them. As they were double the number of the troops under Berry's command, he very judiciously continued his retreat till he got to more advantageous ground—having taken care to send off an express to Colonel Wolseley, at Enniskillen, acquainting him with the situation of his army, and desiring prompt assistance Of two roads leading to Enniskillen from Lisnaskea, Berry took that which had a short time before been made through bogs and low grounds, nearer to Lough Erne than the old way, as being more secure, and having several passes on it much easier to defend than the other. On this road he retreated in good order, the enemy still following him at some distance, till he came to a narrow Causeway across a bog, about a mile from Lisnaskea. Two horsemen could scarcely pass abreast at this part of the road, which was about a musket shot in length, and here Berry resolved to halt, and to repel the enemy, till the arrival of the expected aid from Enniskillen. He placed his Infantry and Dragoons in a thicket of underwood at the end of the Causeway, drawing a body of horse a little further off as a reserve, with which he proposed to support the other, and he gave the word " *Oxford* " In a very short time Colonel Anthony Hamilton, second in command to General McCarthy, came in view with a considerable body of men. Alighting from his horse, he ordered the Dragoons with him to do the same, and very bravely advanced near the end of the Causeway, his men firing briskly at the the Enniskilleners It pleased God, however, on this, as well as on many other occasions during the Campaign, that after many vollies of shot from the Irish, not one of them took effect upon the Protestants, who, being the better marksmen, killed twelve or fourteen of them on the Causeway, and wounded Colonel Hamilton in the leg On receiving the wound he retreated a little, and mounting his horse, ordered another officer to lead on the men Their second Commander, with some private soldiers, fell dead in a few minutes from the shots of the ambuscade in the thicket, upon which the rest began to retreat ; while their opponents, raising a shout, and crying out that the rogues were running, took to the bog on each side of the narrow road, over which the horse passed back with rapidity, and quickly turned the retreat into a disorderly flight The Enniskillen horse soon overtook the foot soldiers and dismounted Dragoons, among whom they made a great slaughter, chasing them through Lisnaskea, and nearly a mile beyond it " ᵢ CHAPTER XII.

Fermanagh, Cavan and Monaghan follow the example of Antrim—The " No Popery" password, when, and by whom, introduced—The York Declaration— Battle of Newtown Butler—Mr Walker and Mr. Hamilton deputed by Derry and Enniskillen to organize a general password— What it was, by whom adopted, and how used—Declaration of the " Enniskilleners"—The Protestants fly to Londonderry for shelter—History and description of Londonderry—The brave " Enniskilleners" defeat Lord Galmoy—Their password at the battle of Belturbet—Description of Enniskillen—James the Second lands at Cork, with French troops, and proceeds to Dublin—His cruelty and infatuation—Makes an expedition to the north, and returns to the Metropolis—Act of Attainder and Proscription.

On the fifteenth of December, 1688, the Protestants of the counties of Down, Fermanagh, Cavan and Monaghan, formed similar societies to those of the " Antrim Association ; " the only difference being, that while the *password* of the latter was " *Oxford,*" the *password* of the former was " *No Popery* " This password was adopted upon the suggestion of an English emissary, sent over to communicate with the Irish Protestants, by the Earl of Danby, who was a member of the ORANGE CONFEDERATION," formed at Exeter ; and who first promulgated the password " *No Popery,*" at the conquest of York, on the 22nd of November, 1688   The particulars connected with this event, are thus recorded by Macaulay, page 397, and who copies from Sir John Reresby's memoirs, and from Clark's life of James the Second, page 231   In the city of York there was a small garrison, under the command of Sir John Reresby   (The Earl of) Danby acted with rare dexterity.   A meeting of the gentry and freeholders of Yorkshire had been summoned for the twenty-second of November, to address the King (James the Second,) on the state of affairs.   All the Deputy Lieutenants of the three ridings, several Noblemen, and a multitude of opulent Esquires, and substantial Yeomen, had been attracted to the Provincial Capital Four troops of militia had been drawn out under arms, to preserve the public peace   The common Hall was crowded with freeholders, and the discussion had begun, when a cry was suddenly raised, that the Papists were up and were slaying the Protestants.   The meeting immediately separated in dismay   The whole city was confusion   At this moment Danby, at the head of about one hundred horsemen, rode up to the militia, and raised the cry " *No Popery !* " " *A Free Parliament !* " " *The Protestant Religion !*" The militia echoed the shout.   The garrison was instantly surprised and disarmed. The Governor was placed under arrest The gates were closed. Sentinels were posted every where The populace was suffered to pull down a Roman Catholic Chapel ; but no other harm appears to have been done. On the following morning the Guildhall was crowded with the first Gentlemen of the Shire, and with the principal Magistrates of the city. The Lord Mayor was placed in the chair Danby proposed a declaration (similar in substance to that of Exeter,) setting forth the reasons which had induced the friends of the Constitution and of the Protestant Religion to rise in arms This Declaration was eagerly adopted, and received in a few hours the signatures of six Peers, of five Barons, of six Knights, and of many Gentleman of high consideration. This password *"No Popery"* became general, it appears, among the Protestant Associations which were at that time being organized, for self-preservation, in the north of Ireland It is mentioned by Graham, in his "Derrianna," page 141, to have been used by the Enniskillen Protestants, commanded by Colonel Lloyd, at the battle fought near Newtown Butler on the 15th of December, 1688 The noble family of Hill, (now represented by the Marquis of Downshire,) patronised those Protestant Associations as early as January, 1689, and under their auspices one was organized at Hillsborough, in the county of Down Its declaration was in the following words "We declare that we form this protective association for self-defence, and for securing the Protestant religion, our lives, liberties and properties, and the peace of the kingdom, disturbed by Popish and illegal counsellors, and their abettors , resolving to adhere to the Laws and Protestant religion, and to act in subordination to the Government of England, and the promoting of a free Parliament , declaring also that, if we are forced to take up arms, it will be against our inclination, and shall be only defensive—not in the least to invade the lives liberties, or estates of any of our fellow-subjects, no not of the Popish persuasion, while they demean themselves peaceably."

Early in the following year (1689,) the Revd George Walker was deputed by the Protestants of Londonderry, and the Revd. Andrew Hamilton, by those of Enniskillen, to form a grand or general password, for the better recognition and encouragement of the northern Protestants For this purpose they met on the 16th of March 1689, at Lifford, in the County of Donegal, at which place they agreed upon the word "*I AM*," as a general grand password . Mr Hamilton carrying it to Enniskillen, and Mr. Walker to Londonderry It was selected from that portion of the Holy Scriptures, which forms the fourteenth verse, of the third Chapter of Exodus "And God said unto Moses, *I AM THAT I AM* And he said, thus shalt thou say unto the Children of Israel . *I AM* hath sent me unto you " The particular manner in which this password was introduced, divided and given, it may not be expedient now to detail Lifford, the place selected f   [illegible]   and at which the password was agreed upon, is a post and market Town, and the Assize Town for the County of Donegal, and was a Parliamentary Borough prior to the Irish union with great Britain It stands on the eastern verge of the County of Donegal, at the formation of the River Foyle, by the Rivers Finn and Mourne. It is but half a mile west by north from Strabane, of which it appears rather a Suburb, than a separate town. It is 14 miles south west from Londonderry, and 102 miles north west from Dublin The bridge at Lifford is remarkable chiefly as the place at which the united streams of the Finn and the Mourne take the name of the Foyle, and as the thorough-fare which connects Lifford with Strabane The town is built at a place where several roads, traversing some of the best cultivated parts of the county of Donegal converge, all leading to the Bridge which affords a passage over the river running between the Counties of Donegal and Tyrone. The Lifford property was originally granted by James the First to Sir Richard Hansard, in pursuance of the plan for "the plantation of Ulster" It was subsequently purchased by Mr Creighton, ancestor to the present proprietor, the Earl of Erne.

Shortly after Mr Hamilton's arrival at Enniskillen, the Protestants of the County Fermanagh publicly declared the objects of their "Orange Confederation." The following is an extract from their "Declaration " "We also declare that we have armed in self-defence, to act in subordination to the government of England, for the security of the Protestant Religion, our Lives, Liberties, and Properties and that although we will admit no persons but Protestants into our Association, yet, will we defend even Papists from violence, whilst they remain peaceable and quiet." *Vide* "Defence of the Loyal Orange Institution of Ireland," page 20, Archer, Bookseller, Dame Street, Dublin, 1825

The "Declaration" from which the foregoing is an extract, was made by the brave followers of King William, who afterwards so nobly distinguished themselves, upon so many hard fought fields, under the title of "Enniskilleners " No person can peruse their "Declaration," and compare it with the one drawn by Bishop Burnet, and adopted in the Cathedral of Exeter, under the immediate sanction of the Prince of Orange, but will at once see the exact similarity. And again, when compared with the "Declaration," which, to this day, appears in the front page of every Book of the "Orange Constitution and Laws," who can fail to be struck with the resemblance, to acknowledge the paternity, or not to behold in every feature the exact lineage and descent ? Well, indeed, may the present "Declaration" set forth that the Orange Society "disdains the badge of Faction—that it takes its stand upon the principles of the glorious Revolution of 1688—and that its foundations were laid in the fields of Protestantism and British Liberty." In the spot solemnly set apart for sacred purposes within the hallowed walls of an English Cathedral Church, were the outlines of "*THE ORANGE CONFEDERATION*" first traced upon paper, and by a Bishop of the Church of Christ. Under the Royal sanction of England's King and England's Deliverer, were those outlines sent forth for the general adoption of Protestant Britons; and to this day they bear the impress of the same Religious and Benevolent features, the same Royalty and the same Loyalty which distinguished their parentage and promulgation.

Tyrconnell, the Popish Viceroy of Ireland, with a view to carry into effect his intended extirpation of the Protestants of that Kingdom, and the eventual subjugation of England to the Hibernia-Romish yoke, by a series of the most cruel persecutions, caused the "Antrim Association," with the Protestant inhabitants of the district immediately surrounding Londonderry, to retire for shelter to that City, and to close its gates in the face of the forces sent against them. This heroic act was performed on the seventh of December, (O. S.) 1688.

> On came the foe in bigot ire,
>   And fierce the assault was given;
> By shot and shell, 'mid streams of fire,
>   Her fated roofs were riven,
>
> But baffled was the tyrants' wrath,
>   And vain his hopes to bend her;
> For still 'mid famine, fire and death,
>   She sung out "No Surrender!"

Some description of this far-famed City, and some glances at its history, may be here expected. The "maiden City of Londonderry" stands on the banks of the Foyle, 69 miles north west of Belfast, and about 113 from Dublin. It is the Capital of the County of the same name, and is situated on an oval hill, usually called "the Island of Derry." It is nearly insulated by a majestic sweep of the broad and voluminous Foyle, and commands a panoramic view of a country rich in both natural and cultivated beauty. A writer of no mean eminence quoted by the Parliamentary Gazeteer, says, "if historical recollections endear this place to every lover of liberty, its situation and time worn walls must render it interesting to all admirers of picturesque scenery." Another writer says, "the situation of Londonderry is, I think, the finest of any Town or City in Ireland. Indeed with the exception of Edinburgh, I do not know any Town in the United Kingdom so well situated as Londonderry. The Foyle, a fine broad river, makes a noble sweep on one side of the Town, and expands immediately below it into a wide estuary, which terminates in the broad waters of Lough Foyle. On all sides of the Town, is seen a succession of deep valleys and corresponding heights, exhibiting every attraction which wood and cultivation can bestow." A third writer says, "it is impossible to approach the venerable and heroic City, without being struck with its apparent fitness for resisting the assaults of a besieger. Its great natural strength is at once apparent , and as we advance nearer, and note the high and thick walls by which it is surrounded, we become convinced that the brave and earnest hearts by which it was defended, and who obtained for it and themselves, imperishable names in history, might have scorned the attacks of any enemy but famine." The County of Londonderry, of which this "Maiden City" is the Capital, was possessed at the earliest dawn of record by the Septs of O'Neills, O'Laughlin and O'Cahan The O'Neills were of the elder and Royal branch of their name, and had their residence at the ancient fortress of Grianan of Aileach, on the border of the County of Donegal, and immediately west of the City Liberties. The walls of Londonderry are now its most ancient remains. They were erected during several years, commencing in November, 1609, and cost, together with the gates, £8,357, (an enormously large sum at that time) A description of the walls, written in 1818, says, "the City of Londonderry is now compassed by a very strong wall, excellently made, and neatly wrought, being all of good lime and stone , the circuit whereof is two hundred and eighty-four and two third perches, at eighteen feet to the perch , besides the four gates which contains eighty-four feet, and in every place of the wall it is twenty-four feet high, and six feet thick The gates are all battlemented, but to two of them there is no going up, so that they serve to no great use ; neither have they made any leaves for their gates, but make two draw-bridges serve for two of them, and two portcullices for the other two The bullwarks are very large and good, being in number nine, besides two half bullwarks , and for four of them, there may be four cannons, or other great pieces , the rest are not about so large, but wanteth very little. The rampart within the City is twelve feet thick of earth all things are very well and substantially done, saving there wanteth a house for the Soldiers to watch in, and a sentinel house for the Soldiers to stand in in the night, to defend them from the weather, which is most extreme in these parts " During the celebrated siege in 1689, the rampart or bastion at the north west corner was called the Double Bastion, from it being divided by a wall, which reached from the face to the middle of the gorge, and was erected in consequence of the Bastion being situated on a descent. That farthest east, in the north wall, was called the Royal Bastion, from its bearing the Red Flag of defiance to the enemy, surmounted with the memorable words, "NO SURRENDER !" The next farthest east was called the Hangman's Bastion, from the circumstance of a person being nearly strangled upon it, while attempting an escape, by means of a cord. The next farthest east was called the Gunner's Bastion, from its being near the master gunner's house That on the north east corner was called the Coward's Bastion, from its being most out of the way of danger, and yet served by unduly large numbers of men That on the south east corner, the Water Bastion, from its being washed by the Tide. The farthest west, on the south wall, was called the Newgate Bastion, from its being near that gate. That next farthest west, the Ferry Bastion, from being situated opposite the Ferry. And that at the south west corner, the Church Bastion, from being situated near the Church. In 1826, the central western Bastion was modified for the reception of the beautiful and appropriate monumental pillar, called "Walker's Testimonial." Though most of the guns used during the memorable siege have been converted to such peaceful purposes as protecting the corners of streets, and holding fast the cables of ships, yet a few are still preserved as memorials on the Bastions —particularly four at Walker's Testimonial, and six at the south west Bastion. The piece called "*Roaring Meg*," from the loudness of her utterance during the siege, measures eleven feet in length, and four and a half in extreme circumference, and stands in good condition, mounted on a carriage, in the Court House yard. The Bishop's Gate is a Triumphant Arch, erected to the Memory of William the Third, in 1789, by the Corporation, with the concurrence of the Irish Society, at the Centenary of the opening of the Gates. The nucleus of the original Derry was entirely Ecclesiastical, and consisted of Churches, and the abodes of Ministers and Students. In 546 St. Columb, when twenty-five years of age, founded here the first of his Ecclesiastical Establishments. This structure was built at the side of a grove, which gave the name Derry to the locality. In 776 and 783, the Religious Establishment of St. Columb was destroyed by fire. In 812, the Danes destroyed the re-edified structure, and put the Clergy and Students to the sword. From thence to 1641, various were the changes that took place in the possession of Derry. In this memorable year of Protestant massacre, the Romish insurgents desiderated the surprise and capture of Derry, as an object of prime importance; but their plot against the City miscarried, and Derry became the Chief place of refuge in the north for the despoiled and alarmed Colonists from England and Scotland. From 1641 to 1689, Derry passed through various scenes of slaughter, pillage, and famine. But the great siege in the latter year figures so celebriously in history, was so severe and continuous in its sufferings, and so important and glorious in its results, as to eclipse the fame of the City's first and second sieges. The flight of O'Donnell and of the Earl of Tyrone in 1607, and the rebellion of Sir Cahir O'Dogherty in 1608, placed the whole of the County and City of Londonderry, in common with five other Counties, at the disposal of the Crown. James the First, in order to support his power, determined to make use of the Protestant Religion, as a means of establishing the plantation and settlement of the forfeited lands. With this view, he applied to the City of London, and offered to grant to the Citizens a great part of the forfeited estates, as an induce out to them to unde... the proposed plan of settlement. The

Citizens accepted the offer, and on the 29th of March, 1613, King James granted them a Royal Charter. A body of twenty-six men, consisting of Govenor, and a Deputy Governor, and Assistants, were appointed by the Common Council, to manage the estates—the one half of them to retire annually, and be succeeded by persons newly elected. This Body, commonly called the "Irish Society," as constituted by a renewed Charter of Charles the Second, after the Restoration, still exists, and exercises its power Their estates were erected into one Shire, called the County of Londonderry, and immediately after the granting of the first Charter, were distributed in portions among the different London Companies or Guilds, and into a remainder, to belong to the "Irish Society," or general Corporation. The company of Goldsmiths, received as their portion the south east Liberties of Derry—the Haberdashers, Bovevagh—the Vintners, Bellaghy—the Merchant Tailors, Macosquin—the Grocers, the precinct of Muff—the Fishmongers, Ballykelly—the Ironmongers, Aghadowey—the Mercers, Moyvanaway—the Clothworkers, part of Coleraine—the Skinners, Dungiven—the Drapers, Moneymore—and the Salters, Magherafelt. Four of the Companies, the Goldsmiths, the Haberdashers, the Vintners, and the Merchant Tailors, have, at various times sold their proportions in perpetuity, principally to the Families of Beresford, Richardson, Ponsonby, Alexander, and Conolly. The County of Londonderry, up to the period of the Protestant Colonization, was one of the most desolate tracts in Ireland, but in consequence of the introduction of all classes of artisans, and the skilful inculcation of habits of industry and independence, it immediately began to acquire an entirely new face as to both its physical and its social condition. The native Irish have gradually returned and multiplied till they nearly equal the descendants of the Protestant Colonists in number, but they are still decidedly inferior to the others in habits of enterprise and comfort.

In 1689 the Protestants of Fermanagh formed themselves into a Regiment of twelve Companies, and under the command of the Governor of Enniskillen, Gustavus Hamilton, they fortified that Town, and declared for King William. Shortly after they were summoned by Lord Galmoy to surrender, to whose demand they returned a firm refusal. So soon as his Lordship received the reply of the men of Enniskillen, he marched his forces to Crom Castle, within sixteen miles of the Town, where he halted ; and after reconnoitring the place, he deemed it more prudent to retire to Bellturbet, in the County of Cavan. On his retreat, his Lordship was closely pursued by the Enniskilleners, under the command of Colonel Lloyd. Pressing close upon Lord Galmoy, the Enniskillen men forced him to battle between Newtown and Bellturbet, in which engagement his forces were totally routed, and his ablest General, McCarthy, taken prisoner. The Protestants, whose password that day was OXFORD, (the *password* of the "Antrim Association,") fought with undoubted bravery ; and it is affirmed by the most impartial historians, that Lord Galmoy lost in the action, upwards of two thousand men ; five hundred of whom were drowned in the Lake while endeavouring to escape, and three hundred were made prisoners. The "Enniskilleners" have been distinguished upon many a hard fought field, and they continue so to the present hour. A slight sketch of this far famed place may therefore be looked for :

Enniskillen is a port and market town, a Parliamentary Borough, and the capital of the County of Fermanagh. The main body of the Town stands upon an Island, in Lough Erne, and is distant from Cavan 25 miles, 75 from Belfast, and 80 north west by north from Dublin. The ground between upper and lower Lough Erne, is about four and a half miles, in a straight line, and consists chiefly of low meadow land, adorned with wood, diversified with arable swells and sylvan knolls, and flanked by slopes and hills of various dress and contour, and of a high aggregate amount of beauty. The Island upon which the main body of the town is situated lies about one mile and a half above the debouch of the River Erne into the lower Lake. Abundance of wood, and the broken surface of the country, gives sufficient shade to the landscape which, on all sides of this celebrated town, images the still, deep, broad waters, that surround it. The great Island of the Town is connected with the two suburbs by two Bridges The principal street extends with considerable spaciousness and some slight sinuosity, from Bridge to Bridge. The entire appearance of Enniskillen, including the arrangement of the streets, the cleanliness of the thoroughfares, the character of the houses, the opulence of the shops, and the dress of the inhabitants, is very greatly superior to that of the vast majority of Irish Towns ; and would put to blush the boasted spruceness and finery of some of the second Boroughs of "merry England." The only buildings which existed on the site of the Town, previous to the English "plantation" of Ulster, was a small Fortalice of the Maguire's, and it passed into English possession during Tyrone's last rebellion William Cole, Esq, one of the Grantees of land in the new "plantation" of Ulster, and afterwards Sir William Cole, obtained by Letters Patent from James the First, four Town lands adjoining, and one third of the Island of Enniskillen. So rapidly did the Town rise under the encouragements of its founder, Sir William Cole, that in 1641, it covered the greater part of the Island, and formed an important asylum and protection for the Protestants during that bloody period. The Enniskilleners are famed for their energy, bravery and freedom. In the war of the Revolution, the Towns people were greatly strengthened by the accession of their Protestant brethren from all parts of the surrounding country. When Lord Tyrconnell sent to them two Companies of the Irish Army, they refused admission to the Force, elected Sir Gustavous Hamilton as their Governor, proclaimed William and Mary, and heroically commenced a series of

defiances, contests and exploits, which terminated in the defeat of Lord
Galmoy before Crom Castle ; in the routing of General McCarthy's army
between Newtown Butler and Lisnaskea, and virtually in the raising of
the siege of Derry   This glorious old Protestant Town gives the title of
Earl, in the Peerage of Ireland, to the noble family of Cole.   The present
possessor being the Grand Master of that Kingdom.

On the 12th of March, 1689, Lord Tyrconnell, who was then in Dublin,
put himself at the head of thirty-eight thousand men, and repaired to
Cork, at which place he was met by his bigot Master, James ; who had
just arrived from France, with five thousand picked troops   The exiled
King, after having put a Magistrate and some other Protestants to death
at Cork, for entertaining opinions favourable to King William, repaired
with Tyrconnell to Dublin, of which City, shortly after his arrival, James
appointed Colonel Lutterell, Governor, and he exercised the most
barbarous cruelties against its Protestant citizens.   James' first expedition
was against the Town of Kilmore, in the County of Cavan, which was
heroically defended by its little garrison.   In consequence of this opposition,
he determined to visit the Protestants generally with the utmost cruelty
After the reception experienced by Lord Galmoy before Enniskillen, James
deemed it prudent to leave its inhabitants unmolested for the present
From Kilmore he marched forward for the purpose of attacking the
renowned City of Londonderry, before the walls of which place he arrived
on the 18th of April, 1689.   Here he tried force, sophistry and persuasion,
to induce its gallant defenders to deliver their liberties into his hands
But all was vain.   The " Maiden City " was not to be wheedled, or intimidated.

> For Derry had a surer guard,
>   Than all that art could lend her ,
> Her 'prentice hearts, the gates who barr'd,
>   And sung out " *NO SURRENDER !* "

Despairing of immediate success, James left General Hamilton (who was
shortly afterwards succeeded by Marshal De Rosen,) in command of the
besieging army, while he repaired himself to Dublin, to meet his Parliament. Here, on the 12th of May, 1689, an Act was passed, by which
two thousand four hundred and forty-one persons were attainted by name,
including 2 Archbishops, 1 Duke, 17 Earls, 7 Countesses, 28 Viscounts,
2 Viscountesses, 7 Bishops, 24 Barons, 35 Baronets, 51 Knights, and 83
Clergymen, all of whom were declared *TRAITORS*, and adjudged to suffer
DEATH, and the *FORFEITURE OF THEIR ESTATES*   Their sole
crime was the maintenance of their Religious and Civil liberties, as by
law guaranteed So diabolical, so general, and so sanguinary a proscription
as this, is probably not to be found recorded in the annals of any country.
It affords proof, melancholy but conclusive, of the *liberty* which was allowed
Protestants by the Roman Catholics of the Irish Nation, in Parliament
assembled !

CHAPTER XIII.

*Trinity College, Dublin—Lutterell's Proclamations—Origin of the " Aldermen of
Skinner's Alley "—The Protestants of Ireland fly to Enniskillen and Londonderry—Letter of the " Inniskilleners," and response of the " Men of Derry."*

On the 11th of Feburary, and before James had proceeded on his
sanguinary tour to destroy the Northern Protestants, he issued a
mandamus to the Provost and Fellows of Trinity College, Dublin, declaring
that he would change their Statutes at his pleasure   He deprived the
Provost and appointed one Doyle to that high post   He also stopped the
annual gift of £388 15s 0d   Not content with altering the Statutes of
the Establishment, and depriving it of its revenues, he turned out the
Vice-Provost, Fellows and Scholars, seized their public and private property, furniture, library, and communion plate, and placing a Roman
Catholic garrison in the College, he converted the Chapel into a Magazine,
and the Chambers of the Fellows and Students into prisons for Protestants !
Soon after a Doctor Moore was nominated Provost, who, to his credit,
preserved the books and manuscripts ; and by his persuasion James was
prevented from converting the College into a seminary for Jesuits.   This
abdicated and banished King by a Royal Proclamation, ordered all the
Churches to be seized under pretence that the Protestants had concealed
arms in them ; and on the 23rd of September, 1689, Christ's Church, Dublin,
and twenty-six others in that Diocese were taken possession of by Governor
Lutterell ; whose heartless soldiers broke open the cemeteries and graves,
and left the dead bodies exposed   On the 13th of July, James issued an
Order prohibiting Protestants from leaving the Parish in which they
resided.   On the 13th of September (only ten days before the Churches
were seized,) he issued a Proclamation prohibiting Protestants from
assembling together in any place of Divine Worship.   And on the 3rd of
May following, Governor Lutterell, in strict accordance with the feelings of
his Master, issued the following manifesto.

PROCLAMATION.

" WHEREAS, it is his Majesty's desire to know the names of all the *Protestant*
   subjects and *Dissenters*, I do, therefore, in His Majesty's name, require
" and order you all, the Ministers and Curates of the several Parishes and Cures of
" this City and Liberties, to bring to me, fairly written, the names of the
" said *Protestants* and *Dissenters*, in a book made for that purpose, that are in the
" several Parishes or Cures   Declaring that it is his Majesty's resolution, to treat all
" such as will not pay obedience to this order, and enter in their names by *Thurs-
" day next* ensuing the date hereof, as spies or enemies"
   " Dated this 3rd day of May, 1690.

"They are to return only from the age of 15, to the age of 80, that are of the
"Male kind, and not of the Female"

By the Governor of Dublin,

Sym. Lutterell"

"*To all the Curates and Ministers of the*
    "*City, Liberty, and Suburbs of the City of Dublin*"

Comment on the foregoing Proclamation would be superfluous : it speaks
for itself   How applicable the words of Dryden,

> "What words can paint those execrable times,
> "The Hero's suff'rings, and the Tyrant's crimes?"

It might be supposed that such a mandate would have satisfied the cruel
bigotry of this infatuated tyrant, and that it would have been sufficient for
his purpose to know the *names* of all the Protestants and Dissenters. Not
content with their names only, he issued the following arbitrary mandate
on the 18th of June following.

PROCLAMATION.

" WHEREAS several disaffected persons of the Protestant Religion, are of late
        come to this City of Dublin, and some of them armed with pistols,
"swords and other weapons, contrary to His Majesty's express commands, by His
" Proclamation bearing date the 20th of May, 1690

" *First*—These are, therefore, to will and require all men whatsoever of the
" Protestant Religion, now residing or being within the City of Dublin, or within
" the Liberties of St Sepulchre and Doner, or Thomas Court, who are not House-
" holders or have not followed some lawful vocation therein these three months
" past, to depart WITHIN TWENTY-FOUR HOURS of the publication hereof, out of the
" said City and Liberties and repair to their respective habitations, or usual places
" of abode in the Country, *UPON PAIN OF DEATH*, or imprisonment ; and
" to be further proceeded against as contemners of His Majesty's Royal command,
" and as persons designing the disturbance of the public peace

" *Second*—And likewise, that all the Protestants within the said City and
" Liberties, not being of His Majesty's Most Honorable Privy Council, or in His
" Army or actual Service, shall, within the time aforesaid, deliver up all their
" arms, both offensive and defensive, and all their ammunition, into his Majesty's
" stores, in the said City, *UPON PAIN OF DEATH*.

" *Third*—And that no Protestant whatever, do presume at his peril, to walk or
" go in the streets, from ten of the clock at night, till five in the morning, nor at
" any time when there is an alarm, in which case, all such persons are required
" for their safety and for the security of the public, to keep within doors till such
" alarm is over.

" *Fourth and Lastly*—For the prevention of riots and unlawful assemblies,
" these are therefore to will and require all the said Protestants, that no greater
" number of them than five shall meet or converse at any time, either within any
" house in the said City or Liberties, over and above the Family of the house, or

"in the Streets or Fields, in and about the same, or elsewhere, hereby declaring
"that all persons who shall offend against any clause in this present order SHALL
"SUFFER DEATH, or such other punishment as a Court Martial shall think fit.
"Dated this 18th of June, 1690.

"By the Governor of Dublin,

SYM. LUTTERELL.

Many of the unfortunate Protestants in the Country parts of the Kingdom who were at that time suffering the most cruel tortures, fled to Dublin
for protection, supposing, as Christians, they would be safe when within
the City, and removed from Country exposure and persecution. But alas!
how sadly were they disappointed! Instead of meeting with protection
from James, they were cruelly driven back into the wildest and most
savage districts of the Kingdom, in the midst of a sanguinary population!
How blind and infatuated must the Bigot have been, even to his own
interests in thus acting? Had he permitted those unfortunate Protestants
to reside in Dublin, the protection he afforded, would have secured to him
their silence, if not their assistance But bigotry being the ruling power of
the infatuated tyrant, he drove them from his shelter, and left them without an
alternative but that of taking refuge in Londonderry or Enniskillen, and
making common cause with the Protestants of those places in declaring for
King William. James having removed the Protestant Aldermen of Dublin
from their offices, they contrived to assemble together in a small house in a
retired part of the City, called "*Skinner's Alley*." In this back lane, they
continued to meet in secret from time to time, till restored to their liberty
and their stations by the "Immortal William." The Society of
"ALDERMEN OF SKINNER'S ALLEY," of which this is the origin,
is still in existence. It is a voluntary Association composed exclusively of
Protestants, and generally of gentlemen connected with the Corporation of
the City of Dublin In the year 1829, (when the writer left Ireland,) it
was presided over by Sir Abraham Bradly King, Bart , and contained over
two hundred members, including amongst other distinguished characters,
the Illustrious Field Marshal, the Duke of Wellington Its members
met annually on the sixth of July (*old style,*) being the anniversary of
the relief of Dublin, by the entry of William into that City in 1690.
Each member wears a silver medal of William the Third, suspended by a
blue ribbon On the one side of the medal is a representation of the
Aldermen seated round a table in a small room, with the motto "*Dumspiro,
spero,*" (whilst we breathe we hope) On the other side is a head of
William the Third, with the words, "*The Deliverer—Sixth July,* 1690."

When Tyranny's detested power,
Had leagued with Superstition ,
And Bigot James, in evil hour,
Began his luckless mission.

> Still here surviv'd the sacred flame,
> Here Freedom's sons did rally,
> And consecrate to deathless fame,
> The men of " SKINNER'S ALLEY "

The union of the Protestant refugees, driven out of Dublin, with those of Londonderry and Enniskillen, caused the two last named places to appear more formidable to the ex-Monarch than he had previously expected The strength forced upon them by the tyranny of James, enabled them to bid defiance to all the efforts subsequently made for their subjugation The Enniskillen men, though small in numbers and feeble in resources, prior to the junction with them of the Dublin Protestants, yet, were they resolved not to surrender their liberties without a struggle. A perusal of the following document, addressed to the Protestants of Londonderry, will establish this fact.

" *To David Cairns, Esq , or the other Officers Commanding in Chief, now in Londonderry*

" GENTLEMEN,

" The frequent intelligence we have from all parts of the Kingdom, of a " general massacre of the Protestants—two Companies of foot, of Sir Thomas " Newcom's Regiment, viz. . Captain Nugent's and Captain Shurloe's, being on " their march to garrison here and now within ten miles, hath put us upon a reso- " lution of refusing them entrance ; our desire being only to preserve our lives and " the lives of our neighbours. This place being the most considerable pass be- " tween Connaught and Ulster, and hearing of your resolution, we thought it " convenient to impart this to you and likewise to beg your assistance, especially " in helping us with some powder, and in carrying on a correspondence with us " hereafter, as we shall, with God's assistance, do with you, which is all at present " from,

" Gentlemen,

" Your faithful friends and fellow Citizens,

" THE INHABITANTS OF INNISKILLEN.

" From Inniskillen,

" December 15, 1688."

The spirited determination of the Enniskilleners as manifested in this letter, was received in Londonderry with the strongest demonstrations of Joy The timid forsook their doubts, and the stout-hearted received a fresh accession of resolution. Two days after the Enniskillen letter was received in Londonderry, the following manifesto was issued by its defenders.

" *To all Christian People to whom these presents shall come, the Mayor, Sheriffs* " *and Citizens of Londonderry, send greeting*:

" Having received information from several credible persons, that an Insur- " rection of the Irish Papists was intended, and by them a general massacre of " the Protestants of this Kingdom, and the same to be acted and perpetrated

" on or about the 9th of this instant, December, and being confirmed in our fear
" and jealousy of so horrible a design, by many palpable insinuations, dubious
" expressions, monitory letters, and positive informations, all conducing and
" concurring to beget in us a trembling expectation of a sudden and inevitable
" ruin and destruction ; we disposed ourselves to a quiet and patient resignation
" to the Divine Providence, hoping for some deliverance and diversion of this impend-
" ing misery ; or to receive from the hands of God, such a measure of constancy and
" courage, as might enable us to possess our souls in patience, and submissively to
" await the issue of so severe a trial.

" Accordingly, when, on the 5th instant, part of the Earl of Antrim's forces
" advanced to take possession of this place, though we looked upon ourselves as
" sheep appointed for the slaughter, and on them as the executioners of vengeance
" upon us, yet, we contrived no other means of escape than by flight, and with all
" precipitation to hurry away our families into other places and countries. But it
" pleased God, who watches over us, so to order things, that when they were
" ready to enter the City, a great number of the younger, and some of the meaner
" of the Inhabitants, ran hastily to the gates, and shut them, loudly denying
" entrance to such guests, and obstinately refusing obedience to us

" At first we were amazed at the enterprise, and apprehensive of the many ill
" circumstances and consequences that might result from so rash an undertaking,
" but since that, having received repeated advertisments of the general design, and
" particular informations which may rationally induce us to believe it, and being
" credibly assured that under the pretence of six Companies to quarter amongst us,
" a vast swarm of Highland and Irish Papists, were on the ways and roads
" approaching to us; that some of the Popish Clergy in our neighbourhood had
" bought up arms, and procured an unusual number of iron chains for bridles,
" (whereof sixty were bespoke at one place,) and some of them seized and now in
" our custody, we began to consider it an especial instance of God's mercy towards
' us, that we were not delivered over as a prey unto them, and that it pleased
" Him to stir up the spirits of the People so unexpectedly, to provide for their and
" our common safety and preservation.

" Wherefore, we do declare and remonstrate to the world that we have resolved
" to stand upon our guard, and defend our walls, and not to admit of any Papist
" whatsoever to quarter amongst us, so we have firmly and sincerely determined,
" to persevere in our duty and loyalty to our Sovereign Lord the King, without the
" least breach of mutiny or seditious opposition to his royal commands.

" And since no other motives have prompted us to this resolution, but the pre-
" servation of our lives, and to prevent the plots and machinations of the enemies
' of the Protestant Religion, we are encouraged to hope that the government will
" vouchsafe a candid and favourable interpretation of our proceedings, and that
" all His Majesty's Protestant subjects will interpose their prayers to God, their
" solicitations to the King, and their advice and assistance to us, on this so extra-
" ordinary and emergent an occasion, which may not only have an influence on the
" rest of the Kingdom, but may have a probable aspect towards the interests of
' the Protestant Religion, and may deserve a favourable regard from all the profes-
" s ... t ... e of in His Majesty's Dominions

" GOD SAVE THE KING '

The memorable defence sustained by the garrison of this "Maiden City," while labouring under the most unparalleled privations, has been recorded by many pens, has been the theme of many tongues, and will live in characters of immortality

> This was the place whose martial sons alone,
> Supported Freedom, and the British Throne;
> Adorn'd the parent stem, from whence they grew,
> Bled to support their rights—and conquer'd too.

CHAPTER XIV

The "Password" of the garrison of Derry, how divided and given—Duke Schomberg lands at Carrickfergus and proceeds to Belfast—He advances to Dunkalk where his army was attacked by sickness—William resolves to proceed to Ireland, and to take upon himself the command of the Protestant army—His Message to both Houses of Parliament—The landing of "the Orange King" signalled through all the Protestant Settlements of Ulster—All hearts filled with joy and hope—Great excitement throughout Ireland—Description of Carrickfergus, (where William landed,) and also of Belfast—He advances from Belfast, through Lisburn, to Hillsborough—Reviews his Army at Loughbrickland, and before leaving, issues a Royal Warrant for the "Regium Donum," to the Presbyterian Ministers of Ulster—He advances through Louth and Meath, to the Boyne—His exclamation on seeing the Irish army—Rise and description of the river Boyne.

The Rev'd Mr Graham, at page 131, of his "*Derriana,*" and Mr Gillespie, at page 143, of his "*Siege of Londonderry,*" mention, that on the 31st of July, 1689, the general *Password* adopted by the garrison, was "*Orange ;*" which word they divided into syllables between the interrogated and the interrogator, after the following manner :

First Interrogator —" Are you for Derry, *or*—Enniskillen ?"

Respondent —" Are you, *an,* enemy, or a friend, to ask me such a question ?"

Interrogator —" *Ge* on man, I mean no offence "

The three syllables marked in *italic* (one in each line,) were thus given and made together the "Password" *or-an ge.*

William having secured the Protestant interest in England, and being made fully acquainted with the deplorable condition of the Irish Protestants, was rapidly preparing for their relief He placed eighteen Regiments of Infantry and five of Dragoons, under the command of Duke Schomberg, with directions to proceed immediately to Ireland Schomberg effected a landing without opposition, near Carrickfergus, in the County of Antrim, on the 14th of June, 1689. From thence he proceeded to Belfast, which important Town he succeeded in taking with but little opposition. From Belfast, Schomberg sent a summons to Carrickfergus, demanding the surrender of that garrison. Compliance was at first refused. But subsequently discovering that the Duke had given orders for a vigorous attack, the garrison capitulated, upon condition of being allowed to march out with the honors of war and to proceed unmolested to Newry. After securing Carrickfergus, Schomberg advanced his army south towards Dublin, as far as Dunfialk, in the County of Louth, intending to move on the Metropolis if possible. A severe malady however, attacked his forces by which he lost nearly 5,000 men ; and the winter setting in earlier than usual, and with great severity, both armies retired into winter quarters

William, finding that his presence had become absolutely necessary in Ireland, resolved upon immediately going over, and taking upon himself the command of the Army He informed both Houses of Parliament of his intention, and from the speech delivered by His Majesty upon that occasion, the following is an extract—it contains an epitome of the whole and is truly characteristic of "the great and immortal King," by whom it was spoken "As I have already ventured my Life, for the preservation "of the Religion, Laws, and Liberties of this Nation, so am I willing "again to expose it, to secure to you the quiet enjoyment of them " William left London on the 4th of June, 1690, and embarked at Highlake, near Chester, on the 11th of the same month, attended by Prince George of Denmark, the Duke of Ormond, and several Officers of distinction

The landing in Ireland, the reception by the people, and the heroic acts of William while in that Kingdom, are related in a variety of Manuscripts, and by a variety of authors. The "*History of the wars in Ireland,*" by an officer in the Royal Army, 1690—the "*London Gazette,*" for the same year—*Villare Hibernicum,*" 1690—the *Life of James the Second,*" Vol. 2—second volume of the "*Memoirs of Bishop Burnet*"—Letters of "*Lauzun to Louvois,*" June 16 and June 26, 1690—Storey's "*Impartial History,*" 1691—"*Historical Collections*" of Belfast, 1817—Gillespie's "*Siege of Londonderry*"—Graham's "*Annals of Ireland*" and Macaulay's third volume of the "*History of England,*" may all be consulted with advantage.

The whole of the Protestant settlements throughout Ireland had been desolated , those in the east, west and south of the Kingdom, had resigned themselves to despair ; but those along the northern coast having communication with Duke Schomberg, who lay at Belfast, had been long expecting the arrival of William. They had long looked to him as their only hope, as, under God their only Saviour and Deliverer , and in every household, and from every hearth, fervent prayers were sent up for his safety and speedy arrival. At length the auspicious day arrived On

Saturday the 14th of June, he landed safely at Carrickfergus, and proceeded the same evening to Belfast. Carrickfergus, the first spot in Ireland honored by the presence of "the Deliverer," deserves a passing notice. Carrickfergus is a sea-port Town and a Parliamentary Borough. It stretches along the Belfast Lough on the Ballinure road, and stands about 10 miles from Lane, 8 miles from Belfast, and 88 from Dublin. The Town consists of the ancient City or walled Town in the centre, the Irish quarter on the west, and the Scotch quarter on the east. The walls were commenced about the year 1576, by the then Lord Deputy, Sir Henry Sidney, and they still to a great extent, may be distinctly traced. The north gate is still standing, and is a pleasing specimen of architecture. The Irish gate was once called the west Suburb, and obtained its present name after the year 1677, when the then Lord Lieutenant, the Duke of Ormond, issued a proclamation ordering all Roman Catholics resident in Cities, corporate Towns, and Forts, to remove beyond the walls. The Scotch quarter is occupied chiefly by Fishermen, and had its name from a Scotch Colony of the same craft of the present inhabitants ancestors, who arrived about the year 1665, from Galloway and Argyleshire, descendants chiefly of the ancient Dalriadians. Carrickfergus Castle, said by some writers to owe its origin to Sir Henry Sidney, by others to Hugh DeLacy, but more generally believed to have been built by John DeCourcey, is the only building now existing in Ireland, which exhibits a specimen of the old Norman military strong-hold. Its site is a rocky peninsula about thirty feet high, shelving considerably to the land, washed on three sides by the Bay, and entirely occupied by the works of the fortress. The site on which Carrickfergus Castle now stands, is said to have been a strong-hold of the Dalriads. It was granted to the celebrated John DeCourcey by Henry the Second; but all the property of DeCourcey subsequently passed into the possession of the DeLacy family. In 1315 it was invested by Edward, brother of "the Bruce" of Scotland. In 1555 the castle was again besieged by the Scotch, but was relieved in the following year by Sir Henry Sidney. During the whole of Tyrone's rebellion, Carrickfergus was the head quarters of the English forces in the north. Various were the scenes of capture and restoration through which this celebrated Castle passed till the year 1690, when the "glorious and Immortal" William of Orange landed at the Town, on his great expedition for the relief of Ireland. A large stone at the extremity of the Quay, is still pointed out, as that on which the great Orange Monarch first set foot in Ireland—it bears the name of "King William's Stone," and is memorable to all classes, even at the present day.

On the road from Carrickfergus to Belfast, William was met and welcomed by his old Marshal, Duke Schomberg. At the entrance to the Town of Belfast, the Magistrates and Burgesses of the Town, clothed

in their official robes, were assembled to meet him   They gave him
a most cordial and gratifying reception   He was surrounded by multitudes of the People, all filled with enthusiasm, all anxious to get a
glimpse of "the Deliverer," and all shouting "*God save the Protestant
King.*"   The night had nearly set in ere William reached Belfast, but
the surrounding counties had signalled to them the arrival of the
Great Prince   The Castle of Belfast boomed forth a Royal Salute, and
Schomberg's cannon—which he had placed as signal guns at different posts
—re-echoed the glad tidings, and filled the hearts of all the Protestant
settlements with joy and anxiety   The peals of the cannon were heard
through Antrim and Down, and ere the clock had told twelve that night,
all the surrounding hills blazed with bonfires, and the whole of the Protestant population bounded with joy.   The next day being the Sabbath, His
Majesty attended Divine Service, when Dr Royce preached an excellent
and appropriate Sermon   His text was from Hebrews, 11th Chapter and
33rd verse—" *Who through Faith subdued Kingdoms, wrought Righteous-*
" *ness, obtained promises, stopped the mouths of Lions* "

The blazing lights from the mountains of Down, were seen by the adverse
party across the bay of Carlingford, and within forty-eight hours after
William's landing, James was in motion from Dublin, to join his Army ,
which lay encamped around Ardee, in the County of Louth   The excitement at this time in Dublin, and generally throughout the Kingdom, was
at the highest pitch   The looks of the persecuted minority betokened the
hopes they entertained of a speedy deliverance ; while those of the
majority, plainly pourtrayed that they felt that the decisive crisis was at
hand, when the cruel tyranny they had practised, would no longer be
yielded to without a death struggle on the part of the oppressed

As it was in the immediate vicinity of Belfast where William first touched Irish ground, as the inhabitants received him with open arms, and as
he made it his first Head Quarters in Ireland, a brief description of the
place may be expected.

Belfast is the largest and most important Town in the north of
Ireland.   It may be called the capital of Ulster, and the Athens of the
Kingdom   It stands at the head of the Belfast Lough, in the County of
Antrim, and is situated 8 miles south west of Carrickfergus, 69 south east
of Londonderry, 75 north east of Enniskillen, and 80 north of Dublin.
It is undoubtedly the first Town in Ireland in enterprise, intelligence and
prosperity   About one-half of the Town stands above, and the other
half below, the debouch of the Lagan water into Belfast Lough   The
environs of the Town, both immediate and more remote, abound in the
amenities of landscape, and blend, in extended views, with a great variety
of such features and groupings as belong strictly to the beautiful, and yet
are nearly allied to the grand.   A Castle, supposed to have been built by

the celebrated John DeCourcey, was erected for controlling the pass across the River Lagan It was inferior in strength to that of Carrickfergus, but was held in conjunction with it, and as a subordinate strength by the English Edward Bruce, in his expedition in 1315, plundered and destroyed the Castle ; and from thence to the year 1571, the Castle of Belfast frequently exchanged masters and underwent dismantling and renovation. It was chiefly, however, in the possession of the O'Neill's. In the last named year (1571,) it appears by the "grand inquisition of the County of Down," that Sir Thomas Smith and his son, received from Queen Elizabeth a grant of Belfast Castle, and of a considerable tract of country around it The conditions of the grant not having been fulfilled, the lands and Castle reverted to the Crown The Earl of Essex subsequently attempted the colonization and settlement of the place ; but it was not till 1604, when Sir Arthur Chichester, (ancestor to the present Proprietor, the Marquis of Donegal,) then Lord Deputy of Ireland, acted energetically in promoting the English plantations in Ulster, obtained a final grant of the Castle and circumjacent lands, from James the First, and it has since continued in the Chichester family. It is at this day the largest commercial and manufacturing Town in Ireland, and is second to none in the wealth, intelligence and industry of its inhabitants, in its sanitary state, or in its public enterprise, and benevolence

From Belfast, William proceeded to Lisburn, and from thence to Hillsborough He had ordered his whole forces to rendezvous at Loughbrickland. From the 14th to the 22nd of June, he was unceasing in his exertions to discipline his Battalions, and to provide for their wants On the last named day, his whole Army, amounting to 36,000 men, passed in review before him While at Loughbrickland, he issued an order to the Collector of Customs at Belfast, authorising the payment of twelve hundred pounds a year to the Presbyterian Ministers of the north, as a reward for their loyalty and as a compensation for their losses This grant was afterwards confirmed by Parliament, and is the origin of the "Regium Donum" annually voted to the Presbyterian Clergy of Ulster

William remained but two days at Loughbrickland, and on the 24th he broke up his camp, and advanced south towards Dublin. As William advanced, James directed his forces to retire from Ardee, and to take post on the south or Dublin side of the River Boyne, a position which he thought it impossible William would be able to force. As the name of the Boyne is associated with every thing sacred in Orange history, and operates as a talisman upon the members of the Order, in whatever country or under whatever circumstances they may assemble, it may be proper here to quote the great modern authority, (Macaulay vol 3. page 492,) for a full description of the incidents connected with this memorable event

On the morning of Monday, the 30th of June, William's army, marching in three columns, reached the summit of a rising ground, near the southern frontier of the County of Louth. Beneath lay a valley, now so rich and so cheerful that the Englishman who gazes upon it, may imagine himself to be in one of the most highly favored parts of his own highly favored country. Fields of wheat, woodlands, meadows bright with daisies and clover, slope gently down to the edge of the Boyne. That bright and tranquil stream the boundary of Louth and Meath, having flowed many miles between verdant banks crowned by modern palaces, and by the ruined keeps of old Norman Barons of the pale, is here about to mingle with the sea. Five miles to the west of the place from which William looked down upon the river, now stands on a verdant bank amidst noble woods, Slane Castle, (the ancient residence of Fleming, Viscount Slane,) now the mansion of the Marquis of Conyngham. Two miles to the east, a cloud of smoke from Factories and Steam Vessels, overhangs the busy town and fort of Drogheda. On the Meath side of the Boyne, the ground still all corn, grass, flowers, and foliage rises with a gentle swell to an eminence surrounded by a conspicuous tuft of Ash trees, which overshades the ruined Church and desolate graveyard of Donore.

In the seventeenth Century the landscape presented a very different aspect. The traces of art and industry were few. Scarcely a vessel was on the River, except those rude corales of wicker-work covered with the skins of horses, in which the Celtic peasantry fished for trout and salmon. Drogheda now peopled by twenty thousand industrious inhabitants, was a small knot of narrow, crooked and filthy lanes, encircled by a ditch and a mound. The houses were built of wood with high gables, and projecting upper stories. Without the walls of the Town, scarcely a dwelling was to be seen, except at a place called Oldbridge. At Oldbridge the River was fordable ; and on the south of the ford were a few mud cabins, and a single house built of more solid materials.

When William caught sight of the valley of the Boyne, he could not repress an exclamation and a gesture of delight. He had been apprehensive that the enemy would avoid a decisive action, and would protract the war till the autumnal rains should return with pestilence in their train. He was now at ease. It was plain that the contest would be sharp and short. The pavilion of James was pitched on the eminence of Donore. The flags of the House of Stuart and of the House of Bourbon waved together in defiance on the walls of Drogheda. All the Southern bank of the river was lined with the camp and batteries of the hostile army. Thousands of armed men were moving about among the tents ; and every one, horse soldier or foot soldier, French or Irish, had a white badge in his hat. That colour had been chosen in compliment to the House of Bourbon. "I am glad to see you, Gentlemen," said the King, as his keen eye surveyed the Irish lines. "If you escape me now, the fault will be mine."

Before proceeding further a short description of "THE BOYNE" so famous and so memorable in Orange history may be expected. It is not only the celebrated, but also the chief River in the Province of Leinster. It rises in the bog of Allen, about a mile and a half south east of Carbery, in the County of Kildare, and drains that portion of the great bog which lies immediately north of the Grand Canal. From its source to its termination in the Irish sea, 3 miles and a half below Drogheda, is about 50 miles. Its chief affluents are the Yellow and the Milltown rivers from the King's County , the Deal from Meath, the Blackwater from Kildare, and the lower and greater Blackwater from Cavan   Through its course in the Counties of Kildare and Kings it is a sluggish and almost stagnant stream , but in the rich champaign County of Meath, and between that County and Louth, it has a delightful variety of motion and scenery—now much disturbed by sharps and rocks, and now stealing silently along considerable flats—now overhung by steep precipices and bold projecting rocks, and now kissing the margin of a gentle declivity, or of a hanging plain—now majestically rippling along a picturesque and bosky dell, and now reflecting the clouds from a mirrory surface, amidst lawns, and parks, and groves, and all the varieties of ornamented demense. Its banks, from the bogs to the sea, however, are in general comparatively high—or at least high enough to form a low land dell . they for the most part slope gradually in wood or verdure to its edge ; and they are thickly studded and in the aggregate profusely embellished by the seats of Noblemen and Gentlemen   Tara Hill, Towns, Castles, Monasteries, and Battlefields on the River's margin, combine to associate its name with multitudinous historical recollections ; and the Abbeys of Clonard, Trim, Bective, Donagmore, Slane, Mellifont, Monasterboice, and Drogheda, on its banks have freely sprinkled its name over monastic annals, and given it the designation of "the Boyne of Science." The river is naturally navigable to Drogheda, three and a half miles from the sea, but is affected by the tide to Oldbridge, which is about two miles and a quarter above Drogheda.

The great battle of the Boyne, which annihilated the power of Popish James, and gave security to "the glorious Revolution" of 1688, extended from the immediate vicinity of Drogheda on the east, to the bridge and village of Slane on the west, a distance of about seven miles, and has left at several points many remains of earthworks, and other traces of military science. The brunt of the engagement was however, chiefly in the vicinity of Oldbridge and the hill of Donore, two miles and a quarter west of Drogheda, and is there commemorated by a stately stone Obelisk of about 150 feet in height   The Obelisk crowns a rock which rises abruptly from the river.

CHAPTER XV.

Relative condition and strength of both armies, and of both positions—the Englishry of Ireland, and the Irishry of the Irish—Death of the Rev George Walker—William wounded in the arm—Reconnoitres the Irish and French army, and prepares to cross the Boyne—The Battle, its sanguinary character and glorious results—Hamilton's "honor" and William's scorn—Loss on both sides—Death of Duke Schomberg.

Each of the contending Princes, whose armies lay on the opposite banks of this river, had some advantages over his rival   James, standing on the defensive, behind entrenchments, with a river before him, had the stronger position ; but his troops were inferior both in number and in quality to those which were opposed to him.   He probably had thirty thousand men.   About a third part of this force consisted of excellent French Infantry and excellent Irish Cavalry.   But the rest of his army was the scoff of all Europe.   The Irish Dragoons were bad ; the Irish Infantry worse   It was said that their ordinary way of fighting was to discharge their pieces once, and then to run away bawling "Quarter" and "Murder"   Their inefficiency was, in that age, commonly imputed, both by their enemies and by their allies, to natural poltroonery   How little ground there was for such an imputation has since been signally proved by many heroic achievements in every part of the Globe   William had under his command near thirty-six thousand men, born in many lands, and speaking many tongues.   Scarcely one Protestant Church, scarcely one Protestant nation, was unrepresented in the army, which a strange series of events had brought to fight for the Protestant Religion in the remotest Island of the west.   About half the troops were natives of England. Ormond was there with the Life Guards, and Oxford with the Blues. Sir John Lanier, an officer who had acquired military experience on the Continent, and whose prudence was held in high esteem, was at the head of the Queen's Regiment of Horse, now the First Dragoon Guards. There were Beaumont's Foot, who had, in defiance of the mandate of James, refused to admit Irish Papists among them ; and Hasting's Foot, who had, on the disastrous day of Killiecrankie, maintained the military reputation of the Saxon race.   There were the two Tangier Battalions, hitherto known only by deeds of violence and rapine, but destined to begin on the following morning a long career of glory.   The Scotch Guards marched under the command of their countryman, James Douglas.   Two fine British Regiments, which had been in the service of the States General, and had often looked death in the face under William's leading, followed him in this campaign, not only as their General, but as their native King. They now rank as the Fifth and Sixth of the Line　The former was led by an Officer who had no skill in the higher parts of military science, but whom the whole army allowed to be the bravest of all the brave, John Cutts. Conspicuous among the Dutch Troops, were Portland's and Ginkell's Horse, and Solme's Blue Regiment, consisting of two thousand of the finest Infantry in Europe　Germany had sent to the field some warriors sprung from her noblest Houses.　Prince George of Hesse Darmstadt, a gallant youth who was serving his apprenticeship in the military art, rode near the King　A strong Brigade of Danish volunteers was commanded by Duke Charles Frederick of Wirtemburg, a near kinsman of the Head of his Illustrious Family　It was reported that of all the soldiers of William these were the most dreaded by the Irish　For centuries of Saxon domination had not effaced the recollection of the violence and cruelty of the Scandinavian Sea Kings ; and an ancient prophecy that the Danes would one day destroy the children of the soil, was still repeated with superstitious horror　Among the foreign auxiliaries were a Brandenburg Regiment, and a Finland Regiment　But in that great array, so variously composed, were two bodies of men, animated by a spirit peculiarly fierce and implacable, the Huguenots of France, thirsting for the blood of the French ; and the Englishry of Ireland, impatient to trample down the Irishry of the Irish.　The ranks of the refugees had been effectually purged of spies and traitors, and were made up of men such as had contended in the preceding century against the House of Valois, and the genius of the House of Lorraine.　All the boldest spirits of the unconquerable Colony had repaired to William's camp.　Mitchelburne was there with the stubborn defenders of Londonderry, and Wolseley with the warriors who had raised the unanimous shout of "Advance" on the day of Newtown Butler　Sir Albert Conyngham, the ancestor of the noble family whose seat now overlooks the Boyne, had brought from the neighbourhood of Lough Erne a gallant Regiment of Dragoons, which still glories in the name of "Enniskillen," and which has proved on the shores of the Euxine, that it has not degenerated since the days of the Boyne.

Walker, notwithstanding his advanced age and his peaceful profession, accompanied the men of "Londonderry," and tried to animate their zeal by exhortation and example.　He was now a Prelate.　Ezekiel Hopkins (Bishop of Derry) had taken refuge from Popish persecutors and Presbyterian rebels in the City of London, had brought himself to swear allegiance to the Government, had obtained a Curé, and had died in the humble duties of a Parish Priest.　William, on his march through Louth, learned that the rich See of Derry was at his disposal　He instantly made choice of Walker to be the new Bishop　The brave old man, during the few hours of life which remained to him, was overwhelmed with salutations

and congratulations.   Unhappily he had, during the siege in which he had
so highly distinguished himself, contracted a passion for war ; and he
easily persuaded himself that, in indulging this passion, he was discharging
a duty to his Country and his Religion.   He ought to have remembered
that the peculiar circumstances which had justified him in becoming a
combatant had ceased to exist ; and that in a disciplined army, led by
Generals of long experience and great fame, a fighting divine was likely
to give less help than scandal.   The Bishop elect was determined to be
wherever danger was ; and the way in which he exposed himself, excited
the opposition of his Royal patron, who hated a meddler almost as
much as a coward.   A soldier who ran away from a battle, and a gownsman
who pushed himself into a battle, were the two objects which most strongly
excited William's spleen.

It was still early in the day.   The King rode slowly along the northern
bank of the River, and closely examined the position of the Irish, from
whom he was sometimes separated by an interval of little more than two
hundred feet   He was accompanied by Schomberg, Ormond, Sidney,
Solmes, Prince George of Hesse, Coningsby, and others.   " Their army is
but small " said one of the Dutch Officers.   Indeed it did not appear to
consist of more than sixteen thousand men.   But it was well known, from
the reports brought by deserters, that many Regiments were concealed from
view by the undulations of the ground   " They may be stronger than
they look," said William ; " but weak or strong, I will soon know all about
them "

At length he alighted at a spot nearly opposite to Oldbridge, sat down
on the turf to rest himself, and called for breakfast.   The sumpter horses
were unloaded : the canteens were opened , and a table-cloth was spread
on the grass   The place is marked by an Obelisk ; built while many
Veterans who could well remember the events of that day were still living.

While William was at his repast a group of horsemen appeared close to
the water on the opposite shore.   Among them his attendants could discern
some who had once been conspicuous at reviews in Hyde Park, and at balls
in the gallery of Whitehall ; the youthful Berwick ; the small fair-haired
Lauzun ; Tyrconnell, once admired by Maids of Honor as the model of
manly vigor and beauty, but now bent down by years and crippled with
gout , and, overtopping all the stately head of Sarsfield.

The Chiefs of the Irish Army soon discovered that the person who,
surrounded by a splendid circle was breakfasting on the opposite bank, was
the Prince of Orange   They sent for artillery.   Two fieldpieces screened
from view by a Troop of Cavalry, were brought down almost to the brink
of the River, and placed behind a hedge.   William, who had just risen
from his meal and was again in the saddle, was the mark of both guns.
The first shot struck one of the hostlers of Prince George of Hesse, and

brought his horse to the ground "Ah!" cried the King, "the poor Prince is killed!" As the words passed his lips, he was himself hit by a second ball, a six pounder. It merely tore his coat, grazed his shoulder, and drew two or three ounces of blood. Both armies saw that the shot had taken effect; for the King sank down for a moment on his horse's neck. A yell of exultation rose from the Irish camp. The English and their Allies were in dismay. Solmes flung himself prostrate on the earth, and burst into tears But William's deportment soon reassured his friends. "There is no harm done," he said "but the bullet came quite near enough." Coningsby put his handkerchief to the wound: a Surgeon was sent for; a plaster was applied; and the King, as soon as the dressing was finished, rode round all the posts of his Army amidst loud acclamations. Such was the energy of his spirit, that in spite of his feeble health, in spite of his recent hurt, he was that day (the thirtieth of June, Old Style,) nineteen hours on horseback.

> "A bullet from the Irish came,
>   Which grazed King William's arm,
> They thought his Majesty was slain;
>   Thank God it done him little harm " *Old Song.*

A cannonade was kept up on both sides till the evening William observed with especial attention the effect produced by the Irish shot on the English regiments which had never been in action, and declared himself satisfied with the result. "All is right," he said; "they stand fire well." Long after sunset he made a final inspection of his forces by torchlight, and gave orders that everything should be ready for forcing a passage across the River on the morrow. Every soldier was to put a green bough in his hat The baggage and great coats were to be left under a guard. The countersign was "WESTMINSTER."

The King's resolution to attack the Irish was not approved by all his Lieutenants Schomberg in particular, pronounced the experiment too hazardous, and when his opinions were overruled, retired to his tent in no very good humour. When the order of battle was delivered to him, he muttered that he had been more used to give such orders than to receive them For this little fit of sullenness very pardonable in a General who had won great victories when his Master was yet a child, the brave Veteran made, on the following morning a noble atonement

The first of July dawned, a day which has never since returned without exciting strong emotions of very different kinds in the two populations which divide Ireland. The sun rose bright and cloudless Soon after four (in the morning,) both armies were in motion William ordered his right wing under the command of Meinhart Schomberg, one of the Duke's sons, to march to the bridge of Slane, some miles up the river; to cross there and to turn the left flank of the Irish army. Meinhart Schomberg was assisted by Portland and Douglas. James, anticipating some such design, had already sent to the bridge a regiment of Dragoons commanded by Sir Neil O'Neil. O'Neil behaved himself like a brave gentleman, but he soon received a mortal wound. his men fled, and the English right wing crossed the river.

This made Lauzun uneasy. What if the English right wing should get into the rear of the Army of James? About four miles south of the Boyne, was a place called Duleek where the road to Dublin was so narrow that two cars could not pass each other, and where on both sides of the road lay a morass which afforded no firm footing. If Meinhart Schomberg should occupy this spot it would be impossible for the Irish to retreat. They must either conquer, or be cut off to a man. Disturbed by this apprehension, the French General marched with his Countrymen, and with Sarsfield's horse in the direction of the bridge of Slane Thus the fords near Oldbridge were left to be defended by the Irish alone

It was now near ten o'clock. William put himself at the head of his left wing, which was composed exclusively of Cavalry, and prepared to pass the river not far above Drogheda The centre of his army, which consisted almost exclusively of foot, was entrusted to the command of Schomberg, and was marshalled opposite to Oldbridge At Oldbridge the whole Irish Infantry had been collected The Meath bank bristled with pikes and bayonets. A fortification had been made by French Engineers out of the hedges and buildings, and a breast-work had been thrown up close to the water side. Tyrconnell was there ; and under him was Richard Hamilton and Lord Antrim.

Schomberg gave the word Solmes' Blues were the first to move They marched gallantly, with drums beating, (the air was "*Lilleburlero*," now called "*The Boyne Water*,") to the brink of the Boyne. Then the drums stopped, and the men, ten a breast descended into the water. Next plunged Londonderry and Enniskillen A little to the left of Londonderry and Enniskillen, Caillemot crossed, at the head of a long column of French refugees. A little to the left of Caillemot and his refugees, the main body of the English infantry struggled through the river, up to their arm pits in water. Still further down the stream, the Danes found another ford In a few minutes the Boyne, for a quarter of a mile, was alive with muskets and green boughs

It was not till the assailants had reached the middle of the channel, that they became aware of the whole difficulty and danger of the service in which they were engaged They had yet seen little more than half the hostile army. Now whole Regiments of Foot and Horse seemed to start out of the earth A wild shout of defiance rose from the whole shore ; one moment the event seemed doubtful ; but the Protestants pressed resolutely forward : and in another moment the whole Irish line gave way. Tyrconnell looked on in helpless despair. He did not want personal courage, but his military skill was so small, that he hardly ever reviewed his Regiment in the Phœnix Park without committing some blunder, and to rally the ranks which were breaking round him, was no task for a General who had survived the energy of his body and of his mind, and yet had still the rudiments of his profession to learn. Several of his best officers fell while vainly endeavouring to prevail on their Soldiers to look the Dutch Blues in the face Richard Hamilton ordered a body of Foot to fall on the French Refugees, who were still deep in the water He led the way, and, accompanied by several courageous gentlemen, advanced, sword in hand, into the river. But neither his commands nor his example could infuse courage into that mob of cowstealers He was left almost alone, and retired from the bank in despair Further down the river Antrim's Division ran like sheep at the approach of the English column. Whole Regiments flung away arms, colours and cloaks, and scampered off to the hills, without striking a blow, or firing a shot.

It required many years, and many heroic exploits to take away the reproach which that ignominious rout left on the Irish name. Yet, even before the day closed, it was abundantly proved that the reproach was unjust Richard Hamilton put himself at the head of the Cavalry, and, under his command, they made a gallant, though an unsuccessful attempt, to retrieve the day. They maintained a desperate fight in the bed of the river, with Solmes' Blues They fell impetuously on the Huguenot Regiments, which, not being provided with pikes, then ordinarily used by Foot to repel Horse, began to give ground Caillemot, while encouraging his fellow exiles, received a mortal wound in the thigh. Four of his men carried him back across the ford to his tent As he passed, he continued to urge forward the rear ranks, which were still up to the breast in water. "On, on, my lads, to glory, to glory" Schomberg, who had remained on the northern bank, and who had thence watched the progress of his troops with the eye of a General, now thought that the emergency required from him the personal exertion of a soldier Those who stood about him besought him in vain to put on his cuirass. Without defensive armour he rode through the river, and rallied the refugees, whom the fall of Caillemot had dismayed "Come on," he cried, in French, pointing to the Popish squadrons; "come on, gentlemen, there are your persecutors" These were his last words. As he spoke, a band of Irish Horsemen rushed upon him and encircled him for a moment When they retired he was on the ground His friends raised him, but he was already a corpse. Two sabre wounds were on his head, and a bullet from a carbine was lodged in his neck Almost at the same moment, Walker, whilst exhorting the Colonists of Ulster to play the man, was shot dead. During near half an hour, the l... .mtori· to rage along the southern shore of the river

All was smoke, dust, and din   Old soldiers were heard to say that they
had seldom seen sharper work in the Low Countries.   But just at this
conjuncture, William came up with the left wing.   He had found much
difficulty in crossing.   The tide was running fast.   His charger had been
forced to swim, and had been almost lost in the mud.   As soon as the
King was on firm ground, he took his sword in his left hand—for his right
arm was stiff with his wound and his bandage—and led his men to the
place where the fight was the hottest   His arrival decided the fate of the
day   Yet, the Irish Horse retired fighting obstinately.   It was long
remembered among the Protestants of Ulster, that, in the midst of the
tumult, William rode to the head of the Enniskilleners   "What will you
do for me?" he cried.   He was not immediately recognized, and one
trooper, taking him for an enemy, was about to fire   William gently put
aside the carbine   "What," said he, "do you not know your friends?"
"It is his Majesty," said the Colonel   The ranks of the sturdy Protestant
yeomen set up a shout of joy.   "Gentlemen," said William, "you shall
be my guards to-day   I have heard much of you; let me see something
of you"   One of the most remarkable peculiarities of this man, ordinarily so saturnine and reserved, was, that danger acted on him like wine,
opened his heart, loosened his tongue, and took away all appearance of
restraint from his manner   On this memorable day he was seen wherever
the peril was greatest.   One ball struck the cap of his pistol; another
carried off the left heel of his jack-boot, but his Lieutenants implored
him in vain to retire to some station, from which he could give his orders
without exposing a life so valuable to Europe   His troops, animated by
his example, gained ground fast   The Irish Cavalry made their last stand
at a house called Plottin Castle, about a mile and a half south of Oldbridge.
There the Enniskilleners were repelled with the loss of fifty men, and were
hotly pursued, till William rallied them and turned the chase back   In
this encounter, Richard Hamilton, who had done all that could be done
by valor, to retrieve a reputation forfeited by perfidy, was severely
wounded, taken prisoner, and instantly brought, through the smoke and
over the carnage, before the Prince whom he had foully wronged   On no
occasion did the character of William show itself in a more striking manner.
"Is this business over?' he said, "or will your Horse make more fight?"
"On my honor, sir," answered Hamilton, "I believe that they will."
"Your honor!" muttered William, "your honor!"   That half suppressed
exclamation was the only revenge which he condescended to take for an
injury for which many Sovereigns, far more affable and gracious in their
ordinary deportment, would have enacted a terrible retribution.   Then,
restraining himself, he ordered his own surgeon to look to the hurts of the
captive

And now the battle was over.   Hamilton was mistaken in thinking that

his Horse would continue to fight.   Whole troops had been cut to pieces.
One fine regiment had only thirty unwounded men left.   It was enough
that these gallant soldiers had disputed the field till they were left without
support, or hope, or guidance, till their bravest leader was a captive, and
till their King had fled.

Of the Irish about fifteen-hundred had fallen ; but they were almost all
Cavalry, the flower of the Army, brave and well-disciplined men, whose
place could not easily be supplied.   William gave strict orders that there
should be no unnecessary bloodshed, and enforced those orders by an act
of laudable severity.   One of his soldiers after the fight was over, butchered three defenceless Irishmen who asked for quarter.   The King ordered
the murderer to be hanged on the spot.

The loss of the Conquerors did not exceed five hundred men ; but among
them was the first Captain in Europe.   To his corpse every honor was paid.
The only cemetery in which so illustrious a Warrior, slain in arms for the
Religion and Liberties of England, could properly be laid was that
venerable Abbey, hallowed by the dust of many generations of Princes,
Heroes and Poets.   It was announced that the brave veteran should have
a public funeral at Westminster.   In the meantime, his corpse was
embalmed with such skill as could be found in the camp, and was deposited
in a leaden coffin.

CHAPTER XVI.

Surrender of Drogheda—Retreat of James, via Kinsale, to France; and advance
of William upon Dublin—Description of Kinsale—Unbounded joy of the
Metropolitan Protestants for their deliverance— William's triumphal entry—
"Enniskillen, Derry, Aughrim, and the Boyne"—The Irish "Rapparees,"
their designs, their mode of arming, their warfare, and their hiding places—
Lord Tyrconnell returns from France to Ireland, accompanied by General St.
Ruth and a French army—General De Ginkell advances against the combined
Irish and French forces—Battle, conquest, and description of Athlone

The victorious army advanced that day to Duleek, and passed the warm
summer night there, under the open sky. The tents and the baggage
waggons were still on the north side of the river. William's coach had
been brought over , and he slept in it surrounded by his soldiers On the
following day, Drogheda surrendered without a blow, and the garrison,
thirteen hundred strong, marched out unarmed

> " The Protestants of Drogheda,
>   Have reason to be thankful,
> That they were not to bondage brought,
>   Though they were but a handful
> First to the Tholsel they were brought,
>   And tried at Millmount after ,
> But brave King William set them free,
>   By venturing o'er the water."—*Old Song.*

James, now bereft of all further hope, resigned his power, and retired
from Dublin to Waterford From thence he proceeded to Kinsale, and
sailed in a French Brig to Brest, in France

As it was from this spot that the infatuated, but cruel James, bid adieu
to the shores of Ireland, a passing allusion to it will readily be excused by
the reader

Kinsale is in the County of Cork ; and is celebrated in Irish history,
from being the residence of the great De Courcy , whose descendent to this
day, by virtue of his tenure of the old Castle of Kinsale, enjoys the title
and nobility of Baron de Courcy and Ringrone Lord Kinsale also enjoys
two of the highest and most distinguished honors in the British dominions
HE IS THE PREMIER PEER IN THE EMPIRE The senior English Duke is
Norfolk, created by Richard the III , the 28th of June, 1483 The senior
English Marquis is *Winchester,* created by Edward the Sixth, the 12th of
October, 1551. The senior English Earl is *Shrewsbury,* created by Henry
the Sixth, 20th May, 1442 The senior English Viscount is *Hereford,*
created by Edward the Sixth, the 2nd of February, 1549 And the senior

English Baron is *Le Despencer*, created by Henry the Third, the 3rd of June, 1269. In the Scottish Peerage *Hamilton* is the oldest Duke, created by Charles the First, in 1643. *Queensberry* is the oldest Marquis, created by Charles the Second, in 1682. *Errol* is the oldest Earl, created by James the Second, in 1452. *Falkland* is the oldest Viscount, created by James the Sixth, 1620. And *Forbes* is the oldest Baron, created by James the Second, in 1440. In the Irish Peerage, *Leinster* is the only Duke, created by George the Third, the 16th of November, 1766. *Waterford* is the senior Marquis, created by George the Third, on the 19th of August, 1789. *Cork* is the senior Earl, created by James the First, 26th of October, 1620. Gormanston is the senior Viscount, created by Edward the Fourth, the 7th August, 1478. While Lord Kinsale dates back his title as Baron, to the reign of Henry the Second, by which Monarch the title was created in the year 1181. Thus then, Lord Kinsale has the honor of standing at the head, as the senior Peer in the Empire. The other distinguished honor which this nobleman enjoys, is the hereditary privilege of wearing his hat in the Royal presence, granted to John de Courcy, Earl of Ulster, by John, King of England ; and exercised by the present Lord Kinsale, in the presence of George the Fourth, upon the occasion of that monarch's visit to Ireland in 1821. The Duke of Devonshire is the principal proprietor of the town of Kinsale, and his grace usually nominates whom he pleases as its representative.

William, before quitting the Boyne, promulgated an Order, for a General Thanksgiving to the Almighty Disposer of events, for His Divine assistance in the glorious achievement just closed. After leaving a strong garrison in Drogheda, the king advanced his Army on the Dublin road. On the fourth of July, Sir Robert Southwell, Lord Auverquerque, General Scravenmore, the Duke of Ormond, with nine troops of English Horse, and Solmes with his Majesty's Blue Dutch Guards, entered the city. The whole Protestant population turned out to salute them as deliverers. The meeting took place in College Green, on the spot where the Equestrian Statue of King William now stands. One historian recording the events of the day, says, "hundreds embraced "the Soldiers, hung fondly about the necks of the horses, and ran wildly "about, shaking hands with each other." Another, an eye witness of the scene, thus speaks : "How did we see the Protestants on the great day of "OUR REVOLUTION, Thursday the third of July, a day ever to be "remembered by us with the greatest thankfulness, congratulate and "embrace one another as they met, like persons alive from the dead, like "brothers and sisters meeting after a long absence, and going about from "house to house to give each other joy of God's great mercy, enquiring of "one another how they passed the late days of distress and terror ; what "apprehensions they had ; what fears and dangers they were under ; those

"that were prisoners, how they got their liberty ; how they were treated :
"and what, from time to time they thought of things"

On the fifth of July, William advanced his Head Quarters to Finglass,
within three miles of the Castle of Dublin, where he encamped for the
night, and on Sunday morning, the sixth, made his TRIUMPHAL ENTRY
into the City He proceeded forthwith to the Cathedral Church of St.
Patrick, where, in great state and with the Crown upon his head, he
returned devout thanks to Almighty God, for the deliverance of the people
from "Popery and Arbitrary Power," and for "the success and miraculous preservation vouchsafed to himself."

To this day upon the Flags and Banners of all Orange Lodges, in Orange
Vignetts, and generally in all Devices and Emblems of the Orange Body,
may be seen conspicuously emblazoned the memorable words, "ENNIS-
KILLEN, DERRY, AUGHRIM, and the BOYNE." In a history of
Orangism, written in a Country thousands of miles distant from those
places, it may be expected briefly to describe the memorable events which
connect their names with the Order. The brilliant heroism of the men of
Enniskillen, and the perils and privations, the fortitude and fidelity of
those of Derry, have been already alluded to The events of the Boyne
have been also detailed It only now remains to notice Aughrim, with a
passing allusion to the siege of Athlone, which was a precursor to the
victory of Aughrim.

After William's departure from Ireland, about one half that Kingdom
had submitted to the English government. All of the Province of Ulster,
the largest portion of Leinster, and about one third part of Munster,
wore the Anglican garments The whole of Connaught, the largest part
of Munster, and two or three Counties in Leinster, still held out for the
rule of James

Macaulay states (Volume 4, page 58) that the distinction between the
Irish Foot Soldier and the Irish "Raparee," had never been very strongly
marked. After the conquest of Dublin, the Irish army lost what little
organization it had previously possessed, and was turned loose to live by
marauding An incessant predatory war raged along the line which
separated the English plantations from the Irish. Every day companies
of Freebooters, sometimes wrapped in twisted straw, which served the
purpose of armour, stole into the English settlements, burned, sacked,
pillaged, and hastened back to their strongholds. To guard against such
incursions was not easy. To empty the granary, to set fire to the dwelling,
to drive away the cows of a heretic, was regarded by every squalid inhabi-
tant of a mud cabin as a good work. The English complained that it was
no easy matter to catch a "Raparee" Sometimes, when he saw danger
approaching, he lay down in the bog ; and then it was as difficult to find
him as it was to find a hare sitting. Sometimes he sprang into a stream

and lay there like an otter, with only his mouth and nostrils above the water. Nay, a whole gang of banditti would, in the twinkling of an eye, transform itself into a crowd of harmless labourers. Every man took his gun to pieces, hid the lock in his clothes, stuck a cork in the muzzle, stopped the touch hole with a quill, and threw the weapon into the next pond. Nothing was to be seen but a train of poor rustics, who had not so much as a cudgel among them, and whose humble look and crouching walk seemed to show that their spirit was thoroughly broken to slavery. When the peril was over, when the signal was given, every man flew to the place where he had hid his arms, and soon the robbers were in march towards some Protestant mansion. One band penetrated to Clonmel, in the County of Tipperary; another to Maryborough, in the Queen's County; and a third made its den in a woody islet of firm ground, surrounded by the vast bog of Allen, harried the County of Wicklow, and alarmed even the suburbs of Dublin. Such expeditions were not always successful. Sometimes the plunderers fell in with parties of Militia, or with detachments from the English garrisons, in situations in which disguise, flight, and resistance were alike impossible. When this happened, every kerne who was taken was hanged, without any ceremony, on the nearest tree.

Early in the spring of 1691, Lord Tyrconnell returned from France to Ireland. He brought with him a considerable force of French Troops under the command of General Saint Ruth, a Patent of Peerage for General Sarsfield, with money and clothing for the Irish army, and an abundance of French sympathy and support. General St. Ruth is said, by the historian, to have been a man of courage, activity, and resolution, but of a harsh and imperious nature. In his own country, he was cele- brated as the most merciless persecutor that ever dragooned the Huguenots to mass. He was assisted by another General Officer, named D'Usson, who came over from France as his second in command. The great body of the Irish and French forces were posted on the Shannon, chiefly along the coast of Lough Rea, from Athlone to Limerick. The British force was under the command of General De Ginkell (afterwards Earl of Athlone) assisted by Generals Talmash, Mackay, and the Marquis of Ruvigny (the elder brother of the brave Caillemot, who had fallen at the Boyne) as Lieutennants. Towards the close of May, the army was concentrated in and around Mullingar, in the County of Westmeath.

On the sixth of June, 1691, De Ginkell moved from Mullingar. On the seventh he advanced to Ballymore, an ancient fortress, which had recently been fortified by the Irish. This place he besieged and captured. At Ballymore he was joined by the Danish auxilliary force, which had come up to his assistance from Cork, under the command of the Duke of Wir- temburg. The whole army then moved westward, and on the nineteenth of June appeared before the walls of Athlone.

Athlone, says the historian, was perhaps, in a military point of view, the most important place in the Island. Marshal De Rosen, who understood war well, had always maintained that it was there that the Irishry would, with most advantage, make a stand against the Englishry. The Town, which was surrounded by ramparts of earth, lay partly in Leinster and partly in Connaught. The English quarter, which was in Leinster, had once consisted of new and handsome houses, but had been burned by the Irish some months before, and now lay in heaps of ruin. The Celtic quarter, which was in Connaught, was old and meanly built ; The Shannon, which is the boundary of the two Provinces, rushed through Athlone in a deep and rapid stream, and turned two large mills which rose on the arches of a stone bridge Above the bridge, on the Connaught side, a Castle towered to the height of seventy feet, and extended two hundred feet along the river. Fifty or sixty yards below the bridge was a narrow ford.

Athlone is now a market post and corporate Town, a Parliamentary Borough, and a strong and important Military station. It stands on the River Shannon, partly in the Barony of Brawney, County of Westmeath ; partly in the Barony of Athlone, County Roscommon, and very nearly in the centre of Ireland It is cut by the Shannon into almost equal parts, and commands the grand thoroughfare between Dublin and more than one-half of the Province of Connaught It lies about 12 miles north-east from Ballinasloe, 40 from Galway , about 20 south-west from Longford, and 60 west by north from Dublin. This Town combines prime facilities for commerce, military strength, and metropolitan command It is situated within about two miles of the centre of Ireland, and surrounded by a low and practicable country, it sends off in all directions lines of ramifying roads It lies on the great road between Dublin Bay and the West, at the only point where the Shannon can be forded within a stretch of 30 miles. It entirely controls the intercourse between Leinster and most of Connaught, and overlooking a navigable communication, both up and down the Shannon ; as well as eastward and westward at an easy distance by the Grand Canal ; and eastward at not much greater distance by the Royal Canal, it may traffic through all the numerous ramifications of both River and Canals, and outward to the Irish Sea and the Atlantic Ocean Notwithstanding its great natural advantages, the Town of Athlone, when viewed in connection with its size and importance, disappoints all visitors, and disgusts and astonishes many. On the Connaught side the streets and lanes are so irregular, and so blended together, that it is difficult to say where they begin, or where they end ! The best private houses of Athlone and the only street having pretentions to cleanliness, are situated in the Leinster division of the Town A strong Castle too, commands the passage of the Shannon. was built at Athlone, as early as the reign of King John. Walls and the same sides of each of the two divisions of the Town, probably were soon after constructed, and they appear to have been either increased, or at least repaired and strengthened, in the reign of Elizabeth. On the Connaught side, scarcely any traces now exist of either walls or gates, but on the Leinster side, a considerable extent of wall still survives amidst a pressure of obscuring houses, and a gateway, perforating one of the old square Towers, and exhibiting marks of the cannonade upon the Town during the battle under De Ginkell, still affords egress near the River, to a principal thoroughfare towards the north. In the reign of Elizabeth, Athlone Castle was the frequent retreat of the Earl of Essex, during his sojourn in Ireland, and the place where he wrote several of his letters to the Queen. In 1690, after the Battle of the Boyne, Richard Grace, a distinguished Colonel in the service of James the Second, with 3 regiments of Infantry, 9 troops of Cavalry, and 2 troops of Horse Artillery, fortified Athlone in the cause of his fallen master. General Douglas, one of the ablest of William's Officers, approached the Town, at the head of 4 regiments of Dragoons, 2 Batteries of Horse Artillery, and 10 regiments of Foot, and summoned Grace to surrender. The Irish commander refused and is reported to have replied, that he would defend the place till he would eat his boots! Douglas plied the seige with great vigor and bravery, but he eventually discovered that his Artillery train was insufficient for the enterprise, and he subsequently retired unmolested to Mullingar. After Douglas' retreat, the Irish resumed possession of the Leinster side of the Town, repaired such of the fortifications as had been injured, and adopted various measures to render their position in Athlone, as far as they could, impregnable. On the 18th of June, 1691, the main division of the Orange army, under the immediate command of General De Ginkell, appeared within sight of Athlone. On the two following days, he battered the walls on the Leinster side, and succeeded in driving the Irish within their fortifications. On the 21st the Orange forces rushed through the breaches which they had effected and swept the besieged Irish so impetuously before them, that numbers were crused to death in mutual pressure on the Bridge and numbers fell headlong from the battlements, and perished in the River. But the arch of the Bridge, on the Connaught side was promptly broken down by the Romish General. The ford between the two Towns was not only dangerous from its depth and roughness, but so narrow as hardly to admit twenty persons abreast. The Roman Irish, who fired furiously from the Connaught side, were posted in great force behind intrenchments and fortresses, and the assailing forces seemed for the time arrested in their bold attack. De Ginkell believing, the Bridge to be the only practicable passage, raised a wooden work for the purpose of throwing plank over the broken arch. Batteries played from the east side to cover the workmen and from the west side to destroy them. A Serjant and ten privates in armour, rushed from among the Irish to demolish the work, and were all slain. Another Irish party followed, and flung the beams and planks into the River De Ginkell quickly ordered the reconstruction of the work, and succeeded in completing a close gallery over the broken arch The Orange forces now resolved to cross in three simultaneous bodies ; the principal one over this place, and subordinate ones at two other places. Just as they were about to rush upon the designated points, they saw the gallery burnt by the fire of the Irish grenades, and were once more flung helplessly back on their inventive resources. On the 30th, the day after the last repulse, and while the Romish forces were insolent from a sense of security, a party of two thousand of the Orange army, headed by their most distinguished leaders, rushed at an appointed signal into the ford of the River, intrepedly advanced across the water amid a tremendous fire from the enemies works, gained the opposite bank, and were speedily joined by parties along the Bridge, and by Pontoons.

Fifteen hundred Grenadiers, each wearing in his hat a green bough, mustered on the Leinster bank of the Shannon. Many of the men doubtless remembered, that on that day year, they had, at the command of King William, put green boughs in their hats on the banks of the Boyne. Guineas had been liberally scattered among these picked men ; but their alacrity was such that gold could not purchase. Six Battalions were in readiness to support the attack. Mackay commanded He did not approve of the plan : but he executed it as zealously and as energetically, as if he had himself been the author of it. The Duke of Wirtemberg, Talmash, and several other gallant officers, to whom no part in the enterprise had been assigned, insisted on serving that day as private volunteers ; and their appearance in the ranks excited the fiercest enthusiasm among the soldiers

A peal from the steeple of the Church gave the signal. Prince George of Hesse Darmstadt, and Gustavus Hamilton, the brave Chief of the " Inniskilleners," descended first into the Shannon Then the Grenadiers lifted the Duke of Wirtemberg on their shoulders, and with a great shout, plunged twenty a-breast, up to their cravats in the water The stream ran deep and strong ; but in a few minutes the head of the column reached dry land Talmash was the fifth man who set foot on the Connaught shore Quickly they mounted the breaches which had been previously battered open on the river side of the fortifications, and struck such astonishment and panic into the Romish forces, that the latter either fell or fled, while their Orange assailants were masters of the Town within half an hour of their commencing the crossing of the water. Over 1,200 of the Irish forces were slain, and the Catholic garrison, consisting of 500 men, surrendered as prisoners The main body retreated beyond the river Sack, towards Aughrim, there to receive in a few days, their still more signal defeat. Athlone gives the title of Earl in the Irish Peerage to the De-

Ginkell family, the descendants of Godard De Ginkell, William's heroic General.

> " Athlone is lost, without some timely aid,
> At six this evening, an assault was made,
> When under shelter of the British cannon,
> Their Grenadiers in armour took the Shannon.
> Led on by brave Captain Sandy's who, with fame,
> Plung'd to his middle in the rapid stream
> He led them on with such undaunted ire,
> They gain'd the bank in spite of all our fire "

After the conquest of Athlone by the English, Saint Ruth pitched his camp near the ruins of the old Castle of Aughrim, about thirty miles from Athlone, on the road to Galway, where he determined to await the approach of De Ginkell, and to give him battle.

CHAPTER XVII.

Description of Aughrim—Religious Bigotry of St. Ruth—The Irish and French Retreat to Aughrim, and are followed by the English under De Ginkell—Description of the Battle Ground at Aughrim—The Fight—Its Dogged Character, and Doubtful Results—Death of St. Ruth, and Defeat of the Irish and French Forces —Advance of the British to Galway, which is taken—Flight of the Irish to Limerick, whither they are pursued by De Ginkell—A Parly, Terms are granted, and Limerick Surrenders.

There are not less than four *Aughrims* in Ireland. One is the name of the most southerly of the three great head streams of the splendid River Ovoca. Another is the name of a small Village in the County of Wicklow. The third of a Parish in the County of Roscommon. And the fourth of a Village in the County of Galway; which last named is "THE" Aughrim celebrated in history, and memorable in importance. This Village stands on the main road between Dublin and Galway, 29 miles east of the latter, and 3 south-west of Ballinasloe. Its present population is about 500. In the 13th century, a Priory for Augustinian canons was founded at Aughrim, by Theobald Walter, the first Butler of Ireland The Village has a clean and comparatively snug appearance It consists of various short streets, chiefly of cottages or cabins, and borrows much ornament from the neat Parish Church, and the embowered Glebe House on its flank. The land in the vicinity, consists of light and indifferent meadow and field pasture, the greater part of which is reclaimed morass, low, flat, monotonous and moist Mr. Griffith, in his survey of Ireland, describes the bog about Aughrim, as amongst the wettest he had ever met with, and the centre as nearly occupied with Lakes. An expanse of gentle declivity, or hanging plain, a little north-east of the Village of Aughrim, in full view from the Dublin and Galway road, and now disposed of in a series of green pasture fields, is celebrated as the scene of the last of the great Irish battles between the forces of James the Second, and those of William the Third. The battle was fought on the 12th of July, 1691, and was an immediate sequent of the expulsion of James' troops from Athlone.

During the few days which remained to the French General, he exerted himself to the utmost, to win the hearts of all who were under his command. He administered to his troops moral stimulents of the most potent kind He was a zealous Roman Catholic ; and it is probable that the severity with which he had treated the Huguenots of his own country ought to be partly ascribed to the hatred which he felt for their doctrines. He now tried to give to the War, the character of a Crusade The Clergy were the Agents whom he employed to sustain the courage of his Soldiers. His whole Camp was in a ferment with Religious excitement. In every Regiment Priests were praying, preaching, shriving, holding up the Host and the Cup While the Soldiers swore on the Sacramental Bread not to abandon their Colours, the General addressed to the Officers an appeal, which might have moved the most languid and effeminate natures to exertion They were fighting, he said, for their Religion, their Liberty and their Honor.

The spot chosen by Saint Ruth, on which to bring the fate of Ireland to issue, seems to have been selected with great judgment His army was drawn up on the slope of a hill, which was almost surrounded by a red bog. In front, near the edge of the morass, were some fences, out of which a breastwork was without difficulty constructed.

On the eleventh of July, De Ginkell advanced his Head Quarters from Athlone to Ballinasloe, then about four miles from Aughrim. From Ballinasloe he rode forward and reconoitred the Irish position On his return, he gave orders that amunition should be served out, that every musket and bayonet should be got ready for action, and that early on the morrow (the twelfth day of July O S.) every man should be under arms without beat of drum Two Regiments were to remain in charge of the Camp . the rest, unincumbered by baggage, were to march against the enemy.

Soon after six, the next morning, the English were on the way to Aughrim. But some delay was occasioned by a thick fog which hung till noon over the moist valley of the river Suck. A further delay was caused by the necessity of dislodging the Irish from some outposts , and the afternoon was far advanced, when the two Armies at length confronted each other, with nothing but the bog and the breastwork between them. The British and their Allies, were under twenty thousand ; the Irish and French over twenty five thousand.

Ginkell held a short consultation with his principal Officers Should the attack be instant, or wait till the next morning? Mackay was for attacking instantly; and his opinion prevailed At five the battle began The English Foot, in such order as they could keep on treacherous and uneven ground, made their way, sinking deep in mud at every step, to the Irish works But these works were defended with a resolution, such as extorted some words of ungracious eulogy, even from men who entertained the strongest prejudices against the Celtic race Burnet says, "they maintained their ground much longer than they had been accustomed to do" Storey says, "they behaved themselves like men of another nation." And the *London Gazette*, describing the battle, says, "the Irish were never known to fight with more resolution" Again and again, says Macaulay, the assailants were driven back Again and again they returned to the struggle Once they were broken, and chased across the morass but Talmash rallied them, and forced the pursuers to retire The fight had lasted two hours . the evening was closing in, and still the advantage was on the side of the Irish. Ginkell began to meditate a retreat The hopes of Saint Ruth rose high "The day is ours, my boys," he cried, waving his hat in the air "We will drive them before us to the walls of Dublin" But fortune was already on the turn, Mackay and Ruvigny, with the English and Huguenot Cavalry, had succeeded in passing the bog at a place where two horsemen could scarcely ride abreast Saint Ruth at first laughed when he saw the Blues in single file, struggling through the morass under a fire which every moment laid some gallant hat and feather on the earth "What do they mean?" he asked : and then he swore it was a pity, to see such fine fellows rushing to certain destruction "Let them cross, however," he said "The more they are, the more we shall kill." But soon he saw them laying hurdles on the quagmire A broader and a safer path was formed , Squadron after Squadron reached firm ground , and the flank of the Irish Army was speedily turned The French General was hastening to the rescue, when a cannon ball carried off his head

> "Aughrim is now no more, Saint Ruth is dead ;
> And all his guards are from the battle fled !
> As he rode down the hill, he met his fall,
> And died a victim to a cannon ball
> With him our lives and fortunes all decay,
> For now the unthinking cowards fall away"

Mackay and Ruvigny with their Horse, charged the Irish in flank Talmash and his Foot, returned to the attack in front with dogged determination The breastwork was carried The Irish still fighting, retreating from inclosure to inclosure. But as inclosure after inclosure was forced, their efforts became fainter and fainter. At length they broke and fled Then followed a dreadful carnage. The conquerors were in a

savage mood. A report had been spread among them, that, during the
early part of the battle, some English captives who had been admitted to
quarter, had been put to the sword. Only four hundred prisoners were
taken   The number of the slain, was, in proportion to the number
engaged, greater than any other battle of that age. But for the coming
on of a moonless night, made darker by a misty rain, scarcely a man would
have escaped. The obscurity enabled Sarsfield, with a few Squadrons which
still remained unbroken, to cover the retreat. Of the conquerors six
hundred were killed, and about a thousand wounded.

The Protestant army slept that night on the field of battle. On the following day they buried their companions in arms, and then marched westward, towards Galway, in pursuit of the flying enemy. The vanquished
were left unburied, a strange and ghastly spectacle. Four thousand Irish
corpses were counted on the field of battle. A hundred and fifty lay in one
small inclosure , a hundred and twenty in another. But the slaughter had
not been confined to the field of battle. One who was there has left of record,
that, from the top of the hill on which the Celtic camp had been pitched,
he saw the country, to the distance of near four miles, white with the
naked bodies of the slain. The plain looked he says, like an immense pasture
covered by flocks of sheep. As usual different estimates were formed even
by eye witnesses. But it seems probable, that the number of the Irish
who fell, was not less than seven thousand. Soon a multitude of dogs
came to feast on the carnage. These animals became so fierce, and acquired such a taste for human flesh, that it was long dangerous for men to
travel the road otherwise than in companies. One stream of the fugitives
ran towards Galway, and another towards Limerick   The roads to both
Cities were covered with weapons which had been flung away in the flight.
Ginkell offered sixpence for every musket. In a short time so many wag-
gon loads of them were collected, that he reduced the price to two pence.

Ginkell pursued his victorious course to Galway, which he soon captured.
From thence he pushed on to Limerick ; to which he speedily laid siege.
The Irish for some time held out, but Ginkell determined on striking a
bold stroke   No point of the circle of the whole fortifications was more
important, and no point seemed more secure, than the Thomond Bridge ;
which joined the City to the Camp of the Irish Horse on the Clare bank
of the Shannon   He laid a bridge of Tin Boats on the river, crossed it
with a strong body of troops, drove before him in confusion fifteen hundred
men ; and thus executed this part of his plan with great vigor, skill and
success.   Shortly after this briliant achievement, the Irish proposed a
parley, terms were granted them, and Limerick surrendered.

CHAPTER. XVIII.

Formation of various Protestant Associations throughout Ireland—Aldermen of Skinner's Alley—'Prentice Boys and the Boyne Society—A Sign but no Password Resolution of the Irish Parliament in 1695 in favor of the Boyne Society.—Expulsion of Edward Forbes and endowment of Trinity College—Proclamation of the Lord Lieutenant of Ireland, and of the Lord Mayor of Dublin—Address of the House of Commons to the Lord Mayor and Sheriffs for preserving the Statue of King William of Glorious Memory—The Lord Lieutenant's Reply to the House of Commons—Proclamation of the Lords Justices in 1714—Spread of Loyal associations in England—Declaration of the Nobility, Magistracy and Gentry of Yorkshire in 1745—Sir Richard Musgrave's authority quoted—Admission of Dr. Doyle, Roman Catholic Bishop of Kildare and Laughlin, in 1828—The Marquis of Drogheda—The Sassenachs—Description of Tipperary—The White-boys—The Defenders—Extracts from a Dublin Magazine in 1791.

THE Irish Protestants of the Metropolis, and throughout the Northern Counties, now relieved from bondage and persecution, in many places formed Societies, to perpetuate to the latest posterity, the remembrance of the great and good Prince who had delivered them from " Popery and Arbitrary Power." The Society of "ALDERMEN OF SKINNER'S ALLEY," has been already mentioned. It was confined to the Protestant Freemen and Freeholders of the City of Dublin. Londonderry followed next, with the Association called the "'PRENTICE BOYS," which body continues to this day, to celebrate the virtue, fortitude and heroism of the youth of the place in defending the renowned walls of their " Virgin City." The "'*Prentice Boys*" of Derry, like the " *Aldermen of Skinner's Alley,*" was merely local. Enniskillen followed close upon the steps of Derry, in the organization of the "BOYNE SOCIETY." It was distinguished from the Associations of Dublin and Derry, in its extension to various parts of the surrounding neighbourhood, by means of branch or auxiliary Clubs.

The Irish being entirely subdued after the capitulation of Limerick, large guerilla parties of them, called " *Rapparees,*" spread themselves over different parts of the Kingdom, and carried on a long and harrassing warfare against the Protestant Settlements. The nocturnal assassinations, the houghings of cattle, the burning of buildings, and the other dreadful atrocities which attended this desultory, but sanguinary, warfare, led to the extension of the " *Boyne Society,*" into many neighbourhoods, where it was used by the persecuted Colonists, as a means of self-protection and mutual recognition. These Societies had a *Sign*, but no *Password*. It was given by the Enniskilleners in remembrance of the wound which

William received at the Boyne, while contending for the "Protestant Religion and the Liberties of England" It was made by putting the open left hand upon the right shoulder, (the spot where William was wounded,) and was answered by the other party holding his right arm across the breast, as if in a sling, (the manner in which William held the bridle reins when he led the final charge across the Boyne.)

These "*Boyne Societies*" proved of the utmost importance to the peace of the Country, the safety of Protestants, and the security of their Settlements. King William declared they formed an asylum for the English, Scotch and Continental Protestants, who were scattered in various small Colonies and Settlements throughout the Island ; and the Parliament, in the year 1695, passed a Resolution upon the subject of them in these words   "*Resolved,* "that whosoever shall affirm that Loyal Societies are illegal, shall be "deemed a promoter of the designs of King James, and an enemy of the "Laws and Liberties of the Kingdom "

Fourteen years after this event, a grant of £5000, was made to the University of Trinity College, Dublin, because that learned Body had expelled one of its members, for speaking dishonorably of the Memory of "the Great and Good King William." The following Resolution, copied from the *Journals of the Irish House of Commons for June* 1709, *will show this fact*

"*Resolved* —That this house taking into consideration the proceedings of the "University of Trinity College, near Dublin, in censuring Edward Forbes, by de- "gradation and expulsion, FOR SPEAKING DISHONORABLY OF, AND ASPERSING, THE "GLORIOUS MEMORY OF HIS LATE MAJESTY KING WILLIAM III,, and also the steady "adherence of the Provost and Fellows to the late happy Revolution, &c , do address "his Excellency the Lord Lieutenant, that he will lay before her Majesty, the humble "desire of this House, that £5,000, he *bestowed* by her Majesty, on the Provost, "Fellows, and Scholars of Trinity College, near Dublin, for erecting a *public* Library "in said College."

In the following year, to wit, in the year 1710, an attempt was made to destroy the Equestrian Statue of King William, erected in College Green, Dublin This daring act of Romish spleen, called forth a burst of Protestant indignation from one end of the Kingdom to the other. On the 26th of June, a Royal Proclamation was issued by His Excellency the Lord Lieutenant and the Privy Council, offering a reward of one hundred pounds, for the discovery of the perpetrators ; and in three days after, the Royal Proclamation was followed by a similar document from the Lord Mayor and the City Council of Dublin, offering an additional reward of Fifty pounds, for such information as would lead to the discovery of the offenders Here is a copy

"A PROCLAMATION,

" By the Lord Mayor of the City of Dublin

" WHEREAS the City of Dublin, in honour of his *Majesty King William*
"*the Third of blessed Memory*, our great Deliverer (under God) from
" *Popery* and *Arbitrary Government*, have erected a large and sumptuous Statue
" in College Green, in token of the deep and grateful sense they retain of their de-
" liverance, and with design to transmit the MEMORY of that GLORIOUS PRINCE to the
" latest posterity —Nevertheless some *Persons disaffected* to her MAJESTY, and to
" the happy Revolution, did on the last Sunday night, break and deface the said
" Statue, and thereby, as far as in them lay, offered the basest indignity to the
" Memory of that *Prince*. The insolence and ingratitude of which action is so uni -
" versally resented by the City, that, by an Act of Assembly, I am directed to re-
" quire all and every the Officers of the City, and particularly the Constables, im-
" mediately to make the strictest search and inquiry in all places within this City,
" for the discovery and apprehending the persons guilty of the aforesaid Misdemeanor.
" And as a further encouragement to any Person or Persons who shall discover the
" said Offenders and their Accomplices, so as they or any of them may be convicted,
" I am, by the said Act of Assembly, empowered to give *Fifty Pounds Reward* to
" such discoverer, over and above the *One Hundred Pounds Reward*, appointed by
" his Excellency the Lord Lieutenant, and the Lords and others of her Majesty's
" most Honorable *Privy Council* of this Kingdom, by their proclamation, dated the
" 26th instant

" And I do hereby desire the several Justices of the Peace, and Aldermen of this
" City, before whom any Persons suspected of the said offence shall be brought, in the
" most strict and careful manner to examine such Persons, and the Evidences which
" shall be produced against them, and such Examinations, when taken in writing, to
" send to me, to the end, that the most effectual methods may be pursued, to expose
" and punish such enemies to our peace and happiness —Dated at the Tholsel of
" the City of Dublin, the 29th June, 1710.

" JOHN PAGE.

" GOD SAVE THE QUEEN "

*Address of the Irish House of Commons to the Lord Mayor, Sheriffs, Commons
and Citizens of the City of Dublin, with their answer —Extracted from the Commons
Journals of the 17th and 18th of AUGUST, 1710.*

" Resolved, *nemine contradicente*, that the thanks of this House be given to the
" Lord Mayor, Sheriffs and Commons of the City of Dublin, (who erected a Statue
" of King William the III., of Glorious Memory,) FOR THEIR ZEAL AND CARE IN
" REPAIRING THAT NOBLE MONUMENT OF THEIR GRATITUDE TO OUR LATE DELIVERER
" FROM POPERY, SLAVERY AND FRENCH POWER, AND SUPPORTING THE HONOR AND
" MEMORY OF THAT PRINCE, IN SO SOLEMN AND PUBLIC A MANNER "

" *Ordered.*—That Mr Parry, Mr B Burton, Sir W. Fawnes, and Mr Walton,
" do attend the Lord Mayor, Sheriffs, Commons and Citizens of Dublin, with the
" said resolution "

" Mr Parry reported from the Committee appointed to attend the Lord Mayor,
" Sheriffs, Commons and Citizens of the City of Dublin, with the thanks of this House,

" FOR THEIR GREAT ZEAL AND CARE IN REPAIRING THE STATUE OF HIS LATE MA-
" JESTY, KING WILLIAM THE III, OF GLORIOUS MEMORY, IN SO SOLEMN AND PUBLIC
" A MANNER, that they had attended the Lord Mayor, Sheriffs, Commons, and Citiz-
" ens accordingly, and that they were pleased to return the answer following:
" The great honor the House of Commons have done this City, in placing so distin-
" guished a mark of their favor on them, for erecting a statue in memory of our
" Great Deliverer, King William the III, and FOR THEIR ZEAL IN RE-ADORNING
" THE SAME, will always encourage the City, to vindicate the honor of that Glorious
" Prince, and the late happy Revolution —Ordered—that the said Answer he en-
" tered on the Journals of this House."

*Answer of his Excellency the Lord Lieutenant to an Address from the Irish
House of Commons, thanking his Excellency for issuing a Proclamation, offering a
reward for the discovery of the villains who defaced the Statue of King William,
in College Green, in the year 1710.*

. " Gentlemen,—I am very well pleased, that my endeavours for the discovery
" of this villainous attempt, have been pleasing to you.   I had been THE MOST UN-
" GRATEFUL of all men living, had I not done what lay in me to that end ; and I AM
" SURE THAT YOU, NOR I, NOR ANY GOOD PROTESTANT, CAN NEVER DO TOO MUCH, TO
" SHOW THE ETERNAL VALUE WE RETAIN FOR THE MEMORY OF THAT GREAT PRINCE."

Proclamation of the Lords Justices and Privy Council of Ireland in the year
1714

" PROCLAMATION

" WILL Dublin Jo Tuam, Kildare, Whereas, notwithstanding a former Pro-
" clamation issued, promising a reward to such as should discover and
" apprehend the person or persons, who had formerly defaced the Statue erected at
" College Green at the expense of the Citizens of Dublin, and in honor of his late
" Majesty, KING WILLIAM THE III, OF GLORIOUS MEMORY, for the issuing of which
" the Commons of Ireland, soon after in Parliament assembled, made an humble
" address of thanks to the then Lord Lieutenant of this Kingdom, for his care and
" vigilance in issuing thereof . yet nevertheless, THE SAME BASE AND VILLAINOUS ACT
" has been since practised, by some PROFLIGATE AND INFAMOUS PERSONS, DISAFFECTED
" TO HIS MAJESTY'S GOVERNMENT, AND HAPPY ESTABLISHMENT ON THE THRONE OF THESE
" NATIONS, AND TO THE LATE HAPPY REVOLUTION, who on the 13th day of February
" last, (being the day of the late King William and Queen Mary's Ascension to
" the Throne,) offered great indignities to the memory of his said late Majesty, by
" taking the Truncheon out of the hand of the said Statue, so erected IN MEMORY
" OF THAT GLORIOUS PRINCE, by whom (under God,) this Nation in the year of our
" Lord ONE THOUSAND, SIX HUNDRED, EIGHTY AND EIGHT, was delivered from Popery
" and Arbitrary Power : We the Lords Justices and Council, having A JUST ABHOR-
" ENCE OF ALL SUCH DISAFFECTED AND VILLAINOUS PRACTICES, do hereby declare, that
" ALL PERSONS CONCERNED IN THAT BARBAROUS ACT, ARE GUILTY OF THE GREATEST
" BASENESS, INSOLENCE, AND INGRATITUDE, and for discovering the author or authors
" of that villainy, we do hereby publish and declare, that we will give the neces-
" sary orders for the payment of

"TWO HUNDRED POUNDS STERLING,

"to such person or persons as shall discover, take and apprehend, all or any of
"the persons guilty of the said offence; and in case any of the persons concerned
"therein, shall make a full discovery of his accomplices, so as one or more of
"them may be brought to condign punishment, such discoverer, besides the said
"reward, shall have HIS MAJESTY'S MOST GRACIOUS PARDON, for the same.

"Given at the Council Chamber in Dublin, the 17th day of March, 1714."

"Alan Broderick, Canc. Inchiquine, Mount Alexander, Tyrawley, Wm Whit-
"shed, John Forster, Edward Crofton, Henry Tichborne, Thomas Knightly, Gus.
"Hamilton, Theop. Butler, John Allen "

"GOD SAVE THE KING "

During the years which intervened between 1740 and 1750, a vast
number of Associations, similar to the "Boyne Society," were formed in
various parts of England. The following short extract from a Declaration,
made in the year 1745, by the Lord Archbishop of York, Lords Lieutenants, Nobility, Deputy Lieutenants, Justices of the Peace, Clergy,
Gentlemen and Freeholders of Yorkshire, who entered into an Association,
on the 24th of September in that year, is itself sufficient evidence of the
fact   "We do voluntarily and willingly bind ourselves, every one of us
"to the other, jointly and severally, in the bond of one firm and Loyal
"Society, and do hereby promise, with our whole powers, bodies, lives
"and estates, we, and every one of us, will stand by, and assist each other,
"in support and defence of His Majesty's sacred Person and Government;
"and will withstand, offend and pursue, as well by force of arms, as by
"all other means, all Popish traitors "   &c. &c

Sir Richard Musgrave, Baronet, M. P., states in his " Memoirs,"
Volume 1, page 36, that in the year 1759, an alarming spirit of insurgency
appeared in the South of Ireland, which manifested itself by numerous and
frequent risings of the lower class of Roman Catholics. They were
dressed in white sheets, armed with guns, pikes and pistols   They
marched through the country in military array, preceded by the music of
bagpipes, or the sounding of horns   In their nocturnal perambulations,
they enlisted, or pressed into their service, every person of their own
Religion, who was capable of serving them   Those they bound by oaths
of secrecy, and of fidelity and obedience to their Officers   In the
examination of Dr James Doyle, Titular Bishop of Kildare and Laughlin,
before the Lords Committee in 1828, he admitted that at this period, the
Roman Catholic Clergy, as well as the Roman Catholic Officers, were
nominated by, and subject to obedience and allegiance to, King James,
his Son, "Prince Charlie" the Pretender, and the House of Stuart   The
pretext the insurgents made for rising was to redress the following
grievances—the illegal inclosure of Commons—the extortion of Tythe
Proctors—and the exorbitant fees exacted by their own Clergy

They committed dreadful barbarities on such persons as refused to obey their mandates, or refused to join their confederacy—they cut out the tongues of some , they amputated the noses and ears of others ; in other cases they compelled them to ride many miles on horseback, naked and bare-backed , in some instances they buried them naked in graves, lined with prickly furze up to their chins , they plundered and burned houses , they houghed and maimed cattle , they seized arms and horses ; which they rode about the country ; and they levied money, at some times even in the open day   Their real object was to drive out the English Settlers, to extirpate the Protestant Religion from the land, and to separate the Island from England.

In the year 1762, the Marquis of Drogheda was sent with a large force to subdue them in the Province of Munster.   On the night of the day on which he arrived at Cloghean, in the County of Tipperary, a large number styled "White-boys," well armed, and headed by the Rev Nicholas Sheehey, a Roman Catholic Priest, assembled close to the Town, and were on the point of attacking it , which caused his Lordship to double the guard, and resort to other precautions to prevent surprise   "*Father*" Doyle, Parish Priest of Ardfinnan, endeavoured by false representations to deceive the Marquis , but he failed in the accomplishment of his purposes, and Sheehey was taken prisoner, tried, found guilty, and executed at Clonmel, Mr. Conway, a respectable and wealthy Irish Roman Catholic gentleman, residing at Paris, regularly remitted money to them, by order of the French Government.   The Earl of Carrick, Sir Thomas Maude, Bart. (afterwards created Lord De Montalt,) the Rev Mr Hewston, William Bagwell, and John Baganall, Esqs , took an active part in suppressing them in that part of the Kingdom   For the energy displayed by those Noblemen and Gentlemen, in counteracting and defeating the schemes of these wicked men, they were vilified and slandered with every term of opprobrium— they were called "English Dogs," "Bloodhounds," "Heretics," "Sassanaghs," &c , &c (Sassanagh, in the language of Ireland, is a term applied to Saxons and Foreigners) As the county of Tipperary is crimsoned, in the notoriety of blood, some description may be expected of this celebrated, but wicked locality.

Tipperary is an inland County, in the Province of Munster, and ranks with Cork and Galway as one of the three greatest Counties in Ireland The Coriondi and the Unice or Uodiæ of Ptolemy, are supposed by Sir James Ware, to have occupied the country which now constitutes the County of Tipperary, and the Counties adjoining it in the west and south west   Sir James thinks also, that the ancient territory of Corca-Eathrach comprehended the portions of the Golden Vale which lie around Cashel , and which vale is probably the most fertile and luxuriant tract of country under the dominion of the British Crown   This gorgeous dale of almost

perpetual soil is everywhere rich, everywhere beautiful, everywhere picturesque and exultant , yet it is specially sparkling and magnificent immediately
around the town of Tipperary—provided with splendid villas, gemmed
with garden, orchard, and mimic grove, and above all, powerfully and
most picturesquely foiled, first by the verdant slopes and gentle sky-line
of the Shevenamuck hills, and west by the sublime escarpments and the
cloud-cleaving summits of the Galtee mountains   The luscious sweetness,
the brilliant beauty, and the thrilling power of Golden Vale, no powers of
our pen can describe , though, we are sorry to say, the district around it,
is associated with the very quintessence of predial disturbance   Of other
districts in this county, Sir James Ware says, the ancient territory of
Eoganacht, was occupied by a Sept of its own name around Thurles—the
ancient Hy Fogarty was occupied by the Sept of O'Fogarty, also in the
vicinity of Thurles—the ancient Hy-Kerin was the country of the Sept of
O'Miagher, which is now identical with the Barony of Ikerrin, which is
pronounced alike and differs only in the spelling—and that the ancient
territory of Muscraige-Thire was the land of the Sept of Kennedy, and
was formed of what is now known as the Baronies of Upper and Lower
Ormond.   These territories seem to have been divided, during the early
periods of Irish history, between the princes of the Dalcassian race, who
governed Thomond or North Munster, and the princes of the Eoganacht
or Eugenian Sept, who governed Desmond or South Munster   These two
sets of princes, alternately possessed the paramount sovereignty of all
Munster, and soon after the landing of the Danes on Ostmen, Feidlim
Mac Crimtham, Prince of Desmond, was King of all Munster, and held
his Court at Cashel   We pass over the antiquities of Tipperary, including
the various buildings on the Rock of Cashel—the fortifications of Clonmel
—the walls and gates of Fethard—the Castle of Cahir—the Abbey. of
Holycross—the Pillar Tower of Roscrea—the Castle of Nenagh—the Caves
of Michelstown, (one of the richest natural curiosities in Europe)—all
the ancient monastic institutions with which Tipperary abounds—and all
its fierce and bloody struggles from the days of Cormac MacCullinan, the
King of Munster and Bishop of Cashel,. in the tenth century, down to
the present day, as too long even for notice   Only one spot in
the county we shall further mention, which is Slivenaman, the cele
brated mountain where the unfortunate Smith O'Brien, Mahar, Dillon,
and other leaders, so recently raised the standard of revolt against the
British Government   Slive-na-man is called in Irish "Shabh-na-mhan,
Fionn-na-Heirin," which means "the mountain of the fair women of
Ireland "   For this appellation tradition assigns the following whimsical
origin.   Fin Mac Comhal (Cual), wishing to take a wife, and being puzzled which to choose among the fair daughters of his land, caused all the
beautiful women of Ireland to assemble at the foot of this mountain,

declaring that which ever first reached the summit should be his wife
Fin then proceeded to the top, and having taken his seat on the Druid's
Altar that crowns it, made a signal to the group of anxious fair ones who
waited below.   Away they went, through wood and heath, and furze, over
crag, mountain and stream.   Graine, daughter of Cormac, monarch of
Ireland, arrived first at the summit, claimed the hand of the Fenian Chief,
to whom she was accordingly united   "This mountain," says Mr. and
Mrs. Hall, "may be emphatically termed an Ossianic locality, being associated in tradition with the deeds of that celebrated Bard, and his father,
Fin Mac Comhal, the Fingal of MacPherson ; many of whose poems, until
a very recent period, were repeated by several of the inhabitants."   This
mountain has a summit altitude of 2,364 feet above sea level   It presents
to the spectator, a beautiful outlined dome, and commands one of the
richest, and most varied, and most extensive panoramic views in Ireland.
The railroad from Dublin to Cork, by way of Clonmel, passes along the
eastern base of the whole group, or rather across the table land of connection between it and the Booley Hills

From the year 1761 to 1763, the most savage brutalities continued to be
perpetrated in blood-stained Tipperary, sometimes under the name of
Rapparees, sometimes under the designation of *Levellers*, and at other times
under the cognomen of *White-boys*   In 1763 the *Hearts of Oak* appeared
in Ulster   These were put down, temporarily, but, in 1769 and 1770, again
arose, and committed frightful depredations, under the name of *Hearts of
Steel*   After that, *Right-Boys* filled Munster with savage atrocities ; while,
in the North, not less abominable and daring deeds were done by confederates, calling themselves *Defenders*

These *Defenders*—partly from the name they assumed, and partly from
the misrepresentations of Lord Gosford, (hereafter referred to at length
were believed by many, to have been driven to act on the *defensive*, and to
organize for self-protection, by the violence committed against them by
the Protestant population of the County Armagh   To show that such an
opinion is totally erroneous, we shall here copy an extract from the Report
on the state of Ireland, made by a select Committee of the House of Lords,
in 1793, who took evidence, and were specially appointed to enquire into
the nature and origin of this *Defenderism*.

"The people at this time called ' Defenders,' are very different from those who
" originally assumed that appellation and are all, as far as the Committee can
" discover, of the Roman Catholic persuasion.   They first appeared in the County
" Louth in considerable bodies, in April last, several of them were armed ; they
" assembled mostly in the night and forced themselves into the houses of Protes-
" tants, and took from them their arms   Their measures appear to have been
" concocted and conducted with the utmost secrecy, and a degree of regularity and
" system not usual in people of such mean condition, and as if directed by men of
" of   r rank "

It will thus be seen, upon the very highest authority, that instead of the Protestants of Armagh, driving the Roman Catholic population to acts of organization and retaliation in 1795, (as alleged by Lord Gosford,) that the House of Lords declared, in 1793, that "they first appeared in the County of Louth, which was, and is a Roman Catholic County, and in which the few scattered Protestants who inhabited it, could have committed against their ten-fold more numerous Roman Catholic neighbours, no act of oppression or cruelty. But we must quote further from the Report of the Lords Committee. Their Lordships say :

"Sums of money to a considerable amount have been levied, and still continue "to be levied, upon the Roman Catholics in all parts of the Kingdom, by subscrip-"tions and collections at their chapels and elsewhere; some of which levies have "been made, and still continue to be made, under the authority of a printed "circular letter, which has been sent into all parts of the Kingdom; a copy of "which letter we think it our duty to insert herein :

"Sir,—By an order of the sub-committee, dated the 15th of January, I had the "honor to forward you a plan for a general subscription, which had for its object "the raising of a fund for defraying the heavy and growing expenses incurred by "the general committee in conducting the affairs of the Catholics of Ireland. As "usual mistakes have occurred in the transmission of these letters, owing to my "ignorance of the address of many of the Delegates. I am directed to inform you "that such a plan is now in forwardness throughout the Kingdom. A measure so "strongly enforced by necessity, and so consonant to justice, cannot fail to attract "your very serious attention. The committee having the most perfect reliance in "your zeal, are confident you will use your best exertions to carry this necessary "business into full effect.

"Signed by the Secretary of the Sub-Committee."
"Dublin, February 5th, 1793."

Thus then appears, upon authority that is indisputable, that instead of the Orange system driving out the Romain Catholic population ; or instead of the Orange Lodge causing the formation of counter associations ; that the Roman Catholics were the aggressors, and that the Romish combinations existed, and that subscriptions were made "*at the Romish Chapels*, and elsewhere," to promote Romish plots, fully two years before the forma_tion of an Orange Lodge was dreamed of in Ireland. In truth so early as the month of November 1791, the treasonable Association of "*United Irishmen*," was organized in Dublin, and it is recorded that money was raised by subscriptions, to arm a Body of Men in Dublin, under the title of "*National Guards*," with a green uniform, and buttons inscribed with a Harp, divested of the Crown, to denote the intended abolition of the English Monarchy. The intended muster of this rebellious Body on the 9th December, 1791, was frustrated, by a Royal Proclamation, issued by the Irish Goverment on the very day preceding the intended meeting.

The excesses of the Rapparees continued till about the year 1786, when

they were succeeded by a continued series of outrages committed by persons
styling themselves "White-boys" and "Right-boys;" and who, in every
respect except the name, resembled the "Rapparees," whose vile principles
and wicked conduct they seem to have inherited.   Their proceedings,
chiefly directed against the Protestant Clergy, were not the wild and extravagant efforts of rash and ignorant peasants, but a dark and deep laid scheme,
which must have been planned by men skilled in the Law, and in the
artifices by which it might be evaded   A combination was formed under
the sanction of an oath, not to take Tythes, or to assist any Clergyman in
drawing them.   A form of Summons to the Clergy to draw their Tythe,
penned with legal accuracy, was printed at Cork, and circulated with great
diligence through many parts of Munster   In order to make the combination general, some of the most active and intelligent members of it, administered oaths to all the lower classes of the people, at the Roman Catholic Chapels and at the Fairs and Market Towns.   These traitors soon proceeded from one act of violence to another, and established such a system
of terror, that Landlords were afraid to distrain for rent, and Merchants
and others were intimidated from suing by civil process for money due by
note, or otherwise   They took arms from Protestants, and levied money
to buy ammunition   They broke open gaols , set fire to hay and corn stacks,
and even to houses, especially those occupied by the army.   At length they
had the audacity to threaten Cork, Limerick and Ennis with famine, and
took measures to prevent farmers and fishermen from conveying supplies
of provisions to them

In 1784, the "Defender" and "Peep-of-Day" systems commenced   The
"Defenders" were exclusively Roman Catholics, upon whom the mantle
of the "Rapparees," the "White-boys," and the "Right-boys," seems to
have descended   The "Peep-of-Days" were made up chiefly of sour-tem-
pered and republican Presbyterians, who have since seen through, and
bitterly repented of their folly , but who were at that time, anxious to cast
off British connection, and to establish a Democratic form of Government
in the Island   They were at first bitterly hostile to the Roman Catholics,
and committed many gross outrages upon them   After the introduction
of Orangeism, the more moderate of the "Peep-of-Days," joined that
Body, but the great bulk of them joined the "United Irishmen."

Up to this period, all parties in the State pretending favor or support to
British connexion, joined in paying homage to the Memory of King William.
The following extract from a *Dublin Magazine*, published in 1791, will show
the feeling entertained by all classes at this period   "Dublin, November 4.
"King William's birth day was celebrated with an unusual degree of *éclat*.
"The VOLUNTEER CORPS appeared in full strength, and under the command
"of their patriotic and beloved general, EARL CHARLEMONT, proceeded to
"the Statue of the great Deliverer of these Countries from Tory tyranny,

" round which they fired three *feu de joies.* In the evening the respective
" Corps, and various other Constitutional and Patriotic Bodies, dined
" together, and poured forth copious libations TO THE IMMORTAL MEMORY
" OF THE PRINCE OF WHIGS. The Troops in the Garrison, also fired three
" vollies in College Green, and His Excellency the Lord Lieutenant, the
" Lord Mayor, Lord Chancellor, Sheriffs, &c. &c., went in state round
" the Statue of King William, and also round that of George the II, in
" Stephen's Green, as is usual on such occasions."

CHAPTER XIX.

*The French Revolutionary mania—The Irish Roman Catholic Committee—Savage
attack on the Protestant settlement at Forkhill in the County Armagh—Perfidious proceedings of the Roman Catholic Committee—Organization of the Society
of United Irishmen—The King(George the Second,) and the Protestant Gentry,
openly patronise the "Boyne Society," whose members are speedily enrolled and
armed as Yeomanry Corps—Description of Bandon—First enrolment of the
Orange Yeomanry in Cork and Wexford—Description of Kerry, Limerick,
Mayo, and Sligo—Circulars from the War Office, and from the Lord Lieutenant,
to enrol and arm the Orange Yeomanry.*

ABOUT the year 1790, the mania of the French Revolution commenced
to be sown among the "Defenders" and "Peep-of-Day" Boys. The
Roman Catholic Priests of Ireland, of which the Revd. "Father Quigly"
was one of the most conspicuous and active, were the Agents of France.
They eulogised every thing French, and used all their influence with the
people, to indoctrinate them with a hatred of everything appertaining to
England, and a love for every thing coming from France. A few zealous
and hot-headed Republicans, were found among the Presbyterians of the
north, to preach up the doctrines of "Liberty and Equality," the "Age
of Reason," and the "Rights of Man." Both parties cordially hated each
other, yet, both parties as cordially desired the overthrow of British rule
—The one to establish the Romish Religion, under the protection of France
—The other Independence and a Republican Goverment. At this period,
and for some time previous to it, the "Roman Catholic Committee" sat
in Dublin, and was composed of all the respectable Roman Catholics of the
Kingdom. At a meeting of this "Committee," held on the 15th of November 1783, Sir Patrick Bellew, of Barmeath, Bart, in the Chair, it was
" *Resolved*—That we feel ourselves particularly called on to declare, that
" this Committee consists of every Roman Catholic Nobleman and Gentle-
" man of landed property, and of other Gentlemen chosen by their fellow-
" subjects of that persuasion, in Dublin and other parts of the Kingdom."

" *Resolved*—That thus constituted, we have, for several years past, been the "medium through which the voice of the Roman Catholics of Ireland has "been conveyed, and the only one competent thereto."

During the whole of this time, the "Defenders," incited by Demagogues, and led by their Priests, were pursuing their career of guilt and blood; were committing acts so barbarous, that even Savage Nations would blush to imitate them ; but no attempt was made by the "Catholic Committee," to soothe their passions, or stay their hands. A few of their acts must speak for the multitude ; there being no time to copy many.

Richard Jackson, Esq , of Forkhill, in the Country of Armagh, died on the eleventh of January, 1787, and devised an estate of about £4000 a year for the following charitable purposes. That his Demense, consisting of about 3000 acres, should be colonized by Protestants of the Established Church, and that four School Masters should be established on it, to instruct, gratis, children of every religious persuasion. In the year 1789, the Trustees obtained an Act of Parliament, to enable them to carry the provisions of the Will into execution. They appointed the Rev. Edward Hudson, Rector of Forkhill, Agent, to transact the business of the Charity. The Roman Catholics who lived in the neighbourhood, who were all "Defenders,' of a savage race, and descendants of the "Rapparees," declared without reserve, that they would not suffer the establishment to take place ; and they soon put their menaces into execution. They twice fired at Mr. Hudson, with the intention to take his life. On one occasion, an assassin was sent from a Roman Catholic Chapel, while the Congregation were assembled at Mass, to the road side, where Mr Hudson was passing by, and he deliberately fired at him with a Musket, from behind a bush , but providentially the Horse instead of the Rider, was killed. The new Colonists were hunted like wild beasts, and treated with savage cruelty ; their houses were demolished, and their property was destroyed. The treatment of Alexander Barclay, one of their Schoolmasters, in the month of February, 1791, will show the ferocious conduct of these savages. In the evening, a number of them rushed into his house, threw him on his face, three of them stood on him, and repeatedly stabbed him. They then put a cord round his neck, which they tightened, so as to force out his tongue, which they cut off. They next cut off the four fingers and the thumb of the right hand ; then left him on the floor, and proceeded to use his wife in the same manner ! To add to their barbarities, they cut off her tongue and four fingers with a blunt weapon, some of them holding up the woman's right arm, while the others were engaged in the inhuman action. After committing these acts of barbarity, they battered and beat her in a dreadful manner. Her brother, a little boy of thirteen years of age, had come from Armagh that morning to see her. They cut out his tongue, cut off the calf of his leg, and then left all three in that situation !

The "Catholic Committee," then sitting in Dublin, seeing that it would materially advance their designs, and remove many obstacles which obstructed their nefarious plots, resolved, if they could possibly effect it, to form a junction with the republican and disaffected Presbyterians, then known as "Peep-of-Day" Boys. For this purpose the "Committee" met on the 23rd of March, 1792, and framed a Declaration of their political tenets, which was signed by Dr. Troy, the Titular Archbishop of Dublin, Edward Byrne, and Richard McCormick. With this document they appointed Sir Thomas French, Christopher Bellew, James Edward Devereux, Edward Byrne, and John Keough, Esqs., to proceed to Belfast, at which Town they arrived on the 12th of December, 1792. At Belfast they were met by Theobald Wolfe Tone, Esq., and other leaders of the revolutionary party. Here they concerted together for some time, and held communication as to the best means of overturning British connexion, and upsetting the existing constitution. After some time spent in these treasonable proceedings, they set out for London, to present a loyal and dutiful Address to His Majesty! From this period the "Catholic Committee" continued to sit 'till the Rebellion of 1798. Their meetings were constant, and with the aid of French money, Revolutionary publications, and active Agents, they succeeded, to a great extent, in uniting the two hitherto hostile factions, ("Defenders" and "Peep-of-Day" Boys,) into one phalanx, called "United Irishmen."

The horrible cruelties inflicted upon the Protestant Colonies, added to the settled organization of the "Catholic Committee," and the Society of "United Irishmen," tended greatly to the spread of the "Boyne Society," before alluded to. Many Noblemen and Gentlemen of property and standing lent their influence to the Society, and openly encouraged its extension. So effective and material were the exertions of the members of the Boyne Society, in the protection and encouragment of the Protestant settlements, that His Majesty George the Second, openly supported them, and declared they were the great mainstay of the Church and English connection in that Kingdom. For this Royal and manly declaration, His Majesty was voted an Address by the House of Commons, in 1736, "for " giving additional strength to the Protestant Interest, and securing to all " future ages the Laws and Liberties of this Nation, in the full manner we " now happily and thankfully enjoy them." Wherever the "Rapparees," " the White-boys," or the "Right-boys" spread their nefarious doctrines, or promulgated their bloody codes, there were the members of the " Boyne Societies" found struggling against them.—There were these volunteer defenders of their Country found on " watch and ward," to guard property, protect life, and preserve British Connexion. During the whole of this gloomy period, England was engaged in a sanguinary and protracted war; all her troops were employed abroad, not a man was to spare for home service. The protection of Ireland was, therefore, necessarily dependent on the united services of the Protestants enrolled in these Clubs The Nobility and Gentry of the Kingdom, seeing the effective services which these societies rendered, applied to the Government, to have them enrolled and armed, and placed upon a more efficient footing. The Island was at this time menaced with an Invasion from France, and every effort was being made by the disaffected within, to be prepared for an event, which they looked upon as the signal for separation from England, and the restoration and establishment of the Romish religion The Government, alarmed at the danger, external and internal, were but too glad to yield to the representations of the Protestant Nobility and Gentry of the Kingdom, and the members of the " Boyne Societies," were speedily armed and enrolled as " Yeomanry Corps," for the protection of the Country, and the preservation of the public peace Ulster being the strong hold of the Protestant Settlements, the "Boyne Society" spread rapidly through it , and their members being now armed and drilled as Yeomanry Corps, the open movements of the disaffected were curbed, and law and order in the northern Province, placed comparatively in the ascendant.

The dreadful ravages which had before disgraced Ulster, now set in with renewed vigor, in the southern and western portions of the Kingdom , the Counties of Cork, Clare, Galway, Kerry ,Limerick and Waterford bearing an unenviable notoriety in the catalogue of guilt. The southern Protestants, beholding the beneficial effects of the northern unions, now, for the first time, exerted themselves to organize " Boyne" Societies The following is a return of those first formed in the Counties of Cork and Wexford

Name of Association	When formed	By whom Commanded
" Boyne "	1776	...Colonel Bagwell, M P
"True Blue"	1776	... ...Colonel Morison.
" Union " .. .	1776	.. .Captain Hickman.
" Culloden" .	1777	. Counsellor Bennet
" Enniskillen" . .	1777	..Captain J. Connor
" Aughrim"	1778	.Major E. Jameson
" Independent " . .	1781	. . Colonel the Hon. Richard Hare, M.P.
" Muskeny True Blues"	1781	. Lieut Col Hutchinson

These Associations were voluntary , they at first received no pay, found their own clothing and appointments, and assembled regularly for drill and exercise Shortly after their formation, they were armed and paid by the Government, and their Officers commissioned by His Majesty, George the Third The eight Corps above named, formed "the Cork Boyne Society." In the year 1793, Colonel Bagwell was appointed their GRAND MASTER, Colonel the Honorable Richard Hare, (afterwards Lord Ennismore,) Deputy Six similar Clubs were established at this time, in Bandon, in the same

County, out of which was formed the "Bandon Legion," comprising three Corps of armed volunteers, called respectively, the

"Bandon Boyne,"
"Bandon Union,"
"Bandon True Blues."

A short description of Bandon, so celebrated for its Loyalty and Protestantism, may here be given :

Bandon is a considerable Town, in the county of Cork. It is built on both sides of the River Bandon, and is distant about 15 miles south west from Cork, and about 142 from Dublin. In the civil wars of 1641, Bandon was placed under the governorship of Lord Kinnalmeaky, second son of the Earl of Cork, and became the retreat of the multitudinous Protestants from Clonakilty and the other parts of the surrounding country. There being no other walled Town in the south west part of the county of Cork, not only did the men, but the Protestant women and children (of which there were upwards of one thousand,) also sought, and obtained shelter within the walls of Bandon, from the bloody massacre of 1641. The ground upon which the Town now stands, was purchased in the year 1602, by Mr. Richard Boyle, afterwards the first, and the "Great" Earl of Cork. He purchased from the party to whom it had been granted after O'Mahony's forfeiture for sharing in the Desmond rebellion. His Lordship by bold energy, indomitable enterprise, and a liberal expenditure of money, soon converted a scene of stillness and sterility, into a large, orderly and busy haunt of men. His object was to make the Town exclusively Protestant, to encourage enterprise and industry, and to secure the repose of all dwellers within it. In a letter written by his Lordship to Mr. Secretary Cook, in the year 1632, he says, "the place in which the Town is situated, "is upon a great district of country that was within the last 24 years, a "mere waste bog and wood, serving for a retreat and harbour to wood-"kernes, rebels, thieves and wolves. It is now surrounded by strong walls, "and otherwise fortified ; provided with two churches, two session-houses, a "strong bridge over the river, two market houses, and ample accommodations "for traders. It occupies an area of 27 acres, and is inhabited by such neat, "orderly and religious people, as it would comfort any good heart to see "the change." His Lordship adds, in the same letter, his desire to have Bandon in the south, to rival Londonderry in the north. Though for many years exclusively Protestant, the chief part of the population of Bandon is now Roman Catholic. The largest portion of the property has passed out of the Boyle Family, and now belongs to the Duke of Devonshire. The remainder being divided between the Earls of Bandon, Cork, and Shannon.

The earliest associations formed in the County of Wexford, were the following :

I

Name.	*By whom Commanded.*
"Ogle's Blues,"	Captain, the Right Hon. George Ogle, M P.
"Ballaghkeene Blazers," ..	Captain, Hawtry White.
"Wingfield Yeomanry," ..	Captain, John Hunter Gowan
"Bantry Williamites,"	Captain, Lord Loftus, (afterwards, Marquis of Ely.)
"Enniscorthy Rangers,"	Captain, Archd Hamilton Jacob.
"Wexford True Blues,"............ .	Captain, James Boyd. -
"Newtown Barry Britons,"	Captain, the Right Hon J. Maxwell Barry, M. P., (afterwards, Earl of Farnham)
"Saunder's Court Invincibles," ...	Captain, the Earl of Arran

Similar Societies were formed about this time, in the Protestant Settlements in Kerry, Limerick, Mayo, Sligo, and Tipperary.

As these five Counties were then, (and comparatively, are even yet) "outside the pale of civilization," so far as regards Protestant colonization and settlement, some allusion to each locality will be readily excused.

Kerry—Was the County that gave birth to the celebrated Daniel O'Connell It lies on the west coast of Ireland, and is the first land washed by the waters as they are blown across the broad Atlantic, from the American Continent. Muckross " Abbey," The "Lakes of Killarney," the Crags of the "O'Donoughoo of the Glens," and of the " Macgillicuddy of the Reekes," are all within this celebrated locality

Limerick—Is at the outlet of the Shannon It is the spot where the last stand was made by the Irish army in favor of King James. In the City of Limerick (which is the capital of the County,) the remnant of the Irish forces, under the immediate command of Sarsfield, took refuge, and from behind its well defended walls, caused the " Siege of Limerick," so much renowned in Irish history. The beauty of the "Limerick Lasses," the bravery of the " Garryowen Boys," and the musical charms of " Garryowen to glory " are celebrated in innumerable Irish ballads. The superiority in texture elasticity and finish, of the "Limerick gloves," is admitted in every part of the Empire.

As a somewhat lengthened description has been already given of Tipperary, it only now remains to notice Mayo and Sligo

Mayo—Is a large maritime county in the Province of Connaught It was included in the grant which Henry the II. made in 1180 to William Fitz-Adelm de Burgho, and it was so soon colonized by the English, that in the reign of Henry the III., a strenuous, but vain effort was made to dispossess them. William de Burgho, Earl of Ulster, was assassinated in 1333, immediately after which, some of the young branches of the Burke family, seized the Counties of Mayo and Galway, appropriated these territories to their own use, renounced English names, laws and alliances, identified themselves and their followers with the native Irish, and success-fully established a sort of rude independence. At this revolution the two leading De Burghos, who mastered Mayo and Galway, took the names respectively of MacWilliam Oughter and MacWilliam Eighter. From this time till the reign of Queen Elizabeth, the MacWilliams exercised sovereign rule, and during their administration, the Blakes, the Brownes, the Kir-wans, the MacDonnels, and other families, from Ulster and the South of Galway, settled within their territories. In 1575, the reigning MacWilliam, accompanied by the heads of the clans of O'Malley and O'Donnel, made their submission to the English Government at Galway. The Burkes, with the O'Donnels, the Joyces, and other families, afterwards arose against the English Government; but in July 1586, Sir Richard Bingham marched into Mayo, at the head of a considerable force, razed several castles of the Burkes and O'Donnels, scoured the whole country from south to north, and utterly overwhelmed the Irish force, in a pitched battle at Ardnaree.

From this county there has been of late years, a great outpouring of the population by emigration—the deaths by starvation and poverty were said to be very numerous—the estates of many of the old Families have been forfeited in the "encumbered Estates court," and there has been a large influx of English and Scotch farmers. In addition, many hundreds of the native inhabitants, are said to have conformed to the Protestant religion. Near Castlebar in this County, is the residence of General the Earl of Lucan, celebrated in the Crimean War reminiscence. His Lordship is the descen-dant of Sir Richard Bingham above named.

Sligo—Is a maritime county in the north of the Province of Connaught. Some antiquarians think, that the people called Nagnatae, Magnatae, or Magnati, by Ptolemy, were the original inhabitants of the territory, which now constitutes the County of Sligo; that their "eminent City" of Nagnata, or Magnata, stood on the present site of the town of Sligo, and that the river Libnius or Leboeus, which watered their capital, was the Sligo or Lough Gill river. Sir James Ware is one of the great antiquarians who hold this opinion; but Baxter, and others, assign the honors of the Nagnatae, to the town of Galway, and the river Corrib. The territorial divisions of this County, long before the entry of the English, were nearly coincident with the present Baronies; but called by different names; their designations then were Gregraria, now called Coolavin—Luigne, now Leney—Coranna, now Corran—Crioch Cairbre, now called Carbery, &c. &c. The family and descendants of Roderic O'Conor, the last native monarch of Ireland, in their struggles to retain or re-acquire possession of the province of Con-naught, made the territory of Sligo, the seat of the chief portion of their wars. In 1200 after Cathal Croobhderg, or Cathal of the bloody Hand, had been dethroned by his kinsman Carrach, who was supported by the

Anglo-Normans under De Burgho, Hugh O'Nell, chieftain of Tyrone, made an attempt to reinstate Cathal, and suffered defeat near Ballysadere. During the general insurrection in the latter part of the reign of Elizabeth, the English army, under Sir Conyers Clifford, were surprised and slaughtered in Sligo, by the Irish forces under O'Ruarc or O'Rourke, chieftain of Breffney. In the great rebellion of 1641, the insurgents held possession of the county, and though in 1645, they were driven out of the town of Sligo and repulsed in an attack upon it, by Sir Charles Coote, they eventually recovered it, and continued to hold it, till near the conclusion of the war. In the war of the Revolution, the adherents of James II. held the county, and the only reverse of any importance they met with, was on their advance to Sligo; from the "Enniskillen men." In 1798, a smart skirmish was fought near the village of Collooney, between the French invaders, under General Humbert, and a portion of the Limerick Militia, under Colonel Vereker. Cromlechs and other supposed Druidical monuments, are numerous throughout the County. Several remarkable caverns occur, the origin and use of which are unknown. Raths or Hill Forts every where abound. The principal Castles, which figure either in historical record, or in their own surviving ruins, are those of Castle Connor, Rallee, Lackan, Roslee, Ardnaglass, Ballymote, Sligo, Bahy, Newtown, Ballinafad, Lough Gara, and Memleck. The number of old monastic structures are too extensive to enumerate, from the Priory, Abbey, Cathedral Church, and Monastery, down to the establishment of Knight's Templars, at Templehouse. Sligo is the only County in the Province of Connaught, that has maintanied through out all changes, its Conservative character. Colonel Percival, the Hon. Henry King, Mr. Cooper, Mr. Wynne, Mr. Ffolliootte, Sir Robert Gore Booth, Mr. Ormsbey Gore, and all its representatives, for a great number of years past, have been Conservative.

The Town of *Sligo* is a Seaport, about 104 miles north west of Dublin, and is the capital of the County. Dr. MacParlan, Mr. Fraser, Mr. Inglis, Mrs. Hall, and other writers upon Ireland, describe the environs of Sligo, as possessing the elements of scenic power and beauty, and an aggregate amount of loveliness, brilliance and magnificence, unsurpassed in any other place they ever visited. The ruins of the Dominican Abbey of Sligo, founded in 1252, are extensive, well preserved, and of extraordinary artistic interest. Three sides of a spacious square of cloisters still remain, each side covered with an arched roof, and presenting to the interior, a series of beautifully carved little arches about four feet in height. Almost all the little pillars between these arches, are peculiarly ornamented ; one in particular is very unique, having a human head cut in the inside of the arch. Sligo was first made a borough town by Charter, in the reign of James the First. In 1207 the town with its Castle was burned by O'Donnel. In 1394, the town was again spoiled and burned by MacWilliam De Burgho. In 1645, an

Irish force of 2000 foot and 300 horse, surrounded the town, and were with great slaughter, repelled and defeated by the garrison, chiefly of English Royalists.

Not only at the eventful period preceding the rebellion of 1798, but even for many years afterwards: in fact during the whole crisis of the French war, and while Rebellion joined to invasion every hour threatened to burst forth like an avalanche, upon doomed Ireland, the government had to rely almost solely upon the devoted loyalty, the patriotic virtue ; and the heroic valor of the Orangemen, to ward off the impending storm. From 1795 to 1809, confidential circulars were forwarded from the war office, and from Dublin castle, to all the leading Orangemen, urging upon them, the enrolment and arming of the " loyal yeomanry," it being well known, that in almost every instance, these " loyal yeomanry," were exclusively Orangemen.   The following are copies of some of those circulars ; signed by the celebrated Lord Castlereagh (afterwards Marquis of Londonderry,) then Secretary at war, and by Sir Edward Baker Littlehales, then Chief Secretary to the Lord Lieutenant of Ireland.

" DUBLIN CASTLE, 16th April, 1798.

SIR,—As it may be expedient, in case of invasion or other emergency, to augment the yeomanry establishment, particularly the infantry, and as much confusion and inconvenience might result from the adoption of such a measure without previous arrangement, you are requested to report to me for his Excellency's information, what number of men of approved loyalty, not exceeding 50, you can add to your corps on the following conditions :

The men to be immediately enrolled, to take the oath of allegiance, as prescribed by the Act, and to declare their willingness to undertake permanent duty as yeomen when called upon by Government.   Until so called upon, they are neither to be clothed, paid, armed, or disciplined, but to consider themselves as a supplementary force, ready to supply vacancies in the corps, or to turn out in defence of their country, should the Lord Lieutenant require their services, in which case they are to be provided by Government with arms and accoutrements.

As soon as I am favoured with your answer, I shall have the honor of transmitting to you his Excellency's further pleasure upon the subject.

I have, &c.

(Signed,)   CASTLEREAGH."

Extract of letter, 6th May, 1798.

" I have also his Excellency's commands to signify to you, his approbation of your immediately enrolling in your corps such a number of men of approved loyalty, not exceeding 50, as shall be ready to engage, according to the terms proposed in my letter of the 16th of April ; it having been understood that the men are not to be either clothed, armed or paid, unless the Lord Lieutenant in case of emergency should find it expedient to avail himself of their services. The names and the oaths of allegiance to be transmitted to the War Office as speedily as possible.

I have, &c.

(Signed,)   CASTLEREAGH."

" WAR OFFICE, Dublin Castle, 4th April, 1799.

SIR,—I am commanded by the Lord Lieutenant to acquaint you, that the Lurgan corps of infantry, under your command, is from the date of this letter established at the numbers detailed as follows ;

Establishment of Captain Brownlow's corps of infantry.

Permanent sergeant   1
Sergeants.............................   6
Trumpeter and Drummer...................   1
Rank and file (dismounted infantry)........... 150
                                              ———
            Total................ 158

I have, &c.

(Signed,)   CASTLEREAGH."

" DUBLIN CASTLE, 12th September, 1808.

SIR,—Circumstances having rendered it expedient, that the yeomanry infantry should be increased in a limited degree, the Lord Lieutenant has been induced to take into consideration the loyal offer for augmenting the corps under your command, which has been for some time before the Government ; and his Grace having decided to approve of an augmentation of four sergeants and 83 privates (infantry) to the corps, I have to request that you will, as soon as possible, transmit to me a roll, in the enclosed form, of the names of the persons willing to join the Lurgan corps, who are fit for service, and for whose loyalty, character, and conduct you can be responsible ; when the roll shall have been received at this office, and duly examined, the augmentation will be immediately placed on the regular establishment, and orders will be made for the issue of arms and accoutrements.

I am to observe, that from the date of the addition to your corps being placed on the establishment, the members of the augmentation will become entitled to pay, and the usual allowance for clothing, in the same manner as the rest of the corps. But I am to state that previously thereto, they are to transmit a similar offer of service through the Brigade Major, and to agree to the arrangement for exercising in Battalion as has been adopted by the corps, which they are to join.

P.S.—It should seem desirable that the corps should be divided into two companies ; and should it meet your concurrence, you will be pleased to transmit the names of such gentlemen as you may wish to have appointed officers.

I have, &c.

E. B. LITTLEHALES."

Captain Brownlow,
    Lurgan Infantry, Lurgan. '

CHAPTER XX.

Efforts of the "Catholic Committee" to unite the "Defenders" and "Peep-of-day
Boys"—Description of Armagh County and City—Indiscreet effects of a united
assembly at Tertaraghan—Fathers Quigly and Treaner enter into a covenant
with Messrs. Cope and Atkinson—The Priests violate their engagements, rally
their forces, and attack the Protestant settlements at the Diamond—Spirited
resistance of the Protestants and defeat of their assailants--Description of the
Diamond—Evidence of Lord Gosford—Letter of the late Mr. Verner, M.P.,
(Father to Sir William Verner, Bart., M. P.)

From 1791 to 1798, the "Catholic Committee" were active and vigilant,
to unite the several disaffected bodies throughout Ireland, to coalesce with
France, in an endeavour to cast off the English government. The better
to effect their designs, two Roman Catholic Priests, accompanied by two
Protestant Gentlemen, (Napper Tandy and Wolfe Tone, Esquires,) were deputed by the "Committee," to visit the northern Province, and to endeavour, if possible, to unite the "Peep-of-day Boys," (disaffected Presbyterians,) and the "Defenders!" the latter exclusively Roman Catholics.
Through the instrumentality of the four Delegates, assisted by several
active local Agents, a temporary, but most alarming amalgamation was
effected. Immediately the system of outrage commenced, and the reign
of terror was renewed, with fearful atrocities, and immunity from punishment. Up to this period, the "Peep-of-day" crimes were chiefly committed against Roman Catholics, the Protestants of the Established Church,
were the particular objects of vengeance ; and in the neighbourhoods of
Charlemont, Lurgan, Loughgall, Newtown Hamilton, Portadown, Rich
Hill, and Tandragee, in the County of Armagh, they may be said to have
been almost driven from their homes and possessions.

As the County of Armagh was the scene of so much disturbance at this
period ; as it was also in this County that the Orange Society was first
practically organized in Ireland, some slight description of the County
and City may be expected.

Armagh is an inland County of Ulster, extending from Lough Neagh
to the northern boundary of Leinster. It is bounded on the north west by
Tyrone, on the north by Lough Neagh, on the east by Down, on the south
by Louth, and on the west by Monaghan and Tyrone. The boundary line on
the north west is the River Blackwater. According to Dr. Beaufort's esti-
mate, and to Sir Charles Coote's statistical survey of the County, its area
contains upwards of 454 English square miles, or 290,786 English acres. The
estates of the County consist of Freehold, Church, and College lands ; but

the two last, in many parts of the County, considerably exceed the first. Leases in perpetuity are few in number and small in value. The principal landed Proprietors are the Earl of Charlemont, the Earl of Gosford, Lord Lurgan, the Duke of Manchester, Sir William Verner, Bart., Sir Capel Moléyneux, Bart., Mr. Hall of Narrow Water, and Mr. Cope of Loughgall.

Armagh City (which is the capital of the County,) is an ancient Royal Borough, and the Ecclesiastical Metropolis of Ireland. It is 15 miles north west from Newry, 31 south west from Belfast, 66 south east from Londonderry, 41 east from Enniskillen, and 65 north by west from Dublin. The City occupies the summit and gently sloping sides of Druimsailech, ("the hill of willows,") and is immediately environed with a rolling or softly tumulated country of beautiful contour. The environs of the City, and even the site, were formerly patched with lake, marsh, bog, and such dense woods and thickets as were impervious to the sunbeams, and prevented the free circulation of the air. Even so late as the beginning of the 18th century, a small Lake called Luppan, remained in the very Town, at the foot of Market Street, and abounded with Eels. But the marshes have been drained, the bogs converted into meadows or corn fields, the offensive Lakes annihilated, the woods and thickets cut down or thinned, and the whole surface so improved and embellished as to present an unwrinkled and unmarred face of health and beauty. The Callan and the Ballinahone rivers traverse the environs, the former on the west, and the Callan on the east ; they form a confluence at a point half a mile from the City's northern extremity, and both are spanned by Bridges carrying across the numerous lines of thoroughfare. The approaches from the south and the north, pass through quite a museum of luxuriance and beauty, which increases in wealth and attraction till the Town is entered. It is said that a Cathedral was erected in Armagh in the year 445, by St. Patrick. The City flourishes early and prominently in the ancient literature of Ireland. Its early history is, however, so shrouded in feature that its true lineaments cannot be seen, and its later history is such a uniform series of plundering and bloody incident on the part of the Danes and Irish septs, as to possess very little real interest. A City called Eamania ("the noble City") is said by Irish tradition, to have been built on or near the site of Armagh, by a Scottish Prince, upwards of two centuries, or according to O'Connor, 353 years before the Christian era. This city claims to have been the capital of the Province of Ulster, and the Royal Seat of the Kings of the North. Colgan affirms that in his time, the ruins of the City were standing. Camden says, that the ruins of the Royal palace of the city, which both he and Speed, who wrote in 1614, call Owen Maugh, were still visible near Armagh. O'Halloran, a modern author, also affirms their existence at the time he wrote. The whole story, however, about the City of Eamania, rests upon the mere legends of Bards and the traditions of Ecclesiastical authors. Previous to the English conquest of Ireland, Armagh suffered more of the horrors of fire, plunder and the sword, than probably any other Irish Town of its size. From time immemorial it has been the scene of many a deadly feud and bloody engagement—in wars, at one time waged between the Irish Chieftains themselves—at other times, between the Irish Danes and Ostmans—and afterwards, between the Natives of the Country and the invading armies of England and Scotland. In 670, 687, and 778, it was burnt. It was plundered eight times in the ninth century; and thirteen times in the three following centuries, it was plundered, burnt, or otherwise laid waste by the Danes. It was pillaged by De Courcy, Fitz-Adelm, and De Lacy, during the English conquest of Ulster. It was frequently burnt in the civil wars during the reign of Elizabeth. During the 1641 massacre, the whole County of Armagh was marked by scenes of peculiar atrocity; and in later years, the savage barbarities committed by the "*White-boys,*" "*Defenders,*" "*Peep-of-day Boys,*" and others, show that the inhabitants of this County, up to a very recent period—say to near the commencement of the present century—had lost but little of that ferocious and bloodthirsty spirit, which distinguished their ancestors.

The Roman Catholic Priests and Population, temporarily strengthened by the junction of the deceived and disaffected Presbyterians, acting on the advice of Tandy and Tone, knew no bounds to their zeal to banish the "*Sassenach,*" and to re-possess the ancient domains of their ancestors. But, like other zealots engaged in a bad cause, and using vile means to effect vile ends, their zeal outstripped their discretion. So powerful did they appear in their own estimation, that, without the consent of their Dublin Leaders, under whose authority they had hitherto acted, they had the daring temerity to appear in arms in the open day. On the 14th of September, 1795, they assembled in great force, and well armed, in the Parish of Tentaraghan, in the County of Armagh, and fired at the persons, and into the houses, of the Protestants in that neighbourhood. The Protestant population, alarmed for their safety, fled to the neighbouring hills, carrying with them such arms and ammunition as they were able to procure. The insurgents followed in pursuit, and during three days (the 15th, 16th, and 17th of September 1795,) a sort of guerilla fire was kept up by the alarmed Protestants, who had sought refuge in the mountain fastnesses. On the morning of the 18th, the Rev. "*Fathers*" Quigly and Treaner, Roman Catholic Priests, called upon Archdall Cope, Esq., of Loughgall, a Magistrate of the County, assuring him of their desire to effect a reconciliation, and to restore the country to quiet and tranquility. Mr. Cope was a Protestant Gentleman, the proprietor of considerable property, and possessing much local and personal influence. He had just sent off despatches to the Military stations at Armagh and Charlemont, stating the alarming condition of affairs, and urging the necessity for prompt military aid. Overpowered by the persuasions of the Priests, and relying upon the sincerity of their professions, he consented to countermand the orders he had previously issued, and to accompany their Reverences to the vicinity of the insurgents. The Priests proceeded directly to the leaders of the rebel party, and Mr. Cope passed on up the hills to communicate with the affrighted Protestants. After some consultation, both parties agreed to "bury the hatchet," and "smoke the pipe of peace." For this purpose they repaired to Crowhill, the residence of Joseph Atkinson, Esq., a Magistrate of the County. Here regular peace articles of mutual forbearance and reconciliation were drawn up and signed ; each party entering into recognizances to keep the King's peace, and to act as loyal subjects in dutiful submission to the Laws and constituted Authorities. The Priests signed the writings and became bail and sureties for the insurgents.

After thus entering into a solemn treaty, and obligating themselves by a written bond, the Priests and their followers perfidiously broke through their engagements. Immediately after leaving Crowhill, on the evening of the same day, and while the ink was yet scarcely dry on the paper that witnessed the obligation, one party of them fired at Mr. Atkinson, while others of them set off to the mountains of Pomeroy and Ballygawley, in the County of Tyrone, to inform their friends that the Army was not coming, and that all they had to do, was to turn out, join their confederates then in arms, and they would exterminate Protestantism from the country. After three days' successive recruiting, they returned in full force, and attacked a Protestant settlement, at a small village called " *The Diamond,*" close to the Blackwater river, which separates the counties of Armagh and Tyrone. The firing of shots and the shouting of the insurgents, as they advanced along the roads, alarmed the scattered Protestants, who fled from their houses, carrying with them their families, and hoping they might be enabled to get into Charlemont, at which post there was a small Military garrison. Approaching the house of a man named William Winter, close to Diamond Village, he refused to retreat, and bravely fired upon the Romish party as they advanced. Overpowered by numbers, Winter was obliged to yield, but made good his retreat from the end of his house, into the village. The spirited resistance which he had offered, emboldened the Protestant party retreating through the village, to stand fast, and under the leadership of Thomas Wilson, to meet the enemy with a bold front. A regular engagement ensued, the little village became the scene of a sanguinary strife, and some two or three hundred ill-disciplined but stout-hearted Protestants, *pro aris et focis*—for their religion and fire-sides—bravely bore up against an infuriated rabble of some eight hundred or a thousand men, maddened to phrenzy by a belief, that they were engaged in a crusade to restore their religion, and to recover the possession of the estates of their ancestors. The Protestant party, bravely encouraged by

Winter and Wilson, had possession of the houses, and eventually succeeded in driving back their assailants, and proclaiming themselves masters in the strife. Four of the Protestant party were killed, and some 37 or 38 wounded. Of the assailants 48 were killed, but how many wounded was not ascertained, as they were carried off by the insurgents when retiring. This conflict has ever since been known as "the Battle of the Diamond."

As there are several places called the "Diamond," in Ireland, it may be necessary here to say, that the Diamond alluded to, is the name of a small hamlet, about two miles from Loughgall, in the Parish of Kilmore, and County of Armagh. On the west border of the Parish, and about two miles from Loughgall, are the intrenchments and ruins of Castleran, and about three quarters of a mile from these, is the little hamlet called the Diamond. It is situated in a glen, and is celebrated as the scene of "the Battle of the Diamond." The *Parliamentary Gazetteer*, Vol. 2, page 516, thus describes this event : "The two parties of predial insurgents, known to local history "as the Defenders and Peep-of-day Boys, having fought several skirmishes, "and sustained mutual losses of blood and life, agreed upon a truce, and "appointed a meeting for negotiation, to be held in the house of a man "named Winter, in the Village of the Diamond. At this meeting a "Roman Catholic Clergyman on the one part, and a Protestant Gentleman "on the other, bound themselves for their respective parties, that peace "between both should be strictly preserved for a period named. The Pro-"testant Gentleman (Mr. Atkinson, J. P.,) was fired at on his way home, "after having affixed his name to the Treaty, and his party was on the next "day, attacked by above 700 of the Defenders. But it is asserted that "these Defenders were ignorant of the fact that an armistice had been "agreed upon. Thus exasperated, both parties prepared for a resort to "arms ; both assembled in large numbers ; the one upon the hill that "overlooked the Diamond, and the other upon the hill opposite ; each "having laid in a large store of provisions and ammunition, and each being "amply provided with weapons. The Battle took place on the 21st of "September 1795, and happily before much mischief was done, although "several lives were sacrificed. The parties were separated by the timely "arrival of the Military. Out of this affray—preceded as it undoubtedly "was by many other unhappy quarrels, and a terrible state of insubordi-"nation in the County of Armagh—arose the Orange Institution." The apology here offered for Priest Quigly and the Roman Catholic party, called Defenders, can scarcely be received. It is in the last degree apocry-phal, that they could have been ignorant, on the day following the armistice, that any such thing had occurred—that they could have been ignorant that articles of peace had been signed, and that both parties had returned to their respective homes, 24 hours after the occurrence of the event itself. The attempt to assassinate Mr. Atkinson on his return home, might have occurred in ignorance of the peace treaty ; but the assemblage of over 700 men on the following day, to exterminate, if possible, the Protestant party, could not have taken place, without a full knowledge of the events which distinguished the preceeding day.

As much misrepresentation prevails, not only as regards the organization of the Orange Society in 1795, but also as regards the events which preceded that organization, it cannot but be interesting to the reader, as also conducive to the ends of truth, that documents of the most unquestioned authenticity should be referred to, and the evidence of the most respectable and the best informed drawn out. The late Lord Gosford was, at the time, Governor of the County of Armagh. He was a Whig Nobleman, entertaining extreme liberal views towards the Roman Catholics ; very anxious, if not to justify, at least to extenuate much of their bad conduct ; and to cast censure and odium upon the Protestant party in the Kingdom, to whom, politically, he was opposed. In 1835, his Lordship's son, the present Lord Gosford, (who inherits his Father's principles,) was summoned before the select Committee of the House of Commons, appointed to enquire into the nature, extent, and tendency of the Orange Society ; and his Lordship appeared as the chief evidence against the Orangemen. From the Journals of the House, the following extracts are taken.

" *Question* 3250.—Your Lordship will find in the evidence of Colonel Verner, now shown to you; and the evidence of the Rev. Mortimer O'Sullivan, that the first Orange Lodge was formed on the 21st of September, 1795, on the evening of the day of the battle of the Diamond ?—*Answer.* It was about that time, as well as I recollect ; but I cannot say precisely.

Question 3251.—The question to Colonel Verner is, " Was there not an assault on the Protestants, previous to the establishment of the Orange Institution, which led to the conflict at Diamond Hill ?" The answer is, " There was." " When was that ?" "The 21st of September, 1795." Will your Lordship have the goodness to read the address of the late Earl of Gosford, then governor of the County of Armagh, and the Resolutions of the magistrates, and the names of the magistrates present on that occasion ?—*Answer.* On the 28th day of December, 1795, certain magistrates and gentlemen were convened in Armagh. At a numerous meeting of the magistrates in the County of Armagh, convened at the special instance of Lord Viscount Gosford, Governor, his Lordship having taken the chair, opened the business by the following Address :—Gentlemen: Having requested your attendance here this day, it becomes my duty to state the grounds upon which I thought it advisable to propose this meeting, and, at the same time, to submit to your consideration a plan which occurs to me as the most likely to check the enormities that have already disgraced this county, and may soon reduce it into the greatest distress. It is no secret that a persecution, accompanied with all the circumstances of ferocious cruelty which have in all ages distinguished that dreadful calamity, is now raging in this county. Neither age, nor even acknowledged innocence as to the late disturbances, is sufficient to excite mercy, much less afford protection. The only crime which the wretched objects of this merciless persecution are charged with, is a crime of easy proof; it is simply a profession of the Roman Catholic faith. A lawless banditti have constituted themselves judges of this species of delinquency, and the sentence they pronounce is equally concise and terrible; it is nothing less than a confiscation of all property and immediate banishment. It would be extremely painful, and surely unnecessary, to detail the horrors that attended the execution of so wide and tremendous a proscription; that certainly exceeds, in the comparative number of those it consigns to ruin and misery, every example that ancient or modern history can afford. For where have we heard, or in what history of human cruelties have we read, of more than half the inhabitants of a populous county deprived at one blow of the means as well as of the fruits of their industry, and driven, in the midst of an inclement winter, to seek shelter for themselves and their helpless families where chance may guide them. This is no exaggerated picture of the horrid scenes now acting in this county; yet surely it is sufficient to awaken sentiments of indignation and compassion in the coldest heart, those horrors are now acting, and acting with impunity. The spirit of impartial justice (without which law is nothing better than tyranny,) has for a time disappeared in this county, and the supineness of the magistracy in this county, is a topic of conversation in every corner of this kingdom. It is said the Catholics are dangerous; they may be so; they may be dangerous from their numbers, still more dangerous from the unbounded views they have been encouraged to entertain; but I will venture to assert, without fear of contradiction, that upon these very grounds those terrible proceedings are not more contrary to humanity than they are to sound policy and justice. I have the honor to hold a situation in this county which calls upon me to deliver my sentiments, and I do so without fear or disguise. I am as true a Protestant as any man in this room, or in this kingdom. I inherit a property which my family derived under a Protestant title, and, with the blessing of God, I will maintain that title to the utmost of my power. I will never consent to make a surrender of Protestant ascendancy to Catholic claims, with whatever menaces they may be urged, or however speciously or invidiously supported. Conscious of my sincerity in this public declaration, which I do not make unadvisedly, but as the result of mature deliberation. I defy the paltry insinuations that malice or party spirit may suggest; I know my own heart, and should despise myself if, under any intimidation, I could close my eyes against such scenes as present themselves on every side, or shut my ears against the complaints of a persecuted people. I have now acquitted myself to my conscience and my country, and take the liberty of proposing the following Resolutions :—1. That it appears to this meeting that the County Armagh is, at this time, in a state of uncommon disorder: That the Roman Catholic inhabitants are grievously oppressed by lawless persons unknown, who attack and plunder their houses by night, unless they immediately abandon their lands and habitations.

2. That a Committee of magistrates be appointed to sit on Tuesdays and Saturdays, in the Chapter room of the Cathedral Church of Armagh, to receive informations respecting all persons, of whatever description, who disturb the peace of this county.

3. That the instructions of the whole body of magistracy to this Committee shall be, to use every legal means within their power to stop the progress of the persecution now carrying on by an ungovernable mob against the Catholics of this county.

4. That said Committee, or any three of them, be empowered to spend any sum of money for information or secret service, out of the funds subscribed by the gentlemen of this county.

5. That a meeting of the whole magistracy of this county be held every second Monday, at the house of Charles McReynold's, to hear the reports of their Committee, and to give further instructions, as the exigency of the times may require.

6. That offenders of every description in the present disturbances shall be prosecuted at the public expense, out of the funds subscribed by the gentlemen of this county; and to carry this resolution into effect it is, Resolved, that Mr. Arthur Irwin be appointed law agent to the magistrates. The above resolutions being read, were unanimously agreed to, and the Committee nominated. Lord Gosford having left the chair, and Sir Capel Molyneaux being requested to take it,—Resolved, that the unanimous thanks of this meeting be presented to Lord Viscount Gosford, for his proper conduct in convening the magistrates of the county, and his impartiality in the chair.

Question 3277.—Have you ever seen those Resolutions before in any other shape?—*Answer*. Yes; I have seen them in print, from what I have found in drawers of my own in looking over papers. I have seen a good number lying there that had been printed, and my impression is that they were circulated through the Country and printed for distribution.

Question 3278.—Your Lordship was then a very young man?—*Answer*. Yes; I think I was at Oxford at the time.

Question 3279.—About that time were you in the County?—*Answer*. I think it is very likely I may have been, as I generally spent my vacations there.

Question 3280.—Has your Lordship any recollection of any of the outrages committed at that time, or any means taken to protect the Catholics, for whose protection this was issued?—*Answer*. Yes; I recollect being told, and I have no doubt of the fact, from the variety of ways in which I heard it and the persons who mentioned it to me, that it was thought necessary by my father, Lord Gosford, the governor, to put soldiers into houses of Roman Catholics for the purpose of protecting them against the threatened attacks of the Protestants.

Question 3281.—Your Lordship will find that the Battle of the Diamond, when the first Orange Lodge took place, was on the 21st of Sept; here are resolutions passed on the 28th day of December, representing half the population as placed out of the pale of the law by a banditti assuming to themselves the whole control of the management of the County, was there a cry at that time accompanying that visitation?—*Answer*. I always understood that on the houses of the Roman Catholics there was written "To Hell or Connaught," and I believe it.

Question 3282.—Were not those considered Orangemen who took those steps to drive the Catholics out of the County at that time?—*Answer*. Not having been an Orangeman myself, I can only speak from the statement made to me: the statement made to me is, that the first Orange Lodge took place in September and those resolutions in December. I should think they alluded to parties of Protestants. banded together, but whether under the form of Orangemen I cannot say.

Question 3283—Your Lordship then finds the first Orange Lodge in the County of Armagh, according to the best evidence now to be procured upon the subject from those connected with the Orange Institution itself, was established on the 21st of September, in the year 1795, and that they had been scarcely three months in existence when—that institution professing to be established for the preservation of the public peace and the maintenance of order—the county is in a state of the most frightful disorder, and outrages of an appalling nature are perpetrated, and half the population driven as outcasts from the county with "Hell and Connaught" inscribed on the doors of the Catholics ; is it fairly to be presumed that that was the result of the Orange System being introduced into that County?—*Answer.* That may be matter of opinion, but I think that the conclusion may be a fair one.

Question 3284—This document appears to be perfectly correct ?—*Answer.* Yes.

Question 3285—Did you ever hear it called in question ?—*Answer.* I never heard any part of it called in question as to its contents or as to its truth, I have heard it objected to by many persons who disapproved of it.

Question 3286—You never heard it impeached by authentic documents?—*Answer.* No : I go further than that: I am sure my Father would not have said one single thing he did not believe to be true, and that he was fully convinced of the correctness of the charges made in that statement.

Question 3287—He states " where have we heard or in what history of human cruelties have we read, of more than half the inhabitants of a populous county deprived at one blow of the means as well as of the fruits of their industry, and driven, in the midst of an inclement winter, to seek for shelter for themselves and their helpless families where chance may guide them ?' That appears in the body of the statement ; all these circumstances, according to this paper, were perpetrated against Catholics, as appears upon the very face of the document itself ?—*Answer.* I always understood these threatening notices to have been directed against the Catholics solely.

Question 3288—There is not appended to this a single name but one of a Roman Catholic, Mr. Owen O'Callaghan ?—*Answer.* That is the only Roman Catholic there.

Question 3289—You have at the head of it the Earl of Gosford, your late Father. Sir Capel Molyneux, Baronet. William Richardson, the member for the County, three gentlemen, who were then in the Church and died Bishops, and several Clergymen, but all staunch friends of the Protestant Establishment, anxious for its preservation, unanimously adopting the resolutions submitted by the Earl of Gosford, unanimously thanking him for his conduct in calling them together, and not one expressing the slightest dissent from the sentiments he uttered in proposing these resolutions ?—*Answer.* I see here that three of the signatures to those were Clergyman, and afterwards Bishops; their names were, Hugh Hamilton, Charles Warburton, and William Bisset, the one Bishop of Ossory, another afterwards Bishop of Limerick or Cloyne, and William Bisset was Bishop of Raphoe, and died such.

Question 3648—Your Lordship did not mean to intimate that the parties pointed at by that speech were Orangemen ?—*Answer.* No. I am sure I did not intend to give any such evidence; I merely stated they were Protestants, and I stated that I did not know whether Orangemen had extended so far, I spoke to the impression I had.

Question 3649—Is not your Lordship aware that the parties who had been banded together on different sides, and who had been committing outrages reciprocally on one another, were " Peep-o-day Boys," and the " Defenders," prior to that period ?—*Answer.* I believe the " Peep-o-day Boys" and the " Defenders" were prior to that.

Question 3650—Were not the persons who had been interrupting the peace of the County, from the time at which your Lordship's Father was appointed Governor of the County up to the time of his delivering that speech at Christmas 1795, Peep-o-day Boys ?—*Answer.* I do not know under what sort of denomination the people went at that time; they were Protestants.

Question 3651—In what age of life was your Lordship at that time ?—*Answer.* I suppose 18 or 19.

Question 3652.—Is it not upon your Lordship's recollection that you heard of the Peep-o-day Boys ?—*Answer.* Yes, I have heard of them.

Question 3653.—At that time ?—*Answer.* No. I think it must be prior to that time ; but I cannot speak clearly from memory.

Question 3654.—Is your Lordship aware of the fact that the persons who were Peep-o-day Boys were Presbyterians and not Churchmen ?—*Answer.* I cannot answer that question.

Question 3655.—Is your Lordship aware of the fact that the Orangemen were on the other hand Churchmen at the institution of the order ?—*Answer.* I have understood originally the Orangemen were composed of Churchmen, and I have heard that afterwards, Dissenters were admitted, and I believe that was so. I can know nothing of that but from hearsay.

Question 3656.—Your Lordship has as much reason to be of that opinion as you have to be of several opinions, your Lordship has expressed yesterday on several matters ?—*Answer.* Yes ; I think that the original institution of Orangemen was confined to the Church of England ; but at the same time, I do believe there was a great number admitted into it that were Protestants and not Church of England men.

Question 3657.—Is not your Lordship aware that the parties who compelled their Presbyterian tenants to become Orangemen, were the Lords Hertford, Abercorn, Londonderry, Northland, and Messrs. Cope, Brownlaw and Richardson, did you not hear that those noblemen and gentlemen compelled their tenants to join the Orange Institution ?—*Answer.* Never, a great proportion of the persons named lived not in any County that I am connected with, but many of them in the County of Down, and the others in the County of Antrim ; but with respect to one name, Mr. Richardson, whom I knew intimately, a connexion of my own, my own positive belief is, that he never did attempt to coerce his tenants to join the Society ; that is contrary to any communication I ever had with him.

Question 3661.—Does not your Lordship think it improbable that Mr. Sparrow, your relative, the Father of Colonel Verner, and Dean Blacker, and those gentlemen, would have become Orangemen themselves, if they had thought the Orange

Association was properly to be described as "a lawless banditti"?—*Answer*. It certainly would be a very surprising thing if they did after signing such a paper as that.

Question 3662.—Taking all these circumstances into consideration, and the fact that there never was an Orange Lodge existing in Ireland till September 1795, that the speech in question delivered by your Lordship's Father was delivered in December 1795, three months after the first Orange Lodge in Ireland, was formed, and considering that upon this occasion, to the resolutions were affixed the signatures of the three gentlemen referred to, does not your Lordship think the great probabilities are, that the reference by your Lordship's Father to this "lawless banditti," must have been to the "Peep-of-day Boys," and not to the Orange Institution?—*Answer*. I have stated that. I could not speak positively to the "Peep-of-day Boys" My belief is, it alluded to Protestants, but under what name or title they went I cannot say.

Question 3663.—Is it probable, taking into consideration the circumstance, referred to, that the reference could be to the Orange Institution?—*Answer*. If so there is a great inconsistency in it certainly.

Question 3664.—Is not your Lordship quite aware that the Orange Lodges in Ireland were extremely few indeed between September 1795 and the 1st January 1796?—*Answer*. I can form no opinion upon that; I cannot state how rapidly they were spread.

Quesiton 3665.—Your Lordship was nearly of age in 1796; is not your Lordship aware that it was in the year 1796 the Orange Institution spread in Ireland? *Answer*. I think it was about the time of Lord Camden's being Lord Lieutenant.

Question 3666.—Just before the invasion of Ireland by the French, which was at Christmas 1796; is not your Lordship aware, as a matter of notoriety, it was in the year 1796 that the Orange Institution spread in Ireland?—*Answer*. I think it was.

Question 4071—Your Lordship on the last day, stated that in that portion of Ireland when Orangeism prevailed, the Calendars were much lighter than they were in other parts where Orangeism does not prevail, where the Calendars are tremendously heavy in the point of crime: Your Lordship was interrogated with regard to the County of Armagh having been once proclaimed?—*Answer*. Yes I think I recollect it.

Question 4072—In the "*Collectanea Politica*" of the transactions of Ireland, third volume, by William Wenman Seward, Esq. Your Lordship will find at page 179 a proclamation by Lord Camden in the year 1796, given at the Council Chamber, Dublin, 2nd of December 1796; "We, the Lord Lieutenant, do by and "with the advice of his Majesty's Privy Council, in pursuance of and by the "authority to us given by the said act of Parliament by this our proclamation "declare that part of the parish of Newry, and also that part of the parish of "Armagh which are situated and lying in the said barony of Onealand West and "County of Armagh aforesaid, to be in a state of disturbance or in immediate "danger of becoming so; of which all justices of the peace and other magistrates "and peace officers of the said county, and all others whom it may concern are to "take notice." Has there in point of fact, ever since the year 1796, which is very recently after the formation of the Orange Association in that county, ever been an instance of the proclamation of the whole or any part of the County of Armagh?—*Answer*. Not that I am aware of: I gave the same answer yesterday, there might have been some portions of the county of Armagh proclaimed adjoining to other counties, but that I do not know of the County Armagh, being affected by any proclamation.

Question 4073.—Nor does your Lordship know of any proclamation affecting any part of it, but that there may have been?—*Answer*. I was at college at that time. I do not recollect the circumstance. I might have got letters and heard reports, some might have been wrong and others not. I can give the impression on my own mind : I have no recollection of that circumstance.

Question 4074.—Your Lordship has not a recollection of any other proclamation?—*Answer*. No, I have not, and I rather think there has been none.

Question 4075.—On the former occasion the committee had not before them the authority they now have, to show that is was matter of history that the departure of those Roman Catholics from the County of Armagh was in consequence of the contests between the "Peep-o'-day Boys" and "Defenders."

"In the same book Seward's *Collectanea Politica*, at page 191, it is thus stated : "The contentions which continued in Ulster between the Peep-o'-day Boys and the "Defenders obliged many Roman Catholic families, particularly of the lower "class, to flee from the County of Armagh, and seek refuge amongst the inhabit-"ants of Connaught. This circumstance occasioned the following address from a "respectable meeting, held in that County, to such of their Roman Catholic "brethren as had been driven from their country by the late cruel persecution." Your Lordship sees, that that statement in the book refers to the transaction of which your Lordship gave evidence. This flying away of the community of Roman Catholics from Armagh would appear to be the result of the contentions in that county between the Peep-o'-day Boys and the Defenders?—*Answer*. I can give no opinion upon that.

Question 4076.—Does it not appear from that passage?—*Answer*. It may be the inference from that passage ; but I have no recollection of the particulars of that period, so as to enable me to say whether that is correct or not.—(*His Lordship referred to the book*.)—I believe that many Roman Catholic families did flee from the County of Armagh to Connaught as here stated, but really whether that was occasioned by previous fightings between Peep-o'-day Boys and Defenders, or any other party whatever, I have no recollection, nor can I form an opinion.

Question 4077.—Does not that passage refer to the same transaction which the speech you gave in evidence on the first day of your examination of the late Lord Gosford referred to ?—*Answer*. I think it refers to the period, the speech referred to was in December 1795.

Question 4078.—Does not that purport to refer to the same transaction that the late Lord Gosford's speech purports to refer to, namely, the flying away of part of the Catholic Population of Armagh ?—*Answer*. I cannot tell until I see what is the period which Mr. Seward refers to, he does not specify what year.

Question 4079.—If your Lordship will have the goodness to refer to the following passage you will see the date ?—"On the 8th of April 1797, a meeting of "freeholders and freemen was held in the Royal Exchange, on proposition to "address his Majesty to dismiss his Minister for ever."—*Answer.* I do not see any date referring to that period.

Question 4080.—By the context it appears that the historian is relating transactions of the year 1797, the date immediately preceding this statement is the 18th March, 1797, therefore he is here giving the political transactions of the year 1797; and in this passage he states that " the contentions which continued in Ulster between the Peep-o'-day Boys and the Defenders, obliged many Roman Catholic families, particularly of the lower classes, to flee from the County of Armagh, and to seek refuge among the inhabitants of Connaught." The late Lord Gosford's speech being delivered in December, 1795, does your Lordship entertain any doubt that the transaction here referred to is the same as that referred to in his speech?—*Answer.* I cannot take upon me to say that the historian in 1797 alludes to the transactions which occurred in 1795.

Question 4081.—He has not stated that the emigration was in 1797, but a matter which had previously taken place?—*Answer.* It might or it might not.

Question 4082.—Did you ever hear of two flights of great bodies of Roman Catholics from Armagh?—*Answer.* No, I do not think I did; I heard of but one of that description when " To Hell or Connaught" was written on the doors of their houses."

The following letter, written by a most respectable resident magistrate of the County, so faithfully describes the events referred to in the preceding evidence, that it is here copied.

From the late James Verner, Esq., M.P., (Father to Sir Wm. Verner, Bart., M.P. for the County of Armagh), to Joseph Pollock, of Carnbane, Esq.

" CHURCH HILL, 9th March, 1807.

"SIR,—On my return from Dublin yesterday, I was favored with your letter of the 3rd inst. As I don't recollect to have attended more than two meetings of the magistrates, held at Armagh in 1795 and 1796, at which Lord Gosford was present, I cannot give you any detail of their various proceedings, or of the application made, which induced Lord Gosford to publish the handbill you allude to, and which was circulated over the Kingdom, and left *gratis* in the houses of several of the inhabitants of Dublin. I cannot say that I ever heard of any " famous speech " made by his Lordship at any of these meetings; and I am inclined to think that the same handbill was, previous to its publication, revised by the Rev. Mr. Bisset, of Loughgall, who appeared to me to be very much in the confidence of Lord Gosford. Whether it is reported accurately by Messrs. Hay, Gordon, Plowden, and O'Halloran, I cannot say, not having one of the originals, or even read the publications of these historians. The disturbances of 1795 seemed to me to be chiefly confined to that part of the County in which I reside. I had information in that year, that meetings were held at night, and that persons were administering oaths, for which they received a shilling from each individual. I never learned the tenor of the oath; and, in addition, persons went about the neighbourhood taking arms out of the houses of Protestants. In September, 1795,

I happened to be a few days in Belfast, and on my return I was stopped within two miles of my own house, by persons who said the country was much alarmed by a mob of armed men, who went to the houses of Protestants and fired shots, declaring that they would drive every Protestant out of the country. The morning following, I heard a constant discharge of guns, about two miles from my own house, in the lands of Anaghmore, and was informed that an attack had been commenced by the Catholics, and the Protestants were assembling in arms to defend themselves. The day following, the engagement was renewed, and I went for a party of the North Mayo Militia at Dungannon, and marched them to Anaghmore, when I was informed that Mr. Archdall Cope and his brother, and two or three other Magistrates had been there before me, and had taken some of the principal persons of each party to Mr. Atkinson's house, and that written articles had been entered into and signed, of amity, and bound in a sum for the due performance. Hearing, however, that this agreement was not likely to avail, and that the Catholic party expected strong reinforcements, and would commence hostilities on the following morning, I set out about three o'clock on that morning, with the same party of the North Mayo, towards Anaghmore and Loughgall, and found all quiet there. On my return home I was told the Catholic party were in great force at the Blackwater Foot, ("the Diamond,") and I could distinctly hear the shots. Immediately I had horses prepared, mounted four of the North Mayo, one of my sons, and servants, and proceeded expeditiously as an advance to reconnoitre towards the place. They, having intimation of my coming, crossed the River Blackwater in boats, and as we approached the village, ("the Diamond,") a number of shots were fired at us, and a constant fire was kept up by the Insurgents from the Tyrone side of the river. We returned back having secured *   *   * prisoners.

" I was now told there was to be no disturbance : but on the night of the 21st September, a number of persons were collected by the Catholic party between Armagh and New Town Hamilton and other parts, and they attacked the houses of some Protestants, particularly one named Winter, on the estate of Robert C. Cope, Esq., and in a short time a general engagement took place, and several of the Catholic party were killed. At this time, the whole country for miles around me, were rising in every direction in despair ; and on that day, I heard that the Messrs. McCann, of Armagh, with a party of cavalry, arrived after the affray was over, and took some prisoners. There also assembled a vast number of Catholics from the mountains of Ballygawley and Pomeroy, to assist on the morning of the 21st, but hearing that I was on the alert, and had secured the boats on the Blackwater river, they were prevented from rendering their friends that effective assistance they might otherwise have done. It has been often asserted, that this interference of mine was adverse to the Catholics, and it is not forgiven or forgotten to this day. Soon afterwards I attended the first meeting held at Armagh, at which Lord Gosford and many Magistrates attended. It appearing then to me, that Lord Gosford and a number of his party were prepossessed in favor of the Catholics, and did not give that credit or attention, which I expected for my exertions, though I endeavoured to assure them, that from every enquiry, I had reason to believe a conspiracy was hatching ; yet I found that Mr. Richardson, of

Rich Hill, (this gentleman was one of the Representatives of the County in Parliament,) and a few other gentlemen only supported my opinion. I left the meeting in disgust, and only once after went to another meeting, where Mr. Richardson's conduct was arraigned. From this time, party began to show itself strongly in the County, and Lord Gosford, the Messrs. McCann, of Armagh, and others, openly espoused the cause of the Catholics.

" The Protestants soon afterwards, began to look for the arms of which they had been robbed, and committed excesses on the houses of some persons where they found them, and in the houses of others, who had appeared so treacherously in the battle. These sad occurrences were consequent upon, and were subsequent to the outrages committed by the Catholic party, and their perfidy at the Battle ("the Diamond.") The Protestants who attacked the houses and demanded the restoration of their arms, were called " *Rackers* ;" and many of the Catholic party who were concerned in the battle, and in the outrages which preceded it, whether from fear of disclosure of their guilt, or otherwise, left this part of the country and went to Connaught, saying they were persecuted by the Protestants, and that justice was not to be expected from the Magistrates of this County. From this circumstance arose the vulgar cant phrase, " *to Hell or Connaught.*" The mania of migration for Connaught, so far took possession of the minds of the peasantry compromised by outrages, that many took the opportunity of breaking their own windows, and other trifling articles, to obtain presentments at the Assizes for sums of money which they might swear to as compensation for their loss. With these sums, they were enabled to maintain themselves, and to have money on their arrival in Connaught. I think it probable, that about this time, Lord Gosford published his " speech," as it is called.

" I believe in 1796, Lord Camden (at the time Lord Lieutenant of the Kingdom), called a meeting of such gentlemen of the county of Armagh, as were then in Dublin, at which I attended, and I believe fifteen or sixteen noblemen and gentlemen who had estates in the County, were present. Lord Gosford put a question to me at the meeting, " *whether I was not the person who banished the Catholics from the County of Armagh* "? This led to an explanation and detail of many particulars I have herein mentioned. After the fullest and freest explanation upon all points, I was not a little gratified to hear the Chief Secretary, Mr. Pelham (afterwards Earl of Chichester,) say to the whole meeting, that " I acted just as he would have done."

" I think it probable, that about this year, commenced the system of ORANGEMEN, which I hear has increased to near thirteen hundred Bodies. But as my family are considered the original institutors of those Bodies, I can assure you, that the first institution began near Caledon, in the County of Tyrone, (close to " the Diamond ;") and though it may not be credited, I can also assure you, that I am not, nor ever was, a member of any Orange Society; though I am a friend and supporter of their principles, as a loyal subject, and a supporter of the Laws and Constitution; and I am firmly persuaded, that there is no part of the oath of an Orangeman, which tends directly or indirectly, to persecute a Catholic on account of his religion.

" I fear I have deviated materially from the subject and enquiring of your letter, and that little information or satisfaction can be had from this ; standing as I did,

and do, on the ground and opinion which I first entertained, viz: that the insurrection of the "*Defenders*" in 1795, was a prelude to the fatal conspiracies and
rebellion of 1798. From several circumstances, and from observations I have made,
I was and am convinced, that Lord Gosford was partly imposed on by party spirit
and electioneering partiality, and partly by the false representations made to him
by the Priests and the Catholic party. The Rev Mr. Bisset of Loughgall, and
Dr Lodge of Armagh, must recollect what passed at the meeting of Magistrates,
but I don't suppose any documents were kept.

"This is the first time I have committed to paper the proceedings of 1795 and
1796, as far as my recollection at present serves me. .Was I to hold any conversation with the two gentlemen I .have named, possibly we might be more
accurate and satisfactory

"I regret that I cannot assist your endeavours to contradict the publication of
Mr. O'Halloran I did not think that at this day, there would be any allusion from
that party, to what passed in 1795.

"I don't recollect to have heard of any burning in Market Hill, in 1796 or
maiming the inhabitants ; and I must suppose that this was exaggeration, to
strengthen Lord Gosford's "speech" and publication.

"I am Sir, with much esteem,

"Your very obedient servant,

"JAMES VERNER.

"To Joseph Pollock, Esq.

   "Carnbane, Hillsborough."

Thus it will be seen that Lord Gosford, instead of being able to establish the allegation of outrages committed by Orangemen, was forced to
admit that the crimes complained of were perpetrated by the "Peep-of-
Day Boys," and not only so, but that afer the institution of Orangeism,
outrage diminished, and the disturbed County of Armagh became one of
the most peaceable in Ireland—it was *a proclaimed* District before 1795,
but never since So much for Orangeism, upon the admission of its
greatest adversary

CHAPTER XXI.

Evil effects of Paine's writings—Alarming state of Ireland—First planting of
Orangeism in Ulster, and statement of various writers upon that subject—Initia-
tion of George the Third, the Prince of Wales, (afterwards George the Fourth,)
and of Prince Frederick, Duke of York—Incorporation of the " BOYNE *" with*
the " ORANGE *" Society in 1795—Evidence of Sir William Verner, Bart. M.P.—*
Sir Richard Musgrave's description of the early Orangemen—Spread of the
" UNITED IRISHMEN*," and efforts of the Orangemen to counteract them—The " early*
Fathers " and Founders of Orangeism; who they were, with a sketch of their
personal characters, and a review of their opinions and objects—the Signs, Pass-
words, and Lecture of the first Irish Orangemen.

The seven years which intervened from 1793 to 1800, may be termed the
most critical and appalling in the history of Ireland—the political horizon
was overshadowed and all things looked doubtful and gloomy.   The artful
writings of "*Tom Paine*" superseded the Inspired Word in the dwellings
of a large portion of the Protestant population—the entire Romanist peasantry panted for the moment of revolt,—the Tyrant of France every hour
threatened the shores of the Island with invasion, and no Troops could be
spared to protect them—the spirit of Loyalty languished and declined—the
stoutest heart quailed before the impending storm— and the sword which
was to have struck from the Diadem of Britain, its Hibernian Jewel,
appeared suspended by a silken thread only.   At this momentous juncture
it was, that the ORANGE SYSTEM sprang into life in Ireland.   Like a
meteor of resplendent power, it penetrated the mental gloom which at that
period enveloped the faculties and clogged the energies of the Protestant
population, and speedily extending its sphere of action, it appalled the
Traitor, and cheered the drooping spirit of the faint-hearted Loyalist—restored his confidence, knit up his tenderest affections with kindred spirits,
and gave him assurances of immediate safety and of ultimate triumph.

In tracing the true period of the Society's origin in Ireland, it may be
proper to quote the authority of an enemy. W. F. Finn, Esq., M.P., was a
Roman Catholic gentleman of some standing ; he represented at one time,
the City of Kilkenny in parliament, and was Brother-in-law to the celebrated Daniel O'Connell. In a speech delivered by him in the British
House of Commons on the 4th of August 1835, as reported in the "*Mirror*
of Parliament," Vol. 30, he thus spoke :

" It is well known that these Orange Societies began in blood and crime.
"They began in 1795, and have continued the fruitful source of disturbance
" of the tranquillity of Ireland from that time to the present."

In a pamphlet printed by Mr. McKenzie, Merrion Row, Dublin, in the year 1809, the origin of the Irish Orange Association is stated in the following words. "At a time when the Loyalists of the County of Armagh "endured much persecution, in the latter part of the year 1793, or the "beginning of 1794, they were in so much dread, that they had regularly "appointed patrols to watch their houses and properties at night ; each of "these parties had countersigns or watchwords, in case of their meeting "each other, that they might be enabled to distinguish themselves from "the *Defenders*. Out of these watchwords, and the necessity of guarding "against hostile intrusion the Orange System first arose."

In an address put forth by the Grand Orange Lodge of Ireland, and published in the *Downshire Protestant* so late as the 9th of July 1858, the origin of the Orange Institution in Ireland, is stated in the following words.

"Its first Lodge was initiated immediately after the successful defence "of the Protestants, known as the battle of the Diamond. The disorgan- "ized state of society at that period, rendered it imperative upon loyal "men to unite for the protection of their lives and properties. The "Orange Institution had never any other object in view than the main- "tenance of the British Crown, the protection of life, and the defence of "the Protestant religion. It has been in existence for sixty-three years, "and has never had anything to conceal, as to its aims, principles, and ob- "jects ; and nothing to retract, deny, or to be ashamed of."

In a work upon the same subject, published by I. I. Stockdale, 7 Pall Mall, London, it is said at page 6, to have "originated in consequence of a "breach of Faith on the part of the Roman Catholics, and other disaffected "persons, headed by two priests, (one of whom was afterwards hanged,) "on the 21st of September 1795." From the pamphlet of the late Mr. Giffard (before referred to,) published by James Charles, of Mary Street, Dublin, in the year 1813, the following extract is taken. "The enlarged "Institution was copied from one, which, since the Revolution, has existed "in the Fourth Foot, a Regiment raised by King William, into which "Orange Lodge several Princes of the House of Hanover, have not thought "it beneath them to be initiated : we believe the King (George III.) was ; "we know that the Prince of Wales (George the IV,) and Prince Frederick "(the Duke of York,) were made Orangemen."

It is not a little remarkable, that so late as 1835, (exactly a quarter of a century after Mr. Giffard wrote,) his words should have been confirmed by a gentleman of undoubted veracity and possessing principles not very favourable to modern Orangeism ; we allude to Colonel Wilbraham, M.P., who, in a speech made in the House of Commons, 11th of August 1835, as reported in the "*Mirror of Parliament*," Vol. 30, page 2418, thus spoke :

"I find in the letter of the Illustrious Duke, (Cumberland.) so often

"alluded to to-night, it has been alleged that the only Regiment, in which
"he was aware of the existence of an Orange Lodge, was the Fourth
"(Infantry) Regiment. I must take the liberty of saying, that I have had
"the honor to be a member of the Institution established in that Regi-
"ment. The Lodge to which the Illustrious Duke has alluded, is of a
"totally different character from those which at present exist in different
"parts of the country. It is in fact, a Lodge of a purely Military Char-
"acter. It was instituted by William the Third, and the only resemblance
"which it bears to the Orange Lodges of the present day is, that its mem-
"bers are allowed to wear a badge which consists of a riband *half Blue and*
"*half Orange* in colour. I cannot however, venture to assert, that nothing
"approaching to a Declaration of political opinions formed any test or
"qualification as to the admission of those who desired to be enrolled
"amongst its members. The qualification for the admission to it was,
"either to have served four or five years in the Regiment, or to have per-
"formed an actual Campaign. It was as a Candidate who had acquired
"the latter qualification, that I obtained admission to that Body."

It would appear from this statement, that the Lodge in the Fourth Foot
was actually "*instituted by William the Third*,"—that its members wear
"*a badge*" of distinction, which consists of "*a ribbon half Blue and half
Orange*"—and that there is, even yet in it something "*approaching to a
declaration of political opinions*." that forms a "*test or qualification for
the admission of those who desire to be enrolled amongst its members*." It
being now of a purely Military character, as stated by Colonel Wilbraham,
(who was himself a member of it,) may have been done to evade the Army
Regulations promulgated against "Secret Societies" in the Service; and so
to preserve and perpetuate a Lodge, so ancient, so honorable, and so distinguished, as that now existing, in the Fourth Regiment, which proudly
traces back its origin, direct to the hand of the "GREAT DELIVERER"
himself.

Sir Richard Musgrave, Baronet, M.P. at page 82 of his "Memoirs," &c.
states that "in Commemoration of that victory (*the Diamond*,) the first
"Orange Lodge was formed in the County of Armagh on the 21st of Sep-
"tember 1795, though the name of Orangemen existed for some time
"before."

All the writers quoted. agree in fixing the date of the Society's origin in
Ireland, at the 21st of September 1795. Mr. Giffard, however, appears a
little more ample, and somewhat more satisfactory. His statement is, that
though its Irish origin was on the day named, it was then only copied and
enlarged from the Order as it existed in the Fourth Regiment of Foot,
since the days of King William. This statement is in entire conformity
with that of Mr. Rogers, before quoted; and if it needed additional confirmation, that confirmation will be found in the fact, that the "General

Declaration" adopted in 1795, and still in use, is but a transcript in substance, of the Declaration adopted under the immediate auspices of the Prince of Orange, at Exeter, on the 21st of November, 1688.

It would seem as if the " Boyne Society," before referred to, was at this period, (1795,) incorporated into the Orange. For many years after, the warrants for holding Lodges, the certificates granted to Members, and other documents connected with the Society, prove this fact. They were nearly all couched in this language, " the Orange or Boyne Society."

As it is a matter of the highest importance to faithful and impartial history, that every authority which can throw light upon the events of this period, should be quoted ; there has been already given the evidence of Lord Gosford, followed by that of Mr. Verner. The statements, if not discrepancies, of the noble Lord and the honorable Commoner, may be further elucidated and explained, by some further extracts from the evidence taken before the House of Commons Committee, in 1835. Touching the origin of the Orange Society, Colonel (now Sir William) Verner, M.P., is asked :

" *Question* 80.—Was not there an assault made upon the Protestants previously to the establishment of the Orange institution, which led to the conflict at Diamond Hill ?—*Answer*. There was.

Question 81.—When was that ?—*Answer*. The 21st September 1795.

Question 82.—Was not the Orange institution first formed in the village of Diamond ?—*Answer*. It was. The first Lodge was formed after an affray between the Protestants and Roman Catholics ; there had been a previous skirmish, and an engagement entered into upon the part of the Roman Catholics by their Priests, and upon that of the Protestants, by Mr. Atkinson, a gentleman of property. This the Roman Catholics violated, and commenced what is called the battle of the Diamond. The Protestants were successful, and the breach of faith caused them to form themselves into a Society.

Question 105.—You stated to the Committee that the Orange Society existed in the year 1795 ?—*Answer*. It originated in the year 1795.

Question 106.—Can you charge your memory in what part of the year it was ; was it before or after the battle of Diamond Hill ?—*Answer*. It was supposed to have originated upon that very day ; What I have always understood was that after the fate of the battle of Diamond Hill, the first Orange Lodge was established.

Question 107.—Who do you consider, in the battle of Diamond Hill, was the aggressor, which party ?—*Answer*. The attack was made upon the Protestants."

Touching the original purposes of the Orange organization, Colonel Verner is asked :

" *Question* 6.—Can you state what was the original intention of the formation of that Society ?—*Answer*. The original intention of the Orange society was to support the Constitution of the Country and allegiance to His Majesty in opposition to Societies of a rebellious and treasonable nature, to join the government in protecting the Country in case of foreign invasion, and for purposes of self-defence."

The efforts made by the disaffected, especially by the " United Irish-men," to warp the loyal intentions of the Orangemen and to induce them to swerve from their allegiance ; are thus alluded to by Colonel Verner.

" *Question* 273.—Is there another paper you wish to submit ?—*Answer.* There is another document which I beg to submit to the Committee ; it is dated " Ballygawly, October 30th, 1798." At this time there were many outrages committed, the country was in a very disturbed state and the Protestants and Orangemen were very fre-quently accused of being the aggressors. I recollect a circumstance which took place about the time the Yeomanry were first embodied ; they wore round hats, the edges of which were trimmed with white tape ; complaints were made of houses having been entered and in one or two instances it was stated that some of these persons had on hats bound with white tape, evidently implying that they were Yeomen. On one of those occasions there were one or two hats left behind, when it appeared that they were done round the edge with chalk to imitate the hats of the Yeomanry ; a meeting took place, at which the following resolutions were passed, the 30th of October, 1798 : " We the undermentioned members of different Orange Lodges in the neighbourhood of Clogher, Augher, Ballygawly and Augh-nacloy having been informed that many irregularities have been committed in some Orange Societies in this district, and that a few members of the same have been guilty of acts of disorder, which may, if not suppressed, throw an odium on a loyal and well-intended institution, do unanimously enter into the following resolutions :—*Resolved*, That we will meet once every month for the purpose of receiving information against any Orangeman who may stand charged with impro-per conduct, and should the complaint appear to us to be well founded, that we will deliver up the Offender to the next Justice of the Peace, and at our expense carry on a prosecution against him.

Resolved, That though we have to lament the mis-behaviour of a few, we must applaud the conduct of the great body of Orangemen, and should any attack be made on any person merely for his being an Orangeman, that we will at our ex-pense carry on a prosecution against such offender or offenders.—*Resolved*, That should it appear upon proper inquiry that any Master has privately admitted into the secrets of an Orangeman any person of improper character, that we will apply to the District Master to remove such Master, and report him unfit for acting under that capacity.—*Resolved*, That it be requested our District Master may at each of our monthly meetings lay before us the names with places of abode, of each person who may from time to time be admitted as a member of any Orange Lodge within this district. *Resolved*, That we will for the future alternately meet at the towns of Augher, Clogher, Aughnacloy, and Ballygawly, and that the next meet-ing shall be held at Augher, on Friday the 30th November next, at the hour of twelve o'clock."

It is signed by twenty persons, nine of whom were magistrates and members of the Orange Society. I beg to read the address of the United Irishmen of the County of Armagh to the Orangemen, and the answer. There is no date to the address, but the answer is dated the " 21st of May, 1797." The address is in these words :—" We have heard with inexpressible sorrow that those men whose wicked designs have already rendered our County infamous through Ireland, are again endeavouring to establish amongst you their abominable system of rapine and murder, persecution and bigotry. To us, the motives of their conduct have been long obvious; permit us, therefore, to explain to you the diabolical principles on which they act, and to contrast them with the genuine precepts of Christianity and reason which influence *United Irishmen*. The men who have hitherto led you astray are anxious to turn those differences of religion which result from abstruse and perplexed questions in theology, into fixed principles of hatred and animosity. What is the ultimate intent of this odious attempt? Is it not that whilst you are employed in idle contentions with your neighbours about heaven, they may enjoy and monopolise the good things of earth? You quarrel with your fellow-citizens about another world. They and their betters laugh at the silly dispute, and riot in the luxuries and pleasures of this. Their safety and power is built upon the disunion of the people, and, therefore, they urge you to commit the most atrocious crimes against society, for matters of as little import to true religion as that which agitated the Blefuscans and Lilliputians, mentioned in Gulliver's Travels, when they slaughtered each other about breaking eggs at the broad or narrow end. Brethren, as long as your attention is engrossed with these absurd disputes, which do not originate in religion, but in that bigoted zeal which dares trammel Christianity in the dogmatic creeds of particular sects, so long will you be ruled with a rod of iron by men who have overwhelmed the people with taxes, who have destroyed our commerce, annihilated our manufactures, placed us under military government, transported our fellow-subjects without trial beyond sea, and when we gently remonstrated against these evils, branded us with the odious name of refractory rebels. Have not the Ministry, whose creatures your leaders avowedly are, overwhelmed us with debts and taxes? Do they not persist in maintaining all the corruptions which they have introduced into the Constitution? They obstinately resist a reform in Parliament, because, if the people were fairly represented, their abominable system of corruption must be annihilated They oppress you with unjust burdens to support their extravagance, and with the very money which they tear from you and your families, they are enabled to purchase votes in the House of Commons and thereby overwhelm you with fresh taxes and fresh impositions. They grudge you the common necessaries of life, and their revenues arise not from taxes laid on articles of luxury, but from matters essential to your very existence. Even salt is not permitted to pass untaxed. Look now at these men who thus scourge the people with scorpions. You will see them and their creatures wallowing in wealth, indulging in the wantonness of unbridled luxury, laughing at your contentions, and fattening in your misery. The poor starve that pensioners may riot in excess. Placemen, and the Whores of placemen, squander that money, for the want of which your wretched families endure hunger and cold. Even Germans and other foreigners feast sumptuously at your expense. It is your business, it seems, to till the ground, it is theirs to enjoy the crop. You labour and feed them; your tyrants use your donations, yet despise and trample on the donors. Know that, if union prevailed amongst you and your fellow-citizens, you would discover that the present Ministers and their creatures are your enemies, and not "United Irishmen." They wish to engage you in religious battles for the same reason that Henry the Fourth wanted to lead his people to the Holy War at Jerusalem, namely, that they may turn your attention from their own misdeeds, and their own unjustifiable assumptions of power. Consider now, on the other hand, what are the objects of "United Irishmen." *Union, peace, love, mutual forbearance, universal charity,* and the active exercise of every *social virtue.* We know that true religion consists in purity of heart, in love to GOD, peace and good will to men. We persecute no man for speculative opinions in theology; we know the mind of man is free, and ought forever to remain unfettered. Our principles lead us to wish for a reform in Parliament, because it is to us indubitably clear that the present system of things is inconsistent with your happiness as well as ours, and erected in violation of the common rights of man. Already we have forgiven you the injuries you have committed against us; we offer you the right hand of fellowship, and entreat you to co-operate with us in that great work which we are able and ready to effect, whether you aid us or not."

I shall now read the answer of the Orangemen to this address:—" Your plans and schemes are now before the Select Committee of the Houses of Lords and Commons, and such measures, we trust, will be adopted, as will purge the land of your ringleaders, and we are happy to find that lenient measures will be adopted towards those among you, who, penitent for the crimes ye have committed, and the crimes ye intended to commit, throw themselves on the mercy of our rulers. The blood of four soldiers of the Monaghan Militia who were shot a few days ago at Blaris Camp; and the blood of the unfortunate wretches who shall suffer for connecting themselves with ye, will at an awful tribunal be demanded at your hands. The unfortunate soldiers took an oath of allegiance to their King at the time they were enlisted; but ye tempted them with a promise of making them officers in your new diocese, and succeeded in making them perjure themselves and thereby brought them to an untimely end. In future we desire you will not call us friends as ye have done in your last address. We will not be your friends until you forsake your evil ways, and until we see some marks of contrition for your past conduct; neither do we wish to hold any intercourse with you, for evil communication corrupts good manners as well as good morals. We are satisfied in the enjoyment of what we can earn by our honest industry, and neither envy those above us, nor desire to take from them a single farthing of their property; we wish you to be of the same mind."

Referring again to the origin of the United Irishmen, and also to the origin of the Orange Society, Colonel Verner says:—

" *Question* 288.—Is there any thing you would wish to correct in the evidence you gave on a former day?—*Answer.* There is. I refer to my statements of the origin of the United Irishmen's Society and the Orange Society. I have since ascertained that the United Irish Society was established on the 14th of October 1791 at Belfast, and the Orange Society, as I have already stated, on the 21st September, 1795."

The evidence given before the same committee, by the Rev. Mortimer O'Sullivan, D.D. Rector of Killyman, is very full and ample upon these and other points. Some extracts are here given. Upon the formation of the Order, the Rev. Doctor thus testifies :

"*Question* 582.—In what did this battle (the Diamond) originate?—*Answer.* I cannot say, the country was for some time in a state of great distraction and alarm. Respectable persons advanced in years, have assured me that their dangers were very great, and that shots having been often fired into their houses at night, it became not unusual for Protestants before retiring to rest, to place their beds among the barricades, by which they endeavored to secure the windows. It is not wonderful that in a state of things like this, men so harassed should be desirous of trying the issue of a decisive combat.

Question 583.—Were they successful in establishing this truce?—*Answer.* No; on the day after the truce was made, the Roman Catholics violated it; the Protestants retired, and the Roman Catholics in very great numbers attacked the village; the conflict seemed to be a matter entirely between the Peep-o'-day Boys, and the Roman Catholics, and Protestants in the neighbourhood of all denominations united for the defence of the town, and a second and a very sharp engagement took place. In this also the Protestants were successful, and on the battle day the fisrt Orange Lodge was formed.

Question 584.—Did this first Orange Lodge consist of Protestants of all descriptions or merely Presbyterians?—*Answer.* I believe the first Orange Lodge consisted exclusively of members of the Church of England. The first engagement at the Diamond was between the Peep-o'-day Boys and the Defenders; the second was one in which Protestants of all denominations associated for the defence of the country, and the members of the first lodge, I believe, were of the Protestant establishment.

Question 585.—This was the first organization of the Protestants of the Church of England in the north?—*Answer.* Yes.

Question 586.—The Protestants of the north, you say, took very little part in the engagements the first day?—*Answer.* I cannot discover that they took much."

The cause why Orangeism was first instituted, is thus given by Doctor O'Sullivan.

"*Question* 545.—What was the cause of their institution, and what were the objects they had in view?—*Answer.* The objects they had in view were self-defence, the maintenance of the Protestant religion, and of British connexion. The immediate causes were the disorders of the Country; which rendered life insecure and threatened to overpower the law."

Touching the exclusion of Roman Catholics from the Society of Orangemen, the Reverend Doctor thus testifies.

"*Question* 807.—You have stated in your former evidence, page 38, that the Orange Society is not designed to give offence, though exclusive; how do you justify the exclusion of Roman Catholics?—*Answer.* The principle of exclusion was not hostile, but cautionary. A main object of those who framed the Orange Society, was the support of the Protestant Religion; they apprehend that the church of Rome must desire its destruction, and therefore, as a caution, Roman Catholics were excluded. There were also especial reasons for their exclusion. At the time when the Orange Society was instituted, the great majority of Roman Catholics in the County Armagh, in which the Orange Institution commenced, were enrolled in the Defender system. The oath of the Defenders had already become an oath of fealty to France, and it is very natural that the Orange Society should reject from its body a class of persons, the great majority, if not all of whom, were sworn by oaths that rendered it impossible they could'take in sincerity the engagements of Orangemen.

Question 808.—From an utter incompatibility of views?—*Answer.* From an utter incompatibility of views. This was, as it might be said, a local necessity. Besides this, there was what Orangemen consider an incompatibility in the Roman Catholic system; they looked upon it that the Roman Catholic religion was in its nature intolerant, and that it held the doctrine of the right of persecuting, and even putting to death, for what was called heresy, and also held the doctrine that the members of the Church of Rome could not be bound by any obligations, even the obligation of an oath, if the interests of their Church required that it should be disregarded. Looking upon those peculiarities of the Romish system, it naturally followed that Orangemen were not disposed to admit into their body professors of such a creed."

James Sinclair, Esq., J.P. of Holly Hill, near Strabane, in the County of Tyrone, a very decided enemy of Orangeism, admits in his evidence before the Committee, that great numbers of the "*Peep-o'-day Boys*" joined the "*United Irishmen.*" He is asked:

"*Question* 5169.—You can hardly say whether the Peep-o'-day Boys, who were Presbyterians, may not have merged into the United Irishmen, who were mostly composed of the Church of England?—*Answer.* I know that a great many of the Peep-o'-day Boys were United Irishmen."

Another evidence brought before the Commons Committee, in 1835, by the Roman Catholic party, was James Christie, Esq., of Kircassock, in the County of Down, a member of the Society of Friends (Quakers.) Even this gentleman is obliged to admit, that when Orangeism went into operation in Ireland, the outrages of the "*Peep-o'-Day Boys*" and "*Defenders*" ceased. Here are a few extracts from his evidence, given on the 10th July, 1835.

"*Question* 5570.—Will you state what you recollect of the outrages that were then committed?—*Answer.* It commenced in 1794, but the greatest depredation was committed in the Spring of 1795; it commenced in the neighbourhood of Church-hill, between Portadown and Dungannon and then it extended over nearly all the Northern Counties, commencing at where the County of Armagh and the County of Down end, at Newry, round by Antrim, Down and Tyrone, and I believe in a very short time it extended to the County of Derry, but not to such an extent as in the other Counties. Then, in the course of time, after the Catholics were many of them driven from the County and took refuge in different parts of Ireland, I understood they went to Connaught. Some years after, when peace and quietness were in a measure restored, some returned again, probably five or six years afterwards ; they got some employment ; some were weavers and other things ; but they staid out of the Country while they thought their lives were in danger ; but the property which they left was transferred in most instances to Protestants ; when they had houses, and gardens, and small farms of land, it was generally handed over by the landlords to Protestant tenants ; that occurred within my own knowledge.

Question 5571.—Are you aware whether some of them had considerable interest in those houses and lands, whether they had, owing to the increased value of land and laying out of money upon the property, a valuable interest in some instances ? —*Answer.* I am not aware that any of them had ; I think most of them were tenants at will, but there were some cases where they had life leases.

Question 5572.—Generally speaking, was the property transferred by the landlords from the Catholic to Protestant tenants ?—*Answer.* I know some cases of it, but I cannot say that it was general, but I do not live in the part of the Country where the greatest mischief was done.

Question 5573.—Were there many Catholic houses destroyed ?—*Answer.* A great many ; sometimes I heard of 12 or 14 houses wrecked in a night, and some destroyed ; I pitied them very much in the straits they were driven to.

Question 5574.—This was about the Spring of 1795 ?—*Answer.* The Spring of 1795 was the worst, but it did not end there, it continued much longer.

Question 5575.—Up to what period did it continue ?—*Answer.* For two or three years, it was not quite so bad in 1796 and 1797 as it was earlier, but after this wrecking and the Catholics were driven out, what was called the Break-of-day party, merged into Orangemen ; they passed from the one to the other, and the Gentlemen in the County procured what they termed their Orange warrants to enable them to assemble legally as they termed it ; the name dropped and Orangeism succeeded to Break-of-day Men.

Question 5576.—From the time they were called Orangemen did you hear afterwards of the name of Break-of-day Men ?—*Answer.* I cannot say that I never heard it, but it was not a general application given.

Question 5577.—Did you hear it with regard to any body of men, subsequently in existence, after the name of Orangemen was adopted ?—*Answer.* No, I never heard it applied to any body of people after the Orangemen had lodges, as they termed it, I think the name of Break-of-day Men completely subsided.

Question 5578.—Did the Orangemen consist of the same class of persons as those that compose the Break-of-day Boys ?—*Answer.* I suppose they did, but I cannot say, because I did not know any of them personally to identify them, the same people that made use of intemperate language towards the Catholics, whilst the Break-of-day business existed were the same people that I saw afterwards walking in the Orange processions, but I cannot say further than that.

Question 5579.—Did you hear at the time, and do you believe, that many men who had been United Irishmen became Orangemen ?—*Answer.* I have little doubt of that, and I believe it.

Question 5580.—Were they moderate or violent ?—*Answer.* I believe that those who went under the denomination of United Irishmen were more violent than the others.

Question 5581.—How would you account for that ?—*Answer.* They made them-selves more conspicuous in the Country, by doing violent acts towards the Catholics than those that had not originally been connected with that party.

Question 5582.—The United Irishmen became Orangemen ?—*Answer.* Yes, and there were very few of them that did of the Protestant party ; fear was one motive, as well as inclination.

Question 5583.—Were the United Irishmen composed in the beginning principal-ly of Protestants, or of Presbyterians, or of Catholics ?—*Answer.* I believe it began among the Presbyterians, it is the general opinion they were the first movers of it."

A very full and most accurate description of the leading events of this critical period will be found upon reference to the Speech of Colonel Verner, delivered in the House of Commons on Tuesday, December 5th, 1837, when moving for a return of the correspondence had between the Irish Government and the honorable and gallant member himself, upon the subject of his dismissal from the Magistracy, for having toasted at an election dinner "the battle of the Diamond." In that Speech, it is abundantly proved, that at the memorable era that called the Orange Society into existence, the State of England was most critical. Britain was then struggling against the designs of foreign and domestic enemies— engaged in an expensive and perilous war—suffering from a scarcity of grain and an accumulation of taxes—a large portion of the subjects of the Empire excited by dangerous and treasonable Associations, and even the very life of the King attempted. England was unable to give to Ireland that military assistance which "secret and treasonable associations of dan-gerous extent and malignity" from within, and a threatened invasion from without, imperatively called for. All authorities, Whig and Tory alike, confirm the truth of the allegation. The facts were proved on the trial of Jackson—they are admitted in the memories of Wolfe Tone, and in the confessions of McNevin and Emmett. The Viceroy of Ireland, in his Speech to the Irish Parliament in 1796, states the existence of the "Secret and treasonable associations, of dangerous extent and malignity ;" that the country was at that period, "the scene of insurrection and outrage," and that "the King had been obliged to direct an addition to be made to the regular forces in Ireland, by troops sent from Great Britain." In an Act of Parliament passed the very same year, that Irish Orangeism sprung into existence, (1795,) it is declared, that "several parts of Ireland are disturbed by treasonable insurrections of persons assuming the name of *Defenders.*" In another Act, it is stated that, "traitorous insurrections have arisen, principally promoted and supported by persons associating under the pre-tended obligation of oaths unlawfully administered." In a third Act, it is de-clared to be "necessary in order to deter men from entering into conspiracies to murder, to increase the punishment of persons convicted of such horrid crimes." And in a fourth Act it is set forth that, "tumultuous risings have of late happened in Ireland, and that the persons engaged therein, had practised various secret contrivances for being supplied with and keeping arms and ammunition." These several Acts of Parliament, are a sufficient answer to the statements put forth by Lord Gosford—they are not the mere emanations of one mind, nor the passing ebullitions of mere party ; but the deliberate expressions of the legislature—of the crown—the Lords and the Commons. They prove that, instead of the Society called " *Defenders*, being an organization for defensive purposes, against Protestant aggressions, they were formed to promote, and did promote, "treasonable insurrections ;" that they " conspired together for purposes of murder ;" and that their " secret contrivances to supply themselves with arms and ammunition " had alarmed the Government, the Legislature, and all His Majesty's peaceably disposed Subjects. The then Noble Viceroy of Ireland, in his Speech to both Houses of Parliament, in October 1795, alluding to the spirited conduct of the loyal Orangemen, who had been the first to step forward and to enrol themselves at this early and critical period, uses the following language :

" At a time when the ambitious projects of our enemies have threatened to interrupt the happiness and prosperity of his people, by making a descent on this Kingdom and Great Britain, His Majesty has been graciously pleased to direct an addition to be made to the regular troops in this Kingdom, by troops sent from Great Britain, the greater part of which is already arrived ; *and in pursuance of His Majesty's commands, I have also encouraged the loyalty and zealous disposition which has generously displayed itself to associate in arms for the better security of property, and the preservation of tranquillity and good order."*

Indeed so great was the terror at this time, and so thankful were the Government and Magistrates—so anxious were they to encourage the patriotic efforts of the early associated Orangemen, that they lost no occasion to second their views, and to express public thanks and gratitude for their services. The following is a copy of a Preamble and Resolutions adopted by the Magistrates of the County of Tyrone, assembled at Quarter Sessions, at Dungannon, the 15th of July, 1796.

" Whereas we have observed with much concern, that great pains have been taken in many parts of this country, to excite discontent among His Majesty's faithful subjects, thereby to alienate their affections from his Person and Government, and to induce them to be willing to change our excellent free Constitution for the system of anarchy and confusion which is now threatening desolation over other parts of the world.

" And whereas, we have reason to believe that such miscreants have carried their wickedness so far as to hold treasonable correspondence with the French, with whom His Majesty is now at open war, to invite them to invade this Kingdom, and, as an encouragement, have held out the following audacious falsehood, viz., that His Majesty's subjects in this Kingdom are ready to rebel against him, and to adopt their principles ; and that a few, seduced by the emissaries of the French, *through the management of a desperate and traitorous society,* have bound themselves by oaths, to be ready in furtherance of their purposes, in case of invasion, either to join them or to rise and to take possession of our country and the property of its peaceable inhabitants.

"Now we, whose names are hereunto subscribed, sincerely attached to our most excellent Constitution, sensible of the benefits we enjoy under the mild Government of our Most Gracious Sovereign, and of the present prosperous state of the country—prosperous to a degree heretofore unexampled—where wealth and comfort are sure to follow honest industry—unwilling to put at hazard these solid advantages, and, abhorrent of the machinations of a set of desperate adventurers, who, without property themselves, aim at that of others, and hope to rise in wealth and consequence in a general confusion;

"*Resolved*—That we will, at the hazard of our lives and fortunes, support and defend our Gracious King, George the Third, against all foreign and domestic enemies.

"That we will discourage and oppose all treasonable and seditious practices, and resist all attempts to disturb the peace of the country; and further, should His Majesty in his wisdom require such exertion, that we will embody ourselves for his defence and for the protection of our lives and properties, and enrol ourselves, under such officers as he shall commission, and with their assistance and under their command, will train and discipline ourselves, so as to be able to render him the more effectual service, and frustrate the hopes of the traitors and banditti, who vainly rely upon finding the country naked and defenceless, should the regular troops be drawn off to oppose an invading enemy."

Northland.	R. Linesay.
Castle Stuart.	James Verner, M. P.
James Stewart, Bart.	T. Caulfeild, M. P.
James Richardson.	W. J. Armstrong.
T. Knox, M. P.	Edward Evans.
John Staples, Bart.	A. Stewart.
Robert Lowry.	T. Foresythe.
T. K. Hannyngton.	Samuel Strean.

All the Orange Lodges formed at this time were enrolled as Yeomanry Corps; and the Lord Lieutenant of Ireland, in His Excellency's address to both Houses of Parliament, 16th of January, 1797, thus speaks of their zeal and patriotism.

"I have beheld, with pleasure, the zeal and alacrity of His Majesty's regular and military forces, and the prompt and honourable exertions of the yeomanry corps, whose decided utility has been so abundantly displayed. *I have not failed to represent to His Majesty, this meritorious conduct of his faithful subjects in Ireland, and am expressly commanded to convey to them, his cordial acknowledgements and thanks.*"

On the 18th of March in the same year, the same high authority addressed the House of Commons in these words.

"The dangerous and daring outrages committed in many parts of the Province of Ulster, evidently perpetrated with a view to supersede the laws and prevent the administration of justice, *by an organized system of murder and robbery*, (the "*Defenders*,") have lately increased to so daring a degree in some parts of that Province, as to bid defiance to the exertions of the civil power, and to endanger the lives and properties of His Majesty's subjects in that part of the kingdom.

"These outrages are encouraged and supported *by treasonable associations, to overturn our happy Constitution*. Threats have been held out against the lives of all persons who shall venture to disavow such, their treasonable intention. The frequent treasonable assemblages of persons, and their proceeding, by threats and force, to disarm the peaceable inhabitants—their endeavours to collect great quantities of arms in obscure hiding places—their assembling by night to exercise in the practice of arms—their intimidation, accompanied by the most horrid murders, to prevent His Majesty's faithful subjects from joining the yeomanry troops established by law—their having fired on some of His Majesty's Justices of Peace, and threatened with murder any who shall have the spirit to stand forth in support of the laws, which threats have been recently exemplified—their attacks on the military, by firing on them in the execution of their duty—have so totally bid defiance to the ordinary exertions of civil power, that I find myself obliged, by every tie of duty to His Majesty, and of regard to the welfare of his faithful subjects, to provide for the public safety by the most effectual and immediate application of the military force entrusted to me.

"I have accordingly ordered the General commanding in that Province, to dispose of and employ those troops under his command, with the assistance and cooperation of the yeomanry, to suppress these outrages, &c

"I have the satisfaction of informing you, that by the firm and temperate conduct of the General, and the troops under him, and the zealous co-operation of the yeomanry corps, a very considerable number of arms has been taken," &c. &c

The vigorous measures adopted by the executive against "*the Defenders*," partially suppressed that murderous association ; and its members, with others, organized themselves under the title of "*United Irishmen*;" but the latter appear to have been just as seditious as the former. The following extract from a Proclamation, issued by the Lord Lieutenant and Privy Council of Ireland, and dated at Dublin Castle, the 17th of May, 1797, will show this

"That there exists within this kingdom a seditious and traitorous conspiracy, by a number of persons styling themselves *United Irishmen*

"That they have frequently assembled, in large armed bodies, and plundered of arms the houses of many of His Majesty's loyal subjects in different parts of the kingdom, and cut down and carried away great numbers of trees, wherewith to make handles for pikes and other offensive weapons, to arm their treacherous associates, and have audaciously attempted to disarm the district yeomanry crops enrolled under His Majesty's commission for the defence of the realm

"We do hereby strictly charge and command all our officers, civil and military, and all other of His Majesty's loving subjects, to use their utmost endeavours to discover all pikes, pike-heads, concealed guns and swords, offensive weapons, or ammunition of any kind whatsoever.

" And we do hereby strictly charge and command all officers, civil and military, and all others, His Majesty's faithful subjects, to be aiding and assisting in suppressing all treacherous, tumultuous, and unlawful assemblies, and in bringing to punishment all persons disturbing or attempting to disturb the public peace."

These are the descriptions of " seditious and traitorous" persons—these the beloved and patriotic " *United Irishmen*," whose example, even at this distant date, and in this distant country, the Irish Roman Catholic newspapers and orators, hold up as Martyrs for Ireland, and guides for the imitation of Irishmen!!! Surely "no mistake" can exist about the disloyalty of such men, had they only the power to carry out their feelings and desires.

Another extract or two may be given, as connected with the events of this period, to show in what light the loyal yeomanry—who were nearly every man Orangemen—of Ireland, were then held by all in authority. In the speech of the Lord Lieutenant, on proroguing the Irish Parliament, 3rd July, 1797, the following language occurs :

"The powers with which you entrusted me, by the suspension of the Habeas Corpus Act, have enabled me to bring to light and to disconcert *the formidable and secret conspiracy* (" *United Irishmen*,") which had been formed for the total overthrow of your establishments, the destruction of property, and the dissolution of Government This conspiracy has been so fully unfolded by your wisdom, that it can no longer spread itself under the insidious pretence which it had artfully assumed, of improving the Constitution.

"I cannot too often repeat my full sense of your wisdom, in the establishment of district corps. I have the most satisfactory accounts of their improvement in discipline, as well as of their exertions in quelling and preventing insurrection. And I have myself witnessed the unexampled exertions, good conduct, and military appearance of the corps of the metropolis, whose increasing and unwearied vigilance, at a most important crisis, checked every attempt to produce confusion by riot and tumult, at the same time that it destroyed the hopes of our enemies, and restored confidence to the country in general."

The Noble Lord concluded his speech in these words :

" We have a common and a sacred cause to defend ; the independence and Constitution of Great Britain and Ireland, from which both kingdoms have derived innumerable blessings, under His Majesty's auspicious reign. They were purchased by the dearest blood of your ancestors, in a crisis not less formidable than the present I trust we shall not fail to imitate the great example, and that we shall be enabled, by similar courage and continued firmness, to transmit to our posterity, inviolate, that invaluable inheritance which their valour rescued, and their perseverance preserved."

The following is the text of two "*Circulars*," which were addressed from Dublin Castle in this year, to the Captains commanding the Yeomanry corps ; who were in fact the masters of the lodges, and the yeoman volunteers, their members.   The first is dated August 25, 1797, and the second December 18, 1797.

"Sir,—His Excellency has directed me to express, in the strongest terms, the very high sense he entertains of the exertions which have been so conspicuously and so universally displayed by the district corps. in preserving the tranquillity of their several districts.   W. ELLIOTT."

"Sir,—I have His Excellency's particular injunctions to convey, in the warmest terms, to yourself and to the officers and privates under your command, his high approbation of the zeal which you have manifested by your regular and assiduous attention to your military duty, and which is no less honourable to yourselves than it has been conducive to the protection and security of your country.

PELHAM. "

Though the following letter was written in the subsequent year, (1798,) yet because it is so intimately connected with the subject matter now under consideration, it is here inserted.   It is addressed to Joseph Atkinson, Esq. J. P. of Crowhill, one of the " early Fathers," and founders of Orangeism, who bore a conspicuous part at the affair of the Diamond.

" Armagh, September 5, 1798.

" Sir,—I am desired by Major-General Goldie to know from you, what number of loyal men you can bring forward, in case of necessity, to join your corps, and act under the yeomanry standing orders as supernumerary men, and for whom you think you can be responsible.   " H. ARCHDALE, M.B.

" To Capt. Atkinson, &c."

Upon two separate occasions, the thanks of both Houses of the Irish Parliament, were voted to the Orange yeomanry of Ireland.   Upon one of those occasions, in 1798, the thanks of the House was accompanied by the following order.

" That there be laid before it a return of all corps, &c., in order that such return may be entered on the Journals of the House, and the patriotic example of such voluntary exertions be transmitted to posterity.   J. LEY."

Such were the efforts that now seem to be forgotten ; or if remembered, are only thought of to be rebuked !   And such was the conduct of the men, whom it has now become fashionable to condemn as "disturbers of the peace" and tranquillity of the country !   At a subsequent period—the very year of the Union with Great Britain—the following "circular" was addressed by the Right Honorable Charles Abbot, (afterwards Speaker of the House of Commons,) to the Captains Commanding the Irish Volunteer Corps of Yeomanry.   It is dated " Dublin Castle, 31st October, 1800.

"Sir,—His Excellency is desirous of taking this opportunity to express the high degree of satisfaction with which he has witnessed the loyalty, zeal and spirit, universally displayed by the yeomanry of this country. whose exertions have already so materially contributed to its security, and which, he is persuaded, will ever be in readiness to maintain the blessings of peace by the promotion of good order amongst all His Majesty's subjects.

                              "CHARLES ABBOTT."

If further should be needed, to prove the dangerous and treasonable acts of the "*Defenders*" and "*United Irishmen*" on the one hand, and to exhibit the patriotism and valor of "*Orangemen*" and "*Yeomanry*" on the other; it may be found upon reference to the Acts of Parliament, 36 George III, Chapter 6, passed early in the year 1796; and the 37 of George III, chapter 10, intituled

" An Act to enable certain inhabitants of the county of Armagh, who have been injured in their persons and properties, to receive compensation," &c.

The preamble to the first of these statutes is in the following words, and proves clearly, not the innocent and self-protective character given to the "Defenders" by Lord Gosford, but the deep and atrocious nature of that treasonable conspiracy.

" Whereas, during the year 1795, several parts of the kingdom were disturbed by the treasonable insurrections of persons assuming the name of " *Defenders*," and the lives and properties of many peaceable and faithful subjects destroyed, and several of his Majesty's Justices of the Peace and other Officers and persons, in order to preserve the public peace, the lives and properties of his Majesty's faithful subjects, and to suppress and put an end to such transactions, have apprehended several criminals, &c, and without due authority have sent other accused and suspected persons out of the kingdom, and also seized arms and entered into the houses and possessions of several persons, and done other acts not justifiable by law, but which were yet so much for the public service, and so necessary for the suppression of such insurrections, and for the preservation of the public peace, that the persons by whom they were transacted ought to be indemnified."

An able writer in the *Church* newspaper, (21st of April, 1841,) gives a very faithful description of the affairs of this period, and of the circumstances attending the origin of the Society at the Diamond.

The societies of *United Irishmen*, were first instituted in the North of Ireland, about the year 1791. Their *professed* object was to obtain parliamentary reform, and catholic emancipation; but whatever the real views of these societies had been at first, in a short space of time they were very well disposed to imitate the example of France,—to separate Ireland from Great Britain,—subvert the established Constitution of the kingdom, and form a Republican government. Ulster, during the progress of the French revolution, had early manifested a strong republican feeling, by rejoicings at, and different commemorations of that event, and by the public addresses of the citizens of Belfast to the National Assembly. Those societies exerted the most unwearied diligence in gaining over persons of activity and talent throughout the kingdom, and in preparing the public mind, by their publications, for the execution of their future purposes. In the summer of 1796, they solicited and were promised French assistance; at which time there were in Ulster

100,000 organized men, well provided with arms and ammunition, and only waiting for the arrival of foreign aid to take the field. At this time, while the North
was preparing for rebellion, the leaders, desirous of strengthening their cause, and
apprehensive that the French might be deterred from a *repetition* of their attempt
at invasion, by the loyal disposition manifested throughout Munster and Connaught,
determined to direct all their energies to the propagation of their doctrines in these
Provinces, which had hitherto been but very partially infected. By what magic,
then, was the South so suddenly and so completely allured into the conspiracy? Was
it the cry of parliamentary reform and catholic emancipation, which in the North
had been employed with such good effect, to *cloak the real designs* of the conspirators.
The evidence furnished by the reports of the " commitees of secrecy " of both houses.
of parliament, will solve this important question :—

  " In order to engage the peasantry, in the Southern counties, the more eagerly
" in their cause," says the report of the House of Commons, " the United Irish-
" men found it *expedient*, in urging their general principles, to dwell with *peculiar*
" energy on the *supposed oppressiveness* of tithes, (which had been the pretext for
" the old *Whiteboy*-insurrections,) and with a view to excite the resentment of the
" Catholics, and to turn that resentment to the purposes of the party, *fabricated*
" and *false tests* were represented as having been taken to exterminate Catholics,
" and were industriously disseminated by the *emissaries* of treason, throughout
" the provinces of Leinster, Munster and Connaught. Reports were frequently
" circulated among the ignorant of the Catholic persuasion, that large bodies of
" men were coming to put them to death. This fabrication, however, extravagant
" and absurd, was among the many wicked means by which the deluded peasantry
" were engaged the more readily in the treason." And, says the report of the
secret committee of the House of Lords. " It appeared distinctly to your com-
" mittee, that the stale pretexts of Parliamentary reform, and Catholic emancipation,
" were found *ineffectual* for the seduction of the people of those provinces, and
" therefore the emissaries of treason, who had undertaken it, in order to prevail
" with them to adopt the system of organization, first represented that it was
" necessary in their own defence, as their protestant fellow-subjects had entered
" into solemn league and covenant to destroy them,—having sworn to wade up to
" their knees in Popish blood. The people were next taught to believe that their
" organization would lead to the extinction of tithes, and *to a distribution of*
" *property*. Under the influence of those false, wicked, and artful suggestions,
" the organization was gradually extended through the other three provinces, and
" the measures thus adopted completely succeeded in detaching the minds of the
" lower classes from their usual habits and pursuits, insomuch that in the course
" of the autumn and winter of 1797, the peasantry of the Midland and Southern
" counties were sworn, and ripe for insurrection."

  From those authentic documents it is evident that the basest frauds and falsehoods were too successfully practised to poison the minds of the Roman Catholic
peasantry against their Protestant countrymen. These wicked arts and lies had
already succeeded in organizing the entire of the Catholic population in the North
and the consequence was, continual hostile and rancorous collision between them
and the rural Protestants, wherever they met, whether in town or country, fair or

market. It is but right, however, to state, that the Presbyterian North, which at the first had been so active in endeavouring to effect a revolution, soon saw the full extent of their error. The termination of the French revolution in a military despotism, and the religious character which the rebellion assumed in the provinces of Leinster, Munster and Connaught, clearly exhibiting a determination on the part of the Romanist to destroy Protestantism, root and branch, out of the land—to establish Popery in all its pristine power and haughtiness on its ruins, and to seize upon all Protestant property, and the acts of savage cruelty which they perpetrated upon unoffending and defenceless Protestants of all sexes and ages, re-enacting the bloody scenes of 1641, all contributed to open their eyes to a view of sober and rational liberty, and to the unchanged and unchangeable nature of Popery. Afterwards in the hour of need, the Presbyterians of the North boldly stood forward to defend their King and Country, her Altars and Institutions, as men resolved to do or die; and at this day, Protestant Ulster is, under Providence, the strong arm and safeguard of Protestant Ireland.

From the year 1791 and 1795, it may easily be imagined that a little or no good will subsisted between the Popish and Protestant population of the North, The former were at this period, known by the name of "*Defenders.*" They had objects unknown to, and distinct from the conspiracy into which they had first been initiated, and separate laws and leaders of their own choice. The *false and wicked representations* made to them, of an intention of the Protestants to murder them by wholesale, or to drive them out of the country, produced an effect different from that designed by the United Irishmen of 1791: an *imperium in imperio* was established among them: and thus, while the Popish traitors *seemed* to act in concert and cordiality with the revolutionary party, they were in fact, working out their own ends, under the advice and direction of a power which is too prudent to appear in the field, until success appears to be certain, and as their numbers increased and good news from the South reached them through their emissaries, they waxed bolder and fiercer, and became daily more insolent and aggressive. "Those men who are called Defenders," says Wolfe Tone, "are completely organized on a "military plan, divided according to their several districts, and officered by "persons chosen by themselves. The principle of their union, is implicit obedience "to the orders of those whom they have elected for their generals, and whose "object is the emancipation of their country, the subversion of English usurpation "and the bettering the condition of the wretched peasantry of Ireland; and the "oath of union asserts, that they will be faithful to the *united nations* of France "and Ireland." Such were the Defenders, and composed, on the same incontrovertible authority, of *Catholics only.*

"In June 1795," Mr. Tone further states, "their organization embraced the entire Roman Catholic peasantry of Ulster, Leinster, and Connaught." About the same time, owing to arrangements devised towards the end of the previous May, the leaders were enabled to ascertain the numbers at their disposal; and in July, at the Fair of Loughgall, in the County of Armagh, the "Defenders" commenced offensive operations. In the morning of that day, large bodies of strangers were observed entering the town; many of them were seen, during the day, penetrating and passing through the groups occupied in traffic, taking but little interest in the business of the market, but, as was afterwards conjectured, testing, by signs and questions, who was of their party. On a sudden, the Protestants found themseves furiously assailed; and after making faint resistance and suffering dreadfully, were driven out of the Fair. They rallied, however, and after hard fighting, remained at night in possession of the town. From that day, until the 21st of September, the country was at the mercy of an ungovernable mob. The "Defenders," foiled in their open attempt, returned to their ordinary practice of more guarded atrocities. Protestants, if found alone, were beaten or killed; their houses were attacked at night, and if not well secured, were plundered; and night and day, they were subjected to a most galling and distressing espionage,—about the middle of the month, it was discovered that the "Defenders" were encamped,—that they had congregated some thousands, it was said, in numbers, and that they had drawn a trench, constituting a sort of fortification around them. The name of the place where they had encamped is *Annaghmore,* and is in the immediate neighbourhood of a village called "*The Diamond.*" The townland, upon which the camp was pitched, was inhabited exclusively by Roman Catholics. The animosity of the opposite party had taken so decided a turn, that the "Defenders" remained under arms for three successive days, challenging their opponents to fight it out in the field; for such Protestants—as were in the neighbourhood—collected and sheltered themselves on eminences, from which the fortifications of their enemies were commanded, and during two successive days and nights an intermitting fire of musketry was kept up by the misguided and misgoverned belligerents.

So far the battle lay between two parties,—one consisting of sworn traitors, the other of loyal men, compelled in self-defence to hostile resistance. The time, however, was at hand, when men of a different character and station were to take a share in the conflict. As peaceful, but resolute Protestants stood together within hearing of the sound of war, comparing and commenting on the rumours, which were thickly and rapidly scattered over the country, they asked each other,—was it right that they should leave the few, among whom they had friends, to continue the combat with so disproportionate numbers? They learned that auxiliaries hourly swelled the ranks of the "Defenders,"—should they leave the Protestant side deserted? The result of such conference was what might have been expected. Volunteers from various parts of the country hastened to the fight, and the challengers felt that they could not long maintain their position. The dangers sure to result from the continuance of a strife, which must speedily bring into action the entire population of the country, became manifest, and efforts were made, by persons of influence on both sides, to procure a suspension of hostilities. A meeting was accordingly obtained in a house in the "Diamond;" the Rev. Mr. Treaner, a Roman Catholic Priest, appeared on the one side; Mr. Atkinson, of Crow-hill, a gentleman as remarkable for personal strength and courage, as for other qualities which ensure popular esteem, answered on behalf of the other. And a deed, imitating all proper forms of law, was framed, binding the Priest and the Protestant gentleman as sureties for the respective parties, in a penalty of £50, that peace should be kept strictly on both sides, for a period at least long enough, to promise a tranquil winter. The truce was proclaimed, and the opposing parties began to disperse. As Mr. Atkinson rode homewards from this work of peace and mercy, he was way-laid, and fired upon ; he escaped unhurt, and said, with his ordinary composure, to some Protestants whom he met a few moments after this treacherous and ungrateful attack upon his life, "The truce is proclaimed, boys, but you'll do well, some of you, to keep for a while within call."

This treaty, however, was but a *ruse* practised to gain time, obtain expected succour, and ensure the success of a renewed attack. Rumours were spread among the Protestants, that parties of "Defenders" were on their march from the adjacent counties, and were coming with the most determined purpose of destruction, well armed, and in considerable numbers. Some Protestants went forward, hoping, that by occupying one or two important passes, they could hold them in check. Owing to this, the village of "The Diamond," was left unprotected, when an unexpected attack was made upon it. The parties who had taken possession of the passes did not know how they had been duped, until fugitives from "The Diamond," summoned them back to its defence.

One, and the most violent of the parties which came to the breaking of the treaty, was from the South ; they were distinguished by a uniform of white jackets and were called from the dress, "Bawning Boys ;" a corruption of " Boughilee Bawn," or " *White Boys*." This party was most conspicuous for its zeal, and most truculent in its menaces. " We'll spare," was their cry, "neither the grey head, nor the white. No pity for the infant or the old ! No pity for body or beast ! slaughter and wrecking for everything English."—[*i. e.* Protestant.]

Such were the cries and the purposes with which the " Defenders," strengthened and rendered furious by their auxiliaries, attacked the village and the house where they had recently prayed forbearance and sworn to be peaceful.

The day on which the celebrated battle of "The Diamond " was fought, is handed down to the remembrance of posterity, by the name of " Running Monday,"—from all parts of the country, crowds hastened to the stormed village. On this eventful day, Protestants gave proof, that they felt their own best interests at stake, and left their menaced homes, with arms in their hands, under the strong conviction that a war of extermination had commenced against them, and that they must either go to meet the enemy, or abandon their possessions. The result of the struggle was long uncertain. As the dangers increased one after another, the gentry appeared among their sore-pressed Protestant brethren, and revived their courage The names of many gentlemen of high birth and noble fortune, could be mentioned,—then boys of sixteen years of age, who escaped from their guarded homes, to make at the " Diamond," their first essay of manhood, *and who have never since deserted the good cause, to which, in that hour of peril, they so early and gallantly devoted themselves.*

The " Defenders " were far better supplied with ammunition than the Protestants, and it was their evident policy to prolong the combat at a distance, until the fire of the opposing party became silent. Symptoms at length were discerned, that ammunition was getting scarce, and the courage of the enemy was proportionally excited. Doubt and apprehensions were beginning to spread through the ranks of the less numerous and worse supplied Protestants, and a dread that everything was lost, if their great want remained long unprovided. Late in the afternoon, two gentlemen were seen riding at a fiery pace, their horses covered with foam, into the little village of Moy, and halting at the door of the only house where gunpowder was vended. The door was open when they reined in their panting horses; before they had sprung to the ground, it was closed and barred. "Knock you," said one of them, "I go for the key." There was a forge near the shop, and the smith at the door; "Hand me your heaviest sledge," said the gentleman, and armed with this ponderous implement, he struck two blows, such as, it is said, there was but one man beside him in the district, capable of delivering. To such ungentle constraint the door soon yielded, and after supplying themselves abundantly with the material of war, and throwing ample payment for the powder and the burglary on the counter, they turned their foaming steeds towards the battle-field, and rode the race thither with unabated rapidity.

The "Defenders" had been encouraged, by the slackening fire of their opponents, to quit their fastness, and advance to a closer and more bloody encounter. They were welcomed with a sudden startling cheer: it was raised for the two riders from Moy, and was repeated when a few score firelocks had been charged. And the "Defenders" still, though somewhat less spiritedly than at first, marched up towards the "Diamond" a party of the Protestants shouldered their muskets and stept out to confront the foe. Their heavy and fatally directed discharge decided the battle: it checked the "Defenders;" and before the second volley was fired, they were rapidly running away.

About this time, the military from the fort of Charlemont made their appearance. They consisted of some companies of "Invalids," and were supported by two pieces of artillery. Some Protestants were on the hill when the army approached: an officer was sent up to them, to give notice that the King's troops were at hand, and to deliver the customary orders.—"Tell your commander," said one of the combatants, "that he came too late to stop the fight." "And you may tell him, forbye," said another, "that although we know nothing of discipline, we can shoot *straight!*"

Thus ended the celebrated battle of the "Diamond."—The disorders by which it was preceded, were contests between an organized multitude, who designed the extermination of Protestants, the seizing of their property, and the re-establishment of Popery, on the one side; and loyal men and Protestants on the other, who were compelled to seek in their own resolution that protection which *the law did not, or could not, afford them.*

Out of the circumstances of this memorable battle THE ASSOCIATION OF ORANGEMEN HAD ITS RISE. Seeing the benefits to be derived from a strong bond of union, cemented by religion, the Protestants formed themselves into a society through Ireland, for *mutual defence*, and assumed the name of ORANGEMEN, in honour of their great deliverer from Popery in 1688,—King William the Third, of glorious and immortal memory. Scarcely were they well organised, when the Irish Rebellion of 1798 burst forth; and then did appear the wisdom of the step they had taken. They proved themselves the bond of union, as they will ever do, between England and Ireland; and under Providence, the saviours of their country from the united assaults of Popery and Treason.

Sir Richard Musgrave observes of the Orangemen of that day, that they were merely a society of loyal Protestants, associated and bound together for the purpose of maintaining and defending the Constitution in Church and State, as established by the Prince of Orange at the late Glorious Revolution, which they regarded as a sacred and solemn duty. It confers distinguished credit on its members, that they united and stood forward for this truly patriotic purpose, unsupported and unprotected by the great and the powerful, to whom their motives and the nature of their Institution was misrepresented by disaffected persons, who were well aware that such an Association of genuine loyalty and patriotism must at all times prove a firm barrier to their nefarious machinations. The lower class of Protestants, remembering their deliverance through the immortal Prince of Orange, and actuated by an invincible attachment to their king, their country, and their liberties, stood forward at that perilous crisis in the spirited defence of British connexion, and avowed their unalterable determination to stand or fall with its maintenance. As they increased a spirit of loyalty increased with them, and strength and confidence succeeded to the place of supineness and despondency. Supported by a consciousness of the goodness of their cause, and by the protection of Heaven, they persevered under every insult, difficulty and danger in their magnanimous resolution. Their numbers and influence rapidly extended, and in a short time they became an irresistible barrier against the further inroads of treason.

The captivating but pernicious doctrines of the "United Irishmen" were still pushed forward; and the members of the "Catholic Committee," aided by Theobald Wolfe Tone, Archibald Hamilton Rowen, and James Napper Tandy, were indefatigable in their exertions to spread far and wide the dogmas of "fraternity and union," as promulgated by the leaders of the French Revolution. Several gentlemen of worth and fortune viewing the Orange Society as the great break-water against the flood of infidel and revolutionary feeling, then rapidly taking possession of the public mind, considered it prudent to lend their countenance and support to the spread of the Institution. Amongst the earliest of the Irish gentry who enrolled themselves as members of the Orange Order, were:—The Right Honorable George Ogle, of Belleview, M. P. for the City of Dublin; Thomas Verner, Esq., Sovereign of Belfast; The Right Honorable John Maxwell Barry, of Newtown Barry, M. P. for Newtownlimavady; The Right Honorable Patrick Duignan, M. P. for Armagh; John Claudius Beresford, Esq., M. P. for Dublin; John Hunter Gowan, Esq., of Mount Nebo, in the County of Wexford; John Gifford, Esq., High Sheriff of Dublin City; Mervyn Archdall, Esq., of Castle Archdall, M. P. for the County of Fermanagh; Sir Richard Musgrave, Baronet, M. P. for the Town of Lismore; and Wolsley Atkinson, Esq., of Armagh.

The speeches made by those gentlemen upon a variety of occasions, their private letters written to correspondents in several parts of the Kingdom, and their many conversations, yet remembered by their children and by their friends, clearly prove what were the views and objects of the earliest founders of the Association, the necessities out of which it sprung, the ends it sought to attain, and the means by which those ends were to be accomplished.

These gentlemen remembered with gratitude to Almighty God, the great Revolution of 1668, by means of which the illustrious House of Hanover was seated on the British Throne, and popular and constitutional remedies established against the despotism of abused and irresponsible power. They considered the maintenance of the Liberal and Protestant principles then established, a sacred duty, securing as they did to all classes of British subjects, liberty without license, authority without insolence, power without oppression, and freedom, religious and civil, unstained by intolerance and unmixed by bigotry.

Popery was viewed by them as a system of despotism, and as forging manacles, spiritual and temporal, to enslave the human mind. Entertaining this view they believed, that in resisting Popery they were really benefitting Papists, curbing the despotic power which enthralled them, and affording them an opportunity of escape from its meshes. But they viewed the religion of Rome not only hateful on account of its intolerance, but also on account of its hostility to all Protestant Governments, and especially to that of Great Britain. Hence their opposition to entrusting any post or place of political or military trust, within the keeping of an Irish Roman Catholic. And hence, also, together with their dread of auricular confession to the Priest, their determination not to allow any one of the Romish faith, no matter how loyal his professions, or respectable his standing, to become a member of the Orange Society. They believed that if a member of the Romish Church was a true and sincere believer in the faith he professes, he must, of necessity, disclose and make known to the Priest at Confession, all secrets, no matter how solemnly given ; and that, if a true and sincere Orangeman, he must of a like necessity, be a hypocrite to his Church ; that, in fact, the Priest was a spy, acquainted with the secrets of every household. Hence their resolve to admit no Roman Catholic within the pale of Orangeism. Viewing the Pope as the centre of Romish unity ; as the head of a despotic power the most secret, the most irresponsible, and the most dangerous in the world ; that united millions of men in every quarter of the globe, in a politico-religious body, acting together as one man, to promote the ascendancy and dominancy of their Church, and to crush all other denominations, as schismatical and heretical ; and seeing that Protestantism, from the very nature of that freedom of thought, of speech, and of action, which it inculcated, led to division, to numerous sects, and could only present to its opponents a disjointed and divided front ; they gave a helping hand to Orangeism as being calculated to unite the discordant Protestant elements ; to harmonize the various creeds and sects into which it was divided into one family of brotherhood and affection, and by such a system of union and fraternity, enable the members to resist the encroachments of Popery against their liberties, civil and religious.

In planting this great Association throughout Ireland they did not confine it to the narrow borders of an exclusive or privileged class ; it was not limited to the castle of the noble, to the hall of the knight, or to the mansion of the squire—its foundation was laid upon a broader and firmer basis. It was made the most endearing child of the people, to be nursed and nurtured in the workshop of the artizan—the fairest flower to be watered and shaded in the garden of the yeomen,—it was given a niche in the halls of the noble,—and the lily of its colour, emblematic of its principles, was found alike in the court yards and shrubberies of the squire and in the stinted rood of earth which surrounded the cabin of the lowly poor. The first Irish Orangemen were taught to respect the hard hand of labour, the iron nerve of manly independence,—they were instructed not to court the rich, to flatter the powerful, to dread the enemy, or to pander to the tyrant,—they were told to respect the good and virtuous, and to shun the evil and vicious ; to "labour zealously and earnestly to preserve the spirit of unity in the bonds of peace," and to inculcate upon all classes, the duty which they owed to their God, to their country, and to themselves.

Such undoubtedly were the opinions, the views, and the feelings of the gentlemen named. And assuredly no men were more capable of forming correct opinions upon the state of Irish society and of Irish parties in the days in which they lived, than they were. Mr. Ogle, of Belleview, was esteemed as one of the most able and eloquent men of the age in which he lived, and in Irish annals his name will be handed down to the latest posterity as holding a high place amongst the poets, orators, and statesmen of "the Green Isle." His "*Molly Asthore*," is of all ballad music one of the most sweet and pathetic on record :

MOLLY ASTHORE.

By the Right Honourable George Ogle, M. P., addressed to Miss Mary Boyce, of Bannow, County Wexford.

" As down by Bannow's banks I strayed, one morning in May ;
The little birds with blithsome notes, made vocal ev'ry spray.
They sang their little tales of love, they sang them o'er and o'er ;
Agrammachree my collien oge, my Molly Asthore.

" The daisy pied and all the sweets, the dawn of nature yields ;
The primrose pale and violet blue, lay scattered o'er the fields.
Such fragrance in the bosom lies, of her whom I adore ;
Agrammachree my collien oge, my Molly Asthore.

" You said you lov'd me, Molly dear, Ah ! why did I believe ?
  Or who could think such tender words, were meant but to deceive !
  Your love was all I asked on earth, kind heaven could grant no more ;
  Agrammachree my collien oge, my Molly Asthore.

" O ! had I all the flocks, that graze on yonder yellow hill ;
  Or lowed for me the numerous herds, that yon green pastures fill :
  With her I love, I'd gladly share, my kine and fleecy store :
  Agrammachree my collien oge, my Molly Asthore.

" I laid me down upon a bank, bewailing the sad fate,
  That doom'd me thus, the slave of Love, and cruel Molly's hate.
  How can she break the honest heart, that loves her in its core ?
  Agrammachree my collien oge, my Molly Asthore.

" Two turtle doves above my head, sat cooing on a bough,
  I envied them their happiness, to see them bill and coo.
  Such fondness once to me was shewn, but now, alas ! 'tis o'er,
  Agrammachree my collien oge, my Molly Asthore.

" Then fare thee well, my Molly dear, thy loss I e'er shall moan,
  While life remains in George's heart, 'twill beat for thee alone.
  Though thou art false, may heaven on thee, its choicest blessings pour,
  Agrammachree my collien oge, my Molly Asthore."

Mr. Ogle's "*Gualtherus and Griselda*," and his various translations
from Boccace, Petrarch, and Chaucer, place his name eminent amongst
the learned host.   His eloquence in the House of Commons was at all times
freely admitted.   He represented as well the City of Dublin, the Metropolis of Ireland, as the County of Wexford, in Parliament ; and the standing
toast, to this day remembered by the Gentlemen of Wexford, was " GEORGE
OGLE AND THE PROTESTANT INTEREST." He raised and equipped, solely
at his own expense, a Yeomanry Corps, called "OGLE'S BLUES." He
was a member of His Majesty's Most Honorable Privy Council, and died
Grand Master of the Orangemen of Ireland.   Mr. Verner, was the oldest
Son of the late James Verner, Esq., of Church Hill, M. P. for the Borough
of Dungannon ; and brother to the present Sir William Verner, Baronet,
M. P. for the County of Armagh.   He was for many years, the Sovereign
and Chief Magistrate of Belfast.   He married in early life, Miss May,
daughter of Sir Stephen May, Knt, and died in London, England, about
five years ago.   Mr. Maxwell Barry, of Newtown Barry, was highly
distinguished as a public and parliamentary speaker.   He was a member
of the Privy Council, and one of the Lords of the Treasury.   He represented the County of Cavan in Parliament, and succeeded to the Farnham
title and estates upon the death of his uncle, the last James Maxwell,
Earl of Farnham.   Mr. Duignan, was a member of the Privy Council,

and Judge of the Irish Prerogative Court. Both at the Bar and in the House of Commons, he was distinguished as an able, acute and vigorous debater. He died while filling the position of Grand Secretary of the Grand Lodge of Ireland. Mr. Beresford was a Banker in Dublin, a Member of the House of Commons, and a near connexion of the Marquis of Waterford. He was a gentleman of great personal influence, and succeeded Mr. Duignan as Grand Secretary of the Grand Orange Lodge of Ireland. Mr. Gowan, of Mount Nebo, was a Magistrate of the County of Wexford, and by a special commission from the Irish Viceroy, was appointed a Justice of Quorum for the Counties of Wexford, Wicklow, Carlow, Kilkenny and Waterford. He was particularly conspicuous in suppressing the insurrections and outrages which disgraced that portion of the Empire between the years 1780 and 1798. For his distinguished services at that period, he was offered by the Viceroy of Ireland (His Grace the Duke of Rutland,) the honor of Knighthood, which he declined. In 1785 he had a silver coffee urn and two silver cups, of the value of 150 guineas, presented to him by a Deputation, consisting of the Marquis of Ely, Loftus Hall—the Earl of Arran, Saunder's Court—the Right Hon. George Ogle, M. P., Belleview—Henry Hatton Esq., M. P., Great Clonard—and Colonel Le Hunt, of Artrammon. These valuable gifts bore the following inscription :

" Presented
at
Spring Assizes, 1785,
to
Mr. John Hunter Gowan,
by
the Grand Jury,
and several
Noblemen and Gentlemen,
of the
County of Wexford."

In 1798, when the French threatened to invade the Kingdom, and the dreadful rebellion of that memorable year, raged in all its terrific fury, Mr. Gowan was one of the first to step forward and ensplrit the loyalists to a vigorous and manly opposition. He raised a troop of Horse and a corps of Infantry, called the "Wingfield Yeomanry," of which he was appointed by the Irish Viceroy, Captain Commanding. He was present and in command of his Corps, at the battles of Tubbernerin, Gorey, Bally-ellis, Ballyrahan, Whiteheaps and Arklow. At the former his horse was shot under him, and at the latter he was wounded, the third finger of the left hand being shot away. The insurgents while in possession of Wexford. issued a Proclamation, offering a high reward for his apprehension. The

Proclamation is set forth at length in Taylor's History of the Irish Rebellion Mr Giffard of Dublin, was High Sheriff of that City, and for many years one of the most able and distinguished members of the Civic Corporation He possessed a vigorous intellect, was the chief contributor to Faulkner's "*Dublin Journal,*" and died deputy Grand Master of the Grand Orange Lodge of Ireland Mr Archdall, of Castle Archdall, was a General in the British Army, and lost his right arm with the gallant Sir Ralph Abercrombie, in Egypt. He represented the County of Fermanagh in Parliament, up to the period of his death, when he was succeeded by his Nephew, the present member. The General was for nine years Grand Master of Ireland Sir Richard Musgrave, of Myrtle Grove, Baronet, was Member for the Borough of Lismore, an active Magistrate, a good public speaker, and as a public writer, able, learned, and argumentative. His "Memoirs of the Irish Rebellions," evince deep research, and a thorough knowledge of the subjects treated of He was the Grand Treasurer of the Grand Lodge of Ireland. Mr. Atkinson of Crowhill, was a Country Gentleman of some estate, and possessed much local respect and influence He was a Magistrate of the County of Armagh, and the Grand Secretary of that County. His name is attached to many of the earliest Warrants for holding Lodges of the Association

Such were the first Chiefs of Orangeism in Ireland—the men who watched by its cradle in infancy—under whose auspicies it was given forth to the public—and who became the exponents of its principles and designs, and the guardians of its character and honor

> Though dead, they speak in reason's ear,
> And in example live,
> Their Faith, and Hope, and mighty Deeds,
> Still fresh instruction give.

The first and the great object of those gentlemen appears to have been, to unite all Loyal Protestants in the bonds of one association, to preserve the unity and integrity of the Empire. They evidently desired to unite all for good purposes ; not for evil ones. Nor was this great bond of fraternity and union which they laboured so constantly to extend, ever sought to be promoted by any other means, than those which were peaceable and loyal In truth all the members were solemnly pledged, not only to be "aiding and assisting the Civil and Military powers in the just and lawful "discharge of their official duties, when called on ," but also to be "aiding "and assisting every Loyal Subject, of every Religious Persuasion, in "protecting him from violence and oppression." In short, they sought by peace and concert, to secure to themselves, and to generations unborn, the supremacy of Law, Order and the Constitution ; the maintenance and freedom of the Protestant Religion , and the perpetual connexion of Ireland with England, as an integral portion of the British empire. They sedulously inculcated the Divine precept, to " do good unto all men, more especially to those who are of the household Faith." They loved all men, but their love for the brotherhood was such, as to lead them to constant vigilance for the preservation and welfare of all its members. They seemed never to forget the dying admonition of the Saviour, "a new commandment I give unto you, that ye love one another." In inculcating this great principle of love for one another, they seem never to have lost sight of the foundation upon which alone all Love should rest, namely, upon Truth. They abhorred the doctrines of dissimulation and time-serving, and constantly exhorted all to follow Truth and Right, wherever they should lead. Even the Love of individual members, or the Union of the whole brotherhood, was never to be pursued beyond the boundary of Truth. Truth and Right was to be the foundation of all their actions. They never alleged that Orangemen were more Loyal, or more Protestant than many others who were not enrolled in the Association ; but they did contend, that when loyal Protestants became Orangemen, their zeal was quickened, and their loyalty and protestantism became more effective for good. Such, and such only, were the doctrines inculcated by the early Fathers of the Institution in Ireland ; and whether they have been adhered to, or departed from, by their followers, it is but justice to the memory of those departed heroes, that their principles of action should be rightly understood, and their doctrines and motives placed fairly before the world.

> "Still o'er these scenes my memory wakes,
> And fondly broods with miser care ;
> Time, but the impression deeper makes,
> As streams their channels deeper wear."

Having thus pourtrayed the characters of the "early fathers" and founders of the Association in Ireland, it only now remains to say what that *system of Mysteries* was, which they founded, and of which so much has been said and written. The whole system, together with many more recent changes, is given in the evidence of Colonel Verner, at the time one of the Deputy Grand Masters of Ireland ; and in the evidence of the Rev. Holt Waring, Dean of Down, and one of the Deputy Grand Chaplains of Ireland, in their evidence before the Parliamentary Committee, in the year 1825.

THE SIGNS.

Place the right hand open, upon the mouth, as if in the attitude of lapping therefrom, the little finger being drawn under the chin. The answer was made by placing the left hand in a similar position, upon the mouth of the other party. (*Note.* For explanation, read the 7th chapter of Judges and the 6th verse.)

LECTURE AND PASSWORDS.

" Have you a Pass ?—I have.
Will you give it to me ?—I'll divide it with you.

Begin ?—Gi—de—on—

GIDEON.

Why do you take Gideon for your Pass ?—Because his name signifies
the cutting off of iniquity from the people ; and he was chosen by the
Lord, to fight His mighty battles in the time of need.

Have you a number ?—I have.

What is your number ?—Three, or else—

What else ?—Three hundred.

Why three hundred ?—Because that was the number tried ; and chosen
by God to sound the trumpets, and to cry to the multitude—behold the
sword of the Lord and of Gideon.

Have you the grand Password of an Orangeman ?—I have.

Will you give it to me ?—I'll divide it with you.

Begin ?—

Do you begin.

Je—ho—vah—Sha—lom.

JEHOVAH SHALOM.

The Lord send peace ! "

For proper explanation there should be read the 6th chapter of Judges,
and the 24th verse. Indeed the whole of the sixth and seventh chapters
of the book of Judges, should be read attentively, in order to understand
the proper bearing and strict applicability of this system, to the times and
circumstances in which the "early fathers" and founders of the Order
lived. It should be ever borne in mind, that the literal signification of
GIDEON, is *the cutting off of iniquity from the people* ; and that the
literal interpretation of JEHOVAH—SHALOM, is *the Lord send peace !*
These being the first, and the grand Passwords of Orangemen, how shame-
fully have such men been misrepresented, as " pledged to wade knee deep
in Popish blood !" The whole foundation of the Order, from its inception
on continental Europe to its Exeter adoption—from its English introduction to its Irish origin—and from its Irish parentage to its Canadian trans-
plantation—all alike prove, that its sole foundation was the Word of God
and its sole designs the security, unity, and freedom of His people.

It may be here remarked that the Reverend and Venerable the Dean of
Down (Holt Waring,) states in his evidence before the House of Lord's
Committee, that the first Password was M-i-g-d-o-l, *(Migdol.)* This,
however, is a mistake, as Migdol was adopted subsequently, and was in
use from 1800 to 1803—the period of the murder of Lord Kilmarden—
when it was again changed. The following is an extract from Mr. Waring's
evidence, in which he mentions this matter :—

*Extracts from the evidence given by the Rev. Holt Waring, before the Select Com-
mittee of the House of Lords.*

" You were a member of the Orange Society ?—I was.

What offices have you held?—I undertook the office of Secretary, to arrange the warrants and other business of the society, which had been in low hands, and was in confusion.

At what period was that?—I believe it was the latter end of 1798, or the beginning of 1799.

Did you hold any other office in the society after that?—No, except that of Chaplain.

What was the object of the society?—The original object of the society was the protection of the persons and property of those who joined in it, that had been most violently assailed in part of the County of Armagh, and their object was self-protection.

Can you give the Committee an account of the Passwords or Signs by which the members of the Orange Society knew each other?—Yes, I believe I can; I believe I recollect nearly all of them.

Did they undergo any change after the time you first became acquainted with them?—Yes, they did, several.

Can you give any particular account of the earliest, and their changes from time to time?—Yes, I can; I have a memorandum with me which will enable me to do so. The scheme and system of the first that was instituted had reference to the exit of the children of Israel from Egypt. It was merely intended as a private or mysterious selection of signs or questions, by which they should know each other, which became absolutely necessary by certain circumstances which had occurred in the County of Armagh previously; and in order that they should know each other for their future protection, they instituted a sort of catechism, question and answer, signs by which they might know each other; and the first was a question: "From whence came you?—From the house of bondage. Whither do you go?—To the promised land. How do you expect to get there? —By the benefit of a Password. Have you that Password?—I have. Will you give it me?—I will divide it with a brother." Then the Password was M-i-g-d-o-l, being the name of a town at which the Israelites encamped."

CHAPTER XXII.

First general meeting of the Orange Society, and formation of the Grand Lodge of Armagh—The Rev. Philip Johnson, Earl O'Neill, and Lord Castlereagh— thirteen Orange Associations armed and equipped by the Government—Remarkable tranquility of the Orange districts—Twenty thousand Orangemen offer their services to General Nugent—The General's reply—General review of the Orangemen by the Commander-in-Chief—Resolutions of the Lisbellaw Orangemen.

ON the 12th of July, 1796, the first general meeting of the Orange Society of Ireland was held. Up to this period there was no Grand Lodge, or governing Body—in fact there was no regularly established organization. Each Society or Lodge, was separate and independent, and this first meeting was convened by a sort of verbal understanding and agreement, to consider the best means of more fully and effectually organizing the Orangemen of Ireland. The meeting was held at Portadown, in the County of Armagh, and was attended by many Gentlemen of fortune and moral excellence. At this meeting, the Grand Lodge of the County of Armagh was formed, and it was allowed precedence over all other Lodges, and the privilege to isuse warrants for the establishment of new Lodges in other parts of the kingdom. Thomas Verner, Esq., presided ; Wolsey Atkinson, Esq., acted as secretary at this meeting.

Sir Richard Musgrave states, in his "Memoirs," &c., that in the month of February following (1797,) the loyal subjects alarmed for their safety, began to form Orange or Boyne Clubs, in the County of Monaghan, where the spread of the society had a most beneficial effect, particularly in detaching the Presbyterian population, from the confederation of "United Irishmen." In the same year, the Orangemen of the County of Antrim, resident upon the extensive estates of the Marquis of Hertford, were organized as a *Posse Comitatus* to assist the Civil Magistrate, and to enforce the due execution of the laws. The Reverend Philip Johnson, Rector of Ballymacash, an active, and benevolent Magistrate of that County, was very active in this organization. A plan for the arming and organization of the Orangemen of the Estate, which included the Parishes of Aghalee, Aghagallan, Ballinderry, Ballymacash, Cromlin, Derriaghy, Glenavy, Lambeg, Lisburn, Maghermisk, Maghregal, and Tullylusk, was drawn up by Mr. Johnson, and by that Gentleman submitted to the Right Honorable the Earl O'Neill, Governor of the County, and to the Right Honorable Lord Viscount Castlereagh, then Chief Secretary for Ireland. By both those

distingushed noblemen, the organization and arming was approved.   The
following corps of loyal orangemen, were accordingly armed and equipped.

Name of the Corps.	Sergeants.	Drummers.	Rank and File.
1. Lisburn Cavalry	3	1	60
2. Maghregal Cavalry	2	1	40
3. Lisburn Infantry	7	1	150
4. Ballymacash Infantry, First Comp.	5	1	100
5. Ballymacash Infantry, Second Comp.	5	1	100
6. Polglass Infantry	5	1	100
7. Ballinderry Infantry	7	1	150
8. Brookhill Infantry	6	1	150
9. Soldierstown Infantry	7	1	150
10. Broomhedge Infantry	7	1	150
11. Glenavy Infantry	7	1	140
12. Aghagallan Infantry	3	1	60
13. Derriaghy Infantry	7	1	150
Totals	71	13	1500

It is a remarkable fact, that when the flames of insurrection burst forth
with so much fury, both at Antrim and at Ballynahinch, at the former of
which the Earl O'Neill was killed, the extensive district of country which
included the twelve Parishes above named, and which lay directly between
the two places (Antrim and Ballynahinch,) was preserved in perfect repose.
Not a hostile shot was fired, nor a human life sacrificed.   Moreover, these
armed Orangemen, not only preserved the peace of their own neighbourhood,
but lying in the direct route between the two disturbed districts, their
union and vigilance prevented the junction of the insurrectionary forces,
effectually cut off all their resources, and frustrated their plans.

In the same year (1797,) a numerous body of Delegates from all the
Orange Lodges in the surrounding neighbourhood, waited on the Rev.
Holt Waring, of Waringstown, (afterwards Dean of Dromore,) a most
respectable and influential Magistrate of the Counties of Antrim, Armagh,
and Down, and authorised that Gentleman, in their name, to address General Nugent, then commanding at Lisburn, and to inform the gallant General, that should an invasion or an insurrection take place (as was then
hourly expected,) they would assemble to the number of 20,000, at four
days' notice, and march under his command, to any part of the kingdom,
where the government might require their services.   The gallant General
gave to Mr. Waring and to the Delegates, a most gracious reception, and
stated that "he was highly honored by such an offer, but that he trusted
"the loyal spirit which they manifested would prevent an insurrection,
"and he hoped that all would soon be enabled to sit down in peace, with
"this pleasing reflection, that the Orangemen had been true to their pro-

" fessions, notwithstanding the false insinuations of the disaffected to
" the contrary, and the artifices used to seduce the loyal from their duty."

Shortly after this occurrence, the Orangemen enrolled in the district of
country surrounding Lurgan, and including a portion of the counties of
Antrim, Armagh and Down, assembled at Lurgan, to the number of at
least twenty thousand, and were there reviewed by the Commander-in-
Chief, Lord Lake, and by General Knox, then commanding the Northern
District.   This fact is proved by Stewart Blacker, Esq., in his evidence
before the House of Commons Committee in 1835.   The following is an
extract from this evidence :

" *Question* 2124.—Did you ever hear that the Orangemen, in the year 1796 or
1797, were reviewed in a body by Generals Lake and Knox, then in command of
the northern district?—*Answer.* I have heard an aide-de-camp of General Knox
who was present on that occasion, who is residing in Dublin at present, General
Owen, state that he went on that occasion from Belfast to Lurgan—that his impression of the state of the country was, that it was in a most frightfully disturbed
state ; that pass-words to which people would attach no particular or definite
meaning, were prevalent among the peasantry, such as " Are you up? Are you up?"
On this progress from Belfast to Lurgan, they saw in their way several bodies of
Orangemen in procession in Lurgan Park, and in the presence of Mr. Brownlow,
the proprietor of that domain, they reviewed a body of nearly 20,000 Orangemen,
who marched past before them ; and on returning the next day to Belfast, a proper feeling of confidence seemed to be restored to the country, and instead of
those indefinite words being used, the general expression that seemed to come from
the peasantry was " GOD save the King."

Sir Frederick Stoven was another witness examined before the same
Committee ; he was Chief Inspector of the Irish Police force, and particularly marked in his hostile feeling against Orangeism.   In his evidence
he is forced to admit, that Ireland was much more tranquil after the spread
of Orangeism, than before the system was introduced   The following
are extracts from Sir Frederick's evidence :

" *Question* 4685.—Are you aware that it is stated in Plowden's History of Ireland,
that about the year 1798, a short time previous to the breaking out of the Rebellion,
a body of men associated themselves in Dublin, under the title of the first National
Batallion, whose buttons were impressed with a harp and no crown, and with a
device over the harp of a cap of liberty upon a pike?—*Answer.* I never heard of it.

Question 4686.—As you are not acquainted with the state of Ireland about 1796,
just at the origin of Orangeism. and as it is important that you should be so, in
order to be able to say whether the present state of Armagh is more tranquil than
it was at that period, your attention is requested to a few passages. Sir Lawrence
Parson (afterwards Earl of Rosse) in a speech to the House of Commons in 1796,
thus expressed himself: " In the county of Armagh an amnesty of both parties
seemed peculiarly necessary, for either under the denomination of Peep-of-day Boys
or of Defenders, almost every man of the lower orders of every sect was implicated

in offences against the law" And a report from the committee of secrecy of the Irish House of Commons in 1798, contains the following passages: "To deter the well-affected from joining the Yeomanry Corps, and to render the administration of justice altogether ineffectual, a most active system of terror was put in operation; persons enrolled in the Yeomanry, magistrates, witnesses, jurors, in a word every class and description of people who ventured to support the laws, became objects of the most cruel persecution in their persons, property, and even in the line of their business, and multitudes were compelled to take the illegal oaths, and profess an adherence to the party as a means of security. In the latter end of 1796 and the beginning of 1797, the loyal inhabitants of Ulster suffered most severely from the depredations of the United Irishmen. Throughout the province they were stripped of their arms, the most horrid murders were perpetrated by large bodies of men in open day, and it became nearly impossible to bring the offenders to justice, from the inevitable destruction that awaited the witnesses or jurors who dared to perform their duty. Your Committee will now shortly trace the measures resorted to for suppressing those disturbances, and for extending protection to the well-affected." Then the report further states, " That the Insurrection Act by which the Lord Lieutenant and Council were enabled on a requisition of seven magistrates of any County, assembled at the Sessions of the Peace, to proclaim the whole or any part thereof to be in a state of disturbance, within which limits this law, giving increased power to the magistracy, was to have operation; many districts in Ulster in which outrages prevailed, occasioned by the activity and persecuting spirit of the United Irishmen, were in the course of the year 1796, and the spring of 1797, put under the provisions of the Act above mentioned. And your Committee have to observe, that although where the law was put in force with activity by the magistrates, very beneficial consequences were found to result from it, yet the treason was then too deeply rooted to yield to this remedy." Having seen what was the state of animosity, as between the Protestants and Roman Catholics, in Plowden, in the very dawn of the existence of Orangeism, and having seen from the report of the Committee of Secrecy what was the unfortunate state of the country in 1796 or 1797, do you consider that the present state of the County of Armagh is worse than it was then, or as bad as it was then, or better than it was then?—*Answer.* With respect to what has occurred between 1796 and this year, from all I have heard and understood, Ireland has been in a fluctuating state, sometimes better and sometimes worse; and this year, and in the last year, Armagh is in a very superior state to what is described by the reports of the Secret Committee, there can be no doubt.

Question 4687.—Then after the Yeomanry system and Orangeism have existed forty years, with the exception of four years that Orangeism was dormant, the state of the County of Armagh is more tranquil than it was at the origin of those institutions?—*Answer* In the years 1795 and 1796 all Ireland was in a state of half-rebellion.

Question 4688.—Are you aware of the fact that, within the last thirty years, the Province of Armagh has never been under the operation of an Insurrection Act?—*Answer.* I know nothing about it, but from what I have heard I should think it has not.

Question 4689 —You are aware that many other parts of Ireland have been under the operation of Insurrection Acts ?—*Answer* Yes.

Question 4690 —Was not there an Insurrection Act called into operation in 1807, which lasted throughout 1808, 1809, and 1810 ?—*Answer.* I was so differently employed in those days that I know nothing about it.

Question 4691 —Are you aware that in 1826 and 1827 the Orange Institution was in abeyance ?—*Answer.* No ; I was abroad then "

The Orange Society was now (1797) rapidly increasing in numbers and respectability, in all parts of the northern Province. ' It will appear from the following resolutions, that at least 315 Lodges had been organized, up to the 4th day of June, 1797 These resolutions are copied, not only as proof of the extent of the order at this date, but also as containing a pretty accurate view of the principles and objects of the members of the Association, at this early period of its existence.

" Resolutions unanimously adopted by the Loyal Boyne Orange Association, No. 315, held at Lisbellaw, County of Fermanagh, on the 4th day of June, 1797, Mr. John Hall, Master, in the Chair ·

" *Resolved*,—That no person shall have admission into our Society until he shall give proper and satisfactory testimony, as to his knowledge of any public or secret conspiracy against our gracious Sovereign, Lord King George the Third, His illustrious House, or the present Constitution as established by law , and that he is not a " *United Irishman*," and never was sworn to the secrecy of any such society, nor never will, unless at the hazard of his life , and that if compelled, he will **give** information on sight to some Magistrate, or Brother Orangeman , to the end, that all dangerous and seditious persons may be brought to condign punishment

" *Resolved*,—That we hold ourselves bound to our God and to each other, in no less a penalty than our *Oaths*, our *Lives*, and our *Properties*, to assist His Majesty King George the Third, and His lawful successors, against His and Their enemies, whilst we reside in His Majesty's Dominions, and whilst He and They shall support and maintain the true Protestant Religion, as declared and established at the Glorious Revolution of 1688, to be the principle for the guide and government of all future monarchs of Great Britain and Ireland

" *Resolved*,—That in case a foreign enemy shall invade this Kingdom, (as is now hourly expected,) we subject ourselves, both by our unalterable principles and sacred oaths, to aid, assist, support and defend his Majesty, our Country and Religion, by all the means in our power, and at the hazard of our lives, if called upon by the civil, military, or other lawful authority

" *Resolved*,—That inasmuch as history and experience have truly informed us that the members of the Popish Church will keep no faith with us, whom they denominate ' *heretics* ;' and that they are also bound by the most sacred and religious ties, to disclose and make known to their Priests at Confession, all secrets, whether of the State or of ourselves ; and also for the reason of their being almost universally disaffected to our good King, that we do therefore declare, that no member of the said Popish Church shall have any inheritance in our loyal brotherhood.

" *Resolved*,—That no member of this Society shall screen or know of any ' *De-*

fender' (so-called,) '*United Irishman*,' or '*Deserter*' from His Majesty's Army or Navy, without giving information thereof to some Magistrate, or other person, that he may be given over to the laws of the land, or to the military authorities.

"*Resolved*,—That every member of this Association, shall be at all times willing to receive arms from His Majesty's Government, for the defence of the country, and to return them when required.

"*Resolved*,—That this Loyal Boyne Orange Lodge, No. 315, will meet on the first day of July, (*Old Style*,) and fifth day of November in each year; provided we are so permitted by a Magistrate, or the Commanding Officer of our County ; in a full body, and decently dressed ; and that we will march to whatever place of Worship we may conclude upon, and return home peaceably and quietly, without molestation to the person or property of any person whomsoever,—and we declare our reasons for so doing are, in remembrance of King William the Third, Prince of Orange and Nassau, who restored to us our liberties and our properties, and who freed us from an arbitrary and cruel power; also in obedience to the wishes and example of our pious ancestors and of the law, which ordains the 5th day of November in every year, to be kept as a day of Thanksgiving to Almighty God."

———

CHAPTER XXIII.

Second General Meeting of the Association, held at Portadown in 1797—The Great Rebellion of 1798—Copy of the First Orange Warrant introduced into the County of Wexford—The First Lodge formed in Dublin, its Meetings and Members, and remarkable entries in its Minute-book—The Antrim Orangemen publish the first Book of Rules—Copy of the Book.

THE Lodges of each County, at this early period of the Association, were separate and independent, and there being no superior degree of pre-eminence or authority, (except what was due to Armagh, as being the County in which the Society was first organized,) each had its own rules, forms and obligations. Some of the principal gentlemen connected with the Institutution, conceiving that it would materially conduce to regularity, efficiency and stability, if a permanent authority should be established, to regulate and control the affairs of the Institution, convened a Second General Meeting of the members of the Association, which was held at Portadown, in the County of Armagh, on the 12th of July, 1797. This meeting was attended by the following Gentlemen :—

Captain William Blacker, *Grand Master*, Armagh.

Thomas Verner, Esq., *Grand Master*, Tyrone, Derry and Fermanagh.

Doctor William Atkinson, *Grand Master*, Antrim.

Thomas Seaver, Esq., *Grand Treasurer*, Armagh.

David Verner, Esq., *Grand Secretary*, Armagh.

John Crossle, Esq., *Grand Secretary*, Tyrone.

William Hart, *Grand Secretary*, Antrim.

Wolsey Atkinson, *Acting Grand Secretary*.

At this meeting the two following resolutions were adopted :—

"1st. *Resolved,*—That all Lodges shall pay an annual sum of three pence for each member, to defray the various expenses incurred by Mr. Atkinson in the issuing of warrants.

"2nd. *Resolved,*—That no Lodge shall be held without a warrant, to be signed by Mr. Wolsey Atkinson, and a seal, with the likeness of King William affixed thereto."

A memorable era in the annals of Ireland now presents itself ; the great Rebellion of 1798 is ushered in, and all its attendant horrors of blood and flame, and suffering, darken the history of this dismal period. "Vinegar Hill," and "Scullabogue Barn," "Wexford Bridge," and "Bloody Friday," will forever imprint their tales of horror upon the escutcheon of Irish Romanism ; while an imperishable mede of praise and gratitude will environ the standard of Orangeism, and hand down to the latest posterity the noble acts of the Orange patriots, who, in that hour of darkness and adversity, proved themselves "the saviours of Ireland."

The Orange Society was first introduced into the County of Wexford in this year. The "*Wingfield Yeomanry*" (Cavalry and Infantry) of which John Hunter Gowan Esq. was the Captain Commanding, was in fact, an Orange Lodge. The following is a copy of the first Orange Warrant brought into the County. The original is in the possession of the writer, and may be seen by any person curious enough to examine it. The ribbon is somewhat faded, the signatures are quite perfect, the seal is small, and the vellum in parts decayed ; but taken as a whole, it is in a state of good preservation.

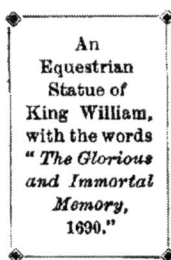

An Equestrian Statue of King William, with the words "*The Glorious and Immortal Memory,* 1690."

Orange Ribbon.

Seal.

"No. Four hundred and six,
February tenth 1798, eight.
By virtue of this Authority,
Our well beloved Brother Orangeman,
JOHN HUNTER GOWAN, Esquire,
of Mount Nebo,
in the County of Wexford,
and District of Gorey,
is permitted to hold a Lodge,
or Brotherly Society,
to consist of true Orangemen,
and to act as Master,
and perform the requisites thereof,

Given under our Seal,
THOS. VERNER, *Gd. Master,*
J. C. BERESFORD, *G. Sy.*
WOLSEY ATKINSON, *G. Secy.*, Armagh."

No. 176, issued to Mr. Verner, in Armagh, was brought up to Dublin in March, 1798 ; it was the first Orange Lodge introduced into the Metropolis of Ireland. Its meetings were held at Harrington's, Grafton street, Dublin. Mr. Thomas Verner was the Master. Its members exceeded three hundred. The names of a few are selected from the long list ; they will speak for the character of the whole. The original minutes of the Lodge were placed in the possession of the writer, through the kindness of Lieut. Col. Verner.

Thomas Verner, Esq., *Master. (This Gentleman was afterwards Sovereign of Belfast.)*

John Claudius Beresford, Esq., *Deputy Master.*

Captain James Verner, *Secretary.*

Frederick Darley, Esq., *Treasurer. (Mr. Darley was one of the City Aldermen, and for many years afterwards Chief Magistrate of Police.)*

David Verner, Esq.

John Verner, Esq.

William Verner, Esq., *(the present Sir William Verner, Bart., M.P. for the County of Armagh.)*

Major Hamilton Archdall.

Rev. Henry McLean.

Rev. John Keating *(Dean of St. Patrick's, and Chaplain to the House of Commons.)*

Richmond Allen, Esq.

Hamilton Maxwell, Esq.

Alderman James Vance.

Authur Kelly, Esq. *(Sovereign of Armagh City.)*

Rev. Charles Cobbe Beresford.

Edmund A. McNaughten, Esq., M.P. *County of Antrim.*

Major William Bellingham Swan.

Rev. John Leslie.

Nathaniel Sneyd, Esq., M.P. *County of Cavan.*

Sir John Ferns, *Knt.*

Colonel John Staunton Rochford. *(Clogrennan Hall, Co. Carlow.)*

Henry Coddington, Esq., *(Deputy Serjeant-at-Arms to the House of Commons.)*

Henry Vaughan Brooke, Esq.

Henry Faulkner, Esq., *(County of Carlow.)*

Hon. Benjamin O'Neill, Stratford, *(afterwards Earl of Aldborough.)*

Rev. Sir Hervy Bruce, *Bart.*

Alderman Jacob Poole.

Rev. Thomas Knipe.

Sir John Macartney, *Bart.*

Right Hon. the Earl of Annesley.

John Stratford, Esq.

Right Hon. Earl of Athlone. (*Note.*—Immediately following the record of the initiation of this Nobleman, the following entry appears in the Lodge book—"*admitted by acclamation, being the only remainder of the Generals of King William.*")

Rev. Henry Roper, D.D.

Right Hon. Patrick Duignan, M.P. and LL.D.

Sir Josiah Barrington, *Knt.*

Major Sandys.

William Hamilton, Esq.

Viscount Corry, (*afterwards Earl of Belmore.*)

John Henry Cottingham, Esq., (*Barrister-at-Law.*)

Rev. Charles Palmer.

Alderman Richard Manders.

Major Henry Charles Sirr.

Hon. Captain De Ginkell, (*present Earl of Athlone.*)

Gabriel Whistler, Esq.

(*Note.*—The following entry appears in the Lodge book, under date of the 23rd of May, 1798. "*The following persons were admitted on the night of their proposal, contrary to rule, in consequence of such numbers hourly pressing forward, owing to the distressed and dangerous state of the Country.*")

Rev. Dean Blacker.

John Giffard, Esq. (*High Sheriff of Dublin.*)

Hon. George De Blaquiere.

Rev. Henry Maxwell.

Trevor Corry Esq. (*of Newry.*)

Rev. William Lyster.

The following names are selected from those persons subsequently admitted :

Major Benjamin Woodward.

James Corry, Esq. (*Secretary to the Linen Board.*)

Rev. Alexander McClintock.

John McClintock, Esq. (*Serjeant-at-Arms to the House of Commons.*)

Lieut. Col. Joseph Pratt.

Sir James Galbraith, *Bart.*

George Ogle Moore, Esq. M.P. *City of Dublin.*

Viscount Kingsborough, (*afterwards Earl of Kingston.*)

Captain Ryan.

Alderman James.

Rev. Mr. Brickle.

Rolleston Nassau Cathcart, Esq.

Rev. Hans Caulfield.

John DeCourcy, Esq.

Rev. William Elliott.

Rev. George Homan.

Rev. Mervyn Pratt.

Andrew Tott Patterson, Esq.

General Robert B. Sparrow.

Henry Colclough, Esq. (*County of Carlow.*)

Hon. General Sir George Lowry Cole.

George Clibborne, Esq. (*Moate, Co. Westmeath.*)

Hon. Major Molesworth.

Lord Viscount Northland.

Hon. Thomas Knox, M.P. *Dungannon, Co. Tyrone.*

The Society at this period (1798,) spread rapidly; the flames of rebellion driving every loyal man into its ranks. It had already taken deep root in the northern Counties, and had included in its ranks many eminent personages, Lay and Clerical, Military and Civil. Early in the year, the Orangemen in the County of Antrim assembled at Lisburn, to deliberate upon the state of the Association in that County, with a view to its more efficient organization. The result of this meeting was the publication of a small pamphlet, defining the principles of the Order, and promulgating certain rules for the good government of its members in the County of Antrim. One of these little pamphlets was given to the writer in the year 1825, by the Rev. Phillip Johnson, Rector of Ballymacash; and as it was one of the very first ever published conveying some definite ideas as to the principles and objects of Orangeism, it is deemed advisable to have it here transcribed.

"ROYAL ORANGE ASSOCIATION, COUNTY ANTRIM DISTRICT.

The Right Worshipful Doctor WILLIAM ATKINSON, of Belfast, *Grand Master.*

The Rev. PHILIP JOHNSON, *Grand Chaplain.*

Brother WILLIAM HART, of Lisburn, *Grand Secretary.*

QUALIFICATIONS REQUISITE FOR AN ORANGE MAN.

HE should have a sincere love and veneration for his Almighty Maker, productive of those lively and happy fruits, righteousness—and obedience to His commands: A firm and steady faith in the Saviour of the World; convinced that He is the only Mediator between a sinful creature and an offended Creator. Without these he can be no Christian. Of a humane and compassionate disposition, and a courteous and affable behaviour. He should be an utter enemy to savage brutality and unchristian-like cruelty. Let him be a lover of society and improving company, and have a laudable regard for the Protestant Religion, and a sincere endeavour to propagate its precepts—zealous of promoting the honor of his King and Country, and a hearty desire for victory and success, but convinced and assured that GOD only can grant it.

A hatred for cursing and swearing, and taking the name of GOD in vain, (a shameful practice) taking all opportunities to discourage it among his brethren

Wisdom and prudence should guide his actions, honesty and integrity influence his conduct, and honor and glory be the motives of his endeavours.

Lastly—he must pay the strictest attention to a religious observance of the Sabbath, and also of temperance and sobriety.

RULES AND REGULATIONS OF THE BOYNE SOCIETY, COMMONLY CALLED ORANGE MEN.

I. We associate for the defence of our persons and properties, and for preserving the peace and good order of our country.

II. That we are exclusively a Protestant Association.

III. That we will to the utmost of our power, defend and support his present Majesty KING GEORGE the Third, the Laws and Constitution of this Kingdom, and the Succession to the Throne, in his Majesty's illustrious House, and ever hold sacred the Memory of our glorious deliverer, William, Prince of Orange.

IV. That we will aid and assist all Magistrates, and all High and Petty Constables, in the lawful execution of their office, when called on.

V. That we will upon all occasions, aid and assist each other, when promptitude and propriety appear to give rise to the necessity of such assistance, and that the same do not exceed the jurisdiction of the law, or tend to promote insurrection, or internal disturbance.

VI. That we are to be true to all brother Orange Men in all their just actions, neither wronging any, or seeing or knowing them to be wronged, and as far as in our power, promote each other's interest and welfare.

VII. That we are not to give the first assault to any person whatever.

VIII. That we are individually bound not only to observe the peace ourselves, but also to be active in preventing all others, of whatever persuasion or denomination (who may come within our knowledge) that may have an intention to do an ill or riotous act.

IX. That we are to meet every first day of July (O. S.) in a full Body, to commemorate the Signal Victory gained by KING WILLIAM, Prince of Orange, at the BOYNE, who bravely supported our rights, and established the Protestant Religion. That on this day we are to walk wherever may be agreed on, always behaving with propriety and decorum.

GENERAL RULES.

I. Any Society whose number shall amount to thirty, one Master and one Assistant ; to fifty, a first and second Master and two Assistants ; Society of One Hundred, first, second and third Master and four Assistants ; to be appointed by the majority of the Society to which they belong.

II. Each Society to have a Treasurer and Secretary, and nine members to act as a regulating Committee; appeals from the decision of which (in cases of trial) may be made to the general Committee, by proper application to the Grand Master.

III. Each member is to attend the summons of any master of a Society, the same to be duly signed and sealed by the seal of the Society ; such summons to specify the purpose for which they may be called.

IV. No fine greater than five shillings and five pence to be imposed in cases where the Committee do not conceive the offence deserving expulsion; all such fines to be appropriated to the use of the district, and lodged with the Grand Master.

V. Each member to have the power of demanding a certificate when he pleases, which upon all demands being paid, must be granted on the next sitting night, unless some sufficient reason be given for the contrary.

General Committee, County Antrim District.

The Right Worshipful Doctor ATKINSON, *Grand Master, Chairman.*

Edward Hogg, Esq., 354, Lisburn.
Rev. Philip Johnson, 317, Ballymacash.
Thomas M'Cully, 224, Soldierstown.
Michael Boomer, 137, Derriaghy.
Stephen Daniel, 238, Belfast.
James Innes, 152, Lisburn.

John Johnston, 244, Lisburn.
Thomas Briggs, 121, Maze.
William Johnston, 143, Ballinderry.
Thomas Shillington, 403, Aghagallan.
William Murphy, 146, Maghragell.

WILLIAM HART, *Grand Secretary.*

REGULATING RULES OF ROYAL ORANGE SOCIETY, NO.

———————————*Master.*
———————————*Secretary.*

I. That no person shall be admitted into this Society, until his name be laid before it one month, and then it shall be decided by

II. That any person admitted to our Society shall pay
admission; and if from any other Society, to produce a certificate of his behaviour and pay   on lodging certificate.

III. That we are to meet once in every month
at   o'clock, and pay each   the club of which to be
shall not exceed   the remainder to go to the stock purse—
absent members to be charged the same as if present.

IV. That any member who has absented himself for three months, and be in arrears to the Society, shall pay   as a fine, unless he can satisfy the Society that he could not attend.

V. That any member who has absented himself and has refused due obedience to the Master and Officers of this Society for three months past, being duly summoned to attend and pay his arrears and fines, and make submission to the Master, shall be fined   or be excluded.

VI. That any regular brother Orange Man may be admitted into our Society, with the consent of the Master and rest of the members, he paying his club.

VII. That no brother not belonging to this Society shall be admitted into it when we are doing business, without the consent of the Master and members present.

VIII. That the Master summoning any member to attend on particular business and he refusing to attend, shall pay   as a fine.

IX. That if any member belonging to our Society give abusive language to another, or is the cause of any disturbance in the Society, or any other place, and judged so by the majority then present, shall pay   as a fine, and on refusal shall be excluded.

X. That if any member curses or swears, or uses any obscene discourse, or offers to lay wagers, or call for drink, without the leave of the Master, or does not keep silence when desired, or comes into our Society drunk, or in any disorderly manner, shall be fined

XI. That no member belonging to this Society shall be aiding or assisting in any clandestine manner in making an Orangeman.

XII. That if the Master do not attend on every sitting night, the Officer next him must officiate as Master for that night, and have the same power as Master for that night.

XIII. That any dispute that may happen between any of our brothers, which cannot be determined by these rules, after being tried by the Committee for regulating this Society, shall be determined by the General Committee.

XIV. The Master cannot forgive any offence that any member is guilty of without the consent of the members, and put to the vote.

XV. On all trials for offences in this Society, the decision of the Committee not considered binding, until approved by a majority of the Society on the sitting night after trial; no trial on a sitting night by the Committee.

XVI. That any member of this Society who may be guilty of such a crime as upon trial shall exclude him entirely from the Society, shall be published in the Belfast "News Letter" and Dublin "Journal."

XVII. That the powers of all Officers belonging to this Society shall cease on the first day of July (N. S.) and the fourth day of November of every year, and the Society shall meet and proceed to the election of their Officers in manner following:

1st. Every member to come prepared with the name of the person (wrote on a piece of paper and folded up) that he thinks most eligible to sit as Master, the same to be deposited in a hat: the member who has the majority of votes to be declared Master.

2nd. To act in like manner for Assistant Master, Secretary, Treasurer, &c., and for nine members to serve as a regulating Committee.

Order of Business each Sitting Night.

1st. Lodge to open with a prayer, members standing. 2nd. Regulating Rules read. 3rd. Members proposed. 4th. Members polled for. 5th. Trials from Committee decided. 6th. Members names called over by Secretary. 7th. Two members standing. 8th. Lodge to close with a prayer, members standing. No drink to be allowed during the business.

Form of Prayer to be used at Opening.

By Order of Doctor WILLIAM ATKINSON, Grand Master of the County Antrim.

Almighty God, and Heavenly Father, who in all ages has shewed thy power and mercy, in graciously and miraculously delivering thy Church, and in protecting righteous and religious Kings and States, from the wicked conspiracies and malicious practices of all the enemies thereof; we yield thee hearty thanks for so wonderfully discovering and confounding the horrible and wicked designs of our enemies, plotted and intended to have been executed against our most gracious Sovereign Lord, King George, and the whole estates of the realm, for the subversion of Government and established Religion; be thou, O Lord, still our mighty protector, and scatter our enemies that delight in blood; infatuate and defeat their counsels, abate their pride, assuage their malice, and confound their devices. Strengthen the hands of our gracious Sovereign, and all that are in authority under him, with judgment and justice to cut off all such workers of iniquity, as turn religion into rebellion, and faith into faction, that they may never prevail or triumph in the ruin of thy Church amongst us; but that our gracious Sovereign and his Realms, being preserved in thy true religion, and by thy merciful goodness protected in the same, we may all duly serve thee with praise and thanksgiving. And we beseech thee to protect the King, Queen and Royal Family, from all treasons and conspiracies; preserve him in thy faith, fear and love; make his reign long, prosperous and happy, here on earth, and crown him hereafter with everlasting glory. Accept also, most gracious God, our unfeigned thanks, for filling our hearts with joy and gladness, by sending thy servant, the late King William, for the deliverance of these nations from tyranny and arbitrary power.

Let truth and justice, devotion and piety, concord and unity, brotherly kindness and charity, with other christian virtues, so flourish amongst us, that they may be the stability of our times, and make this our association a praise here on earth. This we most humbly beg in the name and for the sake of Jesus Christ, our Lord and Saviour. *Amen.*

Form of Prayer to be used at Closing.

O Almighty God, who art a strong Tower of defence unto thy servants, against the face of their enemies; we yield thee praise and thanks for our deliverance from those great and apparent dangers wherewith we were encompassed: We acknowledge thy goodness that we were not delivered over as a prey unto them, beseeching thee still to continue such thy mercies towards us, that all the world may know that thou art our Saviour and mighty Deliverer, through *Jesus Christ.* *Amen.*

CHAPTER XXIV.

First organization of a Grand Lodge for Ireland, and minutes of the proceedings had thereat—First meeting of the Grand Lodge, members present, Grand Officers elected—Particulars of the great rebellion of 1798—Earl of Annesley appointed County Grand Master of Down—Military organization of the Orangemen in Down and Sligo, and gallant conduct of the Coloony Lodge—"Captain Kimlin," A Rebel Leader— Sir Charles Asgill and the Coolatin, Shilelagh and Tinahely Orangemen—Battle of Ballyellis and defeat of the King's forces thereat—the fortunes of the day retrieved by Loyal Orange Lodge 406— admissions of Mooney and Plowden—Loyalty of the Irish Roman Catholics.

The Grand Orange Lodge of Ireland was first organized on the 8th of March in this year. The particular mode in which it was constituted, who were present at the organization, and the proceedings had at the meeting, are all set forth in an addenda to the little pamphlet just copied; and may be found upon pages 6, 7 and 8. At this meeting was sown the germ from which Orangeism in Ireland spread throughout the Kingdom; its proceedings are here copied *verbatim*.

"At a Meeting of Deputies from the following Orange Lodges, to take into consideration the mode of organizing the Orange Men of Ireland, and rendering them more effective in support of their King and glorious Constitution, held in Dublin March 8, 1798.

Present—No. 12, William Blacker, Grand Master, Armagh.

No. 154, Major Molesworth, Cavan *militia*, Master; Captain Moore, Cavan *militia*, Sec.

No. 176, Thomas Verner, Master and Grand Master of Tyrone, Londonderry and Fermanagh; Capt. Beresford, Dublin *cavalry*.

No. 177, Quarter-master, Serjeant Hughes, Cavan *militia*, Serjeant Hamilton Serjeant Gibson, Master, Serjeant Gilchrist, do.

No. 222, Serjeant Little, Armagh *militia*, Master; Serjeant MacClean, and Serjeant Holmes,

No. 235, Serjeant Douglas, Armagh *militia*, Master; Serjeant Sinclair, do.

No. 406, Captain Hunter Gowan, Wingfield Cavalry, Master.

No. 413, Edward Ball, Master; J. Dejoncourt.

No. 414, Lt. Col. Rochfort, Master.

No. 415, Serjeant Major Galloughly, Fermanagh *militia*, Master; Serjeant Price, ditto.

THOMAS VERNER, Esq., being called to the Chair, the following Resolutions were unanimously agreed to:

Resolved.—That it is highly advisable, that a proper correspondence should be forthwith instituted between the different Orange Lodges in this kingdom.

Resolved,—That it is advisable, that a Grand Lodge should be formed for that purpose, to be held in Dublin.

Resolved,—That this Lodge be called, The Grand Lodge of Ireland, for correspondence and information.

Resolved,—For the purpose of carrying the above resolutions into effect, that each County should be divided into Districts, by the Grand Master, and the other Masters of the County.

Resolved,—That each District should have a District Master, to be chosen by the Masters of the Lodges in each District.

Resolved,—That each County should have a Grand County Lodge, to be formed of the District Masters.

Resolved,—That it is advisable that the Grand Lodge of Ireland should be formed by members, to be chosen by ballot by each County Grand Lodge, and that the Grand Masters of Counties, District Masters, and Masters of Lodges in Dublin, on account of their residence, should be members, and that all Masters of country Lodges should be admitted as honorary members, and that each Regiment having one or more numbers, should have a power of choosing one member by ballot to be a member of the said Grand Lodge.

Resolved,—That the said Grand Lodge, when formed, should forthwith choose a Grand Master, to be called Grand Master of Ireland.

Resolved,—That the Masters of Lodges, District Master, Grand Master of Counties, the Grand Lodge of Ireland, and the Grand Master of Ireland, should be re-elected once in every year, one month previous to the first of July.—O.S.

Resolved,—That it is highly advisable that each Master of a Lodge should return the Number of his Lodge, together with the Numbers that compose it, to the District Masters, to be returned by them to the Grand Master of the County, and to be laid by him before the Grand Lodge of Ireland.

Resolved,—That it is advisable that the first meeting of the Grand Lodge of Ireland should be on Monday, the 9th of April, 1798, to be held at the house of Thomas Verner, of Dawson street, Esq., Grand Master of the Counties of Londonderry, Tyrone, and Fermanagh.

Resolved,—That a copy of these Resolutions shall be sent to every Lodge in Ireland.

> THOMAS VERNER, *Chairman, Master Lodge, No.* 176, *and*
> *Grand Master of the Counties of Tyrone, Londonderry, and Fermanagh.*

FORM OF SUMMONS.
ORANGE SOCIETY, No.

SIR AND BROTHER,

Y OU are requested to attend a Meeting of your Society at
    on   the   day of
     at the hour of   o'clock.

Fail not as you are an Orangeman.

        Signed by order of the Master,

                            } *Secretary.*

THE KING AND CONSTITUTION.
LOYAL ORANGE ASSOCIATION, No.

———

WE the Master, Warden, and Secretary of the Loyal   Orange Association, No.   held at
                              in the Kingdom of Ireland, do hereby Certify that Brother
has regularly received the
Degrees of a true Orangeman in this our Association ; and that he has conducted himself, during his stay amongst us, to the entire satisfaction of all our Brethren :—We therefore request that all the regular Orange Associations of the Universe do recognise and admit him as such.

Given under our Hands and the Seal of the Society, this
day of   17

                                                     Master.
                                                     Warden.
Secretary.

———

After the Dublin meeting and organization, the Association spread rapidly in all parts of the Kingdom, and the Executive Government, the Civil Magistrates, and the Military Authorities, vied with each other in promoting the views of the Society, and in extending its organization.

The first meeting of the Grand Orange Lodge of Ireland, was held at the residence of Mr. Verner, Dawson-street, Dublin, on Monday the 9th of April 1798. At this meeting the following members were present.

> Thomas Verner Esq. G. M. Tyrone, (in the Chair.)
> The most Noble the Marquis of Drogheda.
> Captain Blacker, G. M. Armagh.
> Captain Beresford, Dublin Cavalry.
> The Hon. B. O'Neill Stratford.
> The Right Hon. the Earl of Annesley.
> The Right Hon. the Earl of Athlone.
> The Rev. Dr. Keating.
> Captain Hunter Gowan, G. M. Wexford.
> The Right Hon. George Ogle, M. P.
> Frederick Darley, Esq.
> David Verner, Esq.
> John Verner, Esq.
> Major Sirr, G. M., Dublin.
> Councillor Cottingham, G. M., Cavan.
> Right Hon. P. Duignan, LL.D.
> Harding Giffard, Esq.

Hon. J. W. Cole, G. M. Fermanagh.

Hon. Captain De Ginkell.

Captain Moore, Cavan Militia.

Serjeant Hamilton,
Serjeant Hughes,   } Cavan Militia.
Serjeant Gibson,

Alderman Vance.

William Verner, Esq.

Major Swan.

Sir John Ferns.

Serjeant Little,
Serjeant MacCleane,
Serjeant Holmes,   } Armagh Militia.
Serjeant Douglas,

Isaac De Joncourt, Esq.

Alderman Poole.

Major Sands.

Lord Viscount Corry.

Gabriel Whistler, Esq.

Edward Ball, Esq.

Serjeant Major Galloughly,
Serjeant Price,   } Fermanagh Militia.
Serjeant Quinton,

Col. Rochford.

Right Hon. John Maxwell Barry, M. P.

Captain Mervyn Archdall, M. P.

Sir Richard Musgrave, Bart. G. M. Waterford.

Samuel Montgomery, Esq.

Wolsley Atkinson, Esq., Grand Secretary.

The meeting being duly organized by calling Mr. Thomas Verner to the chair, and appointing Mr. Atkinson Secretary, some discussion ensued as to the proper mode of proceeding. The Right Hon. Mr. Ogle, in a very eloquent and impressive speech, seconded by Captain Blacker, proposed that Thomas Verner, Esq., should be the first Grand Master of Ireland. Before putting the motion, Mr. Verner said that as he had no object in view, but the good of the cause and the security of the Kingdom, he thought the first Grand Mastership should be offered to the Earl of Athlone, or to the Marquis of Drogheda, the one as being the only remainder of King William's Generals, and the other as being the descendant of the brave General Moore, distinguished in the annals of the Boyne. The Earl of Athlone and Lord Drogheda, declined respectively the proffered honor, stating that no man could have greater, or even so great, claims as Mr. Verner. The motion was carried by a unanimous vote.

Major Sirr proposed, and Captain Gowan seconded the appointment of Sir Richard Musgrave, Bart. M. P., for Grand Treasurer.

Captain Blacker proposed, and Councillor Cottingham seconded, Mr. John Claudius Beresford for Grand Secretary.

Some discussion ensued about the appointment of Deputies, or Assistants. After which it was agreed that the Very Rev. Dean Keating, Chaplain to the House of Commons, should be the Grand Chaplain—that Edward Turner, Esq., should be Acting Grand Treasurer, and William G. Galway, Esq, Acting Grand Secretary.

A very interesting discussion took place, as to the duty of every Orangeman in the present perilous crisis. It was agreed unanimously, that all should be alert, to thwart the machinations of the seditious, and to give the earliest information to the Magistrates and Military Authorities, of all seditious practices, &c.

A select Committee, consisting of Mr. Giffard and Mr. Montgomery, were appointed to draft rules and regulations, to be submitted for the approval of the Grand Master, and such members as can conveniently attend, at an adjourned meeting to be held in the month of November next, upon the call of the Grand Master.

A vote of thanks was given to Mr. Atkinson, for his zeal and efficiency in the issue of Warrants, and other matters requiring attention.

Also, a cordial vote of thanks was given to Mr. Verner, Grand Master, for his able conduct while presiding, and for his great zeal upon all occasions.

(Signed,)   J. C. BERESFORD, G. S.

Such were the proceedings had, at the first great meeting of Orangemen, for the election of a Grand Master. And assuredly they redound to the credit and honor of the Order. The Noblemen and Gentlemen who attended this meeting, returned to their respective homes, and carried with them the "good seed" of Orange Loyalty, which they lost no time in planting in the honest hearts of their Protestant neighbours.

It was most providential that a Grand Lodge was formed at this period. The events which immediately followed proved the necessity for the organization, and the wisdom and judgment of its founders. Scarcely had the Grand Lodge assembled, and before the gentlemen appointed a select committee for that purpose, had time to draft and report a constitution for the Society,—ere the flame of rebellion burst forth—ere the authority of Britain was set at defiance—and the standard of revolt and blood, of fire, rapine and the pike, was caried aloft by Popish Priests, at the head of Popish thousands, through the hitherto thriving towns and fairest fields of Erin. In the spring of 1798, the plans of the Romish conspirators were disclosed by one of their own party. On the 12th of March in that year, (four days after the organization of the Grand Orange

Lodge of Ireland ;) several of the Rebel conspirators, with their papers, were seized by the Irish Government ; and early in the month of May, Lord Edward Fitzgerald, (the Military Chief of the conspiracy,) was apprehended by Major Sirr, the Grand Master of Dublin. The original plan of the insurgent Leaders, contemplated a general rising of the dis-affected throughout the Kingdom, on the night of the 23rd of May 1798, but the discovery of their plans, and the arrest of their Military Com-mander and other Leaders, frustrated their scheme for a general insurrec-tion. Partial risings of the Romish peasantry, did however, take place, and some rather sharp encounters occurred between the Loyalists and the Rebels on that and subsequent nights, particularly at Naas, Prosperous and Monastereven, in the County of Kildare, and at Carlow.

As the " Orange Yeomanry " were mainly instrumental in suppressing the dreadful Rebellion which burst forth upon the country at this period, it may be necessary here, to recite a few of the most important incidents connected with the memorable event ; together with the part played by the Orangemen on that occasion.

The County of Wexford, (the birth-place of the writer,) was the cradle of the insurrection—there it burst forth in all its terrific fury ; and there its burning lava was quenched in defeat and sorrow. The better to conceal their vile intentions, the Romish Priests and People, had recourse to perjury and to every conceivable species of duplicity and falsehood. Here are a few examples :

The following is a copy of a Loyal address from the Parish of Ballycanow, unanimously adopted at a general meeting of the Roman Catholic inhabit-ants of the Parish, on Sunday, the 1st of April, 1798, and ordered to be forwarded to His Excellency the Marquis of Camden, then Viceroy of Ireland.

" MAY IT PLEASE YOUR EXCELLENCY,—

" We the Roman Catholic inhabitants of Ballycanow, in the County of " Wexford, this day assembled at the Chapel of Ballycanow, holding in abhor-" rence the barbarous outrages lately committed, and the seditious conspiracies " now existing in this Kingdom, by traitors and rebels, styling themselves *United* " *Irishmen*, think it incumbent on us, thus publicly to avow and declare unalter-" able attachment and Loyalty to our most revered and beloved sovereign, King " George the Third, and our determined resolution to support and maintain his " rights, and our happy constitution. And we do further pledge ourselves to " co-operate with our Protestant brethren of this Kingdom, in opposing to the " utmost of our power, any foreign or domestic enemy, who may dare to " invade His Majesty's dominions, or disturb the peace and tranquility of this " Country.

" *Resolved*,—That the above Declaration be signed by our Pastor, the Rev. " Michael Murphy, and a few of the principal Parishioners ; and that the same be

"sent to the Right Hon. the Earl of Mountnorris, with a request that His Lord-
"ship will transmit it to His Excellency the Lord Lieutenant.

    (Signed by)   Rev. Michael Murphy.

                                   Coadjutor Priest.

' James Kenny,	" Michael Connors,
" Patrick Fortune,	" Thomas O'Neill.
" John Murray,	" Peter Hughes,
" Patrick Roche,	" John Beghan,
" Thomas Kelly,	" Anthony Roche,
" Morgan Kavanagh,	" Michael Murphy,
" Thomas Reynolds,	" James Dealy, *Clerk of the Day.*

The Earl of Mountnorris having laid this loyal and dutiful Address and Declaration before His Excellency the Lord Lieutenant, (the Marquis of Camden,) received the following reply.

                            "DUBLIN CASTLE, 16th April, 1798.

"MY LORD,—I have the Lord Lieutenant's commands, to take the earliest "opportunity of acknowledging the receipt of the Address, which was presented "to His Excellency by your Lordship, from the Catholic inhabitants of Bally-"canow.

"His Excellency commanded me to express to your Lordship, the satisfaction "with which he has received their Address, and his entire reliance on the loyalty "and zeal manifested by the persons who have subscribed it.

                " I have the honor to be, &c.

                                CASTLEREAGH."

The Earl of Mountnorris enclosed the Lord Lieutenant's reply to the Rev. Michael Murphy, accompanied by the following note from his Lordship :

" Lord Mountnorris felt highly gratified by being employed to convey the "Address of the Catholic inhabitants of Ballycanow to the Government ; which "was a striking test of their attachment to the Constitution, and which, from his "perfect knowledge of their sentiments, as well as from the proof given by their "Oath of Allegiance, he is convinced they are as anxious to support the Constitu-"tion, as any other members of the community. Should occasion require their "aid, he means to call upon them, persuaded of their anxiety to preserve the "public welfare."

" Camolin Park, April 27th, 1798."

The following is a copy of " the Oath of Allegiance," referred to by Lord Mountnorris, and which was freely taken, not only by the Rev. Mr. Murphy and his flock, at Ballycanow ; but also by nearly all the Roman Catholic Priests and their People, in the County of Wexford.

" I hereby do declare upon the Holy Evangelists, and as I hope to be saved "through the merits of my Blessed Lord and Saviour Jesus Christ, that I will be "true and faithful to His Majesty King George the Third, and to the succession of "his Family to the Throne : that I will support and maintain the Constitution as

" by law established : that I am not a *United Irishman*, and that I never will
" take the *United Irishman's* Oath : that I am bound by every Obligation human
" and divine, to give all information in my power to prevent tumult and disorder:
" that I will neither aid or assist the enemies of my King, or my country ; and
" that I will give up all sorts of Arms in my possession. All the above I volun-
" tarily swear, so help me God and my Redeemer."

This Oath was delivered in a printed form, to each person as he was
sworn ; with a Certificate attached to it, which was couched in the form
following.

" The above Oath was taken on the——day of——1798, before me, by——
of————Parish.

                                                  MOUNTNORRIS."

The short narrative which follows will show, that not only did Father
Murphy of Ballycanow, but that the entire of the Romish Priesthood and
People, openly violated their solemn oaths ; and used their loyal Addresses,
as well as their sworn Obligations, only as a means to lull Executive
suspicion, and to disarm Protestant union and preparation.

On the 9th of June (just 33 days after Lord Mountnorris. letter,) this
same *loyal* Priest, the Rev. Father Michael Murphy, was killed at the
battle of Arklow, while leading on thirty-four thousand Rebels against the
King's Forces ! And every one of the fourteen subscribers to the *loyal*
Address to Lord Camden, were within two months thereafter, either killed
in action with the Royal troops, or subsequently arrested, tried for High
Treason, found guilty and executed ! Such was Romish Loyalty, Romish
Fidelity, and Romish Allegiance, in 1798 ! Are Irish Romanists more true,
or loyal, or dependable, at this day ?

The first actual outbreak of "the great Rebellion of 1798," took place
on the night of Saturday the 26th of May, in that year. The Rev. John
Murphy, Priest of Boolavogue, in the County of Wexford, was the first
who openly raised the standard of revolt. He assembled his deluded flock,
whom he had often harangued, telling them "the hour of liberty had
arrived," and then marched them off to Rockspring, the residence of Lieutenant Bookey, whom they barbarously murdered, and whose residence
they burned, after a most gallant defence by Mr. Bookey and two domestics, then in Rockspring House, named Jacob Ward and Samuel Hawkins.
John Donovan, one of Mr. Bookey's men, fell gallantly by his Master's
side. After the murder of Messrs. Bookey and Donovan, and the destruction of Rockspring, the Priest and his Rebel followers proceded on to
the Village of Oulard, gathering strength on the way, and robbing and
burning all the houses of Protestants as they proceeded. On the following
morning (Whitsunday, 27th of May,) they proceeded to the residence of the
Rev. Robert Burrows, at Kyle, near Oulard. They there deliberately
murdered Mr. Burrows, and five of his parishioners, plundered his dwelling

house, and then set fire to, and totally consumed it.   In the afternoon of
that day, they were strengthened by the arrival of Mr. Edward Roche, of
Garrylough, who was the permanent Serjeant of the Shelmalier Yeoman
Cavalry, and who had been, up to the very moment of the actual outbreak,
looked upon as one of the moderate and respectable Roman Catholics, in
whose loyalty full reliance might be placed, and who was trusted and
confided in by all the neighbouring Protestants.   There were twenty-four
Roman Catholics who had volunteered their services in the Shelmalier
Cavalry ; they were armed, equipped and drilled, marked attention was
paid to them, both by their Commander and their Comrades ; and as a
special mark of confidence and respect, their leader, Edward Roche, was
selected as the Permanent Serjeant of the Corps.   This gratitude and
confidence was requited by the desertion to the rebel camp of Serjeant
Roche and twenty, out of the twenty-four, on the very first day of the Romish insurrection !   Another sad proof of the confidence to be placed in
Romish professions and Romish gratitude !

Almost simultaneously with Father John Murphy's rising at Oulard, the
standard of revolt was unfurled by the Rebels in the vicinity of Ferns and
Newtown Barry, both considerable Towns in the same County.   This body
of insurgents attacked Charles Fort, the residence of Mr. Dawson, which
they plundered, and at which they piked a Protestant domestic, named
Willis, to death.   From thence they proceeded to Ballingale, the residence
of the Rev. Francis Turner, Rector of Edermine.   Mr. Turner was a
most estimable man, who refused to fly when the standard of insurrection
was raised, believing that his conduct was so amiable and benevolent, so
popular and inoffensive, that no party could be found to injure or molest
him.   Not expecting a hostile visit from his Romish neighbours, Mr.
Turner was engaged in the baptism of a neighbour's child, when Ballingale
House was surrounded, the out-offices set on fire, and on the amiable
Clergyman presenting himself, to ask what he had ever said or done, to call
for such treatment, he was instantly fired at, and the side of his face blown
off.   Here they murdered nine innocent and inoffensive Protestants, (two
of whom were the sponsors, and one the father, of the infant just baptized.)
Mr. Turner's body was consumed in the burning ruins of his own dwelling.

The flame of revolt now spread throughout the whole country, and
thousands upon thousands of the insurgents, headed by their Priests,
proceeded by various roads to Corragrewa Hill, on which they established
their Head Quarters.   The Protestant people, in all parts of the country,
fled from their homes, and sought shelter in the Towns and Cities ; their
deserted dwellings were burned, and such of them as were caught were
murdered.

The first encounter between the Rebel forces and the King's troops, took
place on the following day, at Oulard Hill.   The insurgents were in great

force, headed by their Priests, and the Royalists consisted of a detachment of the North Cork Militia, one hundred and thirty strong, under the immediate command of Lieutenant-Colonel Foote ; and the Yeoman Cavalry, under Colonel Le Hunte. The royal forces were surrounded and cut to pieces, the Lieutenant-Colonel and two privates only escaping. Amongst the officers who fell on that melancholy occasion, were Major Lombard, the Hon. Captain De Courcy (brother to Lord Kinsale,) Lieutenants Barry and Williams, and Ensign Ware, all of the North Cork.

The Rebels next directed their movements against Enniscorthy, a large Town on the River Slaney. It was ably defended by the members of a few Orange Lodges, lately organized and armed as yeomanry. But, as the Town was fired in several places, and the masses of the enemy pouring in were so numerous and irresistible, the defenders of the Town were obliged to abandon it, and make their escape as best they could, through the flames, to Wexford. In the defence of the Town, the Orange Loyalists lost ninety of their number, including Captain Pounden of the Enniscorthy Infantry. So soon as the Rebels got possession, the work of plunder and slaughter commenced, and no Protestant who was caught escaped death ! The Rev. Samuel Hayden, Rector of Ferns, a very old and feeble Clergyman, was amongst the murdered, and his body was cast out to be devoured by swine ! Richard Whaley, an aged Loyalist, nearly one hundred years old, was another of the victims of Romish cruelty. After the conquest of Enniscorthy, the Rebel Head Quarters was established at Vinegar Hill, which is in the immediate vicinity, rises in the form of a cone, and completely commands the Town, as also the *Slaney,* which washes its base.

On the night of Tuesday, the 29th of May, the main body of the Rebel forces, under the immediate command of Priest Murphy, (who carried a large crucifix, conspicuously placed before him on the saddle,) marched from Vinegar Hill to the Three Rock Mountain, within three miles of the Town of Wexford. On the following morning (30th May,) a skeleton of the 13th Regiment, consisting of less than one hundred men, with a detachment of the Royal Meath Militia, the whole under the command of General Fawcet, encountered the Rebels at Three Rocks. The forces of the latter were over twenty thousand, and the few troops were speedily overpowered. General Fawcet lost his three Howitzers, had fifty of his little force killed, and twenty taken prisoners. Upwards of twenty thousand Rebels were engaged in this affair at Three Rocks. This defeat of the Royal forces opened the Town of Wexford to the Rebels, into the possession of which they entered on Wednesday the 30th of May. The greater part of the unfortunate Protestants of Wexford suffered, so soon as the Rebels obtained possession of the Town. On the following morning the insurgent forces marched out of the Town, and encamped on the Three

Rocks. Here the whole body was divided into three divisions, com-
manders appointed to each, and particular duties and destinations assigned
them. B. B. Harvey, Esq., was appointed to the chief command of the
body destined to attack Ross, having "Father" Philip Roche, Priest of
Poulpearsey, for his second in command. This division was intended to
open the communication with the County of Waterford, and to effect a
rising of the southern rebels. The second grand division was placed under
the command of Captains Doyle and Redmond, from the Queen's County,
the latter being the nephew of the Rev. Father Edward Redmond, of
Ferns. This body of the insurgents was also accompanied by Priest
Kearnes, and its destination was Newtown Barry. This division was
intended to open up the communication into Carlow and Kilkenny, and to
penetrate into the centre Counties of the Kingdom. The third grand
division was under the command of Anthony Perry, Priest Michael
Murphy, of Ballycanow, and Priest John Murphy, of Boolavogue. It
was destined to march upon Gorey, and from thence, through Arklow and
Wicklow, to Dublin, the Metropolis of the Kingdom, and the seat of
government.

Thus arranged and divided, the whole Rebel force marched from Three
Rocks in the different directions assigned them ; flushed with victory, and
confident of success, from the assurances of their Priests, and from the
vast accessions in number, by which their ranks were constantly augmented.
The first division under Bagnel Harvey, destined to the attack of Ross,
marched by Tagmon to Carrigburn Hill, where Head Quarters were established. The second division, destined to attack Newtown Barry, marched
to Vinegar Hill, on which they took post, intending to occupy Enniscorthy
and to advance up the Slaney to Newtown. The third division, intended
to march direct on the Metropolis, proceeded through Oulard to Corragrewa Hill, where they took post on the night of the 1st of June, throwing
out advanced pickets as far as Ballymenane Hill, within two miles of Gorey.
In the progress of these divisions through the country, the dwellings of
Protestants were consumed, their property of all kinds destroyed, and
such of them as remained at their homes, and were discovered, without
reference to age or sex, were inhumanly murdered.

Soon after the dawn of morning, on the first of June, Mass was publicly
celebrated in the Camp at Vinegar Hill ; and shortly after Prayers, one
half of this division of the Rebel army, was marched off in two columns, on
each side of the river Slaney, to attack Newtown Barry. This Town is
beautifully situated, and was at that time, the property of Colonel Maxwell
Barry, (afterwards Lord Farnham.) It is a "border town," dividing the
Counties of Carlow and Wexford, and is built in a lovely valley, watered by
the Slaney, which passes direct through its centre. A view of the Town
and neighbourhood, from the adjacent hills, is one of the most delightful in

Ireland—it possesses every variety of hill and dale, of wood and water, of natural scenery and delight, rendered still more charming by the taste displayed by resident Proprietors, in adorning and beautifying the scene. Newtown Barry was but thinly garrisoned on the 1st of June, 1798; but what it lacked in numbers, was amply compensated for, in the bravery and endurance of the stout and loyal hearts by which it was defended. Its whole force consisted of 230 of the King's County Militia, commanded by Colonel L'Estrange; 140 of the Orange Yeomanry, under the command of their Master, Captain Kerr, of the Newtown Barry Lodge. In addition to these, there were also 20 troopers of the 4th Dragoons, and 14 of the Carlow Troop, under the orders of Captain Cornwall. The whole strength amounting to 404 rank and file, with two Battalion guns, attached to the King's County Militia. The Rebel force was over 10,000 men, flushed with success, and assured of certain victory by their clerical leaders.

Colonel L'Estrange awaited the attack of the enemy, on some rising ground, about one mile in advance of the Town. After a brisk fire, which continued for some twenty minutes, and the enemy continuing to advance in overwhelming numbers, the Colonel ordered a retreat to Carlow, through Newtown Barry. In passing through the Town, many of the gallant Orangemen refused to retire, deliberately running into their own, and into neighbouring houses, which they barricaded as best they could, and fired upon the enemy as they advanced. Flushed with victory, the Rebels speedily got possession of the greater part of the Town, and immediately commenced the work of plunder and assassination. One wild scene of confusion ensued, the baggage of the army was plundered, the wine cellars and whiskey casks were opened, and in a short period, the Insurgents became one confused drunken and ungovernable mass. The Orangemen under Captain Kerr, finding that many of their comrades had remained in the Town, to defend their homes and families, and were thus left to contend for their religion and firesides, at such fearful odds, now entreated Colonel L'Estrange to return and renew the attack—that the rebels would be in confusion, scattered through the Town—and that their comrades, who had remained and who occupied various houses, would divert the attention of the enemy and divide and distract their aims. Colonel L'Estrange, earnestly pressed, at length yielded, and on again entering the Town, he found the drunken enemy completely disorganized, confusion reigned in every street and road, and the Rebel force fell an easy prey to the handful of steady, but organized, men who, in turn, became their assailants. The mob, intoxicated with success and liquor, fled in all directions, and were pursued for several miles out of the Town, by the few but gallant men who refused to surrender, and who upon that memorable day, preserved untarnished British honor and Orange valor in Newtown Barry.

To Capt. Kerr and the Orangemen of Newtown Barry, belong the chief glory of this victory. They were the men who, after the Militia and other Troops had retired, refused to surrender—theirs was the remonstrance which called back Col. L'Estrange to the attack—and theirs was the individual daring and heroism, (the "over-zeal," if you will,) which enspirited the retiring troops to fresh efforts, and crowned the day with victory and honor. The conduct pursued by the members of the Newtown Barry Lodge upon this occasion, bears a strong resemblance to that of the "'Prentice boys" of Derry, when they closed the gates of that City against the foe. At Derry, the Mayor, Aldermen, Magistrates, and other chiefs of the protestant party, retired —they deemed it "madness" to contend against the overwhelming numbers of the Royal Army then before the City. But the "'Prentice Boys" had stouter hearts—they were "over-zealous" in the good cause—they ran to the City gates, slammed them in the face of their enemies, and loudly denied admission to the foe. The eye of heaven was upon them, and they triumphed! At Newtown Barry, the Orange Yeomanry, like the "'Prentice Boys," were deserted by the Royal officers then in command—the further defence of the Town was pronounced " a rash act," and the mere handful of "over-zealous Orangemen." were pronounced "fools and madmen." They persisted, however, and imitating their Fathers at Derry, they too slammed the doors of their houses in the face of their enemies, and continued by their noble daring the " *no surrender*" practice as of old! Providence blessed their efforts, and Newtown Barry was saved! Nor was this the only fruits of the victory ; for had the rebel forces succeeded in holding the Town, a junction would have been formed with the insurgents in the Counties of Carlow, Kilkenny and Kildare, and thus reinforced, the roads would have been opened to them, to have penetrated with overwhelming numbers, into the heart of the Kingdom.

On the same day, (June 1st, 1798,) that the Orangemen of Newtown Barry defeated the Rebels, and saved their country in one direction, their brethren at Gorey were not idle, or unsuccessful, in another.

Priest Murphy, of Ballycanow, as already mentioned, led his division of the Rebel army through Oulard and Ballycanow, to Ballymenane Hill, within two miles of Gorey, where they encamped, preparatory to the intended attack on the Town. This division of the Rebel forces halted as they passed through Ballycanow, and had Mass celebrated for them. Without waiting for the attack upon the Town, the little garrison of Gorey, consisting of the "Ballaghkeen Blazers," Captain White : the "Wingfield Yeomanry," Captain Gowan ; the "Camolin Cavalry," Lieutenant Smith ; the "Gorey Volunteers," Lieutenant Woodroofe, with 72 Infantry of the line under Captain Elliott, marched out to meet the enemy. The aggregate strength of the whole force was 392 rank and file, all "Orange Yeomanry," save 72. This gallant little force met and defeated the enemy, after a severe contest, in the immediate vicinity of Ballycanow. The battle raged with much fury for upwards of an hour, when Priest Murphy with his followers, were forced to retire, leaving 150 dead upon the field, and securing to the victorious little band two green standards, over 100 horses, with a large quantity of guns, pikes and provisions. Thus were the Rebels twice defeated upon that day, by the bravery of the "Orange Yeomanry."

Priest Murphy's defeat near Ballycanow, brought to his aid the whole force of the Rebel camp from Vinegar Hill, and by the junction thus formed, the united Rebel strength at Corragrewa, exceeded 20,000. On the 3rd of June, the garrison of Gorey was greatly strengthened. There arrived on that day General Loftus, and with him the following forces. The Dumbarton Fencibles, the Londonderry and Armagh Militia Battalions. The Light Companies of the Tyrone and Suffolk Regiments. A Detachment of the Antrim Militia. A portion of the Ancient Britons Fencible Cavalry, under Sir Watkin Wynne, and the Arklow Volunteer Yeomanry, Cavalry and Infantry. Thus reinforced, the garrison of Gorey amounted to from fifteen hundred to two thousand men. On the morning of Monday, the 4th of June, the Military were marched to attack the Rebel camp on Corragrewa. The left wing of the Royal forces, under the immediate command of General Loftus, and comprising the chief portions of the army, advanced along the open road leading direct from Gorey to Corragrewa; while the right wing, consisting of 200 Infantry with 3 guns, the Ancient Britons, and a few Corps of the "Orange Yeomanry," made a detour to the right, and advanced in the direction of Corragrewa, *via* Clough. This division of the Royal forces was a fatal error, and exhibited at once the incapacity of the commanding General. The Rebels, instead of waiting to receive the attack at Corragrewa, broke up their Camp, and advanced through Clough, direct upon Gorey. This was the route chosen for Colonel Walpole's division to march by. The Rebel scouts, observing the advance of Colonel Walpole, carried back the intelligence to Father John Murphy, who was in command; and by the Priest's orders, the Rebel forces concealed themselves behind deep ditches, at a place called Tubberneering, and calmly awaited the approach of the Royal forces. Colonel Walpole threw out no advanced guards, and was completely entrapped—his force was surprised and dispersed, and amongst the slain was the Colonel himself, who paid the forfeit of his life a penalty to his rashness and unmilitary conduct that day. General Loftus, who had still the main body of the army under his command unengaged, instead of attacking the enemy after the surprise and defeat of Colonel Walpole, marched to Carnew, in the County of Wicklow, and from thence to Hacketstown, in the County of Carlow.

The Rebels having now secured the possession of the Towns of Wexford, Enniscorthy, and Gorey, and nearly the whole County, burned and destroyed the property and dwellings of the Protestant proprietors ; and on the 5th of June, they issued a Proclamation declaring that "any one harbouring " Protestants, and not bringing them to the Camp, shall be shot, and have " his house burned."

Having so far described the progress of the second and third Divisions of the Rebel army : a short glance must now be taken at the proceedings of the first, commanded by Bagenal Harvey.

As already stated, Harvey's divisions marched from Three Rock Mountain, on the 31st of May, and took post on Carrigburn Hill on the 1st of June. They remained encamped on Carrigburn during the three first days of June, largely augmenting their strength on each day.   On the morning of the 4th, they broke up their camp at Carrigburn, and advanced to Corbet Hill, close to the Town of Ross, intending to commence the attack upon that Town, early on the following morning.   The garrison of Ross consisted of the following strength.   Detachments of the 5th and 9th Dragoons, Cap. tain Irvine.   Mid Lothian Fencible Cavalry, Lieut. Col. Sir James Fowlis. A detachment of the British Horse Artillery, Captain Thornhill.   The Fourth Flank Battalion, Lieut. Col. Hewitt.   Detachments of the Meath, Clare, and Donegal Militia Regiments.   Dublin County Militia, Col. Lord Mountjoy.   The Ross Yeomen Cavalry and Infantry, and some small parties from other hastily formed Volunteer bodies.   The whole force amounting to about 1500 men, commanded by General Johnson, with Major General Eustace second in command.

The town of Ross is of considerable extent ; it is in the County of Wex-ford, and is situated on the eastern bank of a large river bearing the same name.   The river is very deep, and a bridge was thrown over it by an American Architect, named Cox, in the year 1795.   The bridge is 730 feet in length, and is 40 feet broad.   The town itself is built at the foot of a very steep hill, and is wholly unfortified by any military works of engi-neering art.   The bridge over the Ross river, leads into the Counties of Kilkenny and Waterford, and opens the route directly into the south of Ireland.

On the 5th, General Johnson received a summons to surrender, from the Rebel Commander.   This document was couched in the following terms :

"Sir,—As a friend to humanity, I request you will surrender the Town of New Ross to the Wexford forces, now assembled against it.   Your resistance will but provoke rapine and plunder, to the ruin of the innocent.   Flushed with victory, the Wexford forces, now insurmountable and irrisistible, will not be controlled, if they meet with resistance."

"To prevent the total ruin of all property in the Town, I urge you to a speedy surrender—a surrender which you will be forced to in a few hours, with loss and bloodshed, as you are surrounded on all sides.   Your answer is required in two hours. Citizen Furlong delivers this letter, and will bring the answer."

" I am, &c. &c.

"B. B. HARVEY, M.G.

"Camp, Corbet Hill,

"½ past 3 o'clock, A.M. Tuesday, 5th June, 1798."

As the battle of Ross was one of the most severe that occurred during "the great Rebellion of 1798," a short account of it, as given by an Artillery Officer present, is here transcribed :

"About five in the morning of the 5th of June, the attack commenced. The Rebels advanced, driving before them all the black cattle they could collect, to disorder our ranks and protect themselves, which was in some measure prevented, by a few discharges of grape shot. The action was commenced by the Fourth Flank Battalion ; indeed such a close and well-directed fire I never before witnessed. At near seven o'clock, the Army began to retreat in all directions. I had the honour to command a six-pounder Field Piece. The Rebels pouring in like a flood, Artillery was called for, and human blood began to flow down the street. Though hundreds were blown to pieces by our discharges of grape-shot, yet thousands behind them, being intoxicated from drinking during the night, and void of fear, rushed upon us. The Cavalry were now ordered to charge, when a terrible carnage ensued. They were cut down like grass: but the Pikemen being called to the front, and our swords being too short to reach them, obliged the Horse to retreat, which put us in some confusion. We kept up the action till about half past eight, and it was maintained with such obstinancy on both sides, that it was doubtful who would keep the field. They then began to burn and destroy the Town,—it was on fire in many places in about fifteen minutes. By this time the Insurgents advanced as far as the Main Guard, where there was a most bloody conflict; but with the assistance of two ship guns placed in the street, we killed a great number of them, and beat them back for some time. The Dublin County Regiment, headed by their Colonel, Lord Mountjoy, now made another attack on the Rebels, and the action being revived in all quarters of the Town with double fury, many heroes fell, and among them the brave Mountjoy : this so exasperated his Regiment, that they fought like furies, and now indeed was the scene truly bloody. Our forces being for the third time overpowered, by the weight of such immense bodies pouring down upon us, we retreated beyond the bridge, when General Johnson galloping up, cried out with a loud voice— "Soldiers ! I will lay my bones this day in Ross ! Will you let me lie alone !" These words cheered up the men ; they "huzzad" and followed the General.

"Major Vesey, of the Dublin Militia, the next in command to Lord

Mountjoy, again led his men over the bridge, exhorting them to revenge for the loss of their Colonel. The whole brigade (except some few who fled to Waterford,) were now led on by the General—as brave a Commander as ever drew a sword,—and were determined to retake the Town, to conquer, or "lay their bones" there. Again we opened a tremendous fire on the Rebels, which was as fiercely returned. We retook the cannon which had been captured from the King's forces in a former engagement, and turned them on the enemy. The gun I had the honor to command being called to the Main Guard, shocking was it to see the dreadful carnage that was there. It continued for half an hour obstinate and bloody; the thundering of cannon shook the Town, and the windows were shivered to pieces by the concussion. I believe six hundred Rebels lay dead in the main street of the Town. They would often come within a few yards of the guns. One fellow ran up, and taking off his hat and wig, thrust them up the cannon's mouth the length of his arm, calling out to the rest, "*blood-anounds, my boys, come take her now! She's stopp'd! she's stopp'd!*" The action was doubtful and bloody from four in the morning to four in the evening, when they began to give way in all quarters, and shortly after fled in every direction, leaving behind them all their cannon, baggage, provisions, and several hogsheads of wine, whiskey, and brandy, &c. &c. It was past five before we finally routed them. The computation of their dead, was, as near as I can furnish it, 3,400 buried; 62 cart loads thrown into the river; 60 cart loads taken away by the Rebels. In their flight, several dead bodies were thrown into the houses which were on fire, and were there consumed, so that it was impossible to ascertain the numbers. But from every account I could learn, 7,000 Rebels lost their lives on that day! I know soldiers that fired 120 rounds of ball, and I fired 21 rounds of cannister shot, into masses of closely packed men in narrow streets! So you may think how great was the slaughter."

Such was the narative of an Artillery Officer, who was himself in the midst of the bloody scene. The loss of the King's Troops and Loyalists was very severe. On the news reaching Dublin, the Commander of the forces in Ireland, Lord Lake, addressed a letter to General Johnson, of which the following is a copy:

"DUBLIN, June 9th, 1798.

"MY DEAR GENERAL.—It is with the most extreme satisfaction, that I congratulate you on your late glorious victory over the Rebels; which has rendered such essential service to the country, and gained the applause of every one. Your report of the behaviour of the Officers and soldiers under your command, does them the greatest credit, and will, no doubt, meet with the entire approbation of his Majesty.

"If any thanks of mine can be thought worthy of their acceptance, I beg you to communicate them in the strongest manner possible ; and believe me with the greatest esteem and respect.

"Most truly yours,

"LAKE.

" Major General Johnson, &c."

Similar expressions of thanks and gratitude were conveyed, on the following day, to the gallant general, in a letter direct from His Excellency the Lord Lieutenant.

But the great battle and glorious victory, at Ross, was not the only event, which rendered the 5th of June, 1798, memorable in the annals of Wexford. On this same day, and while the battle yet raged, was the dark, dismal, and bloody tragedy of *"Scollabogue Barn"* enacted. As the disgusting butcheries here perpetrated, have received a world-wide celebrity, and as the particular details are but little known on the western side of the Atlantic, some of them may be here enumerated.

Scollabogue House, together with the estate attached, is in the County of Wexford, and is the property of Mr. King, a Protestant gentleman, and a magistrate of the County. A large number of the Protestants, young and old, male and female, who were found about their dwellings ; and who remained apparently unpartizan spectators of the horrid scenes by which they were surrounded, were made prisoners by Romish gangs, marched to Scollabogue, and there confined. A guard of 300 Rebels, under the command of Captain John Murphy, was appointed over them. Early in the day, one of the Rebels, who had fled from the battle at Ross, came galloping up to Scollabogue House, shouting out at the top of his voice, " Destroy the prisoners ! destroy the prisoners ! our friends are all cut off at Ross !" Captain Murphy said, it should not be done, without orders in writing from the General. In about an hour after, a second messenger arrived at Scollabogue, declaring that "their friends were all destroyed," and calling out to " murder the prisoners !" Captain Murphy again declared, that the prisoners should not be touched without written orders. In some time after, a third express arrived, crying out, " The Priest has sent orders to put all the prisoners to death !" Immediately the Rebel guards stripped off their coats, and deliberately prepared for the bloody tragedy which followed ! They first said prayers, then crossing and blessing themselves in the usual manner, they formed themselves into two divisions ; one to massacre those in the dwelling-house ; the other, those confined in the barn. The first party dragged out thirty-seven from the dwelling-house, and were employed in shooting and piking them ; while the other party surrounded the barn, placed ladders against the walls to stand on, (it was built of stone,) and set it on fire in every direction. The unfortunate Protestant women within, screamed aloud for mercy ; their wailings were mixed with the cries of the children, and the men, pressing

forward as a last effort for life, caught hold of the back door, and endea
voured to force their way out. Their Romish guards observing this, cut
and mangled with pikes all that appeared. At length the weight from the
people from behind, pressing upon their mangled friends in front, forced
the door to give way. But this afforded no relief; for as any one attempted to escape, through the opening thus made, he was instantly
pierced by a number of pikemen, and immediate death terminated his
sufferings. While this cruel scene was being enacted, numbers of the
Rebel guards were engaged in firing in upon the unfortunate sufferers !
This, though not intended as such, was really a mercy, for it put a more
sudden period to their miseries ; or if it was intended to give a more
speedy termination to their sufferings, then how applicable are the words
of Holy Writ, that "the tender mercies of the wicked are cruel !"
Amongst the unfortunate inmates of the barn, was the widow of one of
the North Cork Militia, killed at the battle of Oulard. The poor woman,
finding no way of escape for herself, thought, if possible, to save her child.
She wrapt her cloak about the child, and threw it out of the barn. One
of the sanguinary pikemen observing this, thrust his blood-stained weapon
into the helpless babe, and raising it, like a sheaf of oats, on the end of
his pike, exclaimed aloud, "damn you, you little heretic, get in there,"
and cast it back into the burning elements within the walls ! Another
child, about two years old, crept unperceived under one corner of a door ;
it was soon after observed by a bloody pikeman, who with a savage yell
speedily transfixed the body of the little innocent to the earth ! The
whole number of the prisoners confined at Scollabogue, was two hundred
and twenty four ; twenty of whom were women and children. Out of the
entire number, three only escaped, namely Richard Grandy, Loftus
Frizzel, and Benjamin Lett. Thirty-seven were shot, and one hundred
and eighty-four burned to death ! This was the memorable event at
"*Scollabogue Barn*," the 5th of June, 1798 !

The names of 105 of the sufferers having been ascertained by the author,
they are here transcribed for the information of posterity :

Bell, Thomas.	Kelly, Thomas.
Boyce, Samuel.	Lewis, Richard.
Boyce, George.	Moran, John.
Bassit, Walter.	Macdonald, Thomas.
Box, James.	Monk, Edmund.
Box, Joshua.	Monk, Francis.
Byron, Edward.	Miller, Robert.
Brophy, John.	Neil, William.
Cottom, Samuel.	Neif, Daniel.
Cottom, John.	Presly, David.
Carew, George.	Presly, James.

Cruise, David.
Cruise, George.
Cooke, Robert.
Caroline, James.
Crompton, Samuel.
Chamley, John.
Duffield, John.
Duffield, James.
Dalton, John.
Dobbyn, Patrick, 1st.
Dobbyn, Patrick, 2nd.
Dobbyn, Patrick, 3rd.
Dobbyn, Henry.
Dobbyn, James.
Dobbyn, William.
Davis, Richard.
Daly, William.
Daly, James.
Daly, Sarah.
Eakins, William.
Eakins, Thomas.
Eakins, John.
English, John.
Field, Owen.
Fannin, William.
Finley, Holland.
Gifford, Millward.
Gray, Andrew.
Gray, William.
George, John.
Graham, James.
Graham, George.
Hornick, Philip.
Hogan, William.
Horton, John.
Hogan, James.
Hannard, Joshua.
Hannard, Mary.
Hurley, Edward.
Jones, Samuel.
John, John.
Johnson, William.

Presly, Anne.
Parslow, Thomas.
Parslow, John.
Power, James.
Power, Thomas.
Power, Oliver.
Power, James, Junr.
Pierson, John.
Pyne, William.
Prendergast, Patrick.
Reason, Henry.
Restrick, Edward.
Ryan, William.
Ryan, Eleanor.
Ryan, Mary.
Reel, William.
Rorke, Henry.
Rillagh, Edward.
Richards, Richard.
Sleator, Thomas.
Simmons, Samuel.
Simmons, William.
Sly, Edward.
Sly, William.
Smythe, George.
Shee, Thomas.
Thornton, Edward.
Turner, Samuel.
Taylor, Robert.
Tweedy, John.
Tweedy, William.
Trimble, John.
Thomas, Anne.
Usher, Mary.
Vaughan, Miles.
Whitney, John.
Whitney, Thomas.
Wilcock, John.
Wade, James.
Williams, Margaret.
Younge, Elizabeth.

The Rebel Army broke up its camp at Carrigburn Hill, on the 7th of

June, and marched to Slievequilter, on which mountain they established
their Head Quarters. Here they deposed Bagneal Harvey from the command, and installed Priest Roche of Poulpearsey, (formerly of Gorey,) to
that post. The zeal of the Priests, to fan the flame of rebellion amongst
their flocks was proved in hundreds of instances, at the trials which
followed the rebellion. The gross superstitions and delusions practised ;
were also established in numerous cases. Here are a few ; they must serve
as specimens of the remainder. Priest Murphy of Bannow addressed them
as follows :

" Brethren, you see you are victorious every where—that the balls of the
Heretics fly about you without hurting you—that few of you have fallen, while
thousands of the Heretics are dead—and the few that have fallen, was for devia-
ting from our cause, and want of faith—that this visibly is the Work of God, who
is determined that the Heretics, who have reigned upwards of one hundred years,
should now be extirpated, and the true Catholic Religion be established!"
Their Commander-in-Chief, Priest Roche, collected several bullets, which he
assured them he had caught in the heat of action, at the battle of Ross ! He also
distributed thousands of what he called " Gospels," which were hung round the
neck, suspended by a piece of tape, and which were pronounced to be proof
against heretical artillery ! The following is a copy of one of those " Gospels ' "
which was taken from off the neck of Captain John Hay, one of the Rebel Chiefs,
who was tried and executed at Wexford, after that Town had been re-taken by the
Royal forces.

INRI

" In the　　　　　　✝　　　　　*And of the*
Name of　　　　　　　　　　　　*Blessed*
God,　　　　I H S.　　　　　*Virgin.*

" No Gun, Pistol, Sword, or any other offensive Weapon, can hurt, or otherwise
" injure the person who has this Paper in his possession ; and it is earnestly
" recommended to all Women with child to carry it, as it will be found an infal-
" lible preservation against fatality of child-bed.

" No. 7,601."   Roche."

The charge for these " Gospels " was sixpence each.

To show that the gross superstitions and infamous delusions, practised
by Priests of the Romish Church in Ireland in 1798, are continued to the
present day, and are just as much believed in by their followers in Canada
as in Ireland ; we will only refer to the " Canadian Freeman " Newspaper,
of the 25th of November 1859, (just two months ago.) The Freeman is
edited by Mr. J. D. Moylan, of Toronto, is the reputed organ of Mr.
Thomas D'Arcy Mc'Gee, M.P.P. and the exponent of Roman Catholic
sentiment in Upper Canada. This paper contains under the Editorial
head, what purports to be an account of the " Consecration of the Right
Rev. John J. Lynch, D.D. The Procession. The Ceremony and the

Sermon. Vespers, &c. An interesting Catholic Relic and its history."
Independent of some fifty or sixty Roman Catholic Priests, and other
Authorities in that Church, and some four or five thousand of the Laity ;
there were ten Prelates present, assisting in the ceremony : viz : the
Roman Catholic Bishops of Toronto, Buffalo, Hamilton, Quebec, Dubuque,
Brooklyn, Chicago, Bytown, London and Kingston. After very full and
minute descriptions of the " Cathedral—the Bishops and Clergy—the Ceremony—and the Sermon "—the Editor proceeds to describe the " interesting Catholic Relic," and to give its " History;" which is said to be based
upon the authority of Dr. Wilson, author of the Archæology of Scotland.
Here are the words, as copied from the *Freeman :*

"The Crozier used by his Lordship, Bishop de Charbonnel, on Sunday, (20th
November, 1859,) is a rare and highly interesting relic of old Catholic times,
known among antiquarians as the *Crozier of St. Fillan.* There are many
historic recollections of the most interesting character connected with this remarkable Relic, which we would be anxious to lay before our readers, if our
space would permit. For the present, we shall merely say, that the Crozier, without any doubt, belonged to a very remote period. The Saint, whose name the
Crozier bears, lived in the seventh century, and is honoured in our calendar on
the 9th of January. It is, therefore, a matter of uncertainty, whether the Crozier is so called from its having been used by St. Fillan; or, from its having at
one time contained the relics of the Saint. Be this as it may, certain it is, that
extraordinary powers, and miraculous effects, have been attributed to the Crozier,
and have been traditionally handed down, not alone by its custodiers, but by
many who lived in the neighbourhood where it had been preserved during so
many centuries. It has been for some years in this country, in the possession of
the descendants of the family, to whom it is said to have been given by King
Robert Bruce himself, on the field of Bannockburn. Recently, it was brought by
the Hon. Malcolm Cameron to this city, with the view of inducing the Canadian
Institute to purchase it from its present owner, Mr. Alexander Dewar, of Arran.
It came to the knowledge of W. J. Macdonell, Esq., that this remarkable Catholic
Relic was in Toronto. He applied to the guardian of it, to allow of its being
used in the consecration of Bishop Lynch. The request was courteously complied
with. And thus, after the lapse of, perhaps, more than five hundred years, the
Crozier, which is recorded in the *Acta Sanctorum* to have had great influence in
deciding the fate of Scotland, at Bannockburn, has once more—but for once only
—been converted to its legitimate use by a Catholic Prelate, in the highest exercise of his Episcopal office. The virtues ascribed to the Crozier of St. Fillan, in
his native District, were of a most varied description. It was regarded as *an
effectual cure for Fever,* by administering, or sprinkling with water in which it
had been dipped ; and was no less infallible in cases of *Scrofula, or the King's
evil,* by being rubbed on the affected parts. It was serviceable also as *a Charm*
for the discovery and restoration of *Stolen Cattle,* and generally in all cases of
disease of such."

What is to be thought of a people, who by their Bishops, Priests and Publishers, send forth such trash to the world in the present age ?

But we must return to "the great Rebellion of 1798."

On the 10th of June, the Division of the Rebel Army under the immediate command of Priest Roche, marched from Slievequilter to Lacken Hill, within two miles of Ross ; and on the morning of the 12th, a large column proceeded from the Camp at Lacken, to attack the town of Borris, in the County of Carlow. The defence of Borris was entrusted solely to the members of the Orange Lodge, which had quite recently been formed at that place, aided by a detachment of about 20 men of the Donegal Militia. Borris House, the residence of Walter Kavanagh, Esq., immediately adjoining the town, was used by "the Orange Yeomanry," and the few Donegal men present, as a barracks. Taylor states in his History [page 77,] that "nothing could surpass the determined gallantry of these heroes." Though the town was fired in several places, they held the house against all the force that could be brought against them, and they ultimately beat off their assailants and saved the place. All honor to the Orange Yeomanry of Borris.

We must now leave Father Roche's Division of the Rebel Army on Lacken Hill ; and proceed to a sketch of the proceedings of the other Grand Division, which we parted in scattered groups between Wexford, Vinegar Hill and Gorey.

At Wexford, a *Grand National Committee* was organized, and all Protestants in the town and surrounding country, who had not escaped when the Royal Army retired, were seized and cast into prison. Here they were regularly visited by the priests, urged to conform to the Roman Catholic Church, and to receive baptism at the hands of the Romish Clergy. Many of them pretended conversion, and were baptized by the Priests and Friars, to save death. After baptism, they received "*protections,*" which ran thus :

" Mr. A. B., has complied with every condition required of him, and therefore is to be stopped by no man.

REV. BRYAN MURPHY.

June 4th, 1798."

Here is the copy of another :

"I hereby certify that A. B., of C., in Parish of D., has done his duty, and proved himself a Catholic.

F. JOHN BROE."

Wexford, June 21st, 1798."

Father Broe was a Friar, and very active in the conversion and baptism of the "*Heretics.*" There were six Priests of the name of Murphy, active participants in the rebellion of 1798, namely, Michael of Ballycanow, John of Bolavogue, Eadmus of Wexford, Edward of Bannow,

James of Bargy, and Bryan of Taghmon. Very many of the Protestant prisoners were taken out, shot and piked to death in Wexford, during the period the town remained in possession of the Rebels. A detail of the particulars would be too prolix for this work.

Gorey is a large town, within three miles of Mount Nebo, (the birth-place of the writer.) At this point the Rebels had formed an immense camp ; and from it they sent out scouring parties into all parts of the ad-joining country, destroying the houses and property of Protestants, and arresting and dragging to Gorey, all "Heretics" whom they could dis-cover. These, without reference to age or sex, they confined in a large room over the Market House. Among the old infirm men, crammed into this prison, were William Bryant of Coolook, aged over 70, and William Atkins of Curraclough, aged over 80 years. The condition of the poor Protestants was most pitiable. Day after day, the men were torn from the arms of their beloved wives and children, or distracted mothers and sisters, and murdered in their presence. The widow Carley, near Castle-bridge, and the widow Grindley, near Kilmuckridge, were woeful witnesses of these melancholy atrocities.

Very early in the morning of the 9th of June, Masses were celebrated by the priests in all parts of the Camp at Gorey ; immediately after which the whole force, 34,000 strong, was marched off to attack Arklow, with a view of opening the direct road to Dublin, and, having formed a junction with the Rebels of Wicklow and Kildare, assailing the Metropolis of the Kingdom.

Arklow is a seaport town, in the County of Wicklow, built at the outlet into the Ocean of the celebrated River "*Ovoca,*" about 9 miles west of Gorey, and about 35 miles east of Dublin. A magnificent Bridge, of eighteen arches spans the Ovoca, at this place. When attacked on the 9th of June, the garrison of Arklow consisted of the following : Detachments of the 5th and 9th Dragoons. The Ancient British Fencible Cavalry. A small Detachment of the Royal Irish Artillery. The Durham Fencible Infantry. The Dumbarton and Cavan Militia Regiments. Detachments of the Armagh, Antrim, North Cork and Londonderry Militia Battalions ; together with seven Corps of Orange Yeomanry, viz: the North and South Arklow, the Camolin, Wingfield, Gorey, Coolgreny and Casteltown. Major General Needham was in command. If his energy was not conspicuous, his plan of defence was judicious. The Cavan Militia, called the "*Black Reds,*" to which were attached the various Orange Lodges, that had been organised into volunteer Infantry Corps, were placed under the command of Colonel Maxwell (afterwards Lord Farnham,) and extended in a line from the centre of the Town to the Fishery, with the open Sea on their left flank. On the right, the Durham Fencibles were drawn up, with two Field Pieces, and atttched to them, were the Detachments from the Ar-

magh and other Regiments ; the whole under the command of Colonel
Skerret.   The Dragoon Detachments and Yeoman Cavalry, under the
command of Captain Gowan, were stationed near the Bridge, so as to guard
the Dublin road, and to operate upon either Flank of the Army, as occasion
might require.   The Loyalists who had fled to Arklow for shelter, and who
were very numerous, were stationed in the Barrack.   The Dumbartons,
who formed the advance picquets, were speedily driven in by the advancing
tide of the Rebel horde.   They fell back upon the Durhams and Armagh.
The Rebels fired the town in many places, intending thereby to annoy the
Army and drive them from the positions they occupied.   The wind, however, shortly changed, and the flames and smoke were driven back in the
face of the assailants.   The Rebels pressed on their main forces against
the Durhams, in order, if possible, to turn the left flank ; but Colonel
Skerret maintained his position with unyielding courage.   A large column
of the enemy sought to gain the lower end of the Town by the beach road ;
but here they were bravely confronted by the Cavan " *Black Reds*," and
being charged by the Cavalry Brigade, led by Sir Watkin Wynne, they
were driven back with loss at this point.   They next attempted to force an
entrance near the centre of the Town ; but here too, they were met and
repulsed.   They then tried to enter by the Ovoca ; but here they were met
by the Yeomen Cavalry, under Captain Gowan, and a fearful havoc made
amongst them.   In this encounter, the Captain had the second finger of
his left hand shot away.   His horse was also shot.   The Rebels, thus repulsed in all their attacks, were retiring, but were again rallied by Priest
Murphy of Ballycanow.   In the charge led by this impetuous Ecclesiastic,
he met his death from a Cannister shot, which so disheartened his followers
that they wavered and gave way.   The brunt of the action was borne by Colonel Skerrit's division ; and that gallant Officer, with Colonel Maxwell,
were brilliant examples of steady courage and unyielding determination.
The engagement continued from half past four o' clock till half past eight,
when the Rebels were forced back and retired upon Gorey.   The Arklow
garrison stood to their arms during the night, expecting a renewal of the
attack.

Lord Mountnorris, on viewing the scene of action the following morning discovered the body of the perfidious Priest Murphy of Ballycanow,
who had so often misled his Lordship, and who had so long attempted to
deceive the Country by professions of loyalty.   The *liberal* Lord was highly exasperated, ordered his head to be struck off, and his body to be cast
into a house that was then burning, exclaiming at the time; " let his body
go where his soul is "!   The Priest frequently declared during the battle, to
his deluded followers, that he could catch the bullets, and ward them off at
pleasure.   Unfortunately for himself, he *caught a bullet !*   The Rebel forces,
unpursued by the Army, retired back to their Camp at Gorey.   Here they

committed all kinds of violence and excess, particularly against the Protestant Church of the Town.   They smashed the windows, tore the Prayer
Books to shreds, made saddles of the Bibles and rode upon them, and
conducted two of their Protestant prisoners into the aisle of the building,
and there piked them to death !   They remained in possession of Gorey till
the 19th of June, when they marched to join the Rebel Head Quarters,
established at Vinegar Hill ; at which point, the whole forces of the enemy
were ordered to concentrate.   Here they planted the "*Tree of Liberty,*"
with shouts of " *Vive la Republique,*" and " *Erin go Bragh ;*" and here
the work of blood continued, as of daily practice, for twenty-five consecutive
days !   One authority, the Rev. George Taylor, of Ballywalter, says : " one
" day they were so diabolical as to murder all the Protestants they had ;
" and not satisfied with this, they sent to Wexford for more ; and every
" day parties ranged the Country, dragging forth all they could find, to
" satiate their thirst for blood.   The scarcer they grew, the longer the
" poor victims were kept in torment.   On the first of June, a Protestant,
" who afterwards escaped, by the interposition of a Rebel Captain, being
" in an old Wind Mill, (which formed the condemned cell of the unfortu-
" nate prisoners,) saw a man sitting on the ground, with only a piece of
" blanket covering him ; his eyes were picked out of their sockets, his
" tongue cut out, his head and body swelled to an enormous degree, and
" covered with ulcers.   Not thinking he was alive, till the poor sufferer
" gave a heart-piercing groan, the prisoner was startled, and exclaimed,
" *Good God ! what miserable object is that !*" He was answered by one of
" the Guards, that " *he was under slow punishment !*" This was verified
" upon oath.   None of the Rebels were so blood-thirsty as those who were
" most regular in their attendance on the ordinances of their religion.
" The drunken and careless sort were observed to have the greatest share
" of good nature.   After immolating the victims destined for that
" day, a large Tub of water was brought, which one of the Priests imme-
" diately blessed ; ordering the Rebels to kneel round about.   He, with a
" whisk or broom, then sprinkled them with the water, repeating at the
" same time, the words of the Psalmist again and again, "*Thou shalt purge
" me with hyssop, and I shall be clean : Thou shalt wash me, and I shall be
" whiter than snow.*" Psalms Chap. 51. Verse 7."   In addition to the
evidence of the Rev. Mr. Taylor, (himself one of the captives,) we add
but one more, whose veracity is unimpeachable.   The testimony of this
respected gentleman is given in the following : " When I came to the
" prison door, I was seized by the breast, and thrown amongst the rest of
" the prisoners, where I remained in the deepest sorrow and affliction, be-
" lieving death to be inevitable.   Seeing a man in the prison who had been
" piked the evening before, with signs of life, (he had probably been left
" for dead,) his coat off, his shirt and breeches covered with cakes of blood,

"and his cheeks full of holes, which had been made with the dreadful
"pikes, I drew near and enquired what had happened to him? He told
"me he had been piked the evening before, but had crept in from among
"the dead, who lay before the door, to avoid the heat of the Sun. Look-
"ing out, I saw the Rebels leading up a prisoner, whom they soon after
"shot. Then looking out at the opposite door, I saw, as nearly as I can
"judge, between thirty and forty lying dead, at about three yards distance,
"some of whom I knew, having been in confinement with me, and one
"of them my Brother-in-law. Soon after, we were ordered by the guard
"to kneel down, and each of us to be brought out in turn. Three Rebels
"stood at the door, with pistols in their hands, and as the prisoners were
"brought out and placed upon their knees, they were shot and thrown
"among the dead. Three of them, expecting that they should escape
"death, by renouncing the Protestant religion, and turning Papists,
"called for the Priest. Father John Murphy immediately arrived, and
"laying his hand on their head, repeated some prayers in Latin, I being
"the next, was brought to the door ; a Rebel calling me by name, caught
"the attention of one of the Captains, whose namesake I happened to be ;
"this was fortunate for me, as by this circumstance my life was providen-
"tially spared. A man named Thornton, a resident of Wexford, was shot
"at that instant. The next man who was brought out, broke through the
"crowd, and ran about seventeen perches, when he was met by a Rebel,
"who with a scythe, severed his head from his body, so that it hung down
"upon his breast! In an instant several pikes were fastened in him, and I
"saw him no more. The Priest (Father John Murphy,) walked away as
"unconcerned as if no murder had taken place. Out of twenty-seven
"prisoners then present, only three escaped, viz : Kendrick, who lived near
"Clondau ; William Bennett, who lived near Enniscorthy ; and myself."
From the testimony of other witnesses, it appears that each day, as the
Protestant victims grew scarce, they were kept longer in torment before
despatching them. Mr. Whitney testifies, that "George Stacy and
"several other prisoners, were scourged with lashes made of brass wire,
"and twisted as whip-cord," previous to their being piked. He also testifies that "piking them, but not mortally, was frequently done, for the
"purpose of keeping them in misery. Sometimes (he adds,) they chose a
"stone, with one end small and the other large, and putting the small end
"into the mouth of the expiring victim, would stamp on it with the heel
"of the shoe, till the jaws were extended to the utmost." This piece of
barbarity they perpetrated upon a relative of the writer, Henry Hatton,
Esq. the Portrieve of Enniscorthy. Not less than four hundred Protestants were massacred at Vinegar Hill. From this bloody mountain, parties were sent out to scour the Country in all directions, to bring in the
Protestants to be executed in the Camp. Some of the very aged and

decrepid, were despatched when taken at their own residences. Edward Hawkins, Esq., of Ballycoursey, upwards of sixty years old, and one of the most kind-hearted, amiable and benevolent of men; may be classed in the latter category.

During the period these sanguinary atrocities were being committed at Vinegar Hill, the Royal Forces at Ross and Arklow, were rapidly augmenting. General Johnson was strengthened at Ross, by the arrival of the gallant Sir John Moore (the subsequent Hero of Corunna,) having under his command three splendid Battalions of the Foot Guards, the Roscommon Militia, and the Cheshire Fencible Infantry, and Hompesch's Hussars. These additions, brought up the effective force of the garrison of Ross to seven thousand rank and file. On the 19th of June, General Johnson marched out of Ross, drove the Rebels from Lacken Hill, and took possession of the camp which they had previously occupied at that place. The Rebels retreated from Lacken Hill to the Three Rocks, near Wexford.

On the following day, General Johnson was further strengthened by the arrival of effective reinforcements, ordered up from Duncannon Fort, consisting of strong detachments from the 2nd, the 29th, and the 60th Regiments of the line under the command of Lord Dalhousie. A Brigade, twelve or fifteen hundred strong, was placed under the command of General Moore, and ordered to proceed in the direction of Fookes' Mill, to Long Grage, near Taghmon. Here the General encountered the Rebels from the Three Rocks, about six thousand strong, under the immediate command of Priest Roche. After a severe struggle, in which Major Daniel of the 41st Regiment, and Lieutenant Greene of the Dublin County Militia, were killed, the Rebels were defeated and fled, some to Wexford but the greater part to the camp of Vinegar Hill.

On the same day that General Johnson's Division left Ross, to advance against the enemy posted on Lacken Hill, the Division under General Needham at Arklow, amounting to about three thousand men, were directed to advance against the enemy, then posted at Gorey. The object of these movements was to concentrate the enemy, and force them to a general and decisive engagement. On the approach of General Needham's Division, the Rebel forces at Gorey, abandoned that Town, and retired to Corragrewa Hill, where they encamped for the night ; and on the following day, retired still further, and united with the main body at Enniscorthy and Vinegar Hill. On the following morning, General Needham advanced from Gorey to Oulard, where he established his head quarters for the night. By these movements, Lieutenant General Lord Lake, then commanding-in-chief in Ireland, succeeded in uniting the whole Rebel strength at Vinegar Hill, (a very strong post certainly,) and of surrounding their position, by the whole available force then at his command.

Vinegar Hill was now the only post of importance occupied by the Rebels

—here was seated the head and heart of the insurrection—and from this focus and head quarters, all orders were issued; all commands obeyed. To wave the British ensign on Vinegar Hill, was to crush the heart of the insurrection. The Hill overhangs the large Town of Enniscorthy, its base is washed by the River Slaney, and rises like a cone, from the table land beneath; its approach on every side is steep and precipitous. The Rebels believed the position impregnable, nor did they believe, till the 21st of June, that all the forces in the British Isles could dislodge them from it.

On the evening of the 20th two columns of the British forces, under the command of Generals Johnson and Eustace, advanced from the direction of Ross and Taghmon, and encamped to the right, about a mile distant from the Hill. Shortly after another column, under the command of Lieutenant General Dundas, appeared on the left of the Slaney, and encamped about two miles from the Hill. General Dundas was supported on the right, by a third column, which had approached from the Carlow side, under the command of Major General Sir James Duff. During the night, General Needham's Division arrived on the opposite side of the Hill, and encamped near Saulsborough. The British strength united around Vinegar Hill, on the morning of the 21st of June, 1798, exceeded fifteen thousand men; some of them "the flower of the army," and all animated by the noblest feelings of patriotism, loyalty and courage. Lieutenant General Lord Lake, was present, and in command. The action commenced at half past five in the morning, and ere "the sun had crossed the yard arm," (to use a nautical phrase,) the British standard floated upon the loftiest pinnacle of blood-stained Vinegar Hill! The slaughter in the Rebel ranks was not so great as might have been expected, seeing how completely they were hemmed in. This was owing to a space left unoccupied on the Dublin side of the Hill, which had been assigned to General Needham's Division, and which has since borne the familiar appellation of "*Needham's Gap!*" Through this opening the main body of the Rebel force escaped. This decisive victory, effectually broke the heart of the Rebellion, and drove the Rebels from all their strongholds in the County of Wexford.

Having already noticed the principal events at *Scollabogue Barn* and at *Vinegar Hill*, it remains yet to notice *Wexford Bridge;* and so close our brief epitome of the leading incidents of "the great Rebellion of 1798."

While the important events just referred to, were being transacted at Vineger Hill, Wexford was a prey to the most barbarous cruelties. A Methodist Clergyman, one of the unfortunate prisoners, who, through God's mercy was spared, has left of record the following description of the Wexford tragedies.

" On the 19th of June, the Protestants in Wexford received the heart " rending intelligence, that all the prisoners were to be murdered the next " day. That night also, one of them, while sitting alone in silent sorrow, " heard the *death bell* toll as loud as she had everheard it, and much more

" awful. On the following morning, the never-to-be forgotten 20th of
" June, Thomas Dixon (the Rebel Governor of the Town,) rode to the
" gaol door, and swore that not a prisoner should be alive against sunset.
" He next rode into the street, repeating the same with horrid impreca-
" tions, adding, that "*not a soul should be left to tell the tale!*" Good
" God! how shall I proceed? Neither tongue nor pen can describe the
" dismal aspect of that melancholy day—a day in which the sun did not
" so much as glimmer through the frowning heavens. The Town Bell
" rung, and the drums beat to arms, to assemble the Rebels, for the pur-
" pose of joining those at the Three Rocks, in order to march against
" General Moore's Brigade.   In the evening Dixon assembled the murder-
" ing band, and immediately hoisted that harbinger of destruction, the
" *Black Flag*; which had on one side a *bloody cross*, and on the other, the
" intitials M. W. S. that is "*murder without sin*," signifying that it was
" no sin to murder a Protestant. Having paraded for some time, to give
" more solemnity to the scene, the poor Protestants, who were confined in
" the Gaol and in the Prison Ship, (of which number I was one,) were led
" forth to the slaughter! They were conducted to the Bridge under a
" strong guard of merciless furies; piked to death, with every circum-
" stance of barbarous cruelty, and then flung into the Slaney, to make
" room for more! While this work of blood was going on, a Rebel Cap-
" tain, being shocked at the piteous cries of the poor victims, and possess-
" ing some feeling of humanity, ran to the Romish Bishop, who was then
" drinking wine with the utmost composure, after his dinner; and know-
" ing he could at once stop the massacre, entreated of him "*for the mercy
" of Jesus*," to come and save the prisoners! The Bishop coolly replied
" that "*it was no affair of his*," and requested the Captain "*would
" sit down and take a glass of wine*," adding that "*the people must be
" gratified!*" The Captain, however, indignantly refused the invitation,
" and, filled with abhorrence and distress of mind, walked silently away.
" After this, the sanguinary Pike-men continued butchering the poor
" Protestants on the Bridge. Some they perforated in parts of the body
" not mortal, to increase and prolong the torture; others they would raise
" aloft on their pikes; and while the suffering victim writhed in the extreme
" of agony, his blood streaming down the handles of their pikes, they
" exulted round him with savage joy. In the midst of this terrific scene,
" General Roche galloped up in great haste, and commanded the drums to
" beat to arms, declaring that "*Vinegar Hill was nearly surrounded by
" the King's Troops*," and that "*all should repair to Camp, as reinforce-
" ments were wanting.*" This express had a wonderful effect: the assas-
" sins instantly closed the bloody scene, and fled in all directions, leaving
" three of the prisoners on their knees, namely; William Hamilton,
" William Connor, and Charles Jackson. Some of the Rebel Guards

" returned soon after, and conveyed the prisoners back to the Gaol, who
" had still continued on their knees, without making the least effort to
" escape, being stupified with terror.   Dixon soon returning, evinced that
" his thirst for Protestant blood was not yet satisfied.   He ordered out the
" remainder of the prisoners from the gaol and Prison Ship, the greater
" part of whom were tortured and put to death on the Bridge, in like
" manner as the former.   He then proceeded to the Market House, and
" having fixed his vulture eye on others, had them dragged to the fatal
" Bridge, for execution.   After butchering these, a lot of ten more was
" brought forth, and barbarously murdered, after the like fashion as the
" former.   The third time they took out eighteen, and while on the Bridge,
" engaged in piking them, " Dick Monk " rode into Town from Vinegar
" Hill, with his shoes and stockings off, and shouting " *Damn your souls*
" *you vagabonds, why don't you go out and meet the enemy that are coming*
" *in, and not be murdering thus in cold blood ?*"   Some Protestant women
" followed him, and asked him, " *What news ?*"   He replied, "*bad news*
" *enough ; the King's forces are encamped around Vinegar Hill.*"   He then
" rode towards the Convent.   Shortly after, Priest Corrin was seen running
" towards the Bridge.   There were six of the poor Protestants slaughtered,
" out of the last party that had been taken down, before he arrived ;
" namely ; Philip Bacon, Samual Gordon, William Stedman, Thomas
" Rigly, James Dowzard, and Thomas Shaw, and it was with great diffi-
" culty he prevailed upon them to spare the rest.   The massacre of that
" day, ceased about eight o'clock in the evening.   Out of forty-eight
" prisoners confined in the Market House, nineteen only escaped, one of
" whom is the relator of this narrative.   Their names were,

Bavistor, Joseph.	Mackay, John.
Combes, John.	Mackay, Robert.
Fenlon, Matthew.	Martin, Sandwith.
Hamilton, James.	McCoy, Francis.
Harris, William.	Patchell, James.
Judd, Peter.	Sheppard, William.
Kelly, Matthew.	Styles, Robert.
Kelly, William.	Taylor, George.
Kennedy, William.	Warren, Benjamin.
Kendrick, John.	

" The very awful appearance of this evening, and the bloody scenes of
" the day, alarmed the remaining Protestants, and terrified them beyond de-
" scription ; for the Rebels declared openly, that they would put every
" Protestant, man, woman, and child, to the sword, on the following
" morning.   On the 21st, when the fugitives arrived from Vinegar Hill,
" some were for putting all the prisoners to death ; others for evacuating

" the Town ; and a third party were for fighting to the last. General Moore
" was now on his march from Taghmon ; and Generals Dundas, Duff
" and Loftus, were approaching through Enniscorthy ; and General Need-
" ham through Oulard, to surround Wexford by land ; while eight frigates
" with some gun boats, were riding outside the Harbour. The Rebel Lead-
" ers now saw themselves in a very critical situation ; and being convinced
" that they could not keep the Town, they liberated Lord Kingsborough
" and the other Officers who were prisoners, and sent one of them to propose
" a surrender. The terms offered were as follows : *To deliver up the Town
" of Wexford without opposition; lay down their arms and return to their
" allegiance ; provided their persons and properties were guaranteed by the
" Commanding Officer ; and to use every influence in their power to induce
" the people of the County at large to return to their allegiance also.*" To
" these proposals, General Lake sent the following reply :—" *Lieutenant-
" General Lake cannot attend to any terms offered by Rebels in arms against
" their Sovereign. Whilst they continue so he must use the force entrusted to
" him with the utmost energy for their destruction. To the deluded multitude
" he promises pardon, on their delivering into his hands their leaders, surren-
" dering their arms, and returning with sincerity to their allegiance.*" ·
" After this embassy, General Priest Roche endeavoured to persuade the
" Rebels to go out and meet the Army that was advancing towards the
" town, telling them "*it was better and more honorable for them to fight
" to the last than suffer themselves to be cut in pieces by the King's forces.*"
" All his entreaties were in vain ; they absolutely refused to go on any
" account. The Popish Bishop then ordered them all to kneel down till
" he would give them his benediction ; and in about half an hour there-
" after, the drums beat a retreat. General Roche and his men fled to
" Killinie, in the Barony of Forth, where they were to encamp that
" night, and early next morning to move on to the borders of the County
" of Kilkenny. Perry and his men fled over the Bridge towards Kil-
" muckridge. General Moore's Brigade arrived at the Windmill Hill,
" above Wexford, about five o'clock in the evening, and sent in a Detach-
" ment of two Companies of the Queen's Royals to take possession of the
" garrison. Captain Boyd, commanding the Wexford Yeoman Cavalry,
" with a few of his Troop, were the first that appeared. They came,
" (amidst innumerable blessings,) galloping up to the Gaol door, to see
" the poor prisoners. Many a tear was shed upon this happy occasion
" Description fails in attempting to set forth the emotions which arose in
" the breasts of the poor Protestants who had been doomed to destruction.
" The entrance of the army was peculiarly striking ; for instead of rushing
" in with all the violence of enraged men, as might have been expected,
" they marched along in such solemnity and silent grandeur that not a
" whisper was to be heard through all the ranks. Many wept with joy

" to see their deliverers, who soon opened the prison doors and " set the
" captives free." Thus was the Town of Wexford recovered from
" Popery's persecuting reign, on the 21st of June, 1798, after being in
" possession of the Rebels twenty-three days. Had the army arrived a
" day sooner, they would have saved the lives of ninety-seven Protestant
" victims, who were cruelly butchered on the Bridge—martyrs to con-
" science and Britain."

Thus closed the inhuman butchery at the Bloody Bridge of Wexford.

The following day, Friday, the 22nd of June, was blackened with deeds
just as atrocious as those which dyed the waters of the Slaney, at Wexford.
One division of the Rebel army, as already mentioned, evacuated Wexford,
viâ Kilmuckridge. This body marched through Gorey, and spread itself
in and around the environs of that town, including the villages of Ballycanow, Clough, Coolgreny, Little Limerick, Moneyseed, and Craanford.
Fortunately for them, but few of the Protestant inhabitants in any of
those neighbourhoods had as yet returned to their homes. All who had,
and were discovered, were put to death. That day is yet familiar in the
memory of every Protestant resident in that part of Wexford as *"Bloody
Friday!"* Thirty-seven Protestants were inhumanly butchered on that
day, in and around the immediate vicinity in which the writer was born.
Their names were,—

Bates, William.	Johnston, John, Senr.
Bates, Robert.	Johnston, John, Junr.
Bates, George.	Johnston, Samuel.
Bassit, John.	Jolly, Thomas.
Butler, William.	Kennedy, Joseph.
Butler, Richard.	Lee, Richard.
Buttle, Thomas.	Moore, Daniel.
Buttle, Henry.	Needham, John.
Chase, William.	Ormsby, William.
Cooke, John.	Patchell, Michael.
Dobbin, William.	Rogers, Henry.
Erritt, William.	Read, George.
Erritt, Isaac.	Shaw, Abraham.
Foxton, Thomas.	Stanford, William.
Foxton, Richard.	Tomkin, James.
Gray, William.	Whitaker, John.
Harris, John.	Webster, Robert.
Hogan, Robert.	Williamson, Ralph.
Jones, William.	

After committing these acts of savage barbarity, this division of the
Rebel forces passed on through Hollyfort, Wicklow-gap, and Tinnehaley,

into the mountains of the County of Wicklow, intending to form a junction with the insurgents in that County, and, strengthened by them, to attack Hacketstown, in the County of Carlow. On the morning of the 25th of June, the combined Rebel forces, amounting to upwards of four thousand men, appeared before Hacketstown. The garrison of the place was small. With the exception of a Detachment of fifty men of the Antrim Militia, under the command of Lieutenant Gardiner, the whole strength of the place consisted of the armed Orangemen of the Upper Talbotstown Lodge, (50) ; those of the Shillelagh Lodge, (24) ; the Hacketstown Lodge, (46) ; and the Coolattin Lodge, (30). In all two hundred men, to oppose four thousand ! The Worshipful Masters of the Lodges were in command of their respective corps or companies. Mr. Hume, of Humewood, the Upper Talbotstown ; Mr. Braddell, of Bullingate, the Shillelagh ; Mr. Hardy, of Hacketstown, the Hacketstown ; and Mr. Chamney, of Ballyrahan, the Coolattin. The attack commenced about six in the morning, when the town was completely surrounded by the multitude. Lieutenant Gardiner, seeing that their intention was to surround him, concentrated his small force in the barracks. Captain Hardy, Master of the Hacketstown Lodge, covered the retreat of the Antrims, and fell, mortally wounded, in their defence. His death was deeply deplored by his brethren, and his memory is cherished to this day by the Loyalists of Hacketstown. The Reverend James M'Ghee, who was Chaplain to the Coolkenna Lodge, asked and obtained permission to take a dozen of the Coolattin men with him to occupy a house, placed on an eminence, flanking the barracks, and completely commanding the Rebels' approach. The Antrims having retired to occupy the barracks, followed by their Orange comrades, who contested every street, and lane, and corner as they retreated ; the Rebels advanced with loud huzzas, setting several houses on fire as they entered the town. The rear of the barracks soon became the principal point of attack ; but here the Rebels found themselves, in a narrow street, between two fires. The Antrim's played upon them in front from the barracks, and the Coolattins, under their *Reverend* Commander and Chaplain, from the rear. The Rebels fought well, but the leaden messengers from Mr. McGhee were found to be *too pressing* to be long withstood ! The insurgents were thus driven back from the rear of the barracks, and this part of the town preserved. The engagement throughout, was an obstinate and a bloody one—the contest continued without intermission, and in the midst of smoke and flame, from six in the morning till three in the afternoon. The Rebels retired, leaving the loyal little garrison in possession, with the Royal Standard of Old England still floating from the top of the Barrack pole of Hacketstown. This repulse greatly disheartened this division of the Rebel forces ; they soon after broke into guerilla parties, confined themselves to the bogs and forests of Wexford, and to the mountains of Wicklow ; until their predatory depredations were terminated by the zeal and intrepidity of the Orange Yeomanry of these Counties. Perry, their leader, after having been defeated at Kilcahan Hill, the Whiteheaps, and Slievebuoy Mountain, directed his route to the County of Kildare, and there joined a strong body of insurgents, under the command of Michael Alymer, Colonel of the Kildare Rebel army. The united forces of these Chiefs amounted to about four thousand men. Their plan was to attack the Town of Clonard, a Village situated on the River Boyne, and at the confines of the Counties of Kildare and Meath. From Clonard to advance by Kilbeggan to the Shannon, and surprise Athlone, where, from its being the centre of the Kingdom, they expected great reinforcements.

The Town of Clonard, at that period so important, was wholly bereft of Military aid. Their was not a "red coat" within miles of it, nor could a single Military Detachment be spared for its defence. But there was an Orange Lodge met in the immediate vicinity. Mr. Tyrrell, of Grange Castle, was its Master. Their numbers were few, but their hearts were brave, their hands were steady, and their resolution was unflinching. As the writer enjoyed the personal friendship of Mr. Tyrrell for many years, he prefers copying the description of the events at Clonard given by a historian of admitted veracity, to any picture drawn by his own pen.

Taylor's edition, published by Curry in 1829 ; says, page 153-7. The force at Clonard consisted of a Corps of Yeomen, commanded by Lieutenant Tyrrell, a Gentleman who had never served in the Army, yet upon this occasion he evinced a degree of skill and bravery, which would have done honor to a veteran. When he received intelligence of the enemy's approach, he made every necessary preparation for their reception, which his very limited force would admit. He placed six of the Yeomen, including his own son (a lad only fifteen years of age,) in an old Turret, at the extremity of his garden, which commanded the road the Rebels were to come Such was the rapidity with which the latter advanced, that the firing actually commenced from this quarter upon them, before the entire guard could be collected, and the gate leading into the Court Yard was, under such necessity, closed, to the exclusion of several ; so that when the Lieutenant came to ascertain his strength, he found he had only twenty-seven men, including his three sons, the eldest of whom was but seventeen years old ! Such a critical situation required all the coolness of a man inured to military dangers, and the skill and firmness of an experienced soldier. But although Lieutenant Tyrrell had not enjoyed those advantages, his good sense supplied the want of experience, and his native courage furnished resources adequate to the perilous emergency. He found his men, all of whom he knew, as zealous and as loyal as himself ; determined to maintain their post, and to discharge their duty to their

King and Country, or fall in the glorious cause. After sending a supply of ammunition to the advanced post at the Turret, and stationing out picquets, he retired into his Dwelling House with the main body; from which he selected the best marksmen, and placing them at particular windows, gave directions that they should not fire without having their object covered. He had the rest of the men secured behind the walls and incessantly employed in loading muskets and carbines for the marksmen at the windows. The firing, as has been observed, commenced from the Turret. About three hundred of the Rebel Cavalry, commanded by Captain Farrell, formed their advanced guard, and approached in a smart trot, without apprehending any danger. The first shot, which was fired by young Mr. Tyrrell mortally wounded Farrell. The rest immediately discharged their pieces at the Rebels, and threw them into such confusion that they fled out of reach of the firing. The Rebel infantry now coming up, passed the Turret, under cover of the wall; and numbers were posted behind a thick hedge, on the opposite side of the road, from which they kept up a smart fire against the Turret, but to no effect. After this division had passed the Turret, they were joined by another, which came by a cross road, (for their plan was to surround the House, by advancing in different directions,) and they immediately stationed a guard upon the Bridge, to prevent any reinforcements arriving to the garrison in that direction. In a few minutes, ten or twelve of their guard were shot by the marksmen, from the windows of the House, upon which the rest fled. Not one of the Rebels appeared afterwards on the Bridge; the communication with the Western road was in a great measure preserved—the importance of which, to the little garrison of Clonard, will appear in the sequel. The enemy being thus defeated in their first onset, at both points of attack, became exasperated to extravagant fury, and determined on the most savage revenge. A large party contrived to penetrate into the garden by the rear; and some of them immediately rushed into the Turret. The brave men stationed there, were on the upper floor, and had taken the precaution to drag up the ladder by which they ascended. The Rebels endeavoured to climb up on each other so as to reach the higher story; but they were killed as fast as they appeared. Others ran pikes into the ceiling, and fired through it, but without effect. The conflict was so obstinate and bloody, that twenty-seven of the Rebels lay dead on the ground floor. At length they brought a quantity of straw, and set the Turret on fire, on which two of its gallant defenders, while endeavouring to force their way through the smoke and flame, were instantly put to death. The other four escaped by leaping from a window, twenty feet high, into a hay yard, from whence, under cover of a wall, which divided it from the garden, they fortunately reached the House. Having succeeded so well by the effect of conflagration, the enemy now set fire to the Toll House, and to some Cabins on the left, near the Bridge, for the purpose of embarrassing and confusing the garrison. During this operation, they were seen throwing their dead into the flames, for the purpose of evading discovery. The unequal contest had now lasted six hours ; when, about five in the evening, the approach of succour was descried from the House, and the hopes of the loyal little garrison were so elevated that they fought with renovated vigour. One of the little party, who had been excluded by the sudden shutting of the gates in the morning, finding he could be of no use in defending the House, repaired with all expedition to Kinnegad, and represented the alarming situation of his friends at Clonard. Lieutenant Houghton, with fourteen of the Kinnegad Infantry (all Orangemen,) and a sergeant, with eleven of the Northumberland Fencibles, (this being all the force that could be spared,) immediately marched to their succour. The pass by the Bridge having been kept open, in the manner before related, Lieutenant Tyrrell now sallied from the House, and soon effected a junction with this reinforcement. A few vollies completely cleared the roads ; and having placed the Northumberland and Kinnegad in such situations as most effectually to gall the enemy in their retreat from the garden, the Lieutenant himself undertook the hazardous enterprise of dislodging them from thence. At this time it is supposed, there were four hundred Rebels in the garden. A large body were posted on a mound planted with old fir trees, which afforded considerable protection ; while many lay concealed behind a private hedge, from which they could see distinctly every person who entered the garden, though unperceived themselves. The brave Tyrrell, at the head of a few of his chosen men, now rushed into the garden, and were received by a general discharge from both bodies of the enemy. He immediately attacked the party behind the hedge, which being defeated retired to the mount. Here a warm action ensued ; the enemy appearing determined to maintain this advantageous position ; but the few gallant men by whom they were assailed, though fatigued, and many of them badly wounded, persevered with the most undaunted courage, and maintained such a steady and well directed fire against the mount, that the enemy were at length dispersed, and in their flight the Northumberland Fencibles and Kinnegad Infantry made great havoc among them. Thus, through the favour of Providence, was accomplished as glorious an achievement as had occurred during the whole rebellion, for which Mr. Tyrrell and his few loyal men can never be too much applauded. It was the first check the Kildare Rebels had met, and proved the forerunner of those several defeats, which terminated in their total dispersion." Thanks, and thanks again and again to the little band of Clonard Orangemen. Mr. Tyrrell died a few years ago ; he was the Grand Treasurer of the "*Benevolent Order*" of Orangemen, during the period the writer held the office of Grand Secretary of the same Body.

This body of the Rebels, after having been driven through Carbery, Johnstown, and Nineteen-mile house, in the County of Kildare; succeeded in crossing the Boyne, near Slane, and getting into the County of Meath. From thence they pursued their course to the neighbourhood of Ardee, in the County of Louth, where they were speedily disposed of by the Sutherland Highlanders, (now the 93rd of the line.) Part of them fled from Ardee, towards Garrotstown, in the County of Meath; but being everywhere hotly pursued by the Loyal Yeomany, they broke up and dispersed as a body, and sought protection by coming in, taking the Oath of Allegiance, and thus getting *metamorphosed into loyal subjects!*

We have yet to account for the Rebel division which retreated from Wexford under the command of General Priest Roche, and Father John Murphy. This party proceeded by the Blackstairs Mountain into the County of Kilkenny, and on the morning of the 23rd of June, made their appearance opposite Gore's Bridge, a Village situated on the River Barrow, in the County of Kilkenny. Here they attacked the small garrison stationed at Gore's Bridge, which they defeated, making twenty-four of the Wexford Militia prisoners. The probability is, that most of these men were disaffected. Sixteen out of the twenty-four were Roman Catholics; they were not molested; the remaining eight were Protestants, and were put to death on the following day. From Gore's Bridge the Rebels proceeded through Kellymount, to a hill five miles from Castle-comer, in the range of Mountains called the Ridge, where they encamped on the night of the 24th of June, determining to attack Castlecomer on the following day. The garrison of Castlecomer was about two hundred and fifty strong, and ought to have made a good defence. After hearing mass from Priest John Murphy, the Rebels quitted their Camp at the Ridge, and moved forward for Castlecomer. The Military marched out of Town about the same time to meet their assailants. The Rebel force advanced in good order, and in the most daring manner. The engagement commenced about seven in the morning; a smart fire was for some time kept up, but at length the Military retired towards the Town. The Rebels advanced, and a rather sharp encounter took place at the Bridge; when the Commanding Officer ordered a retreat. The Cavalry, and most of the Infantry obeyed. Some twenty soldiers of the Waterford Militia, all of whom were members of the Orange Body, refused to obey. They placed a non-commisioned officer, who was the Master of their Lodge, at their head, and openly declared "*they would prefer death to dishonour!*" When the Army retreated, the perfidious inhabitants of Castlecomer, (most of whom were Roman Catholics,) set fire to the Town; and the few Waterford men who had disobeyed orders, with about thirty Loyalists of Castlecomer, were all that remained to engage the enemy. Fortunately however, they were speedily reinforced by the timely arrival of Major General Sir Charles

military command of the District, applied to the Government for a pension for the widow of the deceased Orangeman, which was granted.

It is stated in Mr. Wright's "History of Ireland," (*vide vol. 6, chapter 16,*) that after the French had reached Ballinamuck, an attempt was made by the Rebel leaders to advance from Granard to co-operate with them—that several men of property had espoused their cause—and that multitudes from Longford and the neighbouring Counties, were ready to rise at the summons of their chiefs—their plan being to seize the town of Granard, and then march to attack the Town of Cavan, where there was a considerable depôt of arms and ammunition. Fortunately, however, they were attacked and defeated, after an obstinate resistance, by Captain Cottingham, Grand Master of the County of Cavan, who hastily called out the Cavan and Ballyhaise Orangemen, then being enrolled as yeoman ; who fought with admirable skill and bravery upon this occasion and succeeded not only in defeating the Rebels, but also in preventing their junction with the French invaders.

The Coolattin, Shillelagh, and Tinehaly Yeomanry mustered under their respective Masters, Captains Chamney, Nixon, and Morton, rendered the most effective services to the King's troops, at this critical juncture, and were publicly thanked for their zeal and services in "a general order," issued by the Major General, Sir Charles Asgill, then commanding in the Carlow and Wicklow Military District. At the affair of Ballyellis, (30th of June, 1798,) the members of the Orange lodge, No. 406, then organized only four months and a few days, were instrumental not only in retrieving the fortunes of the day, after the ancient Britons had been defeated, but, after a contest which lasted two whole days, during which the town of Carnew was burned, succeeded in defeating the Rebels, and rescuing the country from their grasp. The Revd. George Taylor, Sir Richard Musgrave, and Mr. Jackson, all give full particulars of this event. Here is the account of the first named historian. (*Vol.* 1. *pages* 149, 150 *and* 151.)

"On the 30th of June, information was brought to Gorey, that the "insurgents were advancing in some force towards Carnew—a small town "on the borders of the counties of Wicklow and Wexford, but situated "in the former. General Needham, with the Troops under his command, "was then encamped on Gorey Hill, and being apprised of this circum- "stance, ordered out a reconnoitring party of the Ancient British Cavalry, "and some of the Yeomanry. After marching a few miles, they were "joined by a detachment of the Fifth Dragoon Guards, and some other "Troops, the whole under the command of Lieut. Colonel Puleston of "the Ancient Britons. The whole was about one hundred and fifty "strong. As the patrole advanced, they met a woman who informed "them that the Rebels were near Ballyellis, and that they had not much

" ammunition. The Colonel, turning to his men, swore he would cut them
" in pieces ; and making all speed, he descried them coming along the side
" of Kilkevin Hill.   When the the Rebels saw the Cavalry advancing in
" so rapid and incautious a manner, they instantly quitted the highway,
" and lay down under cover of a hedge, till the Army should come up ;
" having to all appearance abandoned their horses, baggage cars, and
" wounded, which they had brought from the battle of Hacketstown.
" The ditch behind which the Rebels lay to the right, was very high ;
" while on the left was a wall, with a deep dyke between it and the road.
" When the patrole came up, the Rebels opened upon them a tremendous
" fire of musketry, while they were so securely sheltered, that the Cavalry
" could do no execution, being obliged to gallop stooping under cover of
" the hedge.   Not being sufficiently cautious enough to avoid the cars,
" they rode against and overthrew some of them. Those in the rear press-
" ing forward at the same time, and being also obliged to stoop, could
" not look before them, nor suddenly stop, they therefore tumbled, men
" and horses, one over another, whilst some of the horses' feet got fastened
" in the shafts of the cars, so that the road was strewed with men and
" horses, plunging and tumbling about.   The Rebels, taking advantage of
" this confusion, rushed on them, piked and shot twenty-five Ancient
" Britons, eleven of the Fifth Dragoons, and eight of the Yeomanry,
" with two Loyalists who went out with the Patrole, besides wounding
" many.   The remainder passed on through Carnew, and by taking another
" route, got back to Gorey.   During this transaction, the Wingfield dis-
" mounted Cavalry and Infantry, under the command of Captain Hunter
" Gowan came up with the Rebels, and having no particular uniform, the
" enemy thought they were part of their own forces ; but the Yeomanry
" seeing their opportunity, attacked them with great spirit, killed a num-
" ber of them, and then retreated without the loss of a man.   By the
" defeat of the Patrole, the Rebels acquired a supply of arms and ammuni-
" tion, and knowing that Carnew was in a feeble state of defence, they
" resolved on attacking it, but after an uninterupted contest of two days,
" they were repulsed by the gallant Yeomanry, who killed a number of
" them, and drove the rest into the country.   The town of Carnew was,
" however, destroyed."   The reader may be somewhat at a loss to account
for one or two circumstances narrated in the preceding account of Mr.
Taylor.   It will be observed that the Cavalry are termed " dismounted,"
and the force itself is described, as " having no particular uniform."
This requires explanation.   The facts are these.   Mount Nebo, the seat
of Captain Gowan, is about three miles from Gorey and about five from
Carnew.   Ballyellis, where the King's forces were defeated, lies on the
direct road leading from Mount Nebo to Carnew, and is nearly equi-
distant between them.   Upon the day in question, (30th of June,) Cap-

tain Gowan's Yeomanry met in Lodge, within the burned walls of his mansion at Mount Nebo, and were in the act of initiating Lieutenant George Smith of Cummer, when intelligence was brought to them, that about 200 of the King's Troops had passed on the road from Gorey to Carnew to meet the Rebels, then reported to be advancing from the Hill of Killkevin. The Lodge was immediately closed, and the men, who had attended without their military uniform, but who had carried with them their muskets, bayonets and one hundred rounds of ball cartridges each, were ordered by the Captain to fall in, and were instantly marched off in support of the Royal forces. The Cavalry had not time to return for their horses, and united as foot Soldiers with their Brethren of the Infantry. On reaching Moneyseed (a small village about one mile and a half from Mount Nebo,) they could distinctly hear the fusilade in the direction of Carnew. They then quickened their pace, but arrived at Ballyellis too late to assist Colonel Puleston, who had retreated with the remnant of his forces toward Carnew. On arriving at Ballyellis, the Rebels, on seeing the Yeomanry dressed in the ordinary costume of the country, hailed their approach with cheers, conceiving, as Mr. Taylor states, that "they were part of their own forces." They did not open fire upon the insurgents till within ten or twelve yards of them, and then with such precision, as regularly swept down the dense mass that blocked up the highway. After a few such discharges, the rebels retreated in great confusion to Kilkevin Hill, where they were joined by the main body of their forces. Captain Gowan then carried away the wounded of Colonel Puleston's party, and retired in good order toward Carnew. Here he was joined by the Yeomanry from Carnew, Tinehaly and neighbourhood, which were in fact, (like his own Corps,) the members of the Orange Lodges at those places. The regular forces under Colonel Puleston having retired to Gorey, to join the main body under General Needham, the defence of Carnew was entrusted solely to the Orange Yeomanry there assembled. For two successive days they withstood the incessant attacks of the enemy, and at length succeeded in defeating the overwhelming multitude, by which the few but gallant band were assailed. This noble defence of Carnew completely frustrated the plans of the insurgents, prevented the junction of the Rebels from Wicklow and Carlow, with those of Wexford, and left the latter to be dealt with by the Royal forces, unsupported by their comrades from the two former Counties. Do not such services call for gratitude? Are they not deserving of commemoration and record? Even Plowden and Mooney, both Roman Catholic historians, and the bitterest and most unrelenting foes of Orangemen, admit that Ireland was preserved to England by the Orangemen. Mooney says, (page 923,) that the Country was "left to the Orange Yeomen;" and again (at page 931,) that "fully two-thirds of the British force then enrolled, were drawn from the Gentry and Orange Lodges." Yet with such evidence before the world, evidence too, wrung from their bitterest enemies, it is now fashionable to speak of such men as " a faction !"—"A mere set of Orange factionists, got up to insult Her Majesty's *loyal* Roman Catholic Subjects !", The Hessians and other German mercenaries, were loyal to England, and fought her battles in '98, so long as they were paid for it ; more recently still, England subsidized plenty of "Foreign Legions," Prussians and Poles, Portugese and Spaniards, "Turks, Jews, and Atheists," to fight her battles ; and even at this time, the *soi-disant* "Successor of St. Peter" has his heretical Swiss mercenaries, more faithful than his Papal subjects, to keep him in the Papal Chair ! Facts prove that the *loyalty* of Irish Roman Catholics, as a class, to the British Government, is the *loyalty* of the Hessians and Swiss, the *loyalty* of "Foreign Legions" to ——PAY !

CHAPTER XXV.

Address from the Orangemen of Ireland to His Excellency the Marquis of Camden—Adjourned meeting of the Grand Lodge of Ireland, names of members present, and report from the Select Committee—First Rules and Regulations adopted; the Marksman's Obligation, and copy of the Secret Articles.

On the 14th of February, in this year, Captain James Verner and Thomas Verner, Esq., waited upon His Excellency the Marquis of Camden, then Viceroy of Ireland, and presented His Excellency with a Declaration, signed by upwards of 30,000 Orangemen. His Excellency was pleased to express himself most thankful for the Address—and to say that His Majesty and the whole Empire must ever feel grateful for the patriotism and public spirit the Orangemen had evinced. His Excellency ordered the Declaration to be printed and circulated. The following is a copy of it :

"We, the loyal inhabitants of the Province of Ulster, who have been styled Orangemen, in remembrance of our glorious deliverer, King William the Third, think it incumbent upon us at this critical period, to declare our faithful and steady attachment to His Majesty, King George the Third, and to our valuable Constitution in Church and State, as well as our gratitude for the blessings we enjoy under the present government, and our happiness in the suppression of insurrection and rebellion, and the restoration of tranquillity in this province, by the exertions of the general officers and the militia, aided by the zeal of the loyal inhabitants.

" We have read in the public papers with much satisfaction, the declarations of the Roman Catholic inhabitants of several parishes in this province—we have no doubt of the sincerity of these declarations, and that the Roman Catholics of Ireland, sensible of the benefits which they enjoy, will not suffer themselves to be made the dupes of wicked and designing men, for the most diabolical purposes; and we flatter ourselves that such declarations will be embraced, and have the happiest effects in other parts of the kingdom. Such conduct must be acceptable in the eyes of God and man.

" We declare most solemnly, that we are not enemies to any body of people on account of their religion, their faith, or their mode of worship. We consider every loyal subject our brother, and they shall have our aid and our protection.

" Anxious to co-operate in preserving internal tranquillity and repelling invasion should our foreign enemies be desperate enough to attempt it, we take this opportunity of declaring our readiness to undertake any duty in obedience to the commands of his Excellency the Lord Lieutenant."

The adjourned meeting of the Grand Lodge, to receive the report of the Select Committee appointed on the 9th of April, to revise the rules and regulations, was held on the 20th of November 1798. The proceedings are here given at length. They may be found in the minutes of evidence, given before the Select Committee of the House of Commons in June 1835. *See Appendix No. 3, from page 2, to the end of page 6.*

APPENDIX No. 3.
RULES OF SOCIETY, 1799.

Rules and regulations, revised by the Grand Orange Lodge of Ireland, for the use of all Orange Societies.

At a meeting of the Grand Orange Lodge of Ireland, November 20th, 1798.

Present:—Thomas Verner, Grand Master; J. C. Beresford, Grand Secretary; H. A. Woodward; J. S. Rochfort; J. F. Knife; Samuel Montgomery; Harding Gifford; William Richardson; John Fisher; William Corbitt; W. G. Galway; Francis Gregory :—Harding Gifford, and S. Montgomery, Esqs., reported as follows:

REPORT.

Having been honoured by the Grand Lodge with instructions to revise and select a proper system of rules for the government of Orange Lodges, we beg leave to make a report of our progress.

We are happy in being able to say that, in our duty upon this occasion, we received the greatest assistance from the experience of the Grand Master of Ireland, and his Deputy Grand Secretary, who did us the honour of imparting to us their sentiments.

Encouraged by their help, we have ventured very materially to alter the shape of the confused system which was referred to us, preserving the spirit, and as much as possible the original words, except where we had to encounter gross violations of language and grammar.

The general plan of our proceedings has been this;—we have thrown what are, in our opinion, very improperly called the six first general Rules into one plain, short declaration of the sentiments of the body.

Next in order, we have given the qualifications of an Orangeman, selected from the Antrim Regulations; and the rather, as it breathes a spirit of piety which cannot be too generally diffused throughout an institution, whose chief object, whatever political shape it may assume, is to preserve the Protestant religion.

After this comes the obligation of an Orangeman, from which we have struck out the word "Male," as we learn from the Grand Master that it is an unauthor-ized interpolation, and as it it might lead to unnecessary and injurious cavils.

The secret articles are as nearly as possible in their original shape; they have, however, been a little improved in point of language, and two of them, which were mere matter of private economy, are placed among the By-laws.

The Marksman's obligation is, on the suggestion of the Grand Master, here introduced.

Then follow the Master, Treasurer, and Secretary's obligation.

We have endeavored to reduce the general rules, giving hints in our arrange-ment, which may be adopted.

For the same reason which we have given for adopting the qualification of an Orangeman, we have recommended the insertion of two prayers, for opening and closing the Lodge; they are to be found in the Antrim Regulations. We confess, however, that we think the first of them rather too long to have a good effect; but this not being exactly within our line of knowledge, we beg leave to transfer the duty of abbreviating it to some of our clerical brethren.

Nov. 20*th.*, 1798.   { SAMUEL MONTGOMERY,
                                              { HARDING GIFFARD.

RULES AND REGULATIONS, &C., &C.—GENERAL DECLARATION OF THE OBJECTS OF THE ORANGE INSTITUTION.

We associate to the utmost of our power to support and defend His Majesty King George the Third, the constitution and laws of this country, and the succession to the throne in His Majesty's illustrious House, being Protestants; for the defence of our persons and properties, and to maintain the peace of our country: and for these purposes we will be at all times ready to assist the civil and military powers in the just and lawful discharge of their duty. We also associate in honor of King William the Third, Prince of Orange, whose name we bear, as supporters of his glorious memory, and the true religion by him completely established: and in order to prove our gratitude and affection for his name, we will annually celebrate the victory over James at the Boyne, on the 1st day of July, O. S. in ever year, which day shall be our grand Era for ever.

We further declare, that we are exclusively a Protestant association; yet detesting as we do any intolerant spirit, we solemnly pledge ourselves to each other that we will not persecute or upbraid any person on account of his religious opinions, but that we will, on the contrary, be aiding and assisting to every loyal, subject of every religious description.

QUALIFICATIONS REQUISITE FOR AN ORANGEMAN.

He should have a sincere love and veneration for his Almighty Maker, pro-ductive of those lively and happy fruits righteousness and obedience to His

commands; a firm and steady faith in the Saviour of the world, convinced that
He is the only mediator between a sinful creature and an offended Creator. Without those he can be no Christian; of a humane and compassionate disposition, and
a courteous and affable behavior; he should be an utter enemy to savage brutality
and unchristian cruelty; a lover of society and improving company; and have
laudable regard for the Protestant religion, and a sincere desire to propagate its
precepts; zealous in promoting the honour of his King and Country; heartily
desirous of victory and success in those pursuits, yet convinced and assured that
God alone can grant them; he should have an hatred of cursing and swearing,
and taking the name of God in vain (a shameful practice); he should use all
opportunities of discouraging it among his brethren; wisdom and prudence should
guide his actions, honesty and integrity direct his conduct, and honor and glory be
the motive of his endeavors. Lastly, he should pay the strictest attention to a
religious observance of the Sabbath, and also to temperance and sobriety.

OBLIGATION OF AN ORANGEMAN.

I, A. B., do solemnly and sincerely swear, of my own free will and accord, that
I will, to the utmost of my power, support and defend the present King, George
the Third, and all the heirs of the Crown, and so long as he or they support the
Protestant ascendancy, the constitution and laws of these Kingdoms; and
that I will ever hold sacred the name of our glorious deliverer, King William the
Third, Prince of Orange: and I do further swear, that I am not nor was not a
Roman Catholic or Papist, that I was not, am not, nor ever will be, an United
Irishman; and that I never took the oath of secrecy to that society; and I do
further swear, in the presence of Almighty God, that I will also conceal, and
never will reveal, either part or parts of this that I am about now to receive,
neither write it, nor indite it, stamp, stain, nor engrave it, nor cause it so to be
done, on paper, parchment, leaf, bark, brick, stone, or any thing so that it might
be known; and that I am now become an Orangeman without fear, bribery or
corruption.

SECRET ARTICLES.

1. That we will bear true allegiance to His Majesty King George the Third,
and his successors so long as he or they support the Protestant ascendancy; and
that we will faithfully support and maintain the laws and constitution of this
Kingdom.

2. That we will be true to all Orangemen in all just actions, neither wronging
nor seeing him wronged to our knowledge, without acquainting him thereof.

3. That we are not to see a brother offended for 6d. or 1s., or more if convenient, which must be returned next meeting, if possible.

4. We must not give the least assault to any person whatsoever that may bring
a brother into trouble.

5. We are not to carry away money, goods, or anything from any person whatsoever, except arms and ammunition, and those only from an enemy.

6. We are to appear in ten hours warning, or whatever time is required, if
possible, (provided that it be not hurtful to ourselves and family, and that we are
served with a lawful summons from the Master), otherwise we are fined as the
co pa   p

7. No man can be made an Orangeman without the unanimous approbation of the body.

8. An Orangeman is to keep a brother's secret as his own, unless in case of murder, treason, and perjury, and that of his own free will.

9. No Roman Catholic can be admitted on any account.

10. An Orangeman who acts contrary to these rules shall be expelled, and the same reported to all the Lodges in the Kingdom, and elsewhere.

GOD SAVE THE KING.

MARKSMAN'S OBLIGATION.

I, A. B., of my own free will and accord, in the presence of my Almighty God, do hereby most solemnly and sincerely swear, that I will always conceal, and never reveal, either part or parts of this which I am now about to receive; and that I will bear true allegiance to His Majesty King George the Third, and all the heirs of the Crown, so long as they maintain the Protestant ascendancy, the laws and constitutions of those Kingdoms; and that I will keep this part of a Marksman from that of an Orangeman, as well as from the ignorant; and that I will not make a man until I become Master of a body, nor after I am broke; and that I will not make a man, nor be present at the making of a man, on the road, or behind hedges; and that I will be aiding to all true Orange honest Marksmen, nor know him to be wronged of anything of value, worth apprehending, but I will warn him or apprize him of, if in my power lies. All this I swear with a firm and steadfast resolution, so help me GOD, and keep me steadfast in this my Marksman's obligation.

GENERAL RULES FOR THE GOVERNMENT OF ORANGE LODGES.

1. Each lodge is to be governed by a Master, Deputy Master, Treasurer and Secretary; the Master appointed by the Grand Lodge; and the Deputy Master, Treasurer and Secretary, by the Master, with the approbation of his own Lodge.

2. These officers upon their appointment, shall take the following obligations:

MASTER, SECRETARY, AND TREASURER'S OBLIGATIONS.

I, A. B., do solemnly and sincerely swear, that I am not, nor was not, a Roman Catholic or Papist; that I am not, was not, nor ever will be an United Irishman, and that I never took the oath of secrecy to that society.

FOR THE MASTER AND DEPUTY MASTER, (*add.*)

And that I am not now made a Master for any private emolument or advantage; that I have not a sitting in my house for the purpose of selling beer, spirits, &c., and that neither I, nor any other person for me, will admit any one into the society of Orangemen who was or is a Papist, or has been a United Irishman, or has taken their oath of secrecy; and that I will use my authority to keep proper behaviour and sobriety in this lodge, and that I will not certify for any person without having first proved him, and knowing him to be a good character. *So help me GOD.*

FOR THE SECRETARY, (*add.*)

And that I will keep safe the papers belonging to this lodge; and that I will not give any copy of the number of secret articles, or lend them to make an

Orangeman out of the lodge belonging to, or lend the seal, so that it may be fixed to any forged paper, or irregular Orangeman's certificate. So help me GOD.

FOR THE TREASURER, (add.)

And that I will fairly account for all money I have, or shall receive, for the use of this lodge, when called upon by the Master of this lodge, so help me GOD.

3. That a Committee be appointed to conduct the affairs of each lodge, to consist of the Master, Deputy Master, Secretary and Treasurer, and five members, the first of whom is to be nominated by the Master, the second by the first, and so on until the number five be completed.

4. That in the absence of the Master, the Deputy Master shall preside, and in his absence, the senior Committee man who shall be present.

5. That each candidate for admission shall be proposed by one, and seconded by another member of one meeting, and admitted or rejected at a subsequent one.

6. That one negative shall exclude.

7. That any person wishing to become an Orangeman, must be admitted in the lodge nearest his place of abode (except in cities or great towns,) or have a recommendation from that lodge, that he is a proper person, before any other lodge can accept him.

8. That the names of persons rejected in any lodge shall be sent by the Master or Secretary to the District Master, with the objections to such persons, in order that the District Master may communicate to other lodges, as those who are unfit for one lodge must be so for every other.

9. That each member on admission shall pay ———.

10. That all Orangemen shall be considered as members, but none to vote in any lodge except the particular members thereof.

11. All members to be subordinate to the Master or person presiding for him.

12. Any dispute arising, not provided for by the rules, is to be decided by the Committee, and the parties must abide by their decision, on pain of expulsion.

13. That each new Resolution shall remain on the books from one meeting to the subsequent one, previously to its being adopted or rejected by the majority of the members then present.

14. That no election or other business do take place, unless ten members at least be present, providing the lodge consists of so many; if it do not, then two-thirds of the lodge must be present.

15 That no business be done in any lodge after dinner, supper or drink have been brought in, but every motion shall be previously decided.

16. Any new member attending intoxicated, cannot be admitted at that meeting; any old one so attending to be fined.

17. The Secretary is to read out before the books are closed, the names of those persons proposed for the next night.

18. A person is to attend on the outside of the door, while business is going on; and that person to be nominated by the Master or whoever presides at the time.

19. The Master to have full power of fining all disorderly persons to an amount not exceeding ———.

20. No gentleman is to be ballotted for, unless the person proposing or seconding him be present, or some reasonable excuse for his absence be offered.

21. Order of business for each night:—1. Lodge to open with a prayer (members standing). 2. General rules read. 3. Members proposed. 4. Reports from Committee. 5. Names of members called over. 6. Members ballotted for. 7. Members made. 8. Lodge to close with prayer (members standing.)

PRAYER FOR OPENING THE LODGE.

Gracious and Almighty God, who in all ages has shown thy mighty power in protecting righteous Kings and States, we yield thee hearty thanks for so miraculously bringing to light and frustrating the secret and horrible designs of our enemies, plotted and intended to have been executed against our gracious King, our happy constitution, and the true religion established by our glorious deliverer, William the Third, Prince of Orange.

Vouchsafe, O Lord, to continue unto us thine Almighty protection; grant to our pious King, long life, health and prosperity; let thy providence ever guard our happy constitution, and enable us to transmit it to our latest posterity, unimpaired, and improved by our holy religion. Bless, we beseech thee, every member of the Orange institution with charity, brotherly love, and loyalty. Make us truly respectable here on earth, and eternally happy hereafter; these, and all other blessings we beg in the name, and through the mediation of Jesus Christ, our Lord and Saviour. *Amen.*

OR THIS.

Almighty God, and Heavenly Father, who in all ages past hast showed thy power and mercy, in graciously and miraculously delivering thy church, and protecting righteous and religious Kings and States from the wicked conspiracies and malicious practices of all the enemies thereof; we yield thee hearty thanks for so wonderfully discovering and confounding the horrible and wicked designs of our enemies, plotted and intended to have been executed against our most gracious Sovereign Lord King George, and the whole estates of the realm, for the subversion of Government and established religion. Be thou, O Lord, still our mighty protector, scatter our enemies that delight in blood, infatuate and defeat their councils, abate their pride, assuage their malice, and confound their devices. Strengthen the hands of our gracious Sovereign and all that are in authority under him, with judgment and justice to cut off all such workers of iniquity as turn religion into rebellion, and faith into faction, that they may never prevail in the ruin of thy church amongst us; but that our gracious Sovereign and his realms, being preserved in thy true religion, and by thy merciful goodness protected in the same, we may all duly serve thee with praise and thanksgiving. And we beseech thee to protect the King, Queen, and Royal Family, from all treasons and conspiracies; preserve him in thy faith, fear, and love; make his reign long, prosperous and happy here on earth, and crown him hereafter with everlasting glory. Accept also, most gracious God, our unfeigned thanks for filling our hearts with joy and gladness, by sending thy servant, the late King William, for the deliverance of these nations from tyranny and arbitrary power.

Let truth and justice, devotion and piety, concord and unity, brotherly kindness and charity, with other christian virtues, so flourish amongst us, that they may be the stability of our times; and make this, our association, a praise here on earth; this we most humbly beg, in the name and for the sake of *Jesus Christ*, our Lord and Saviour. *Amen.*

FORM OF PRAYER TO BE USED AT CLOSING.

O Almighty God, who art a strong tower of defence unto thy servants, against the face of their enemies, we yield thee praise and thanks for our deliverance from those great and apparent dangers wherewith we were encompassed, we acknowledge thy goodness that we were not delivered over as a prey unto them, beseeching thee still to continue such thy mercies towards us, that all the world may know thou art our Saviour and mighty deliverer, through Jesus Christ. Amen.

RESOLUTIONS OF THE GRAND ORANGE LODGE OF IRELAND.

Resolved,—That new numbers be printed on parchment, and stamped according to the specimen produced, and that any lodge wishing to get them instead of their old numbers, shall have them on paying half-a-crown.

Resolved,—That for all new numbers issued on parchment the sum of 5s. 5d. be paid, half-a-crown for the grand lodge of Armagh, and half-a-crown for the grand lodge of Ireland.

Resolved,—That after the date hereof, every old number renewed, and every new one granted, must be signed by the Grand Master for Ireland, or Grand Secretary for Ireland, and countersigned by the Grand Secretary of Armagh, and that no other shall be valid, and that the Grand Secretary of Armagh do issue them to the Grand Master of Counties, and to no others. Save and except to the Grand Lodge of Ireland, and that he do receive the fee of 5s. 5d., as before directed for each number so granted, and shall make a monthly return to the grand lodge of the numbers by him granted, and to whom.

Resolved,—That in a County where there is no Grand Master appointed, an application for a number must be made to the grand lodge of Ireland.

Many persons having introduced various orders into the Orange Society, which will very much tend to injure the regularity of the institution, the grand lodge disavow any other orders, but the orange and purple, as there can be none others regular, unless issing from and approved of by them.

Resolved,—That the Secretary of the grand lodge do write to Wolsey Atkinson, Esq., Grand Secretary of Armagh, enclosing him the Resolutions, and requiring him to make a return of numbers granted up to this time, and that he do not issue any new numbers until he has the parchment numbers, signed by the Grand Master and Secretary.

Resolved,—That the thanks of the grand lodge be and are hereby given to S. Montgomery, and H. Giffard, Esqs., for their great trouble in revising these Regulations.

Ordered,—That the foregoing Rules and Regulations be printed, under the direction of the Deputy-Secretary, and by him dispersed to Orangemen only.

The grand Lodge will meet, the first Tuesday in every month, at Harrington's, in Grafton street, at 7 o'clock in the evening, and the third Tuesday in every month, at 3 o'clock in the afternoon, at the same place.

FORM OF SUMMONS.

Orange Society, No.

Sir and Brother, you are requested to attend a Meeting of your Society, at on the day of at the hour of . Fail not, as you are an Orangeman. Signed by order of the Master.

Secretary.

FORM OF CERTIFICATE.

Loyal Orange Association, No.

We, the Master, Deputy-Master, and Secretary of the Loyal Orange Association, No. held at in the Kingdom of Ireland, do hereby certify that Brother has regularly received the degrees of a true Orangeman in this our Association : and that he has conducted himself, during his stay amongst us, to the entire satisfaction of all our Brethren. We therefore request, that all the regular associations of the universe do recognize and admit him as such.

Given under our hands and the seal of the Society, this day of

Master.

Deputy-Master.

CHAPTER XXVI.

Resolutions of eight Orange Lodges in the City of Dublin—Liberality of the Orangemen of ancient "Lisnegarvey"—Admirable conduct of the Orangemen of Tyrone—Exposition of Orange principles by the Orangemen of Dublin— The Lord Lieutenant of Ireland declares the Orangemen to be "THE SAVIOURS OF THEIR COUNTRY."

The following is a copy of the resolutions of eight Orange Lodges meeting in the City of Dublin. These resolutions clearly establish the patriotism, the impartiality, the charity, and the truly liberal spirit, of the loyal Orangemen of the Irish Metropolis ; and the more particularly so, as these proceedings occurred at a particular crisis, when religious prejudices ran high, and when every man's mind was more or less excited by the fierce rebellion then raging through the kingdom.

Resolutions of the Loyal Orange Lodges, Numbers 176, 230, 473, 505, 507, 522, " 532, and 598, assembled at Harrington's, Grafton Street, on the 16th Septem- " ber, 1798.

" *Resolved,*—That the fifth rule of our association be now read, (and the same " being read—viz., *that no person shall injure, persecute or upbraid, any one on* " *account of his religious opinions, but that he will, on the contrary, be aiding and* " *assisting every loyal subject, of every religious description.*)

" *Resolved,*—That a committee of nine be appointed, to conduct a subscription
" on behalf of the brave fellows who have been wounded, and the widows and
" orphans of those gallant men who have fallen, gloriously fighting for their King
" and Constitution, in the late actions with the French and Rebel armies, in the
" Counties of Sligo and Leitrim.

" *Resolved,*—That the said committee be empowered to extend the benefits of
" this subscription to all the brave fellows who have been wounded, and to the
" widows and orphans of those who have fallen during the late invasion, and
" whose conduct shall be certified by their Officers, as deserving the notice of the
" committee, without regard to any religious distinctions whatever."

Instead of being governed by religious fanaticism, or led away by
religious intolerance, it will be seen by the foregoing resolutions of the
Metropolitan Orangemen, that where merit was to be acknowledged, or
valor rewarded, or suffering relieved, they allowed no selfish or bigoted
feelings to interfere ; but that all alike participated freely in their generosity, their justice and their love. Nor was it in the chief City of the
Kingdom only, that such sentiments were found glowing in the bosoms of
Orangemen ; the rural Districts, aye, even in "the black North" itself,
the Orangemen were found to vie with their Metropolitan Brethren, in
sentiments of good will, benevolence, and christian charity to all. Let
the following speak for them upon this head ; it emanates from the "hot-
bed of Orangeism," from Lisburn, celebrated as the ancient "Lisnegarvey."

" We, the subscribers, members of the Royal Boyne Society, called Orangemen,
" and others, friends of said Association, being informed that since the commence-
" ment of the rebellion, which has brought disgrace and desolation on many parts
" of this kingdom, the Roman Catholic Chapels in the Parishes of Derriaghy,
" Ballinderry, Glenavy, and Aghagallan, have been set on fire, and nearly consumed,
" by some wicked person or persons to us unknown ; and being convinced that
" said atrocious acts have been committed by the enemies of our King and
" Country, with an intention of exciting the Roman Catholics in this neighbourhood
" to join in the rebellion, or of supporting the groundless calumny, that Orange-
" men are combined to persecute their Roman Catholic brethren, whereas their
" great object is, to preserve our excellent Constitution, and to promote the general
" tranquillity and happiness of the country, having always solemnly avowed that
" they are enemies to none merely on account of their religious opinions. We,
" therefore, have contributed the sums annexed to our names, towards repairing said
" Chapels, and we promise to pay double the sum of our present subscription for the
" discovery and conviction (within six calendar months from the date hereof) of
" the person or persons who have committed said crimes.

	£	s.	d.		£	s.	d.
" Marquis of Hertford	20	0	0	Mr. R. Johnson	1	2	9
" Rev. P. Johnson	2	5	6	Mr. H. Waring	1	2	9
" W. Atkinson, Esq.	1	2	9	Mr. James Wallace	1	2	9
" Rev. Dr. Cupples	1	2	9	S. Delacherois, Esq.	1	2	9

	£	s.	d.		£	s.	d.
" W. Hawkshaw, Esq......	1	2	9	Mr. W. Hunter	1	2	9
" W. Smith, Esq..........	2	5	6	Edward Gayer, Esq.......	1	2	9
" W. Rogers, Esq..........	1	2	9	Mr. John Corkin..........	1	2	9
" Rev. Mr. Fletcher	2	5	6	Doctor Crawford..........	1	2	9
" Mr. Ravenscroft..........	1	2	9	James Watson, Esq........	2	5	6
" R. J. Smythe, Esq........	2	5	6	E. Wakefield, Esq	2	5	6
" P. Stewart, Esq..........	2	5	6	Major John Watson	1	2	9
" W. M'Cance, Esq........	1	2	9	&c. &c. &c.			
" John Russell, Esq........	2	5	6	Amounting to £79	13	10	

" Which sum was divided between the Rev. John Devlin, the Rev. William
" Dawson, and the Rev. William Crangle, for the building and repairs of their
" respective Chapels.

The following resolutions, passed in the month of October, in the same
year, show fully and most clearly, the exertions made by the Loyal Orangemen of Tyrone, to preserve the Brotherhood "void of offence to all men,"
and strictly within the bounds of Christian charity, liberality, and good
will.

" We, the undersigned, members of the different Orange Lodges in the neigh-
" bourhoods of Claugher, Augher, Ballygawley, and Aughnacloy, having been
" informed that many irregularities have been committed in some Orange Societies
" in this District, and that a few (we are happy to say but a very few,) members
" of the same, have been guilty of acts of disorder, which may, if not suppressed,
" throw an odium on a loyal and well-intended institution, do unanimously enter
" into the following resolutions.

" *Resolved,*—That we will meet every month for the purpose of receiving
" information against any Orangeman who may stand charged with improper
" conduct; and should the complaint appear to us to be well founded, that we
" will deliver up the offender to the next Justice of the Peace, and at our expense
" carry out a prosecution against him.

" *Resolved,*—That though we have to lament the misbehaviour of a few, we
" must applaud the conduct of the great body of the Orangemen, and should any
" attack be made upon any person, merely for his being an Orangeman, that we
" will, at our own expense, carry on a prosecution against such offender or offenders.

" *Resolved,*—That should it appear upon proper enquiry, that any Master may
" privately admit into the secrets of an Orangeman, any person of improper
" character, that we will apply to the District Master to remove such Master, and
" report him unfit for ever acting in that capacity.

" *Resolved,*—That it be requested that our District Master may, at each of our
" monthly meetings, lay before us the names, with places of abode, of each per-
" son who may, from time to time, be admitted a member of any Orange Lodge
" within this District.

" *Resolved,*—That we will for the future meet alternately at the Towns of
" Augher, Claugher, Aughnacloy and Ballygawley; and that the next meeting

"shall be held at Augher, on Friday, the 30th of November next, at the hour of
"12 o'clock.

"Ballygawley, October 30, 1798.

"John Crossle, J. P., *District Master,*
"W. C. Lindsay, J. P.,
"Stuart Mulligan, J. P.,
"William Falls, J. P.,
"George Harris,
"Samuel Moffatt,
"Thomas Armstrong, J. P.,
"W. Richardson, Bart., J. P.,
"Hugh Nevin,
"Robert Pettigrew,

"R. C. George,
"Robert Thompson,
"Richard Armstrong.
"William Warnock,
"J. C. Montray, J. P.,
"John Storey,
"Edward Moore,
"James M. Richardson, J. P.,
"William F. Speer,
"Hamilton Harvey."

Notwithstanding all the efforts made by the Officers and Leaders of the Association, to preserve the members "void of offence ;" notwithstanding all their exertions to show that the Society was purely defensive, that it was in no sense an aggressive Body, and that its sole objects were, to protect the Protestant religion, to nurture a spirit of loyalty to Great Britain, and to maintain the integrity of the Empire, and the tranquillity of the Country ; still the malignity of the disloyal was unabated, and their outpourings of slander and misrepresentation relentless and unceasing. These violent and reiterated attacks, drew forth the following Declaration from the Orangemen of Dublin, issued this year.

"From the various attempts that have been made to poison the public mind, "and to slander those who have had the spirit to adhere to the King and Constitu-"tion, and to maintain the Laws, we, the protestants of Dublin, assuming the name "of Orangemen, feel ourselves called upon, not to vindicate our principles, for "we know that our honour and loyalty bid defiance to the shafts of malevolence "and disaffection, but chiefly to avow those principles, and declare to the world "the objects of our institution.

"We have long observed with indignation, the efforts that have been made to "foment rebellion in this Kingdom by the seditious, who have formed themselves "into Societies, under the specious name of *United Irishmen.* We have seen with "pain the lower orders of our fellow-subjects, forced or seduced from their alle-"giance by the threats and machinations of *traitors.* And we have viewed with "horror the successful exertions of miscreants, to encourage a foreign enemy to "invade this happy land, in hopes of rising into consequence by the downfall of "their Country.

"We, therefore, thought it high time to rally round the Constitution, and there "pledge ourselves to each other, to maintain the laws and support our good King "against all his enemies, whether rebels to their God or to their Country, and by "so doing, shew to the world that there is a body of men in this Island, who are "ready in the hour of danger, to stand forward in defence of that grand palladium "of our liberties, the Constitution of Great Britain and Ireland, obtained and "established by our ancestors under the great King William

" Fellow subjects, we are accused of being an Institution founded on principles " too shocking to repeat, and bound together by oaths at which humanity would " shudder. But we caution you not to be led away by such malevolent falsehoods : " for we solemnly assure you, in the presence of Almighty God, that the idea of " injuring any one on account of his religious opinions never entered our hearts. " We regard every Loyal Subject as our Friend, be his religion what it may—we " have no enmity but to the enemies of our Country.

" We further declare that we are ready at all times to submit ourselves to those " in authority under His Majesty, and that we will cheerfully undertake any duty " which they shall think proper to point out to us, in case either a foreign enemy " shall dare to invade our coasts, or that a domestic foe shall presume to raise the " standard of rebellion in this land. To these principles we are pledged, and " in support of them we are ready to shed the last drop of our blood.

" Signed on behalf of the Society,

" Thomas Verner,
" J. C. Beresford,
" Thomas Ball,
" Isaac De Joncourt,"

Enough probably has been quoted to prove beyond question what was the course pursued by the Orangemen of Ireland in the dreadful year of " the Rebellion of '98." The regular troops of the Empire were required for foreign service—a powerful enemy every hour threatened the Country with invasion—in the heart of the Kingdom, the flames of insurrection were laying waste the fairest portions of the land—rooted disaffection to English rule pervaded the minds of the great majority of the people—and even many of those whose hearts were well affected had their voices silenced and their hands tied, by the dread which every where surrounded them. In the midst of this great political paralysis, the gallant Orangemen struck the electric chord which called to remembrance the deeds of the Boyne ; which gave life to the heart, and pulsation to the arm of duty in every grade of society, from the Noble in his castle to the Squire in his country seat ; from the steady Yeoman on his farm to the humble Labourer on the road side ; from the weary and calculating Merchant in his counting house to the toil-worn Mechanic and Artizan at his anvil, in his loom, or on his work bench. The spirit of loyalty thus touched, thus awakened to a sense of duty, and thus encouraged by voluntary combination and by a sense of manly independence, gave peace to Ireland, strength to England, frustrated the designs of France, crushed the treasonable efforts of the disaffected, and earned for the Orangemen the noble distinction conferred upon them by the Irish Viceroy, the Marquis of Camden, of "THE SAVIOURS OF THEIR COUNTRY."

Here we part with "'98," and enter upon the succeeding year, 1799.

CHAPTER XXVII.

Mr. Pitt suggests a Legislative Union between England and Ireland as essential to the security of the British Empire—Violent agitations arise out of the Union scheme—Proceedings of a Select Committee of the Grand Lodge—Prudence and foresight of the Grand Lodge, as displayed in their Address to the Orangemen—"Primitive times," with the "Articles" of Lodge 232, Newry—Close of the Century.

No sooner had the Irish Orangemen succeeded in crushing "the rebellion of '98," than Mr. Pitt and many eminent English Statesmen decided upon a Legislative Union with Great Britain, as the great panacea for Irish agitation, and as the only safe mode of securing the future stability and strength of the Empire.   The announcement of this course of public policy led to the most violent agitations in Ireland ; the whole Kingdom, from Cape Clear to the Giant's Causeway, was one scene of political commotion ; meetings were held, addresses were adopted, resolutions passed, declarations made, and all the public bodies, not the Municipal or Corporate merely, but even the Grand Juries of the Country, entered into the political arena, and gave free vent to their feelings upon the occasion.

Towards the close of the year 1798, Mr. Thomas Verner, Mr. Harding Giffard, Mr. Hunter Gowan, Mr. Beresford, Mr. J. M. Barry, Mr. Ogle, and some other gentlemen of foresight and penetration, anxious to keep the Orange Association, *as a Body*, from being mixed up with the agitation then in its bud, were instrumental in having an Address issued to all the Lodges throughout the Kingdom, warning the members against the wiles of the agitators ; allowing to all the members, not as members of the Orange Society, but as free Citizens of a free State. full permission to take any side they pleased of the question, and to support their views in any and every Constitutional shape they might desire ; but strongly enjoining on them not to permit the matter to be mooted in their Lodges ; but that they should "strictly abstain from expressing any opinion *pro* or *con* upon "the question of a Legislative Union between this Country and Great "Britain, because that such expression of opinion, and such discussion in "*Lodges*, could only lead to disunion ; that disunion might lead to disrup-"tion ; and the disruption of the Society in the present crisis, would but "promote the designs of the disaffected, and in all human probability, "lead to the dismemberment of the Empire."

This Address, so creditable, so paternal, and so patriotic, was followed up by another in the early part of the year.   This document from the pen of the ever vigilant Mr. Verner, the first Grand Master of Ireland, is of sufficient importance to be preserved, and is here given entire.

" DEAR BRETHREN,

" The Grand Lodge of Ireland observe with heartfelt satisfaction, that their " former recommendation to their Brethren, to abstain *as Orangemen*, from any " discussion of the question of *Union*, has had the happiest effects, insomuch as it " has disappointed the sanguine and malignant hopes entertained by the enemies " of religion and good order, and that such discussion would be productive of " discord among Orangemen. They now feel it to be their duty to offer some " further observations on the present juncture of affairs.

" Orangemen in different capacities, as Members of Parliament, Grand Jurors, " Freeholders, and Members of Corporate Bodies, will have opportunities of debat- " ing the important question of *Union*. But it is the earnest entreaty of the " Grand Lodge, that *as a Society* they will continue silent ; for as every Orange- " man, however zealous, may, and no doubt will, conceive different ideas on this " subject, the discussion of a question of such magnitude, involving not only great " imperial topics, but also matters of local advantage and local disadvantage, must " unavoidably create a division in opinion, and 'a house divided against itself " ' cannot stand.' It is therefore recommended to all Orangemen, to keep in mind " the great object for which they have associated, and to avoid, as injurious to the " institution, all controversy not connected with their principles.

" The Grand Lodge most solemnly enjoin Masters of Lodges, and their brethren " in general, most particularly to scrutinize the character of every candidate for " admission, as they understand with indignation, that men notoriously disaffected " have of late had the audacity to offer themselves to some Lodges. It is also " requested that Master of Lodges will discountenance by every means in their " power, even by the imposition of a fine, any imitation of the manners and dress " of traitors, which the Grand Lodge have heard with surprise, has been of late " affected by some of the younger Orangemen. They are the more anxious on this " head, which may at first seem unimportant, as traitors are now busy in boasting " of a coalition with our Association, an opinion which this conduct in known " Orangemen tends greatly to encourage.

" The Grand Lodge further recommend that this Address be read to all Lodges " in Ireland.

"(Signed,)   THOMAS VERNER, *Grand Master.*
"   JOHN C. BERESFORD, *Grand Secretary.*

" January 5, 1799."

Another meeting of the Grand Lodge was held on the 5th of November in this year. No matter of novelty or importance was brought forward. The conduct of the Brethren throughout all the Provinces was highly commended ; and upon motion of the Right Honorable George Ogle, M. P., seconded by the Right Honorable Patrick Duignan, L. L. D., the following Committee was appointed to revise the Rules and Regulations, the Forms,

Obligations, &c. &c., to report at a meeting of the Grand Lodge, to be held on the 10th day of January, 1800.

Thomas Verner, Esq., G.M., of Ireland.
J. C. Beresford, Esq., G.S., of Ireland.
William G. Galway, Esq., Sec. of the Grand Lodge.
The Hon. Major Molesworth, G.M., Dublin Co.
James Henry Cottingham, Esq., G.M., Cavan.
Alexander Kerr, Esq., G.M., Monaghan.
John Hunter Gowan, Esq., G.M., Wexford.
Henry Brooke, Esq., G.M., Donegal.
Col. Rochford, G.M., Carlow.
Rev. Thomas F. Knipe.
John Slack, Esq.
A. Bell, Esq.
Isaac De Joncourt, Esq.
Alderman William James.
Harding Giffard, Esq.
James Hogan, Esq.
Samuel Montgomery, Esq. G.M., Kildare.
Simon Langley, Esq., G.M., Tipperary.
Right Hon. P. Dunignan, L.L.D.
William Furlong, Esq.
Robert Weir, Esq., *(and the Mover,)*
The Right Hon. George Ogle, M.P.

We part with the last year of the last century, by copying the "**Rules and Regulations**, unanimously agreed to by the members of the Boyne Orange Lodge, No. 232, February 11th, 1799." This Lodge sat at Newry, in the County of Down ; and we copy their "Articles," merely as a specimen of the "*primitive times*" in which they were written.

ARTICLE I.

Imprimis, That every Member of our Society shall have been born and brought up in the Protestant Religion ; and if sufficient proof is produced that any one Member deviates in the smallest degree from the true Principles of a Protestant, he shall be excluded.

ARTICLE II.

Every Member of this Society shall meet on the second Monday Evening of every Month, at seven o'clock, at Brother Wm. Blackham's in Boat street ; Lodge Hours shall continue till the Clock strikes nine.

ARTICLE III.

If any Member swear in our Lodge-room, during Lodge Hours, he shall for every Oath, (if heard by two Members) forfeit 2d., and if any Member offer to gamble, make Bets, or give a Brother the Lie, he shall forfeit 2d., and if to fight a Brother 2s. 6d.

ARTICLE IV.

If any Member come into our Lodge-room during Lodge Hours intoxicated in Liquor, he shall for every such Offence forfeit 6½., and the Opinion of four Members shall be sufficient to determine whether he is guilty or not.

ARTICLE V.

If any Member has any thing of Consequence to say, relating to the affairs of the Lodge, he shall stand up and address the Chairman, and any Member attempting to interrupt him in his Speech, shall forfeit 2d.

ARTICLE VI.

If any Member shall leave the Lodge-room during Lodge hours, without leave from the Chairman, and not return again before Lodge hours are expired, he shall forfeit 6½d.

ARTICLE VII.

Each Member shall every monthly Meeting subscribe 6½d. to the Box, and spend 2d.; and every Member shall at least once in six Months pay, or cause to be paid off all arrears due to the Box, or forfeit 6½d. extra.

ARTICLE VIII.

If any Member become sick, lame, or blind, (through the Providence of God) so as to render him incapable of following his lawful calling, and if he has subscribed twelve Months to our Box, he shall be entitled to receive five Shillings and five Pence per Week, during six Months, and if his affliction shall continue longer, he shall receive three Shillings and nine Pence half-penny per Week, and shall continue while he is unable to follow his Business.—No Member shall be relieved from our Stock till he has subscribed twelve Months to our Funds; nor shall any Member, though free of the Box, be entitled to any benefit therefrom till the end of twenty-four hours after his affliction commences, during which time he shall inform the Master or one of the Stewards that he wishes to receive the benefit of the Box.

ARTICLE IX.

No Member shall receive any benefit from our Stock, provided his affliction is known to proceed from the venereal disease, or obtained by fighting, or in any other way not properly connected with his Occupation, or in defence of his Life or Property.

ARTICLE X.

If any Member, while he receives Benefit from our Society, is seen by a Brother intoxicated in Liquor, or gaming in any public Place, or doing any Manner of Business (for which he may receive a Reward) before he has declared off the Box to the Master or one of the Stewards, he shall be excluded our Lodge.

ARTICLE XI.

If any Member depart this Life within two Miles of Newry, every Member shall attend his Funeral or forfeit 2s. 8½d., unless he can prove he was at that Time five Miles from Newry, or unable through Affliction to attend.

ARTICLE XII.

At the Death of any Member of our Society, the Stewards shall pay two Guineas out of our Stock towards his Funeral Expenses, and at the next monthly

Meeting, two Guineas more to his Widow or any other Person to whom he shall bequeath it.

ARTICLE XIII.

Any person who wishes to become a Member of our Society shall be recommended, and his Name given in to the Secretary by a Brother who shall propose him the next monthly Meeting, and if a Majority are in his Favour, he shall be admitted the monthly Meeting following, but no person shall be admitted as a fitting Member in our Society who is under 16 or more than 45 Years of Age and of a good moral Character; and every Person thus admitted shall pay 5s. 5d., 2s. 2d. of which shall go to our Stock, and 3s. 3d., to be spent in the Company then present.

ARTICLE XIV.

No Stranger shall be admitted into our Lodge-room during Lodge Hours, without the Consent of the Master, who shall be responsible that he is an Orangeman, and the Stewards shall request of every such visiting Brother 3d. towards the Reckoning.

ARTICLE XV.

No Member shall be entitled to a Certificate from our Society till he has paid in twelve monthly Subscriptions, and is clear of all Arrears, unless he pay 2s. 8½d. for such Certificate, which shall go to our Stock.

ARTICLE XVI.

If any Member wishes to have the Lodge Night, Lodge Hours, or the Place where the Lodge is held changed, he may propose it, and these as well as any other Questions, for which there is no particular Article, provided it shall always be decided by a Majority of the Members present.

ARTICLE XVII.

The present Master of our Lodge shall continue his Situation while he continues to act worthy the Character of a true Orangeman. The Secretary and Deputy Master to be appointed by the Master. The Chairman and two Stewards shall be changed every three Months, as their names stand in Rotation in the Lodge Book.

ARTICLE XVIII.

The Master, nor any other Member belonging to the Society, shall dispose of any Part of the Society's Property, without the Approbation of every Officer in the Society, then in Being.

DUTY OF OFFICERS.

The Master's Duty is, to see that no improper Person is admitted into our Society, to see that the Stewards do their Duty, to make every new Member perfect in his Duty as an Orangeman, to see that the Members are comfortably accomodated on a Lodge Night, to appoint proper Persons to act as Deputy Master and Secretary, who shall be changed at his Pleasure, to keep a Key of the Box, and be present when any Money is drawn from our Stock for the Use of the Society, and the next meeting Meeting Night to produce it to the Secretary.

The Chairman's Duty shall be to see that good Order is observed during Lodge Hours, not to suffer any blasphemous, disloyal, or debauched Songs to be sung, or Toasts of that Nature to be drank, either by our own Members or Strangers, to see that ... Fine, and that they pay it before they quit the

Room, and to call the Reckoning when the Clock strikes nine, that any Member may depart, who chooses.

The Steward's Duty is, to take Account of all Liquor brought into the Lodge-room, to visit the sick at least once a Week, and to pay them every Saturday their Allowance out of our Stock, to deliver all Summonses, and to see that no Brother is suffered to want during his Affliction, and that he is decently interred after Death.—Also to see that no Member imposes on the Lodge. Each Steward to keep a Key of the Lodge Box, which shall be in the Lodge-room every monthly meeting Night, by a Quarter past seven o'Clock, or forfeit 6½d.

The Secretary's Duty is, to keep a correct Account of all the Transactions of the Lodge, to give every necessary Information to a Brother, when required, to see that no Member is suffered to run in Arrears without informing him, to fill up all Certificates and Summonses, and to give all public Information to the Society, that relates to their Affairs, that comes within his Knowledge.

WILLIAM BLACKHAM senior, Master.
JOHN BLACKHAM, Deputy Master.
JOHN WHITIKER, } Stewards.
JAMES DUNSHEATH, }
WILLIAM CLARK, Secretary.

CHAPTER XXVIII.

First meeting of the Grand Lodge in 1800—Report from the Select Committee, and adoption of new Rules and Regulations—Dangers and temptations placed in the way of the Orange Body—Orangemen still faithful, and the schemes of the disaffected nipped in the bud.

THE first meeting of the Grand Lodge in the year 1800, was held on the 10th day of January, in the City of Dublin. Although the Orangemen did not, as a Body, mix themselves up with the *Union* question, still, considering that it occupied every man's mind, and dwelt upon every man's tongue, it was impossible to conceive that the members of the Orange Association should be free from the agitation and turmoil, at that period every where prevailing. Owing to this agitation, but few attended the meeting, and the only matter of importance transacted, was the reception and adoption of the Report of the Special Committee appointed to revise the Rules and Regulations. The Grand Master presided at this meeting, and the following is a copy of the Rules and Regulations, Obligations and Forms, &c., &c., as reported by the Committee, and adopted by the Grand Lodge. Upon careful comparison, they will be found to differ but little from those adopted in the preceding year. They may be found in the Minutes of Evidence taken before the House of Commons Committee in June 1835, in *Appendix* from page 7 to page 11.

RULES OF SOCIETY, 1800.

RULES AND REGULATIONS *for the use of all Orange Societies ; revised and corrected by a Committee of the Grand Orange Lodge of Ireland, and adopted by the Grand Orange Lodge, 10th January, 1800.*

GENERAL DECLARATION OF THE OBJECTS OF THE ORANGE INSTITUTION.

We associate, to the utmost of our power, to support and defend His Majesty, King George the Third, the Constitution and Laws of this Country, and the succession to the Throne in His Majesty's illustrious House, being Protestants ; for the defence of our persons and properties, and to maintain the peace of the Country ; and for these purposes we will be at all times ready to assist the civil and military powers in the just and lawful discharge of their duty.

We also associate in honor of King William the Third, Prince of Orange, whose name we bear, as supporters of his glorious memory, and the true religion by him completely established in these Kingdoms. And in order to prove our gratitude and affection for his memory, we will annually celebrate the victory over James at the Boyne, on the first day of July, O. S., in every year, which day shall be our grand era for ever.

We further declare that we are exclusively a Protestant association ; yet, detesting as we do any intolerant spirit, we solemnly pledge ourselves to each other, that we will not persecute, injure, or upbraid any person on account of his religious opinions, provided the same be not hostile to the State ; and that we will, on the contrary, be aiding and assisting to every loyal subject of every religious description, in protecting him from violence and oppression.

QUALIFICATIONS REQUISITE FOR AN ORANGEMAN.

He should have a sincere love and veneration for his Almighty Maker, productive of those lively and happy fruits, righteousness and obedience to his commands : a firm and stedfast faith in the Saviour of the world, convinced that he is the only Mediator between a sinful creature and an offended creator : without these he cannot be a Christian : of an humane and compassionate disposition, and a courteous and affable behaviour. He should be an utter enemy to savage brutality and unchristian cruelty, a lover of Society and improving Company, and have a laudable regard for the Protestant religion, and a sincere desire to propagate its precepts : zealous in promoting the honour, happiness and prosperity of his King and Country ; heartily desirous of victory and success in those pursuits, yet convinced and assured that God alone can grant them. He should have an hatred of cursing and swearing, and taking the name of God in vain (a shameful practice) : and he should use all opportunities of discouraging it among his brethren. Wisdom and prudence should guide his actions : honesty and integrity direct his conduct ; and the honour and glory of his King and Country be the motives of his endeavours. Lastly, he should pay the strictest attention to a religious observance of the Sabbath, and also to temperance and sobriety.

OBLIGATION OF AN ORANGEMAN.

I, A. B., do solemnly and sincerely swear, of my own free will and accord, that I will, to the utmost of my power, support and defend the present King, George the Third, his Heirs and Successors, so long as he or they support the Protestant ascendancy, the Constitution and Laws of these Kingdoms; and that I will ever hold sacred the name of our glorious deliverer, William the Third, Prince of Orange: and I do further swear, that I am not, nor ever was a Roman Catholic or Papist; that I was not, am not, nor ever will be a "*United Irishman*;" and that I never took the oath of secrecy to that, or any other treasonable Society : and I do further swear, in the presence of Almighty God, that I will always conceal, and never will reveal either part or parts of what is now to be privately communicated to me, until I shall be authorized so to do by the proper authorities of the Orange Institution; that I will neither write it, nor indite it, stamp, stain, or engrave it, nor cause it so to be done, on paper, parchment, leaf, bark, stick, stone, or any thing, so that it may be known : and I do further swear, that I have not, to my knowledge or belief, been proposed and rejected in, or expelled from any other Orange Lodge, and that I now become an Orangeman without fear or bribery or corruption. *So help me God.*

SECRET ARTICLES.

1. That we will bear true allegiance to His Majesty, King George the Third, his Heirs and Successors, so long as he or they support the Protestant ascendancy ; and that we will faithfully support and maintain the Laws and Constitution of these Kingdoms.

2. That we will be true to all Orangemen in all just actions, neither wronging one, nor seeing him wronged to our knowledge, without acquainting him thereof.

3. That we are not to see a Brother offended for 6d. or 1s. or more, if convenient, which must be returned next meeting if possible.

4. We must not give the first assault to any person whatever, that may bring a Brother into trouble.

5. We are not to carry any money, goods or any thing from any person whatever except arms and ammunition, and those only from an enemy.

6. We are to appear in 10 hours warning, or whatever time is required, if possible, (provided it is not hurtful to ourselves or families, and that we are served with a lawful summons from the Master), otherwise we are fined as the Company think proper.

7. No man can be made an Orangeman without the unanimous approbation of the body.

8. An Orangeman is to keep a brother's secrets as his own, unless in case of murder, treason, or perjury, and that of his own free will.

9. No Roman Catholic can be admitted on any account.

10. Any Orangeman who acts contrary to these rules shall be expelled, and the same reported to all the Lodges in the Kingdom and elsewhere. *God save the King.*

MARKSMAN'S OBLIGATION.

I, A. B., of my own free will and accord, in the presence of Almighty God, do hereby most solemnly and sincerely swear, that I will always conceal, and never will reveal, either part or parts of what is now to be privately communicated to me, until I shall be duly authorized so to do by the proper authority of the Orange Institution ; and that I will bear true allegiance to his Majesty King George the Third, his heirs and successors, so long as he or they maintain the Protestant ascendancy, the constitution and laws of these Kingdoms ; and that I will keep this part of a Marksman from an Orangeman, as well as from the ignorant, and that I will not make a man until I become, and only whilst I shall be, Master of an Orange Lodge ; and that I will not make a man, or be present at the making of a man on the road, or behind hedges ; and that I will be aiding and assisting to all true honest Orange Marksmen, as far as in my power lies, knowing him or them to be such ; and that I will not wrong a brother Marksman or know him to be wronged of any thing of value worth apprehending, but I will warn or apprize him of it, if it in my power lies. All this I swear with a firm resolution. So help me *God*, and keep me steadfast in this my Marksman's obligation.

GENERAL RULES FOR THE GOVERNMENT OF ORANGE LODGES.

1. That every member of the Orange Institution should undergo a new election whenever the Grand Lodge may think it expedient.

2. That each lodge now existing shall, on such occasion, elect by ballot five of its members ; that those five members shall then proceed to re-admit or reject the remaining members of such lodge ; and that each member, as he shall be re-admitted, shall become qualified to proceed with the five original members to the further re-election of others ; but that in the event of any person being discontinued a member of his lodge, or wishing to become a member of another, he cannot be ballotted for in any other, without producing to the Committee of such Lodge a certificate from his former Lodge, specifying the cause of such change, and that he is a fit and proper person to be admitted or continued as an Orangeman.

3. That each lodge shall have a Master and Deputy Master, a Secretary and Deputy Secretary, a Treasurer and five Committee men ; the Master to be appointed by the Lodge ; the Deputy Master, Secretary, Deputy Secretary, and Treasurer, by the Master, with the approbation of his own Lodge ; and the first Committee man by the Master, the second by the first, and so on until the number of five be completed ; the election to each of those offices to take place on the 1st day of June for one year from the 1st July ; which election, and every other change or alteration that may take place, shall be forthwith certified to the Grand Master of the County, or City, to be by him forwarded to the Grand Lodge.

4. The Master, Deputy Master, Secretary, deputy secretary, treasurer, and the five committee men, upon their appointment, shall take the following obligations :

MASTER, DEPUTY MASTER, SECRETARY, DEPUTY SECRETARY, TREASURER, AND COMMITTEE MEN'S OBLIGATION.

I, A. B., do solemnly and sincerely swear, that I was not, nor am not, a Roman Catholic or papist ; that I was not, am not, nor ever will be, an *United Irishman* ; and that I never took the Oath of secrecy to that or any other treasonable society

FOR THE MASTER AND DEPUTY MASTER, (add)

That I am not now made a Master for any private emolument or advantage; that I have not a sitting in my house for the purpose of selling beer, spirits, or any other liquor; that I will not knowingly admit, or consent any person for me shall admit, any one into the society of Orangemen, who was, or is a Papist, or has been an *United Irishman*, or has taken their Oath of Secrecy; that I will use my authority to keep proper behaviour and sobriety in this lodge; and, that I will not certify for any person, without having first proved him, and being satisfied in my conscience that he is a person of good character. So help me GOD.

FOR THE SECRETARY AND DEPUTY SEC., (add)

And that I will, to the utmost of my power, keep safe the papers belonging to the lodge; and that I will not give a copy of the secret Articles, or lend them to make an Orangeman out of the lodge I belong to ; or lend the seal, so that it may be affixed to any forged paper, or irregular Orangeman's Certificate.

FOR THE TREASURER, (add)

And that I will fairly account for all money I have or may receive for the use of the lodge, when called upon by the Master of this lodge. So help me GOD.

FOR THE COMMITTEE MEN, (add)

And that whenever I may be called upon to act, in the absence of the Master and Deputy Master, I will not knowingly admit any one into the Society of Orangemen, who was, or is a papist, or has been an *United Irishman*, or has taken their Oath of Secrecy, and that I will use my authority to keep proper behaviour in this lodge. So help me God.

5. That the affairs of each lodge be conducted by the Master, Deputy Master, Secretary, Deputy Secretary, Treasurer, and the five Committee men.

6. That in the absence of the Master, the Deputy Master shall preside, and in his absence the Senior Committee man who shall be present ; but that no other person whatever, shall have the power of making an Orangeman.

7. That each candidate for admission shall in future be certified to be eighteen years of age; and that he shall be proposed by one, and seconded by another member at one meeting, and admitted or rejected at a subsequent one; but no ballot can take place, unless the person proposing or seconding be present.

8. That one negative shall exclude

9. That any person wishing to become an Orangeman, must be admitted in the Lodge nearest his place of abode, (except in cities or great towns,) or have a recommendation from that Lodge, that he is a proper person, before any other Lodge can accept him.

10. That the names of persons withdrawn and rejected in, or expelled from, any Lodge, shall be forthwith sent by the Master, or Secretary, to the District Master with the objections to such persons, in order that the District Master may communicate the same to other Lodges ; as those who are unfit for one Lodge must be so for every other.

11. That each member on admission shall pay ———.

12. That the Masters of Lodges to make returns to their District Masters, of

the number, names, and places of abode of the members of their respective Lodges, every six months.

13. That in order to establish a fund to defray the various and necessary expenses of the Grand Lodge, in all lodges one-fifth of the sum paid by the members on their first admission, shall be forthwith paid by each, and shall continue to be paid annually, by half-yearly payments, that is on every first day of May, and every first day of November, to the treasurer of their respective lodges, who shall hand over the amount to the District Master, to be by him remitted through the Grand Master of the county or city, to the Grand Treasurer of Ireland; the Treasurer of each Lodge to be accountable according to the return made previous to the days above specified.

14. That as regiments are considered as districts, the Masters of all regimental Lodges do make half-yearly returns of the number, names, and rank of the members of their Lodges, to the Secretary of the Grand Lodge; but that they shall not make an Orangeman except the officers, non-commissioned officers, and privates of their respective regiments; and that they do remit to the Grand Treasurer of Ireland, the half-yearly subscription as well as that which is immediately to take place.

15. That no visitor shall be admitted into any Lodge, unless introduced by a member; and that new members shall not be initiated in the presence of any visitors, save Masters and Deputy Masters.

16. That no Master shall initiate any Orangeman into the purple order, who does not belong to his lodge, or without a written recommendation from the Master of the Lodge to which such Orangeman may belong; and that no member can on any account be raised to the dignity of the purple order, who has not been an Orangeman for twelve months at least, and has attended eight monthly meetings during that period, save in the instance of a member who has been elected to the office of Master, Deputy Master, Secretary, Deputy Secretary, Treasurer, or Committee man.

17. All members to be subordinate to the Master, or person presiding for him, who shall have full power, fining all disorderly persons in an amount not exceeding ————.

18. Any dispute arising, not provided for by the rules, is to be decided by the officers of the Lodge; and the parties must abide by their decision, on pain of expulsion, saving the right of appeal in all such cases to the Grand Lodge.

19. That each new Resolution shall remain on the books, from one meeting to the subsequent one, previous to its being adopted or rejected by the majority of the Lodge then present.

20. That no election or other business do take place, unless ten members at least be present, provided the Lodge consists of so many; if it do not, then two-thirds of the members must be present.

21. That no business be done in any Lodge after dinner, supper, or drink have been brought in; but every motion shall be previously decided.

22. No person attending intoxicated can be initiated at that meeting; any old member so attending shall be fined.

23. The Secretary is to read out, before the books are closed, the names of persons proposed for the night.

24. A person is to attend on the outside of the door, while business is going on; that person to be nominated by the master, or whoever may preside at the time.

ORDER OF BUSINESS FOR EACH NIGHT.

1. Lodge to open with a prayer (members standing). 2. General rules read. 3. Members proposed. 4. Report from Committee. 5. Names of members called over. 6. Members balloted for. 7. Members made. 8. Lodge to close with prayer, (members standing).

RULES FOR THE FORMATION OF DISTRICTS, &C.

1. That masters of counties and cities do divide their respective counties and cities into districts, according to local circumstances, not more than five Lodges to constitute a district, unless they may see reason to extend the number; the Masters of Lodges so forming a district, to elect a Master for that District. Should the choice of a District Master fall on any private member of a Lodge within the district, that then such person shall cease to be a private member of that Lodge—so long as he shall continue in such office.

2. That during the absence, suspension, or non-election of a District Master, the Senior Master in the district shall act for the time, the seniority to be determined by the number of the Lodge to which the Master may belong.

3. That the election to the office of District Master shall take place on the first day of June, for one year from the first day of July.

4. That District Masters shall make returns of the members of the different Lodges within their respective districts, to the Grand Master of their county or city, every six months.

REGULATIONS *for the appointment of Grand Master and Deputy Grand Master of Counties and Cities.*

1. That a Grand Master for each County and City, shall be chosen by the District Master of such County and City, and Deputy Grand Master by the Grand Master; both subject to the approval of the Grand Lodge. Should the choice of a Grand Master or Deputy Grand Master of the County or City, fall on any private member of a Lodge within the County or City of which he is chosen Grand Master or Deputy Grand Master, that then such person shall cease to be a private member of that Lodge so long as he shall continue in such office.

2. That the Grand Masters and Deputy Grand Masters of Counties and Cities, shall be elected on the first day of July in every year.

3. That in any County or City in which there shall be less than three Districts, the senior District Master shall, with the approbation of the Grand Lodge, act as Grand Master for that County or City.

4. That during the absence, suspension or non-election of a Grand Master for a County or City, the Deputy Grand Master shall act; and should the Grand Master and Deputy Grand Master be absent at the same time, or in case both offices should be vacant, then the senior District Master: the seniority in all such cases to be determined by the number of the Lodge to which the District Master may belong.

5. That Grand Masters of Counties and Cities shall be returned to the Secretary of

the Grand Lodge, every six months, such returns as shall be made to them by their District Masters, of the number, names of places of abode of the members of the different Lodges within their respective Counties and Cities ; and that they do remit to the Grand Treasurer of Ireland the half-yearly subscription from such Lodge, as well as that which is immediately to take place.

RULES FOR THE FORMATION OF THE GRAND LODGE.

1. That the Grand Lodge be formed anew.

2. That the Grand Lodge shall consist of Grand Masters of Counties and Cities, their Deputies, District Masters, Masters of Lodges, and in their absence, Deputy Masters of Lodges : from amongst whom shall be chosen a Grand Master for Ireland, a Grand Secretary, and a Grand Treasurer : the election to each of these offices to take place on the first day of July, O. S., every year.

3. That all authority necessary for the avancement and welfare of the Orange Institution shall be vested in the Grand Lodge.

4. That the Grand Lodge do meet in the Metropolis four times in each year, for the general government of the Orange Societies, to wit : on the 7th day of May, the 7th day of August, and the 7th day of November ; and that the Committee do lay before them, at such quarterly meetings, a Report of their proceedings, for the approbation of the Grand Lodge.

5. That the ordinary business of the Orange system be transacted by a Standing Committee, to consist of such members of the Grand Lodge as may be in Dublin ; and to which the Grand Lodge shall have the power of calling in the aid of men of known zeal and talents, not to exceed 21, to be selected by them from the Purple Order; such persons, from the time of their being so chosen, to be considered as members of the Grand Lodge ; provided always that such Committee shall only exist until the 7th day of August next ensuing the day of their being appointed or chosen.

6. That in every meeting of such Committee, in the absence of the Grand Master, the senior member who shall be present will act as Chairman of that meeting, the seniority to be determined by the number of the Lodge to which such member may belong, and that seven shall be a quorum.

7. That the Secretary to the Grand Lodge shall be Secretary to this Committee.

8. That as the office of Secretary to the Grand Lodge is attended with great expense, and requires constant labour and attendance, therefore it is expedient that all the expenses incurred in the execution of that office shall be defrayed by the Grand Lodge, and that the person filling it shall be allowed an adequate compensation for his trouble and attendance, which shall be paid one quarter in advance.

PRAYER FOR OPENING THE LODGE.

Almighty God, and Heavenly Father, who in all ages has showed thy power and mercy, in graciously and miraculously delivering thy Church, and in protecting righteous and religious Kings and States from the wicked conspiracies and malicious practices of all the enemies thereof, we yield thee hearty thanks for so wonderfully discovering and confounding the horrible and wicked designs of our enemies, plotted and intended to have been executed against our Most Gracious Sovereign

Lord King George, and the whole estate of the realm for the subversion of the government and established religion.   Be thou, O Lord, still our mighty protector, and scatter our enemies that delight in blood; infatuate and defeat their councils, abate their pride, assuage their malice and confound their devices. Strengthen the hands of our Gracious Sovereign, and all that are in authority under him, with judgment and justice to suppress and punish all such workers of iniquity as turn religion into rebellion, and faith into faction, that they may never prevail in the ruin of thy Church amongst us; but that our Gracious Sovereign and his realms, being preserved in thy true religion, and by thy merciful goodness protected in the same, we may all duly serve thee with praise and thanksgiving.   And we beseech thee to protect the King and Queen, and Royal Family, from all treason and conspiracies; preserve him in thy faith, fear and love; make his reign long, prosperous and happy here on earth, and crown him hereafter with everlasting glory.   Accept also, Most Gracious God, our unfeigned thanks for filling our hearts with joy and gladness, by sending thy servant, the late King William, for the deliverance of these nations from tyranny and arbitrary power.

Let truth and justice, devotion and piety, concord and unity, brotherly kindness and charity, with other christian virtues, so flourish amongst us that they may be the stability of our times, and make this our association a praise here on earth. This we most humbly beg, in the name, and for the sake of Jesus Christ, our Lord and Saviour.   *Amen.*

FORM OF PRAYER TO BE USED AT CLOSING.

O Almighty God, who art a strong tower of defence unto thy servants against the face of their enemies, we yield thee praise and thanks for our deliverance from those great and apparent dangers wherewith we were encompassed.   We acknowledge thy goodness, that we were not delivered over as a prey unto them, beseeching thee still to continue thy mercy towards us, that all the world may know thou art our Saviour and mighty deliverer. through Jesus Christ   *Amen.*

Though it was a truly gratifying reflection to the wise and patriotic leaders of the Orangemen of that day, to look back upon the course their brethren had pursued in the great crisis through which their country had passed, near the close of the century which had just terminated, still they were not yet wholly free from danger.   Though the Orangemen of Ireland were found true to the obligations of duty and allegiance through all the political convulsions and rebellions ; though they had firmly withstood all the allurements of treason, in however captivating a form presented ; though, in the darkest hours of gloom and dread, they had remained unappalled and unshaken ; though when others, who were appointed and paid by the Executive to discharge high and onerous duties, had meanly skulked or pusillanimously neglected to fulfil the task assigned to them, the Orangemen of Ireland,

"True as the dial to the sun,"

by a firm, but dignified and unwavering deportment, struck terror into the councils of the disaffected, strengthened the authority of the Executive,

and gave vigor and energy to the laws.   But their well proved devotion
was not allowed to slumber.   The far-seeing spirits of the disaffected, the
Napper Tandy's, the Hamilton Rowan's, the Emmet's, the Shears', the
Sampson's, the MacNevin's, and other intelligent and designing leaders of
the disaffected, saw that there was no hope for the success of their schemes
so long as the Orangemen remained faithful.   Once secure their assistance,
or even their neutrality, and English rule in Ireland must cease, except in
so far as it could be secured by the bayonet.   To secure this—the darling
object of the disaffected—no means were left untried, no allurements neglected, no seductive art left unpractised.   Everything that could be said
or written upon the subject of the *Union* was put forth ; the house of
every Orangeman was inundated with pamphlets, speeches, squibs, resolutions, and inflammatory newspaper articles, representing the corruption of
the Government, the sale of the national independence, the general degra-
dation of the people, and the future impoverishment and ruin of the
country ; their religious feelings were appealed to as Protestants, their
national pride was sought to be aroused as Irishmen, their independent
spirit was called forth as freemen : nor were the future sighs of their
children, yet in the womb of time, left unprophesied or undepicted—in
fact, no artifice was left unresorted to to stir up their feelings and to induce them to take part in their struggle.   But the Grand Lodge, with
that foresight and prudent wisdom which had hitherto guided all its proceedings, resolved to nip the machinations of the disloyal in the bud.

CHAPTER XXIX.

Admirable Address of the Grand Lodge on the subject of the Legislative Union between Great Britain and Ireland—Circular of the Antrim Orangemen, the 8th of March, 1800—Calumnies against the Grand Master, Mr. Verner—Resolutions of the factious Lodges—Resignation of Mr. Verner, and meeting of the Grand Lodge consequent thereon—Indignation of the Orangemen of Ireland, and recall of their old Grand Master—Annual Meeting on the 12th of July, 1800, and list of Grand Officers then appointed—List of the "YEAS" and "NAYS" in the Irish House of Commons on the Union question.

ON the 21st of January, 1800, a general and most admirable *exposé* of the opinions of the Grand Lodge upon the subject was issued. After a firm but temperate and argumentative discussion upon the impropriety and inutility of dragging the members of the Order into the arena, either as Unionists or disunionists ; after setting forth the full liberty they enjoyed of giving expression to their sentiments in every other capacity except as Orangemen ; setting before the members a recital of the dangers through which they had passed, the perils they had escaped, and the triumphs that were yet in store for them if they but adhered to the voice of reason and experience : it winds up with a declaration that " No member of the " Society shall be permitted to drag the honorable, and as yet untar- " nished colours of an Orangeman, through the disgraceful slough of a " Union or anti-Union discussion—the portals of your Lodges must not " be defiled by angry discussions upon such questions—and any Orange- " man who may not be contented with the enjoyment of all the liberties " which every other Irish subject of His Majesty, not an Orangeman, " enjoys ; of discussing the matter out of Lodge, let him at once leave " the Society, and not seek to disturb the repose of his brethren by his " own over-heated imagination—if he must be an agitator, let him agitate " to his heart's content *out of Lodge ;* and if, after this, he presumes to " disturb the quiet of his own Lodge, or to set at nought the decision of " his Fathers in the Order, let him at once be brought to trial and ex- " pelled from the ranks of the faithful." This spirited and manly address and declaration brought many on the brink of ruin back to the fold. For a time it cooled the overheated, and restored confidence to the timid and wavering. Some persons, however, in the County of Antrim, endeavoured to defeat the laudable exertions of the Grand Lodge, and to excite a spirit of discontent amongst the members, and, especially, a spirit of hostility and misrepresentation against the Grand Master, Mr. Thomas Verner. It was not to be supposed, however, that such crafty and talented leaders as the Rev. Dr. Snowden Cupples, Rector of Listrum, the Rev. Philip Johnson, Rector of Ballymacash, Dr. William Atkinson, of Belfast, &c., would long suffer the efforts of the agitators to pass unnoticed. A meeting of the County Lodge was convened for the 8th of March, 1800, which resulted in the publication of the following "Circular" to all the members:—

> "*At a meeting of the Grand Lodge of the County of Antrim, duly convened,*
> "*and held in Belfast on the 8th of March, 1800, the following Declaration*
> "*was unanimously agreed to :—*

"With the most sincere regret, we observe an appearance of division and dis-
"cord arise amongst Orangemen, instead of that unanimity which has hitherto
"prevailed, and which alone can give strength and respectability to our Associa-
"tion. It is with reason, therefore, that we hold in high estimation the wholesome
"advice and salutary order issued by the Grand Lodge of Ireland, on the 21st
"day of January last—*to avoid all discussion of the great question of the Union*
"—which advice seems to have been dictated by a prudent foresight of the evils
"with which we are threatened, and well calculated to prevent them. And we
"are surprised that any man, who bears the name of an Orangeman, would treat
"it with disrespect. On that most important, most difficult question, we wish to
"be silent, in obedience to those orders. We are also conscious of our incapability
"to throw light upon a subject which has employed the abilities, and divided the
"opinions, of some of the wisest and most loyal men in the kingdom. We are a
"numerous body, and we hope will always prove a powerful aid to the laws and
"constitution of our country, which we have sworn to support and defend. We
"know that those laws give us no rights as Orangemen to decide upon political
"subjects, and we know that any attempt on our part to overawe the Legislature
"by our numbers, would only bring upon us the merited scourge of those laws
"which we cannot without *perjury* oppose.

"We, therefore, most earnestly call upon the Brethren, who from ignorance or
"inadvertence have been led into a contrary line of conduct, immediately to
"return back to that subordination and obedience to the Grand Lodge, which
"alone can make us respectable, and on which our very existence as a Society
"depends ; and instead of becoming tools to any party, or degenerating into fac-
"tious members of so many political clubs, let us preserve that dignified station
"in which we have hitherto stood, as the strenuous and determined supporters of
"the religion, the laws, and constitution of our country.

"Signed by William Atkinson, Grand Master, William Hart, Grand Secretary,
"and eleven District Masters."

Baffled in the North, the disaffected now sought succour in the Metropolis of Ireland ; the City of Dublin was fixed upon as the general *rendezvous* of discontent. A carpenter named William Hopkins, a publican named George Stokes, a person dismissed from the Sheriff's office named David Martial, with a tailor named Henry Fenwick, all four Orangemen, possessing more tongue than brains, and anxious, upon all occasions, to push themselves into note, were found through the Dublin Lodges representing, or rather misrepresenting, the proceedings of the Grand Lodge, alleging that the members were ruled by *a clique*—that Mr. Verner, the Grand Master, was bribed by English gold, and the tool of the English Ministry—that the Grand Officers were subservient to the Grand Master's wishes—that, in a word, the Society was ruled by the Verners, and that it was necessary for its independence and strength, that the yoke of the Verners should be cast off To all this rigmarole of trash ; all this out-pouring of " envy, hatred, malice and all uncharitableness ;" all this ingra-titude and slander ; what did Mr. Verner oppose ? SILENCE ! Relying on his well established devotion to the cause of Orangeism ; relying on the gratitude of those Orange children, whose cradles, like a watchful parent, he had " watched and warded " with unsleeping vigilance, he allowed the disordered imaginations of the low-minded and the vicious, to vent their spleen and exhaust their wrath unanswered and unnoticed. While the faithful parent paid no attention to the maniac ravings of a few of his un-grateful Orange offspring, who blushed not at offering personal insult, and heaping personal contumely upon his name and family ; he was not un-mindful of, or unmoved by others, who forgetful of the admonitions of the Grand Lodge, persisted in introducing the discussion of the *Union* into their Lodges. This persistence to discuss the *Union* question in some of the Dublin Lodges, and especially the publication of the following resolu-tions from three Lodges, induced Mr. Verner to tender his resignation of the high office of Grand Master.

" At a full meeting of Lodge 652, held in Dublin, on Monday evening the 3rd "of March, 1800, the following Resolutions were unanimously adopted.

" *Resolved unanimously.*- -That as a Loyal and Protestant Association, attached " as we are to our Most Gracious Sovereign and happy Constitution, we cannot, " without the utmost indignation and regret, see a Resolution from the Grand " Lodge, enjoining us to Silence on the momentous question of a Legislative Union.

" That sorry as we are to differ in opinion from the Grand Lodge, we should " consider our silence as being accessory to the annihilation of that Constitution, " which, as Orangemen and Freemen, we have solemnly sworn to support.

" That we consider the Friends of that abominable measure, a Union with Great " Britain, as the greatest enemies of our Gracious Sovereign ; a measure which " would destroy our existence as a Nation, and eventually involve the rights, " liberties, and even the lives, of the People of Ireland.

" That from the above considerations, we solemnly protest against that destruc-" tive measure, and do call upon our Brother Orangemen, by every legal means to " support that Constitution for which we risked our lives and properties in the " hour of danger.

" GEORGE STOKES, *Deputy Master.*
" HENRY FENWICK, *Secretary.*"

" At a full meeting of the Orange Lodge, No. 500, held in Mountmelick, the 4th
" February, 1800, the following Address was unanimously agreed to.

" *To all Brother Orangemen :*—Conscious as we are of our Loyalty to His
" Majesty, George the Third, and of our attachment to the happy Constitution of
" this Kingdom, as established in 1782, we have beheld with surprise and concern,
" an Address from the Grand Lodge to all Orangemen, entreating of them to be
" silent on a question whereby that Constitution is attacked, and whereby the
" Loyalty of the most valuable part of our Countrymen is shaken and endangered.
" We cannot think it the duty of an Orangeman to submit implicitly, in all cases
" of the utmost moment, to the directions of a Lodge which is principally composed
" of persons who are under a certain influence, which is exerted against the rights
" of Ireland ; and while a Lodge under such influence shall give the law to all
" Orangemen, we fear that our dearest interests will be betrayed.   We therefore
" protest against its injunctions of silence ; and declare as Orangemen, as Free-
" holders, as Irishmen, in all the several relations in which we are placed, that
" we consider the extinction of our separate Legislature as the extinction of the
" Irish Nation.   We invite our Brother Orangemen to elect, without delay, a
" GRAND LODGE, which shall be composed of men of tried integrity ;
" who shall be unplaced, unpensioned, unbought ; and shall avow this best quali-
" cation for such a station, that they will support the independence of Ireland and
" the Constitution of 1782.

" (Signed,)   HENRY DEERY, *Master.*
"   JOHN ROBINSON, *Deputy Master.*
"   ABRAHAM HIGHLAND, *Secretary.*"

" ORANGE LODGE, 651.   At a numerous meeting of the Brethren, it was—

" *Resolved unanimously,*—That we deeply regret the necessity which compels
" us to differ from the Grand Lodge, as we conceive no Body of men whatever,
" have so just a right to take into serious consideration the subject of a Legislative
" Union with Great Britain, as Orangemen, who have associated and sworn for
" the sole purpose of supporting their King and Constitution.

" That we see with unspeakable sorrow, an attempt to deprive us of that Con-
" stitution, of our trade, of our rising prosperity, and our existence as a Nation
" and reducing us to the degrading situation of a Colony to England.

" That we consider this measure but an ill return to men who clung to that
" Constitution in the hour of danger and distress, and resigned their lives and pro-
" perties in its support, to have it snatched from them almost at the moment they
" save it.

" (Signed,)   GEORGE GOUNE, *Master.*
"   S. H. SMITH, *Pro. Sec.*

" Dublin, 19th February, 1800."

The Metropolitan factionists now thought they had secured their object ;
they had driven Mr. Verner (who might justly be termed "the Father of
the Faithful" in Ireland), in disgust from the post of Grand Master ; and
they presumed (vain presumption !) that they would now be enabled to
annihilate the Verner influence, and mould the Order to suit the purposes

of a few Metropolitan fault-finders! Immediately on the receipt of Mr. Verner's resignation, the Grand Lodge was specially summoned. It was largely attended; the Country members were surprised and annoyed at the conduct of the Dublin factionists, and the result was a full attendance from almost every County in the Kingdom. The meeting was held on the 25th of March, 1800. The Grand Master of the County of Donegal was called to the Chair, and able speeches were made by many members of distinction. Many of the more bold and enthusiastic spirits of the Association gave vent to their feelings of indignation at the conduct of their Dublin Brethren, while the eyes of not a few of the veterans of the Order, were suffused with tears of sorrow and shame at the black-hearted ingratitude, the unmanly slanders heaped upon their late beloved Grand Master. The few discontented spirits that pestered their Society in Dublin, were silenced by the voice of the Country, and when Mr. Cottingham, Grand Master of Cavan, (seconded by Lord Kingsborough, Colonel, commanding the North Cork Militia), proposed the following Address to Mr. Verner, it was adopted by the whole assembly with a unanimity and cordiality, that clearly evinced the strong emotions then pervading the Orange representatives of Ireland.

"To THOMAS VERNER, ESQ., *Grand Master of Ireland.*

" Sir and Brother,

" We, the members of the Grand Lodge of Ireland, duly and specially sum-
" moned to take into consideration your intended resignation of Grand Master, feel
" it a duty we owe ourselves and our Brethren, to testify our sincere regards for
" you —our perfect approbation of your exertions, and our gratitude for your
" manly and decided conduct in the support of Orange principles, in the worst
" and most dangerous times—to assure you of our most zealous support, and to
" request you will withdraw your resignation, and continue by your influence and
" example, to support and advance the Orange Institution.

" (Signed.) HENRY BROOK, *G. M.*, *Co. Donegal,*
" *Chairman.*

" Grand Lodge,
" 25th March, 1800."

Mr. Verner returned from the North on the 27th, and on being presented with the foregoing Address, sent the following reply :

" TO THE GRAND ORANGE LODGE OF IRELAND.

" Gentlemen and Brethren,

" I have been this day honored with your Address. Gratified and flattered as
" I have been, to the utmost of my wishes, by being placed in a situation to see
" the Orange Institution in four years increase in respectability and numbers, far
" exceeding our most sanguine expectations, it may easily be conceived how great
" has been my mortification to observe, that in opposition to your wise and prudent
" advice, the discussion of a political question had been encouraged, and occa-

" sioned divisions in the Societies of Orangemen—introduced, no doubt, by *persons*
" *who would not be zealous friends* of the Orange Institution. Under those cir-
" cumstances, I was induced to offer the resignation of Grand Master.

" The sentiments expressed in your Address of my conduct, are such as I feel
" with the PRIDE and SPIRIT of an ORANGEMAN, and I should consider myself un-
" worthy of that name, did I not comply with your request, confident, that by
" your steady perseverance, all those temporary divisions will subside, and that
" by our *unanimous* exertions we shall frustrate the expectations of our foreign
" enemies, and defeat the dark and dangerous conspiracies of all rebels and traitors
" to our King and Country.

" I have always obeyed your dictates, I shall continue to do so as long as I have
" the honour to hold the situation in which you have placed me.

" I am, with great esteem and respect,

" Your very faithful humble servant,

" THOMAS VERNER.

" Dawson-street, 27th March, 1800."

The annual meeting of the Grand Lodge, for the election of Grand
Officers, and the transaction of other necessary business, was held on the
1st day of July, O. S., (the 12th), 1800. The Grand Master presided, and
the attendance was respectable. The following is a list of the Grand Officers
chosen at this meeting :

Grand Master—Thomas Verner, Esq., Dawson-street, Dublin.

Grand Treasurer—Sir Richard Musgrave, Bart., Myrtle Grove, Co.
Waterford.

Grand Secretary—The Right Hon. Patrick Duignan, LL.D., Dublin.

Grand Chaplain—The Rev. Alexander McClintock, Drumcae House,
Co. Louth.

Secretary to the G. L.—R. E. Mercer, Esq., Dublin.

A new issue of the Rules and Regulations, with the usual Forms, &c.,
were ordered to be printed, and an Address was adopted to the Orangemen, expressive of the necessity of all the members being alert to guard
against the snares that would be laid to entrap them. Fixed in the strength
of their principles, and full of confidence in the ability and wisdom of the
leaders they had selected, the machinations of their enemies were frustrated, and internal repose and tranquility prevailed in the Order.

As so much has been said upon the subject of the Irish Union with
Great Britain, it may not be amiss here, to leave of record, the names of
the Members of the Irish House of Commons, who voted upon the division
of that measure. They are as follows :

YEAS :—*(for the Union, 140.)*

Aldridge, R.	Bailey, William.
Alexander, Henry.	Beresford, Right Hon. John.
Archdall, Richard.	Beresford, John, Jr.

Beresford, Col. Marcus.
Bingham, John.
Blake, Joseph H.
Blackwood, Sir J. G., Bart.
Blaquiere, Sir John, Bart.
Bothet, Anthony.
Burton, Hon. Col.
Butler, Sir Richard.
Boyle, Viscount.
Brown, Right. Hon. Denis.
Bruce, Stewart.
Burdet, George.
Bunbury, George.
Brown, Arthur.
Bagwell, John, Senr.
Bagwell, Col. John, Jr.
Bagwell, William.
Castlereagh, Viscount.
Cavendish, Sir Henry, Bart.
Cavendish, George.
Chinnery, Sir Broderick, Bart.
Cane, James,
Casey, Thomas.
Cope, Colonel Charles.
Cradock, General.
Crosby, Colonel James.
Cooke, Edward.
Coote, Charles Henry.
Corry, Right Hon. Isaac.
Cotter, Sir James, Bart.
Cotter, Richard.
Creighton, Hon. H.
Creighton, Hon. John.
Crosbie, W. A.
Cuffe, James.
Dunne, General.
Elliot, William.
Eustace, General.
Fitzgerald, Lord Charles.
Fitzgerald, Rt. Hon. William.
Fortescue, Sir Christ., Bart.
Ferguson, Sir A., Bart.
Fox, Luke.

Fortescue, William.
Galbraith, Sir James, Bart.
Grady, Henry Dean.
Hare, Richard.
Hare, William.
Henniker, Colonel B.
Holmes, Peter.
Hatton, George.
Hutchinson, Hon. General.
Howard, Hon. Hugh.
Hancock, William.
Hobson, John.
Jackson, Col. George.
Jephson, Denham.
Jocelyn, Hon. George.
Jones, William.
Jones, Theophilus.
Jackson, Major General.
Johnson, William.
Johnson, Robert.
Keane, John.
Kearny, James.
Kemmis, Henry.
Knott, William.
Knox, Andrew.
Keatinge, Colonel.
Laugrishe, Rt. Hon. Sir H., Bart.
Lindsay, Thomas, Senr.
Lindsay, Thomas, Jr.
Longfield, John.
Longfield, Captain J.
Loftus, Viscount.
Lake, General.
Latouche, Right Hon. David.
Loftus, General.
McNamara, Francis.
Mahon, Ross.
Martin, Richard.
Mason, Right Hon. Monk.
Massey, H. D.
Mahon, Thomas.
McNaughton, E. A.
Moore, Stephen.

Moore, N. M.
Morris, Right Hon. Lodge.
Musgrave, Sir Richard, Bart.
McCleland, James.
McDonnel, Colonel Charles.
Magenness, Richard.
Nesbitt, Thomas.
Newcomen, Sir W. G., Bart.
Neville, Richard.
O'Dell, Colonel William.
Osborne, Charles.
Ormsby, Charles M.
Packenham, Admiral.
Packenham, Colonel.
Prettie, H. S.
Pennefather, Richard.
Prendergast, Thomas.
Quinn, Sir Richard, Bart.
Roche, Sir Boyle, Bart.
Rutledge, R.
Rowley, Hon. C.
Skeffington, Hon. H.
Smith, William.
Sandford, H. M.

Stanley, Edmund.
Staples, John.
Stewart, Sir John, Bart.
Shatton, John.
Stratford, Hon. Benjamin, O'N.
Stratford, Hon. John.
Sankey, Richard.
Stannus, Thomas.
Savage, J.
Toler, Right Hon. John.
Trench, Frederick.
Trench, Hon. Richard.
Trench, Hon. Charles.
Talbot, Richard.
Tottenham, P.
Tyrone, Viscount.
Tottenham, Charles.
Townsend, J.
Tighe, Robert.
Uniacke, Robert.
Verner, James.
Vandeleur, J. O.
Wemyss, Colonel.
Westenra, Hon. Henry.

NAYS :—(against the Union, 121.)

Acheson, Hon. Archd.
Alcock, William C.
Archdall, Mervyn.
Armstrong, W. H.
Burrowes, Peter.
Ball, John.
Ball, Charles.
Barrington, Sir Jonah.
Bushe, Charles.
Blackeney, William.
Burton, William.
Brooke, Henry V.
Balfour, Blayney.
Babbington, David.
Butler, Hon. James.
Barry, Col. John Maxwell.
Corry, Viscount.

Clements, Viscount.
Cole, Viscount.
Cole, Hon. Lowrey.
Carew, Robert Shapland.
Cooper, Joseph Edward.
Caulfield, Viscount.
Coddington, Henry.
Crookshank, George.
Daly, Denis Bowes.
Dalway, Noah.
Dawson, Richard.
Dawson, Arthur.
Dobbs, Francis.
Egan, John.
Edgeworth, R. L.
Evans, George.
Freke, Sir John, Bart

Faulkner, Frederick.

Fitzgerald, Right Hon J

Fortescue, Wm Charles

Foster, Right Hon. John

Foster, Hon Thomas.

French, Arthur

Georges, Hamilton.

Grattan, Right Hon Henry.

Gold, Thomas

Hamilton, Hans

Hardman, Edward

Hardy, Francis

Hoare, Sir Joseph

Hume, William H

Hoare, Edward

Hoare, Bartholomew

Hamilton, Alexander.

Hamilton, Hon A C.

Irwin, H

King, Gilbert

King, Charles

King, Hon. Robert

Kingsborough, Viscount

Knox, Hon. George

King, Hon Henry

King, Major.

Lambert, Gustavus

Latouche, David, Jr.

Latouche, Robert

Latouche, John, Senr.

Latouche, John, Jr.

Leslie, Col Charles Powell.

Lee, Edward

Leighton, Sir Thomas, Bart

Maxwell, Viscount

Montgomery, Alexander

McCartney, Sir John, Bart

Moore, John

Moore, Arthur

Mathew, Viscount.

Mahon, Thomas

Metze, John

Newenham, Thomas

O'Brien, Sir Edward.

O'Donnell, Col Hugh,

O'Donnell, James Moore.

O'Callaghan, Hon W.

Osborn, Henry.

Ogle, Right Hon George.

Preston, Joseph

Parnell, Right Hon Sir John

Parnell, Henry

Plunkett, Wm Conyngham.

Ponsonby, Right Hon W B,

Ponsonby, J. B.

Ponsonby, Major W

Ponsonby, Right Hon. George.

Parsons, Sir Lawrence, Bart.

Power, Richard.

Rochford, John Staunton.

Richardson, Sir William, Bart.

Reilley, William E

Ruxton, Charles.

Ruxton, William P.

Saunderson, Francis

Smyth, William,

Stewart, James.

Skeffington, Hon. W. J.

Savage, Francis.

Synge, Francis

Stewart, Henry.

St George, Sir Richard, Bart

Sneyd, Nathaniel.

Shaw, Robert.

Saurin, Right Hon. William.

Tighe, William

Tighe, Henry.

Taylor, John.

Townshend, Thomas

Taylor, Hon. R.

Vereker, Charles.

Wynne, Owen.

Waller, John.

Willson, E D.

Westly, Nicholas.

Wolfe John.

CHAPTER XXX.

Resignation of Mr. Verner, and appointment of Mr. Ogle, as Grand Master—
Address to Mr. Verner—Attempted invasion of Ireland, by the " COR-
SICAN USURPER," and noble conduct of the Orange Yeomanry upon
that occasion — Address of the Antrim Orangemen—Rooted treason of the
Irish Romanists—Emmett's Rebellion in 1803—Slaughter of Lord Kil-
warden—Orangemen "the Saviours of their Country"—Mooney's description
of Emmet's rebellion—Wright's Narrative of the same event—A full state-
ment of the affair.

At the annual meeting of the Grand Lodge, in the year 1801, Mr. Verner
earnestly solicited and obtained leave to resign the high office of Grand
Master.   It was the wish of the whole Order that he should continue ; but
Mr. Verner desiring to pursue in the Country, and in the bosom of his
amiable family, a more domestic life than that afforded by his constant and
unremitting attendance in the Metropolis, asked permission to retire from
duties so onerous, but yet so honorable.   With this request, the Grand
Lodge could scarcely fail to comply ; and his resignation was—though very
reluctantly—accepted.   Many of the members—even many who differed
widely from Mr. Verner—wept bitterly at the idea of losing the future
superintendence of their "Father and Founder ;" to him they looked up
for advice and counsel in most difficult and trying cases ; his experience
was freely admitted, to his judgment the multitude readily deferred ; in his
wisdom entire confidence was reposed, and his advice was most cheerfully
followed.   Mr. Verner's resignation would, undoubtedly, have cast a gloom
upon the whole Institution, and might have been followed by the most
disastrous consequence, had he not been succeeded in the high post of
Grand Master by one of the most enlightened scholars, one of the most
able statesmen, one of the most accomplished orators, and one of the
most uncompromising Protestants that the Kingdom produced—the Right
Honorable George Ogle, M.P.   The election of Mr. Ogle was, as might
have been expected, by acclamation ; and the resignation of his upright
and beloved predecessor, called forth the following just and well deserved
tribute to his exertions, his fidelity and his worth in times of unequalled
peril.

"To Thomas Verner, Esq., *late Grand Master of Ireland.*

" We the members of the Grand Orange Lodge, impressed with the highest
' sense of gratitude for the important services you have rendered your Country
" by founding our Benevolent and Loyal Institution, avail ourselves of the oppor-

" tunity, which your retiring from the office of GRAND MASTER gives us, to return
" you our most sincere and hearty thanks for your zeal and exertions.

" We beg to assure you, that we will ever cherish those admirable principles of
" Religion and Loyalty upon which you have fixed the basis of our Association,
" and that we will maintain them steadily, as the best and surest foundation upon
" which to rest the preservation of our Institution, the happiness of our Country,
" and the prosperity of our Order

" (Signed,)   GEORGE OGLE, G. M
"   RICHARD MUSGRAVE, G T
"   PATRICK DUIGNAN, G. S
"   R. E MERCER, Sec to the G. L

" Grand Orange Lodge,
" Dublin, 12th July, 1801."

During the succeeding year, 1802, the Orange Society went on increasing in numbers and respectability, and counting within its Brotherhood nearly the whole of the Loyal and Protestant population of the Kingdom. So general was the influence of the Society, and so effective were the exertions put forth by its members in the preservation of Law and Order, that the government were enabled to draw off the military force from the Kingdom, and to trust its security to the Loyal Orange Yeomanry, who in that dread hour of terror, undauntedly moved forward to preserve the homes of their families and the altars of their God

In the year 1803, the war with France was renewed, and the " *Corsican Usurper*," Napoleon Buonaparte, threatened every moment the invasion of the Island The following admirable Address was put forth at that critical period, by the Grand Lodge of the County of Antrim

" As it redounds much to the credit of the Orangemen of Ireland, that they stood
" forward in the hour of danger to defend the religion, the laws and constitution
" of their Country, so the Masters of the several Orange Societies in the County
" of Antrim, assembled in their annual meeting in Lisburn, on the 6th day of June,
" 1803, think it proper to address their Brethren at this juncture, when war is
" renewed with their ancient and inveterate enemy, whose views of ambition and
" aggrandizement have disdained to be confined within due bounds They call
" upon, and urge them by every tie which binds them to the discharge of the most
" important duties, that they will continue to exert all their powers to guard and
" defend those invaluable interests, which are the objects of their Association
" They congratulate their Brethren and their Countrymen in general, on entering
" into the present contest with more favourable prospects than any period of the
" late war presented. They have reason to believe that the number of internal
" enemies is greatly diminished, that the folly and madness of attempting to over-
" turn our happy constitution, established under the auspices of our great deliverer,
" WILLIAM, Prince of Orange, is more evident , and that no man who is not a
" traitor to his Country, will now be disposed to sacrifice these inestimable advan-
" tages which have been matured and confirmed by the wisdom of ages, for such

" speculative doctrines and idle theories as have been demonstrated, when reduced
" to practice, to lead only to anarchy, slavery, and arbitrary power. Strange,
" however, as it may seem, there is cause to fear that some such traitors do exist,
" and therefore, Orangemen are called upon to be on their guard against them, to
" be ever ready, like watchful sentinels at their posts, to defend the constitution
" against the first attempts of all its foes. By so doing, they will hand down to
" posterity the character of intrepid and unshaken loyalty which they have justly
" acquired, and of having materially contributed to the safety and protection of
" their Country.

" Let us ever keep in mind the spirit of our Institution—that we entertain no
" enmity to any man, whatever may be his religion, who is not an enemy to the
" State—and that we consider *every good Subject* as a friend and coadjutor with
" us in the glorious and patriotic cause which animates our exertions. Let us
" *fear God, honor the King, and love the Brotherhood.*"

" (Signed by order,)   WILLIAM HART,

" Co. Antrim, June, 1803 "   *G. Sec., Co. Antrim*

For centuries, the motto of Irish Romanists has been " *England's adversity is Ireland's opportunity.*" It was practically displayed in this year
(1803),—at a later period it was openly promulgated by the late Daniel
O'Connell—and even at this hour, the same sentiment is avowed, and the
same words repeated, by the Roman Catholic organ published in this City.
(*Vide Freeman's Journal for July,* 1859.) When the war of 1803 was
renewed, when every available soldier was drawn off to fight the battles of
the Empire against the Ruler of Gaul ; when every resource the Nation
could command was called into play, in the same cause ; when in fact
" adversity " threatened England on every hand, then it was, that Irish
Romanism seized the " opportunity " to burst into open rebellion, and to
seek the dismemberment of the Empire. Plots were formed, Clubs were
organized and armed, and Delegates sent from the Provincial branches, to
meet in the Metropolis of Ireland, to devise the best plan for a successful
overthrow to British rule. The Irish Roman Catholics, joined to the remnant of the defeated Republicans of the North, sent a secret agent to France
to negociate with that Government for assistance ; and placing an infatuated young gentleman, Mr. Robert Emmet, at their head, they had the
audacity to burst forth into open rebellion on the night of the 23rd of July
1803. As before every effort was made to get over the Orangemen on this
occasion. In Emmet's Address to " the Citizens of Dublin," he strongly
appeals to the Orangemen for support, and without them, seems doubtful
of success. In it he says, " Orangemen ! add not to the catalogue of your
" follies and crimes. Already you have been duped, to the ruin of your
" country, in the Legislative Union. Return from your paths of delusion ;
" return to the arms of your countrymen, who will receive and hail your
" repentance." But as before, all attempts proved vain and delusive. The
Orangemen stood faithful to their professions : and again proved them-

selves to be, as Lord Camden called them, "the Saviours of their Country."
Mr. Mooney, the Roman Catholic historian *(page 1077 and 1078)* thus
describes the outbreak.

"On the morning of the 23rd of July 1803, the Lord Lieutenant (the
"Earl of Hardwicke,) held a council in Dublin Castle, at which Colonel
"Aylmer of Donadea, in the County of Kildare, attended, and gave
"positive information that a rising was intended in that County. Infor-
"mation of a like character was given by a manufacturer in Chapelizod,
"a Village near the City. The Officers of State, present at this council,
"separated at three o'clock. The Lord Lieutenant, attended by a Serjeant
"and twelve Dragoons, drove out to the Lodge, in Phoenix Park, where
"he and the Lord Chancellor, and a party of friends, dined as usual. His
"Excellency repeatedly urged upon his council, the impolicy of spreading
"an alarm through the country, and probably drove out in this unguarded
"way, to allay any suspicions in the public mind that he apprehended
"danger. The Commander-in-Chief of the Forces returned to Kilmain-
"ham. The Lord Chief Justice went out of town. No intimation was
"given to the Lord Mayor, that danger was apprehended. Sir Edward
"Baker Littlehales, Secretary for the War Department, was entertaining
"a party of friends at his apartments in the Castle ; and every department
"of the government seemed to be hushed in the repose of security.

" About nine o'clock in the evening of this memorable day, an unusual
"number of unarmed men, in separate groups, assembled in and about
" Thomas Street, within five minutes walk of the seat of government and
"the chief arsenal.   At ten o'clock, they moved in a body to Mass
" Lane, where they were quickly furnished by Mr. Emmet with pikes and
" other military weapons. As fast as they were armed, they returned to
" Thomas Street. The number of men thus equipped, did not exceed
"two hundred ; but numerous bodies were momentarily expected from the
" country, and they were looked for through every avenue.

" A rocket was let off at ten o'clock, which was the signal for an
" immediate turn out. Mr. Emmet, with his small staff, appeared at that
" moment, dressed in full uniform, their swords drawn, and ready to lead
" the premeditated attack on the Castle. Unfortunately for his plans,
" some drunken persons of the party, who got arms, had misled the men
" in Thomas Street. Ere he took the command, the party was broken
" into two or three fragments ; and when Mr Emmet looked to the men
" with whom he was to capture the Castle, he found that some of them had,
" quite contrary to his instructions, and the proclamation he had intended
" to issue, attacked Yeomen and Soldiers, who had made no resistance.
" Fnding he could not direct a sufficient body to the attack, and also
" finding that the promised supplies from the country did not appear, he
" judged it better to relinquish the attempt, and seek safety in flight to-

" wards the Wicklow mountains. Meantime the mob in Thomas Street,
" not knowing precisely what they were to do, commenced wreaking their
" vengeance upon every obnoxious person that came in their way. The
" infuriate mob attacked several persons they deemed obnoxious, particulaly
" individuals of the Yeomanry Corps. As Lord Kilwarden (Lord Chief
" Justice of the King's Bench,) was returning from his country seat, accom-
" panied by his daughter, Miss Wolfe, and a clergyman, he was attacked
" and killed by this drunken mob. Miss Wolfe ran distracted to the
" Castle, sought the Secretary of War, and from her lips did he first learn
" of the outbreak. All this took place in the short space of twenty
" minutes. The Castle garrison was alarmed soon after the explosion,
" and a force was sent to quell and disperse the scattered parties that were
" found in arms." This is the account of the insurrection of 1803, as
given by a Romish sympathiser. Though the main facts, as stated, are
correct, still the narration contains those sins of omission of, and commission against, the truth, which might be expected from the bias of the
narrator. In addition to Lord Kilwarden, the Lord Chief Justice of Ireland, his nephew, the Rev. Richard Wolfe, Colonel Browne of the 21st
Regiment, three Dragoons of the 16th Regiment, and five of the Yeomanry, in all eleven persons were killed, and several others, including a Cornet of the 16th wounded. (*Vide Mr. Wright's History of Ireland, Vol. 6, Chapter 4.*) Of this insurrection the government seems to
have had no accurate information. In the early part of the day, and indeed
for several days previous to the 23rd, information had been conveyed to the
Castle, of an intended rising of the disaffected on that day. But no certain account was received as to the precise time, or place, or party, when,
or where, or by whom, the blow was to be attempted. The wailing of
Miss Wolfe, the terrified daughter of the murdered Chief Justice of Ireland, was the first information received at the Castle, of the *locale* of the
insurrection, though it was within a stone's throw of that citadel ! Such
was the ignorance, or rather the criminal neglect, of the Lord Lieutenant
(Lord Hardwicke,) and the Castle authorities, upon that occasion. The
Rebels were defeated, their schemes entirely frustrated, and Ireland saved
to the British Crown, but not by the foresight or wisdom of the Executive,
or by the valor of the Royal Forces ; but entirely and exclusively by the
Loyal Orangemen of Dublin. Those who are acquainted with the locality
of that city are aware, that the Castle stands on an eminence, bounded on
the north by Castle Street, and on the west by Werburgh Street ; both
streets uniting opposite Christ's Church, and nearly at the corner of High
Street, which leads directly from the Castle into Thomas Street, the place
of the Rebel rendevouz. At the corner of these streets (Castle and Werburgh,) stands the Church of St. Werburgh, and the next building to the
Church was owned and occupied by Mr. Peter Daly, a respectable citizen

of Dublin, who kept an Hotel, well known to all the citizens as "Daly's Orange House." Two Orange Lodges met in Daly's on the night of the 23rd of July, 1803. Three Soldiers on their way from Stevens' Hospital to attend these Lodges, observed the gathering of several suspicious looking gangs of men in Thomas Street, through which they passed, it being the direct route to Daly's. On arriving at Daly's, they reported what they had seen, and their apprehensions that immediate mischief was brewing. A small depôt of arms was kept at Daly's, belonging to some of the Yeomanry and other armed Loyalists of the city, who resorted to this long room for drill, and there deposited their arms for the double purpose of security and of practice in handling. On the report of the three soldiers, Major Swan, an active and well known Magistrate of the City, who was then visiting one of the Lodges, immediately rose from his seat, and asked permission to retire, "that he might see what was going on in Thomas Street." The Master closed the Lodge business forthwith, and the Orangemen present, amounting to about seventy in the two Lodges, armed themselves from Daly's depôt, and proceeded under Major Swan's immediate command, along High Street to Thomas Street. On arriving near the corner of the last named street, they distinctly saw and heard the Rebel mob, then in the act of piking the Chief Justice and the Rev. Mr. Wolfe. They rushed upon the crowd of armed pikemen but too late to save the life of the noble and venerable Kilwarden, though they captured and made prisoners some forty or more of his assassins. Mr. Wright relates this matter in the following words : "They had "committed several murders besides those already mentioned. Colonel "Brown of the 21st Regiment was met in the street and put to death ; "two Dragoons of the 16th Regiment, carrying expresses were killed, "and two Yeomen were intercepted and slain, and three severely wounded. "A Cornet was dragged out of a carriage, in which he was passing, and "severely wounded with pikes. The bodies of Lord Kilwarden and his "nephew, were found on the spot where they were slaughtered. The "former was not quite dead, and he was carried in a dying state to the "watch-house. A number of prisoners were taken, and one of the officers, "horror-struck at the condition of the dying nobleman, declared aloud, "that he would have a gallows erected at the watch-house door to hang "the villains. Lord Kilwarden, with his well known love of justice, said "feebly, *What are you going to do Swan?* To hang these Rebels, my "Lord, was the reply. *I desire,* said Lord Kilwarden, *that no man shall* "*be put to death but by the laws of his country.* These are said to have "been the last words he uttered." Those of the Rebels that were not slain, or captured, in Thomas Street, fled southward into that part of the city called "the Liberties ;" whither they were hotly pursued by their Orange assailants. They attempted to make a stand at the Upper Coombe, and again at Cross Poddle Lane, but in both instances, were rushed upon by the Orange Yeomanry, who completely defeated and dispersed them. Mr. Emmet's schemes were thus frustrated, the Castle saved from attack, the regular army unemployed, and the Lord Lieutenant and the Irish Government left unacquainted with the danger to which they had been exposed, till after that danger had passed away.   So much for the gallant, but calumniated, Orangemen in 1803.

CHAPTER XXXI.

Death of the Earl of Annesley, and appointment of Lord Lecale to the Grand Mastership of the County of Down—The Ministry of " all the Talents," and Letter of the King to Lord Grenville—Address of the Orangemen to the High Sheriff and Grand Jury of Tyrone—election of Grand Officers in 1807— address to Mr. Ogle and his reply—establishment of Lodges in the Army, and in England and in Scotland.

The appointment of the Right Hon. the Earl of Annesley, to be the Grand Master of the County of Down, has been already mentioned. His Lordship died in the early part of the year 1803, and the Right Honourable Lord Lecale was appointed his successor.   The following is a copy of the correspondence which took place upon that occasion.

To the Right Hon. the Lord Lecale, &c. &c.

" My Lord,—" I had the honour of proposing your Lordship to be Grand Master " of the County of Down Orangemen, at a meeting at Ballynahinch, on the 24th " inst., and I feel sincere pleasure in being able to inform your Lordship, that you " were unanimously appointed to that office to succeed our late steady good friend, " Earl Annesley.

" Signed on behalf of 43 Lodges,

" ROBERT BROWN, D. M. Lecale."

Answer

Ardglace, June 4th, 1803.

" Dear Sir,—" The honour of being at the Head of the County of Down Orange- " men is a favour I never shall forget.   Allow me, however, to regret, that the " death of our late Grand Master is the occasion of my promotion—he was a man, " whose steady, firm, and manly conduct in the support of his King and Country, " must ever render his memory dear to every loyal subject—I may imitate him but " never can exceed him.

" I am Sir, with great esteem, yours,   " LECALE.

" I hope to meet my brother Orangemen at Ballynahinch, on the first of July, " (O.S.) and the Rev. Mr. Wilson will please prepare a sermon for the occasion.'

No matter of importance, connected with the progress of Orangeism, occurred in the years 1804, 5, 6 or 7. The efforts of the disaffected having so signally failed ; all their schemes having been completely frustrated ; the country was allowed to enjoy some little repose from domestic agitation. *"All the Talents"* Ministry, as they were called, were pushed into power in the course of 1807 ; and some little agitation arose out of the circumstance of their pressing upon the King, (George the Third,) what was then called "Catholic Emancipation." The memorable letter of His Majesty, addressed to his First Minister, Lord Grenville ; in which he declared his firm resolve not to concede the measure, allayed the temporary excitement then got up. "All the Talents" retired from office, and "Catholic Emancipation" received *a damper*. Nearly all, if not all, the Grand Juries, Corporations, and other Protestant bodies in Ireland, addressed his Majesty upon that memorable occasion, expressive of their loyalty to the Throne, and of their approval of the sentiments conveyed in the King's letter to Lord Grenville. Amongst the other public bodies that addressed His Majesty, was the High Sheriff and Grand Jury of the County Tyrone. For this address, the Orangemen of that County addressed the Sheriff and Grand Jurors on the 16th of April, in the following language ; the Venerable Archdeacon Caulfield, County Grand Master, in the Chair.

" *To the High Sheriff of the County of Tyrone ; and to William Stewart, Esq.* " *M.P., Foreman, and the other Jurors of the said County.*

" We, the Orangemen of the County of Tyrone, feel ourselves called upon in " these critical times to declare our sentiments in the face of the empire and the " world. It is our glory and our boast to be firmly united in a Society by ties " the most honourable, because they are the most loyal and constitutional. We " are bound to assist the magistrates in the preservation of order and peace—we " are enemies to none but those who would disturb them—the ground on which " we stand is the Glorious Revolution of 1688. It was nobly purchased for us by " the gallant exertions of our ancestors, and cemented by their blood. We hold " it but in trust. We have no right to fritter away the inestimable gift, and we " are therefore resolved to demonstrate ourselves worthy of it, by faithfully " delivering it to our posterity pure and unimpaired. What was effected by their " courage shall never be forfeited by our timidity—what they dared to gain we " dare to defend.

" To that Glorious Revolution we are indebted among other blessings for the " gracious Monarch who so worthily sways the sceptre of the realm, and whose " just sense of the mighty charge with which his family were entrusted, has been " so steadily and publicly avowed from the throne as to insure our gratitude—for " whom we live, and to maintain whose rights we would freely die.

" It is our happiness to find, Mr. Sheriff and Gentlemen of the Grand Jury, that " you are influenced by the same patriotic sentiments, and we request you to ' receive our most cordial thanks for your decided declaration of them at our last " assize

" It is not our concern, and we will accordingly never interfere with any man in
" his religious principles—the gospel found him, and the gospel leaves him a free
" agent;—but while any man, or body of men acknowledge submission or duty of
" any sort or kind to any foreign power whatever, we maintain that such person
" or persons demand the vigilant inspection of our rulers, and should be under
" every limitation the wisdom of Government may suggest, as requisite to preserve
" inviolable the Constitution of our country in Church and State.

" While we thus with heartfelt joy coincide with you, Mr. Sheriff and Gentle-
" men of the Grand Jury, in your manly Address to our Representatives, it is our
" mutual felicity and glory to enjoy so powerful and firm a guardian of our Con-
" stitution, in the Majesty of our Sovereign, whose health may Almighty God
" preserve, and his reign prolong.

" Signed by Order,

" April 16th, 1807."   "JOHN CROSSLE, Co. Grand Secretary."

The Grand Lodge met as usual, on the 1st of July, (O. S.) 1807.   The
following Grand Officers were elected ;

Grand Master.—The Right Honourable George Ogle, M.P., Belleview,
County of Wexford.

Deputy Grand Master.—John Giffard, Esq., Dublin.

Grand Secretary.—The Right Honourable Patrick Duigan, LL.D.,
Dublin.

Grand Treasurer.—Sir Richard Musgrave, Bart., Myrtle Grove, County
of Waterford.

Grand Chaplain.—Rev. William Hamilton, Dublin.

Acting Grand Secretary.—John Brooke, Esq., Dublin.

Acting Grand Treasurer.—Abraham Bradley King, Esq., Dame Street,
Dublin.

Mr. Ogle came up to the Metropolis from his Country seat in Wexford,
and presided at this meeting.   The following fresh testimony of the high
estimation in which that distinguished statesman, orator and author was
held by the Orangemen of Ireland, was presented to him in open Lodge.

" *To the Right Honourable George Ogle, M.P.,*

" SIR AND BROTHER,—Rejoicing to see you once more amongst us, and to hear
" again from yourself those sentiments which have endeared you to the Protest-
" ants of Ireland, we feel that we can offer to you nothing more pleasing than our
" heartfelt congratulations upon the glorious and successful stand lately made by
" our beloved Sovereign, on behalf of the Protestant Church.

" Most sincerely do we pray, that our good King may continue to reign over a
" free and happy people, upon the principles of " *Civil and Religious Liberty,*"
" which called his family to the Throne, and that all his subjects, grateful for the
" blessings of such a reign, may in return, emulate the Constitutional Loyalty of
" GEORGE OGLE."

To this Address, Mr. Ogle returned the following answer :

"FRIENDS AND BROTHERS,—Allow me to express my sincere and heartfelt
" thanks for this fresh and honourable testimony of the confidence you repose in
" me and my principles, and to assure you, that in any state of this country, or of
" myself, no time, no chance, no circumstance, nor any power upon earth, can ever
" shake my inviolable attachment to our happy Constitution in Church and State.

" No oblivion can ever erase from my mind or my heart, what we owe to the
" memory of our great and glorious Deliverer, or those principles which placed
" the Illustrious House of Hanover upon the Throne of these realms, and of what
" we all owe to our good old Protestant King, who stood forward at the late awful
" crisis to support the principles of our glorious institution, to which I am, and
" ever shall be, inviolably bound by every tie human and divine.

" Under these impressions, I hope there can be no occasion for me to say how
" much it will be my pride and my pleasure to advance the prosperity and maintain
" the honour of the Orangemen of Ireland.

" GEORGE OGLE, *Grand Master.*

" Dublin, July 12th, 1807."

At this period, Lodges of the Association had extended, not only into all
the Yeomanry Corps and the Militia Regiments of Ireland, but also into
nearly all the Battalions of the Regular Army, and especially was the
system cultivated in the Royal Artillery ; nearly all the members of which
arm of the service were Orangemen. In this year (1807,) also, the Society
was extended to England, by Orangemen from Ireland, who had migrated
to the sister Kingdom. Some seventeen or eighteen Lodges were organized
in the northern and western Shires, chiefly in the commercial and manufacturing Towns of Liverpool, Manchester, Leeds, Birmingham, York and
Bradford. One or two Lodges were also organized about the same period
in the city of London ; and one at Maybole, in Ayrshire, and another in
the city of Glasgow, both in North Britain. All these Lodges were opened under the authority of warrants, brought over from Ireland by Irish
Orangemen.

CHAPTER XXXII.

When and how a Grand Lodge was first established in England—Colonel Taylor
the first Grand Master of England—Letter from Mr. Nixon to Mr. Verner
21st November, 1808—Removal of the Grand Lodge from Manchester to London
—Address to the King, with his Majesty's reply—Report of the House of
Commons' Committee on English Orangeism.

In the year 1808, the annual meeting of the Grand Orange Lodge of
Ireland was held as usual. No event of importance transpired, and the
Grand Officers of the preceding year were re-elected.

In this year, a Grand Lodge was first organized in England. The
particulars connected with this event may be found upon reference to the
" Report from the Select Committee of the House of Commons, appointed
" to enquire into the origin, nature, extent and tendency of Orange
" Institutions in Great Britain and the Colonies, with the Minutes of
" Evidence, Appendix and Index. Ordered by the House to be printed,
" 7th September, 1835." *Vide Report*, page 4, and *Appendix No. 21, page*
174. It appears that Mr. R. Nixon, of Manchester, was the chief instrument in establishing a Grand Lodge in England. He was a very zealous
and efficient member of the Order ; what might be termed a strong mind-
ed man, possessed of an independent and liberal spirit, and had cultivated
an intimacy with Mr. John Verner of Church Hill, (a younger brother of
the first Grand Master,) with whom he kept up a correspondence on Orange
matters. Mr. Nixon, anxious in the organization of the Society in England, to place its direction in respectable hands, had an interview with
Colonel Taylor, an Officer of distinction, then residing at his seat, Moston,
near Manchester. The Colonel was not only a gallant soldier, but a well-
informed and efficient Magistrate also ; and before connecting himself with
the spread of Orangeism in England, he required Mr. Nixon to furnish
him with the Constitution of the Society, the Obligations of Members, and
any other documents he might be able to afford, calculated to put him in
full possession of the aims and designs of the Association, and the means
by which they were carried out. In the month of May, Mr. Nixon furnished Colonel Taylor with the information sought, accompanied by the following letter :

" Colonel Taylor.   " Manchester, 20th May, 1808.

" Sir,—Enclosed you have the documents, which will assist you to elucidate the
" principles and designs of the Orange Association. I have to apologise for not
" sending them sooner, as it was with difficulty I could procure a printed book

" of the Rules, from which I copied them. I know not that I can furnish any other
" additional information, than what you are already in possession of. Our " General
" Declaration " is the best proof of the Loyalty of our views. Assembling with
" no hostile design to any party, or even the least appearance to party allusion,
" the Societies enjoy their periodical meetings like good subjects, each readily
" contributing his quota, which is reserved for his support in affliction. Meet-
" ing with these views, have not the Society a right to claim the countenance
" and support of the Government? Undoubtedly they have; but especially at
" this crisis, when the overgrown power of an implacable enemy threatens to
" overwhelm us; and when internal dissatisfaction is not altogether extinguish-
" ed.   Surely the good policy of supporting those who are sworn to ' assist
" the Civil and Military powers, in the just and lawful discharge of their duty,'
" cannot be disputed. Leaving the whole to your own judicious government,
" and heartily wishing you success in the object of our wishes.

I have the honour to be, &c.,

R. NIXON.

In the month of September following, Mr. Nixon wrote to Mr. Verner,
in the following terms :

" Manchester, September 3rd, 1808.

" John Verner, Esq.,

"DEAR SIR,—I am fearful you will think me remiss in not writing to you
" before. I entreat you will not construe my silence to any personal disrespect
" or to any lukewarmness in the cause, but solely to the wish I feel to com-
" municate to you all the proceedings connected with the Grand Lodge, and
" with the present state of the Societies here. This I have not been able to
" do before this time, and even now, not completely. I beg leave respectfully
" to direct your attention to my letter of the 2nd of last December, wherein I
" apprised you of the establishment of a County Lodge (for Lancashire on the
" 16th Feb., 1807,) which establishment you were pleased to approve of in a
" subsequent letter to Colonel Taylor. At the following quarterly meeting,
" (December the 29th,) a circular letter of printed resolutions, was received from
" an Orange Lodge in London, proposing to the Societies here, the establishment
" of a Grand Lodge for England, and requesting that Delegates might be sent
" thither on the 4th of January, to assist in such formation, is an object so
" desirable, that the Societies were determined to give all the aid in their
" power; and for this purpose it was resolved, that two Delegates should be
" sent to ascertain the practicability of the measure.

" Mr. James Lever, of Bolton, and myself, were nominated for this business.
" On our arrival in London, we were disappointed to find the Society neither
" so numerous, nor quite so respectable as we anticipated, or as the nature of such
" an establishment requires. We therefore deemed it prudent to withhold our
" countenance from the measure, and the meeting dissolved without adopting any-
" thing whatever towards the plan.

" Notwithstanding our failure in this respect, the members of this County
" (Lancaster,) were so convinced of the necessity, as well as the utility of such a
" formation, that they resolved to try some other expedient, before they altogether

" abandoned the design. The great body of Orange Lodges are centred in this
" and the adjoining Counties. For the better government of these societies, the
" erection of a Grand Lodge in Manchester, became at every succeeding quarter-
" ly meeting, more apparently necessary. The transaction of business with the
" Grand Lodge of Ireland had become extremely precarious: no direct communi-
" cation with any of its leading members: but above all, the declaration in your
" letter of the 22nd of January, that it had "almost ceased to exist," entirely
" convinced the minds of all here, that no general organization or regularity could
" take place, without a Grand Lodge in Manchester, to govern the subordinate
" Lodges. It was accordingly agreed that such a Lodge should, from that meeting,
" be established. In doing this, the Societies have not the remotest wish to deviate
" from the genuine object of the Institution; but on the contrary, are resolved to
" adhere to those fundamental rules, as framed by the founders of our excellent
" Institution.

                                                      I have, &c.,
" John Verner, Esq., Church Hill, Dungannon."   R. NIXON."

The foregoing communication from Mr. Nixon; was clearly indicative of
the views of the Orangemen of England, upon the subject of organizing a
Grand Lodge, to govern the members then rapidly advancing in that
Kingdom. Accordingly a meeting was held at Manchester, on the 4th of
November, 1808, at which it was resolved to organize a Grand Lodge for
England and Wales; and to adopt the Irish Rules and Regulations, Forms
and Obligations, till others could be drawn up, revised and printed, to
suit the special circumstances of England. The City of Manchester was
fixed upon as the seat of the Grand Lodge, and Colonel Taylor of Moston,
near that City, was elected Grand Master of England and Wales, with
Colonel Fletcher of Bolton, Deputy Grand Master; W. A. Woodburn,
Esq., Grand Treasurer; and Richard Nixon, Esq., Grand Secretary.
Immediately on the close of the meeting, Mr. Nixon was deputed to
proceed to Dublin, and to lay before the Grand Lodge of Ireland, a full
report of the proceedings at Manchester. This mission was fulfilled by
Mr. Nixon; but the Grand Lodge of Ireland did not seem to *relish* the
proceedings of their English brethren. They expressed no opinion however,
but informed Mr. Nixon verbally, that their reply would be conveyed in
writing. This was done in time to be laid before the Manchester Grand
Lodge, which stood adjourned to the 26th of the same month. The following is a copy of the response forwarded by the adjourned meeting held
at Manchester, to the letter of the Deputy Grand Secretary for Ireland.

                              " Manchester, 27th November, 1808.
" SIR,—The answer of the Grand Lodge of Ireland, to the communication I had
" the honour to deliver to them, from the Orange Societies of England, was laid
" before the Grand Lodge at Manchester, at an adjourned meeting on the 26th inst.
" I am directed to say, that the information which the Grand Lodge of Ireland
" requires, with respect to the " *date and number of Warrants, and the number of*

" *members composing each Lodge*," will be most cheerfully transmitted, so soon as " a correct return can be obtained from the District Masters, who were ordered to " ascertain those particulars completely by the next meeting, to be held on the " 29th of December next.

" The members of the Grand Lodge here feel extremely anxious to maintain a " good understanding with the Grand Lodge of Ireland, which they will at all " times prove by an invariable adherence to the principles of our excellent " Institution

I have, &c,

" To Mr John Brooke,   " R NIXON, G.S."
" Secretary to the Grand Orange Lodge, Dublin "

It was quite evident, that the Grand Lodge of Ireland were unwilling to permit the Orangemen of England, to separate from under the Irish jurisdiction. They did not, it is true, *refuse* the application for separation, presented by Brother Nixon; neither did they *grant* it. They evaded a direct negative by a sort of " side wind " reply, calling for a return of the dates and numbers of the warrants, under the authority of which meetings were at that time held in England, together with a return of the actual strength of each Lodge, so that they might have full information before them before considering the question. The English Grand Lodge very wisely left unnoticed the rather unkind, if not selfish, disposition, manifested by their Irish brethren, and with much good taste and good judgment, declared at once that they would cheerfully forward the returns asked for. The opinions of the English Orangemen were, however, fully conveyed to Mr. John Verner, in a letter addressed to that gentleman by Mr. Nixon, immediately after the return of the latter from attending the Grand Lodge of Ireland. Mr Nixon's letter to Mr. Verner, was couched in the following terms

" Manchester, 21st November, 1808

" To John Verner, Esq, Dungannon

" Sir,—I have the honour to acknowledge the receipt of your favour of the 14th " of October, and in reply, I beg leave to observe that the establishment of a " Grand Lodge at Manchester, having rendered unnecessary the six Warrants " received from you, I left them, when in Dublin, in the care of Mr William " Buchan, near Grafton Street, where, on application, you will receive them

" You seem to think that the Orange Societies here, have been somewhat " precipitate in their desire for the formation of a Grand Lodge, and you advise them " ' *to wait a little* ' Alas ! Sir, they have but waited too long, and I believe had " that measure been further protracted, it would eventually have ruined every " thing that has been done to advance the cause, and to organize the Societies.

" In my first letter, I clearly evinced the necessity, as well as the prudence, of " our new establishment. There is not, therefore, any occasion for me to repeat " those particulars. When you figure to yourself the situation of the Societies " previous to this, (without means of forming fresh Lodges, or of complying with " the numerous objects for Warrants which came from different parts of the

"Kingdom: or even without the power of punishing refractory Lodges,) I am sure
" you will see the good policy of what has been done.

" Desirous as the Societies here feel, to preserve a friendly connexion with those
" of Ireland, they nevertheless prefer a distinct establisment.

" Meeting for the same objects, and supporting the same principles as their
" Brethren of Ireland, they will always remain united (at least) in sentiment
" with them. Though the discipline of the two Associations must necessarily
" vary, yet of this I am certain, that no material encroachments will be made on
" any fundamental rule, which is considered as the standard of the old, genuine
" principles of our Institution.

I have, &c.,

" R. NIXON, Sec. of Grand Lodge.

The Grand Lodge of England, as now constituted, assumed jurisdiction
over England, Scotland and Wales ; and as Orangeism was, at this period,
pretty extensively cultivated in the Army, (there being scarcely a Regiment
in the service without its Lodge ;) whenever any Corps passed over into
Great Britain, in which a Lodge was established under the authority of an
Irish Warrants, an effort was made to induce the Lodge to give up its Irish
Warrant, in exchange for one from England. This led to the Military
Warrant, under the authority of the English Grand Lodge, being carried
to the garrisons abroad, as also to most, if not to all, the Colonies, and
other Dependencies of the Empire.

In the following year, (1809,) the Grand Lodge of England held its
annual meeting at Manchester. The following Grand Officers were chosen :

Grand Master.—Colonel Taylor, J. P., Moston, near Manchester.

Deputy Grand Master.—Colonel Fletcher, J. P., Bolton.

Grand Treasurer.—John Joseph Stockdale, Esq., London.

Grand Secretary.—William A. Woodburn, Esq., Manchester.

With slight variations, these officers continued in their respective posts
from 1809 to 1821, during all of which period the Grand Lodge held its
sittings at Manchester. One of the last acts of the Grand Lodge,
prior to its removal to the Metropolis, was the adoption of the following Resolutions and Address :

" At a special meeting of the Grand Lodge of Great Britain, held at the " *King's
" Head*" Tavern, Manchester, on the 10th day of February, in the first year of the
" Reign of our Sovereign Lord, King George the Fourth—Colonel Taylor, Grand
" Master, in the chair.

" *Resolved,*—That the Institution deeply laments the death of his late Majesty
" King George the Third, who was to his people a Father, Friend, and King, and
" strongly impressed with the sorrow that now overwhelms our present most
" gracious Sovereign, King George the Fourth, for the death of his Royal Father,
" and his Illustrious Brother, Prince Edward, Duke of Kent, feels it incumbent
" upon all loyal subjects to condole with him upon the severe loss himself and the
" country have sustained.

"*Resolved.*—That the Address now read be adopted, and be presented to our
"most gracious Sovereign, by the Grand Master, accompanied by our brethren, the
"Lords Kenyon, Yarmouth, and Kirkwall.

"(Signed,)

"SAMUEL TAYLOR, *Grand Master.*"

"*To the King's Most Excellent Majesty.*

"MOST GRACIOUS SOVEREIGN,—We, the Grand Master, Officers, and Members
"of the Loyal Orange Institution of England, in Grand Lodge assembled, come
"before your Royal Throne to present our vows of loyalty and attachment to your
"sacred Person and Government.

"In common with all the people of these realms, we deeply lament the loss
"of our late most beloved and benignant Monarch, your father. During the
"period of his mild and gracious dominion, we all enjoyed happiness and prosper-
"ity, far beyond the ordinary portion of humanity. Troubles, indeed, from which
"no condition of mortality is exempt, occasionally visited our lives and chastened
"our felicity ; among these the heavy calamity which fell upon the declining age
"of our venerable King was afflictively pre-eminent; our tenderest sympathy at-
"tended his long protracted sufferings, and though we had continued to hope a
"termination more favourable to his people, we thank the God of infinite mercy
"for the release which he has been pleased to afford.

"Amid all the sorrows which the woes of our Sovereign excited, we were not
"insensible to the favours which we still possess in his Son ; it has been a grateful
"consolation to our griefs, that in his stern dispensation to our chosen and righ-
"teous Monarch, Providence was pleased to provide so excellent and well worthy
"a supporter of the dignities of his Sire. We thank you under the King of Kings,
"most gracious Sovereign, for the blessings which, during your Regency, did accrue
"to this happy land, from the wisdom and integrity of your Government, and the
"greatness and decision of your councils. From the experience of the past we
"look forward to the future with unmingled confidence in your goodness, our
"anticipations of the glories and happiness of your reign, are built upon the sure
"foundation of your Princely ability and virtue. We doubt not that the Almighty
"Being which has hitherto watched over our country, preserved her excellent
"renown, and defended her happy Constitution, will continue his divine protection
"to our gracious Sovereign and Lord. And it shall be our unceasing prayer to
"the same source of bounty and beneficence with his favour to behold our King,
"and so to replenish him with the grace of his Holy Spirit, that he may always
"incline to his will, 'and walk in his way, to endue you plenteously with heaven-
"ly gifts, to grant you in health and wealth long to live, to strengthen you that
"you may vanquish and overcome all your enemies, and finally after this life, that
"you may attain everlasting joy and felicity.'

"We cannot conclude, most gracious Sovereign, without expressing our most
"sincere condolence with the sorrows that now afflict you. The death of a Father
"and a brother is indeed a bitter pang to the filial and fraternal affections. Of
"the latter, your Illustrious brother, his late Royal Highness the Duke of Kent,
"(we may be allowed in this place to say,' had justified the love and affection

" which we feel for every member of your illustrious House, by his manly and
" exalted virtues. We know how deeply this double deprivation must afflict the
" bosom of your Majesty. We cannot offer a sufficient solace to your griefs, but
" the alleviation which your subjects' sympathy, and the comfort which your
" people's love can administer, these we willingly devote, with our liege fidelity and
" duty.

(Seal.)   " SAMUEL TAYLOR, *Grand Master.*"

In consequence of the severe indisposition of His Majesty, the Address
was transmitted to Lord Kenyon, who forwarded the same to Viscount
Sidmouth, Chief Secretary of State for the Home Department, and the
following is a copy of the official reply :

" Whitehall, 14th March, 1820.

" My Lord,—I have had the honour to lay before the King, the loyal and
" dutiful Address of the Grand Master, Officers and Members of the Loyal Orange
" Institution of England.

" And I have the satisfaction to inform your Lordship, that His Majesty was
pleased to receive the same in the most gracious manner.

" I have the honour to be My Lord.

Your Lordship's Most Obedient, Humble Servant.

" SIDMOUTH."

" To the Right Hon. the Lord Kenyon."

In the year 1821, the Grand Lodge was moved from Manchester to
London. This is stated in the Report of the Committee of the House of
Commons, page 3, in the following words : " The Letter Book of the
" Loyal Orange Institution laid before your Committee, commences with
" the year 1808, although Orange Lodges were held in England before that
" time, by Warrants under the Grand Lodge of Dublin. The correspond-
" ence with Mr. Verner shows in what manner the first Grand Lodge was
" established in England. It was formed in Manchester, in 1808, under
" Samuel Taylor, Esq., of Moston, as Grand Master ; and Warrants to
" hold Lodges under the English Institution, were then first granted.
" The Grand Lodge of England continued to hold its meetings in
" Manchester, granting new Warrants, and exchanging English for Irish
" Warrants, to all who sought for them and were qualified to receive them,
" until the year 1821, when it was removed to London, and the first meet-
" ing was held at Lord Kenyon's, on the 27th of April, 1821, his Lordship
" as Deputy Grand Master, in the chair."

CHAPTER XXXIII.

Disturbances in the Manufacturing Districts in England—The Prime Minister and the Secretary of State, both encourage the spread of Orangeism in England—Lord DeWahill's note—Mr. Eustace Chetwood's evidence—Mr. Hulton's letter—The Grand Master calls the Orangemen to arms—Death of the Princess Charlotte of Wales—Address of Condolence to the Prince Regent—Official recognition of the Orange Society by the Crown and the Imperial Authorities—Removal of the seat of the Grand Lodge from Manchester to London—Appointment of His R. H. the Duke of York, as Grand Master, with a copy of His Royal Highness' Warrant.

During part of the time the Grand Lodge continued its sittings at Manchester, several portions of England, particularly the manufacturing districts, were in a very disturbed state, and the Government did not hesitate to avail itself of the aid of Orangeism, to quell disturbance, restore tranquility, and implant feelings of order and loyalty in the minds of the population. The Right Honourable the Earl of Liverpool, first Lord of Treasury at that period, and the Right Honourable Lord Viscount Sidmouth, then Secretary of State for the Home Department, were both exceedingly anxious for the spread of Orangeism in England. Major Chetwood, of Woodbrook, near Portarlington, at that time Grand Master of the Queen's County, and afterwards Lord DeWahill; was a near connexion of the Premier, (Lord Liverpool,) and in constant correspondence with his Lordship. The writer (who for many years enjoyed the friendship and intimacy of the gallant Major,) was informed by him, that Lord Liverpool expressed himself upon several occasions, as deeply anxious for the spread of Orangeism in England, and particularly that it should be inculcated amongst the manufacturing and the mining populations in the north and west of the Kingdom. Upon one occasion Major Chetwood exhibited to the writer, a book of the "Rules and Regulations of the Loyal Orange Society," which had been for some time in the Premier's possession, and which he had returned with these words written on them, in his Lordship's hand writing: "with Lord Liverpool's compliments and thanks for the perusal." As regards the fact that the Home Secretary, the Magistrates, and the chief Manufacturers, encouraged the planting of the Order amongst the people. the evidence given before the House of Commons Committee, (14th of August, 1835, page 33,) is conclusive.

Chetwood Eustace Chetwood, Esq., thus testifies.

" *Question* 614.—Are there not more Lodges in Manchester and its neighbourhood than nine ?—*Answer.* There are several Warrants in the neighbourhood, but they are not considered as attached to Manchester.

" *Question* 615.—Have you any idea of the number in Lancashire ?—*Answer.* I have not. The Orange System was greatly encouraged in Manchester, and in the Manufacturing Districts at the time of the troubles.

" *Question* 616.—What troubles do you mean ?—*Answer.* First, I allude to the time of the Blanketers ; the general troubles in the Manufacturing Districts. Whenever those troubles arose, we always understood that the the Orange System was rather encouraged, because it was found useful in aid of the Magistracy.

" *Question* 617.—By whom was that encouraged ?—*Answer.* The great Manufacturers felt, that their men being embodied in the Orange Society, they were ready at all times to come forward in the suppression of disturbance.

" *Question* 620.—What do you mean by their being encouraged to form bodies ; how could they be useful to suppress disturbances, unless they were in a state of organization ?—*Answer.* Ready to be sworn in as Special Constables ; part of the original Constitution of Orangeism, and the present object of the Orange Institution being, *to be ready at all times to assist the Civil Authorities in the just and lawful execution of their duties.*

" *Question* 621.—You state that the Grand Lodge began first in Lancashire ?—*Answer.* The English Grand Lodge was first established there.

" *Question* 623.—What induced you to propose the transfer of the Grand Lodge to London ?—*Answer.* It was the Duke of York's wish, when he accepted the office of Grand Master.

" *Question* 624.—Do you recollect the time of the Special Commission for the trial of the Luddites ?—*Answer.* I have some recollection of the time.

" *Question* 625.—What part did the Lodges take at that time ?—*Answer.* I was not acting as an Officer of the Institution at that time. I did not commence my office, nor did the transfer of the Grand Lodge take place till 1821 ; but being in communication with the late Colonel Fletcher and others in that quarter, I understood that the Society was considered useful by the Magistrates.

" *Question* 627.—Have you made any communication, at any time, to the Government, as regards the utility of these Institutions to maintain the peace of Lancashire ?—*Answer.* I have had various general conversations with my Lord Sidmouth, when he was in office, but I cannot recollect any thing particular.

" *Question* 628.—Did you state yesterday, that Lord Sidmouth was consulted, when the Grand Orange Institution was established ?—*Answer.* It was merely with reference to the Duke of York's acceptance of the Grand Mastership. His Royal Highness hesitated to accept the office, until the Government appeared satisfied that the Institution was strictly legal."

Evidence, similar in tendency, is given from a variety of sources. When the writer was in Manchester, in the year 1824, there was exhibited to him by Mr. William Beale, of Jackson's Row, off Dean's Gate, a letter from Mr. Hulton, of Hulton, conveying his thanks, on behalf of himself and brother Magistrates, to the Loyal Orangemen of the District, for their

oyal and efficient conduct upon the recent occasion of the public disturbance and riot. This letter from the Magistrates, had reference to what
was called "the Peterloo affair," when the Yeomanry of Lancashire were
ordered out to fire upon the mob, led by Mr. Henry Hunt. At one period
in the year 1817, when a large portion of the Manufacturing population of
England were led away from the paths of constitutional loyalty and
patriotism, to those of combination and intended insurrection, the Grand
Master, Colonel Taylor, called all the Orangemen to arms, in defence
of law and order, in the following terms ; which summons to duty was
delivered by each Master to the members of his lodge.

" *To the Members of the Orange Institution* "

" Moston, near Manchester, March 29th, '817.

" BRETHREN,—I hereby order and command every Orangeman in England, during
"this daring attack on our inestimable Government, to be at his post, ready to
"assist the civil and military powers to the last drop of his blood , and that he
"distinguish himself by wearing his colour on some conspicuous part of his cloth-
"ing—every Orangeman is expected to do his duty"

"SAMUEL TAYLOR, Grand Master, England "

The English Orangemen, like their Irish Brethren, were ready at the
shortest notice, to defend their altars and their homes. And notwithstanding the inflammatory appeals of mob orators , notwithstanding the
pernicious doctrines inculcated by revolutionary publications , notwithstanding the poison sought to be infused amongst the lower classes in the
great manufacturing Towns by secret emissaries , the Orange Body to a man,
not only remained faithful in their allegiance, but won over many from
the ranks of the disaffected, to the cause of loyalty and order Their
firmness presented an immoveable barrier to the advancing tide of anarchy,
and sent back the flood upon the fountain from whence it emanated '
Well indeed might Lord Liverpool be anxious for the spread of such a
system amongst the working men of England—well indeed might Lord
Sidmouth express the pleasure of the Government, at the efficient and
praiseworthy conduct of the Orangemen—well indeed might the great
Manufacturers be anxious for the enrolment of their artizans in such a
Society—and well indeed might Mr. Hulton and the Lancashire Magistrates, return their thanks for the aid they had received from such a Body
of peace conservators

In this year, 1817, the Princess Charlotte of Wales, the only child of
His Majesty George the Fourth, was called to another, and it is to be
hoped, a better world The death of this amiable Princess, (who had been
married to Prince Leopold of Cobourg,) cast a gloom over the whole nation.
By none, however, was the grief more keenly felt, than by the Orange
Body They remembered that her Grandfather (George the Third,) had

been initiated into their Order, when his mental faculties were more vigorous, and that he had been at all times, the unyielding supporter of their principles—they remembered that her Father, the Prince of Wales, (afterwards George the Fourth,) had requested to be introduced into the mysteries of their Loyal and Protestant Order; that he must shortly ascend the Throne, and that through this Princess alone, could he hope to perpetuate the succession. All these circumstances combined, tended to render the painful event peculiarly poignant to all Orangemen. Imbued with these feelings, the Grand Master of England convened a meeting of the Orangemen of that Kingdom, at Manchester, on the 9th of December, when the following Address of sympathy and condolence, was unanimously voted to the Prince Regent.

" *To His Royal Highness, George, Prince of Wales, Regent of the United King dom of Great Britain and Ireland."*

"The humble Address of the Members of the Loyal Orange Institution, " assembled pursuant to notice from the Grand Master, at Manchester.

"MAY IT PLEASE YOUR ROYAL HIGHNESS,—We, his Majesty's most faithful and " devoted subjects, the members of the Loyal Orange Institution of England, with " hearts deeply penetrated with unaffected grief, humbly beg leave to offer to your " Royal Highness our sincere condolence upon a recent catastrophe, which has at " once bereaved your Royal Highness of an only, a religious, and altogether ac- " complished Child, an examplary Husband of his chief pride, and the whole British " Empire of her on whom their hopes and affections were ardently fixed.

" Firmly attached to the Protestant succession in your Royal Highness' Illus- " trious House, we had fondly anticipated the most glorious results from the happy " union of your beloved Daughter with a brave and virtuous Prince; and that it " would have pleased the Almighty long to continue through her the uninterrupted " succession to the crown. By the inscrutable decree of Heaven these pleasing " prospects have been blighted, and we are suddenly plunged into the utmost " disappointment and woe, and the bright star which lately cheered our horizon " has unexpectedly vanished.

" Under a visitation so afflicting, we hope your Royal Highness will derive that "genuine consolation which religion only can impart, and which enabled her, " whose loss we mourn, with pious resignation to exclaim, " the will of God be " done."

" Permit us to assure your Royal Highness, of our firm and unalterable attach- " ment to your Royal Highness' Person and Government, which we are at all " times ready to defend and maintain·

" At the request and on behalf of the meeting, this 9th day of December, 1817,

"SAMUEL TAYLOR, *Grand Master.*

This Address was transmitted by Lord Kenyon, to Viscount Sidmouth, the Home Secretary, by whom it was presented to His Royal Highness the Prince Regent; and the reply was, "that His Royal Highness was pleased " to rec   ····· ··· ···· gracious manner." The Address, it will

be perceived, was signed by Colonel Taylor, in his official capacity as
"*Grand Master*," and its reception by the Regent, and the official answer
through the Chief Secretary of State, was a full recognition of the Orange
Order   Upon many occasions, as will be hereafter shown, the Society was
officially recognized by the Government, not alone by the Regent, but also
by the King, and by His Majesty's Viceroys, as well in Ireland as in the
Colonies   Indeed the Committee of the House of Commons, of which
Joseph Hume, Esq , was Chairman, make no secret of the fact of the
official recognition of the Institution , and openly state, (*Vide Report, page*
18,) "the Orange Lodges have addressed His Majesty, on special occasions
"of a political nature "

The seat of the Grand Lodge of England, was removed from the city of
Manchester, to the city of London, very early in the year 1821   At the
annual meeting held at Manchester immediately preceding the removal to
London, (26th and 27th of June, 1820,) Mr Chetwood Eustace Chetwood,
was authorised to tender the Grand Mastership of the Order to His Royal
Highness the Duke of York.   At the same meeting, as appears by the
Minute Book, page 16, copied into the House of Commons Report,
page 19, it was "*Resolved,*—That this meeting strongly recommends to
"the notice of all Lodges, the Newspaper called the ' *Hibernian*
"*Journal,*' published in Dublin by our excellent brother, John Burke
"Fitzsimmons, Esq., as the only Paper which has avowed spiritfully,
"and maintains undauntedly, the Orange Principles, in defiance of all
"Popish attempts to stifle the swelling chorus of loyalty to our King and
"sincere attachment to our glorious Constitution "   In pursuance of the
understanding come to at the Manchester meeting in June, Mr Eustace
Chetwood communicated with His Royal Highness, who was graciously
pleased to accept the Grand Mastership   Some time elapsed however,
before an official communication was opened with the Duke, making a
formal tender of the appointment   The following reply from His Royal
Highness, will show the date of the tender, together with its acceptance.

"Horse Guards, 8th February, 1821

Sir —I have to acknowledge the receipt of your letter of the 6th instant, and
"to acquaint you, that Mr. Eustace communicated to me the Resolution entered
"into by the Loyal Orange Institution, appointing me then Grand Master, and
"with which I felt much gratified, and I am sorry that my acquiescence therein
"should not have been communicated to you

(*Signed*)   FREDERICK."

" William Woodburn, Esq ,

" Grand Secretary "

On the 18th of March following, His Royal Highness issued his warrant,
in the following am -

"LOYAL ORANGE INSTITUTION OF GREAT BRITAIN.

" *By His Royal Highness Prince FREDERICK, Duke of York and Albany,*
" *Earl of Ulster in Ireland, Bishop of Osnaburg in Germany, a Field Marshal in*
" *the Army, Commander in Chief of all the Land Forces, Colonel of the First*
" *Regiment of Foot Guards, Colonel in Chief of the Sixtieth Regiment, Officiating*
" *Grand Master of the Order of the Bath, High Stewart of New Windsor, and*
" *Warden and Keeper of New Forest, K. G.—K. S. E.—B. E.—M. T.—and C. S.*
—*D. C. L—and F. R. S., &c. &c. &c.*

" In pursuance of the First Article of the printed Regulations of the Loyal
" Orange Association of England, dated the 28th day of June, 1819, I hereby
" constitute and appoint the Right Honourable George, Lord Kenyon, Deputy
" Grand Master; the Right Honourable William, Viscount Lowther, Grand
" Secretary; Colonel Fletcher, Grand Treasurer; and Mr. Chetwood Eustace,
" Deputy Grand Secretary; and I desire that all communications on the affairs of
" the Society, shall, in future, *invariably* be addressed to the Grand Secretary, or
" to his Deputy. I further order and direct, that the next meeting of the Grand
" Lodge be held in the Metropolis, according to the Order of the Deputy Grand
" Master.

" FREDERICK, Grand Master."

" Given at Westminster,
    " the 19th day of March, 1821."

CHAPTER XXXIV.

First meeting of the Grand Lodge in the Metropolis of the Empire—Appoint-
    ment of Lords Kenyon and Lowther—Sir John Newport's question in the
    House of Commons; Lord Londonderry's reply—Various consultations on the
    legality of Orangeism—Evidence of Mr. Chetwood—Ditto of Lord Kenyon—
    Opinions given upon the legality of the Society by Lord Gifford; Mr. Baron
    Gurney; Sir William Horne; Mr. Serjeant Lens, Mr. Adolphus, and Mr.
    Gazelee—Withdrawal of the Marquis of Hertford and Lord Lowther.

The first meeting of the Grand Lodge of England, held in the Metropo-
lis of the Empire, occurred on the 27th of April, 1821, as already shown.
At this meeting, held at the residence of the Right Honourable Lord
Kenyon, 9 Portman Square, the following Grand Officers were chosen:
Grand Master.—His Royal Highness, Prince Frederick, DUKE OF

YORK and Albany, Earl of Ulster in Ireland, Field Marshal, and
Commander in Chief of all His Majesty's Forces, &c. &c. &c., Oatland's
Park, Surry.

Deputy Grand Master —The Right Honourable George, Lord Kenyon, F.S.A., and LL.D., &c &c. &c., *Portman Square, London,* and *Gredington Hall, Flintshire.*

Grand Secretary.—The Right Honourable William, Lord Viscount Lowther, M.P., &c. &c. &c , *Spring Garden Terrace, London , Lowther Castle, Westmoreland , Cottesmore Park, Rutland ,* and *Whitehaven Castle, Cumberland.*

Grand Treasurer.—Colonel Fletcher, J P., &c. &c , *Bolton, near Manchester, Lancashire*

Deputy Grand Secretary —Chetwood Eustace Chetwood, Esq., &c. &c., *Lyon's Inn Chambers, London*

Deputy Grand Treasurer —William A. Woodburn, Esq , &c &c , *Manchester, Lancashire.*

At this meeting, (over which Lord Kenyon presided,) it was " *Resolved* "—That the grateful thanks of this meeting be given, on behalf of the "Loyal Orange Institution of Great Britain, to the Proprietors and "Editors of the *True Briton,* and the *Hibernian Journal,* for the constitu- "tional part which they took, on the introduction into Parliament of the "late Bills for the destruction of the Protestant Religion and the Glorious "Constitution of this country "

Immediately upon the appointment of His Royal Highness the Duke of York, to the Grand Mastership of the Order, being noised abroad, it was taken hold of by the Radical and Romish parties, and especially by a portion of the Press ; the comments of which were not sparing His Royal Highness was attacked in language the most insulting and offensive ; the Society was pronounced illegal, (which by implication, it really was at the moment, owing to the then existing state of the Law for the suppression of Trades Unions, Delegated, and Representative Associations, and other similar Bodies, organized for seditious and illegal purposes,) and at length the subject was brought before the House of Commons, by a question put by Sir John Newport to the Government, on the 21st of June, 1821, asking if the appointment of His Royal Highness was true , and if so, whether it was right or politic, that the Heir apparent to the Throne, and the Commander in Chief, should be placed at the head of an illegal Society ? To which Lord Londonderry, then Secretary of State, replied, that the Royal Duke finding that the Society was illegal, had withdrawn from it

A similar intimation was conveyed to Lord Kenyon, on the following morning, in a letter from His Royal Highness, dated " Oatlands, 22nd June, 1821."

This conversation in the House of Commons, together with the letter of the Royal Duke to Lord Kenyon, led to immediate consultation with the most eminent Counsel in England. Whig and Tory, touching the legality of the Society. The Counsel thus consulted were Mr. Serjant Lens ; Sir William Horne ; Sir Robert Gifford, (afterwards Lord Gifford,) Mr. Gurney ; Mr. Gaselee, and Mr. Adolphus. In the House of Commons Report, Mr. Eustace Chetwood gives the following evidence upon this point :

" *Question* 67.—Where are the Rules and Regulations ?—*Answer.* I have not a " copy of them ; but I have a copy of the Code formed from them. This new " book was formed under the opinion of eminent Counsel.

" *Question* 68.—Were the Rules revised in consequence of the objections of " His Royal Highness ?—*Answer.* The matter was referred to the opinion of the " then Attorney General, I think Sir Robert Gifford ; and I gave all the informa- " tion in my power. It was then thought advisable to consult eminent Counsel, so " as to put the legality of the Institution beyond question. The Counsel consulted " were Sir William Horne, Mr. Serjant Lens, Mr. Gurney, Mr. Gaselee, and Mr. " Adolphus."

" *Question* 79.—Were those steps taken in consequence of the objection taken " by the Duke of York ?—*Answer.* Precisely so.

" *Question* 79.—A case you say was laid before Counsel ?—*Answer.* The then " existing Rules were, by His Royal Highness' command, with the sanction of my " Lord Sidmouth, then one of the Secretaries of State, laid before Counsel, and on " the opinion of Counsel a new set of Rules was framed. Several cases were " laid before Counsel.

" *Question* 80.—Those were drawn by an Attorney ?—*Answer.* Yes.

" *Question* 81.—Who was the Attorney ?—*Answer.* They were all drawn by " Mr. Harman, then of Jermyn Street.

" *Question* 83.—Did you pay him his costs for drawing the Case ?—*Answer.* " Yes, all the costs were paid.

" *Question* 663.—You had occasional conversations with Lord Sidmouth about " the time that the Duke of York was requested to take the Head of the Orange " Institution ?—*Answer.* Yes.

" *Question* 664.—It was the wish of the Duke that everything should be " regular ?—*Answer.* Yes.

" *Question* 665.—Was it at his instance you consulted Lord Sidmouth ?—*Answer·* " It was.

Question 666.—His Royal Highness was unwilling to do anything disagreeable " to the Government of the Country, as it would appear ?—*Answer.* Yes ; or to " connect himself with a Society exposed to the imputation of illegality.

" *Question* 667.—It was deemed by the lawyers consulted, whom you name, " that an alteration should take place in the original Rules of the Institution, as " adopted when in Lancashire, where the first Grand Lodge was held, and they sug- " gested changes ?—*Answer.* They did not so much suggest changes, as to state that " certain parts might be subject to suspicion. The general import, I think, was, " that the Society itself, was not illegal at common law ; but that such and such " parts of the then existing Regulations might be subject to observation.

" *Question* 668.—Its violations of the Statute Law?—*Answer.* Yes; that it
" would be better without those parts, and therefore a change was made.

" *Question* 669.—Had you many interviews with Lord Sidmouth upon that
" occasion?—*Answer.* A great many. I was in general in the habit of calling
" upon him, and conversing with him upon different subjects, but that particularly
" engaged my attention at that time.

" *Question* 679.—Were you on those terms of intimacy with Lord Sidmouth as
" to call upon him, without having to speak to him on important affairs?—*Answer.*
" I was.

" *Question* 680.—Lord Sidmouth knew the capacity in which you called upon
" him about the Orange Institution?—*Answer.* I was in no official capacity then;
" I was referred to him by the Duke of York. His Royal Highness requested me
" to furnish my Lord Sidmouth with a copy of the Rules of the Society at that
" time, to see whether it was objectionable for him to take the office.

" *Question* 681.—What was the observation of Lord Sidmouth upon the subject
" to you?—*Answer.* I cannot recollect his exact observation; but I know that the
" Law Officers, I believe particularly the Attorney General, Sir Robert Gifford,
" were consulted upon the subject.

" *Question* 682.—Was he consulted by Lord Sidmouth?—*Answer.* So I
" understood.

" *Question* 689.—You considered the Orange System a most excellent and
" admirable one?—*Answer.* I never should have belonged to it, if I did not so
" consider it.

" *Question* 690.—Did you ever report to Lord Sidmouth, the strength of the
" System, during the time you were Deputy Grand Secretary?—*Answer.* I never
" did.

" *Question* 691.—In those confidential communications, did you not point out to
" Lord Sidmouth, the value of such formidable support to the Government of the
" country, and point out the importance of the Government encouraging it?—
" *Answer.* I recollect about the year 1820, when the conspiracy of Thistlewood
" and others took place, I have frequently conversed with him upon the subject.
" I can say, that I remarked it was strange, that such a Loyal Society as the
" Orange Institution, should have its main strength among the manufacturing
" classes in the Country, and that in the Metropolis, where Loyalty ought to be
" most encouraged, there was none to counteract sedition and treason—that there
" was no Orange Lodge, (for this was before I knew there was one at Clerkenwell,)
" or at least no respectable one, to counteract the pernicious system then in
" operation; and I think Lord Sidmouth said, that he never had any connection
" with the Orange Society, and knew nothing about it but from my representations.

" *Question* 692.—This was in 1820?—*Answer.* About that time; 1819 or 1820.

" *Question* 698.—You have stated, that you expressed to Lord Sidmouth your
" surprise, that London should not have its Orange Associations, as the manufactur-
" ing classes in the Country had: what parts of the Country did you allude to in
" that conversation?—*Answer.* I alluded to the Manufacturing districts; Lanca-
" shire and the adjoining districts; that was the great seat of the Society."

This testimony all goes to prove three facts; and which three it clearly establishes. *First.*—That while the Society existed at Manchester, and in the manufacturing districts, it was found extremely useful by the Government, the Magistrates, and the Manufacturers, in aid of the Civil Law and Civil Authorities. *Second.*—That its removal to, and its establishment in the Metropolis of the Empire, was, at least, with the knowledge and consent, if not at the instigation and under the direct patronage, of the responsible Ministers of the Crown. And *Third.*—That the law officers of the Crown, and the most eminent counsel in England, were consulted in the revision of the Rules and Regulations of the Society, so as to secure its entire freedom from the imputation of illegality. Upon this latter point also, the testimony of Lord Kenyon, before the same Committee, is ample and satisfactory. His Lordship is asked:

" *Question* 2599.—Can your Lordship state where the first Grand Lodge was " holden, and who was its Master, and in what year?—*Answer.* Colonel Taylor " was the first Grand Master of it. Where it was holden, or when the first Lodge " was held, I cannot tell.

" *Question* 2600.—Was it at Manchester?—*Answer.* Yes.

" *Question* 2601.—Was Colonel Taylor a Magistrate?—*Answer.* I believe he " was. It was upon his death that I was applied to, to become Grand Master.

" *Question* 2602.—In what year was that?—*Answer.* I cannot charge my " memory. It was at the time, I think, under consideration, whether Colonel " Fletcher should not be appointed Grand Master; he was at that time, I think, " Deputy Grand Master.

" *Question* 2603.—Colonel Fletcher of what place?—*Answer.* Of Bolton.

" *Question* 2604.—He belonged to the Institution?—*Answer.* He did; and he " was the principle cause of my becoming a member of it, from the statement he " made to me, of the benefit he conceived the cause of good order received in his " neighbourhood, from the Institution.

" *Question* 2605.—Where was your Lordship initiated?—*Answer.* I think at " Colonel Fletcher's.

" *Question* 2611.—When you were initiated, were there any Oaths administered " to you?—*Answer.* There were.

" *Question* 2612.—Had you any copy of the Rules and Ordinances before the " copy of 1826?—*Answer.* Yes, one of which I have brought here, which was " laid before counsel when their opinion was asked on the legality of the Institu- " tion. Those, I think, were drawn up at that time; meaning that there should " be any alteration from the others which was felt requisite.

" *Question* 2613.—There is no date to this copy which you produce?—*Answer.* " The date is 1821.

" *Question* 2614.—Is there an Oath prescribed in these Rules and Regulations? " *Answer.* The very object in consulting counsel at that time was, because the " Oath was considered to be illegal, to obtain their opinion on the subject; and the " result of the opinion was, that the Oath should be entirely discontinued.

" *Question* 2615.—Do you mean what is called the Orangeman's Oath in
" Ireland ?—*Answer.* Yes, that was discontinued this is the opinion of Mr. Ser-
" jeant Lens. I wish to state to the Committee that he was applied to, because it
" was understood, he was more completely in the confidence of the Whig party at
" the time, and had enjoyed the high approbation and confidence of Mr Fox, more
" than any other eminent man in the law , and the Society were therefore, par-
" ticularly desirous of taking his opinion   The first date, it will be seen, is in
" December, 1821, and the second is January the 16th, 1822.

(*The case laid before Mr Serjant Lens, and his answer, dated December, 1821,*
were handed in   Also the case, and his answer, dated the 16th of January, 1822
And also the answer of Sir William Horne, to the same case, dated the 24th of
January, 1822 , all of which were read as follows ')

" CASE

" The object of submitting the Rules a nd Regulations of the Orange Institution,
" left herewith for your consideration and opinion, is for the purpose of ascertain-
" ing, if a Society so constituted violates the common law, or any existing statute,
" particularly the acts of the 37th of George the Third, Chap 123 , the 39th of
" George the Third, Chap 79 , and the 57th of George the Third, Chap 19

" The 39th of George the Third, recites in its preamble the existence of a
" traitorous conspiracy, the institution of Societies of a new and dangerous nature,
" inconsistent with the public tranquility , particularly certain Societies, United
" Englishmen, United Irishmen, United Britons, and the Corresponding Society
" It then proceeds to state that, *whereas members of many such Societies, have*
" *taken unlawful Oaths, and engagements of fidelity and secrecy, and used secret*
" *Signs, and appointed Committees, Secretaries and other Officers, in a secret*
" *manner, and many of such Societies are composed of different divisions, branches*
" *or parts, which communicate with each other by Secretaries, Delegates or other*
" *wise, and by means thereof maintain an influence over large bodies of men, and*
" *delude many ignorant and unwary persons into the commission of acts highly*
" *criminal and whereas it is expedient and necessary, that all such Societies as*
" *aforesaid, and all Societies of a like nature, should be entirely suppressed and*
" *prohibited, as unlawful combinations and confederacies, highly dangerous to*
" *the peace and tranquility of these kingdoms, and to the constitution of the*
" *Government thereof, as by law established.* It enacts that all the said Societies,
" and all other Societies called Corresponding Societies, shall be suppressed and
" prohibited, as being unlawful combinations

" The statute then proceeds, in the second section, to enact, that all and
" every the said Societies, and also every other Society now established, or here-
" after to be established, the members whereof shall, according to the Rules thereof
" or to any provision or agreement for that purpose, be required or admitted to
" take any Oath or engagement, which shall be an unlawful oath or engagement,
" within the intent and meaning of the Statute, the 37th of George the Third
" Chap 123, or to take any other Oath not required or authorised by law, and
" every Society, the members whereof or any one of them, shall take, or in any
" manner bind hemselves by any other oath or engagement in becoming, or in

" consequence of being members of such Society , and every Society, the members
" whereof shall take, subscribe, or assent to, any test or declaration not, required
" by law , and every Society of which the names of the members, or any of them,
" shall be kept secret from the Society at large, or which shall have any Committee
" or Select Body, so chosen or appointed, that the members constituting the same
" shall not be known to the Society at large, to be members of such Committee
" or Select Body , or which shall have any President, Treasurer, Secretary,
" Delegate, or other officers, so chosen or appointed that the election or appoint-
" ment of such persons to such offices, shall not be known to the Society at
" large , or of which the names of all the members, and of all Committees or
" Select Bodies of members, and of all Presidents, Treasurers, Secretaries,
" Delegates, and other officers, shall not be entered in a book, or books, to be
" kept for that purpose, and to be open to the inspection of all the members of
" such Society.   And every Society which shall be composed of different divis-
" ions or branches , or of different parts acting in any manner separate or distinct
" from each other ; or of which any part shall have any separate or distinct
" President, Secretary, Treasurer, or Delegate, or other officer, elected or appointed
" for such part, or to act as an officer for such part, shall be deemed and taken
" to be unlawful combinations and confederacies   and every person who shall
" become a member of any such Society', and every person who shall, directly
" or indirectly, maintain correspondence or intercourse with any, such Society ;
" or with any division, branch, committee, or other select body, President, Secre-
" tary,Delegate, or other officer, or member thereof, as such , or who shall by
" contribution of money, or otherwise, aid, abet, or support, such Society, or any
" members or officers thereof as such, shall be deemed guilty of an unlawful
" combination and confederacy

" The Fifth Section, exempts Lodges of Freemasons , and the Sixth, specifies
' the terms upon which the exemption shall be obtained

" In passing this Act of Parliament, the Legislature seems to have had two
" objects   First, the suppression of the then existing Societies, mentioned and
" described in the Act   Secondly, the prevention of their institution in future.
" The Legislature had found that the public peace, and the security of the Govern-
" ment, had been endangered by the existence of Societies, the members of which
" took unlawful oaths and engagements of fidelity and secrecy, and used secret
" signs, and appointed Committees and Officers in a secret manner   Societies
" composed of different divisions, branches or parts, which communicated with
" each other, and by means thereof, maintained an influence over large bodies of
" men   It considered secret engagements and signs , secret officers or members ;
" and different divisions, branches or parts of Societies, the nature and tendency
" of which are described in the Act, as mischievous, and the different divisions
" branches or parts, gave a widely extended influence   It found the principle of
" those Associations dangerous, as it gave to men the control and direction of a
" mighty engine, which had been employed for bad purposes, and might be again
" so employed.

" It is submitted however that the Orange Institution is not such a Society, as
" is by the terms and the above referred to made an illegal combination

" and confederacy. *first*, because it was established for Loyal and Constitutional
" purposes alone ; while the Title of the Act describes it to be for the suppression
" of those Societies, which are in exact reverse in their purposes, treasonable and
" seditious : *secondly*, because the Preamble of the Act recites the then existence
" of a traitorous conspiracy with the persons then exercising the powers of
" Government in France, which Government was subsequently recognized by
" England, and a treaty of Peace executed with it, and ultimately displaced for
" the lawful Monarchy of France, wherewith we are now in alliance. And it is
" therefore submitted that the initiatory cause assigned for the enactment of the
" Statute no longer exists , *thirdly*, because the Preamble proceeds to recite the
" institution of divers Societies in England and in Ireland, inconsistent with public
" tranquillity and the existence of regular Government, and particularizes some
" thereof in both countries , and in fact all the illegal Associations then existing,
" without any reference whatever to the Orange Association, though it was in full
" and notorious activity in Ireland at the time of the Statute being proposed and
" discussed, and enacted : *fourthly*, the Preamble recites the several Societies
" referred to therein, as well the named as the unnamed, to have been instituted
" in pursuance and for the effectuation of the aforesaid conspiracy with the
" Government of France, and does not refer to any other design or connection
" whatever. The Preamble also refers to the object of overthrowing the *Ecclesi-*
" *astical* state in England and Ireland, which it is the peculiar purpose of the
" Orange Association to preserve . *fifthly*, because the Preamble refers to the
" Oaths, engagements, signs, and regulations of many of such Societies, and not of
" any other kind   The Preamble also recites, that such Societies have deluded
" ignorant and unwary persons into the commission of acts highly criminal, while
" no criminality whatever was at any time attempted or effected by the Orange
" Association : *sixthly*, because the Preamble recites the expediency of suppressing
" the Societies named therein, and all Societies of a like nature, describing also
" their unlawful character, without any reference to the Orange Association ; and
" the first enacting clause of the Statute, suppresses those Societies alone which
" are named in the Preamble as being unlawful combinations against the King's
" Government and the Public Peace, and extends this suppression to none others.
" except those which are styled *Corresponding Societies*, without any reference,
" direct or implied, to the Orange Association.

      "The Report of the Select Committee of the English House of Commons,
" made to the House in March 1799, about three months before the passing of this
" Statute, and whereupon this Statute was founded, is full of references to the
" several Societies in England, in Scotland, and in Ireland, which were instituted
" *for seditious and treasonable purposes*, but has no reference whatever to the
" Orange Association.

      "This Report, however, refers to the Reports of the Committees of the two
" Houses of the Irish Parliament, wherein the Orange Association of Ireland is
" frequently mentioned, not as a seditious and treasonable Society, but as the
" opposite, and as the impediment to the Society of United Irishmen, which this
" Statute recites and suppresses, as seditious and treasonable.

      "It is submitted that this being a penal statute its letter is not only to be con-

v

" strued favourably for the subject, but entirely to be set aside wheresoever it shall
" appear to be adverse to its spirit.   It is also submitted, that the Orange Associa-
" tion cannot be brought within the original contemplation of the framers of this
" Statute, if we consider its spirit, which nothing except matters of mere form and
" regulation alone can bring the Association within its letter.   It is conceived to
" be as much a breach of the Law, to apply its letter beyond its spirit, as it would
" be to make its spirit extend its letter.

" It should be here observed, that in the Rules of this Association, it is express-
" ly provided, that no Orangeman can, at any time or place, meet, or transact
" business, as forming among themselves a separate or distinct branch or part of the
" Institution, but that any meeting of Orangemen, assembled as such, may elect
" and admit members into the Society at large, provided that five members be
" present.   It may be contended that the Legislature had not said that Societies
" shall be legal or illegal, according to the intentions, or even the professed object,
" of the persons of whom they are composed; but that Societies constituted in a
" certain manner, shall be prohibited.   In some of the Societies suppressed,
" observation was eluded by secrecy, and by the combination of many divisions,
" branches or parts, spread over the Kingdom, a widely extended influence was
" acquired.   It is confidently submitted, however, that this Society is founded
" upon very different principles, and that the members thereof mean what they
" profess.   This Society requires no Oaths to be taken upon the admission of a
" member; it only requires the proposer and seconder of such member, to certify
" that the person proposed is a Protestant of known Loyalty, and has produced
" satisfactory proof of his having taken the Oath of Allegiance before a proper
" lawful authority, and of his having taken the Oaths of Abjuration and Supremacy.

" The proposer and seconder of a Candidate are to satisfy themselves of his
" principles, but the Society prescribes no mode for their enquiry thereon, and
" assuredly wishes them to obtain their assurance legally; this may be done by
" general conversation.   The Society has no division, branches, or parts acting
" separately, for there is only one Grand Lodge: and the Deputy Masters, Secre-
" taries, or other Dignitaries, are not appointed by name for any one place;
" although it may be expected that the permanent residents in and about any
" place, will usually meet, yet there is no reason to infer that no others will join
" them.   Every Secretary has a book to himself, and he enters therein, not what
" is transacted in any particular place, but what is transacted wheresoever he is
" present.   The whole Society is one General Assembly.   A Dignitary acts
" wherever he chances to be, to day in Yorkshire, to-morrow in Cornwall, to day
" with his known friends, to-morrow with strangers.   Nothing depends on place,
" everything on person; and although the Society may obtain an influence over
" large bodies of men, yet they will not delude unwary persons into the commission
" of criminal acts.   It is indeed contended, that inasmuch as the object of the
" Institution, is not to subvert, but to support the Constitution, it is neither within
" the letter nor the spirit of the Statute.   It may be urged, that as the Society
" possesses certain secret signs, it is therefore one of the Societies which the
" Legislature had in contemplation to suppress, but it is submitted, that it is very
" questionable whether secret signs are prohibited by the Act; for although it

" appears that the use of secret signs were, by the Preamble, enumerated as one
" of the characteristics attending the Societies therein specified, and the Preamble
" states it to be expedient and necessary that all such Societies, and all Societies
" of a like nature, should be entirely suppressed and prohibited ; yet as the enact-
" ing part of the first clause only suppresses the particular Societies' therein
" enumerated, and all other Societies called Corresponding Societies, and the
" Second Section does not mention those using secret signs, they are not within
" the provisions of the Statute.

" Your Opinion is therefore requested, whether this Society is a violation of
" any of the Statutes referred to, and if so, you are requested to state in what
" respect. And you are also requested to give your opinion on the legal application
" of the letter and spirit of the above named Statutes to a Society so constituted."

OPINION.

" I have perused the copy of the Rules and Regulations which accompany this
" Case. With reference to the terms and provisions of the Statutes, particularly
" the 39th of George the Third, Chap 79 ; and the 57th of George the Third,
" Chap 19, I am of opinion that the establishment of the proposed Society cannot
" be deemed to be in violation of any of the Statutes referred to, or of the provi-
" sions and restrictions intended to be introduced by the several enactments
" contained in them. It is indeed stated, that the proposers of the Institution
" have purposely endeavoured to avoid that effect, and have surrendered to the
" necessity of conforming to it, many of the Regulations which it might other-
" wise have been thought advisable to have introduced into it It is truly
" observed in the Case, that the circumstances which appear to be stated as
" important in the recital and preamble, are not embodied in the enacting clause,
" and that there is no special enactment against using secret signs. I think,
" therefore, that this Society, if it is objectionable at all, must be so on the
" principles of Common Law, and not as falling within the particular penalties of
" the Statutes It is rightly remarked that, the denomination of loyal, or any
' other epithet which a society affixes to itself, and wishes to announce as the
" object of its institution, will not decide or alter the nature or legal description
" of it No one will, in this case, suspect the sincerity of that declaration, or
" that any other purpose is in view than that which is exhibited But, it must
" be observed, that an Institution of the extent and influence which must, from
" its constitution, belong to the present, may be made an engine of great power,
" if it should be capable of abuse in its application

" It must also be observed, that its object is not distinctly defined, as to the
" nature of what is to be done Its affairs are mentioned in general terms, but
" the " affairs " are not specified , nor are the particular functions or duties which
" the Grand Master has to execute anywhere defined

" The Grand Lodge is, I presume, to be composed of all the members, and there
" is to be no separate division inaccessible to the general body ; and in that and
" other respects, it is clear of the particular objections made to such Societies in
" Section 2 of the 39th of George the Third, Chap 79

" The secrecy of the signs and symbols which may be changed from time to

" time, I cannot help thinking is objectionable ; and if any question were here-
" after to arise on the legality of any of its proceedings, might be urged as a
" circumstance of great suspicion. It is also to be remembered that the Societies
" known as regular Freemason's Lodges, are particularly and specially exempted
" from the operation of the Acts only under certain conditions to be observed in
" future. (See Sections 5, 6 and 7, of the 39th of George the Third.)

" I have thought it right to state thus particularly the grounds and extent of
" this opinion.

" JOHN LENS."

" Serjant's Inn, Dec. 20, 1821."

The above Case, with the opinions of the eminent Whig Serjant at
Law upon it, ought to be deemed full and satisfactory, touching the legality
and constitutionality of the Loyal Orange Association. As however, there
were one or two points upon which some doubts seemed to have been
entertained by Counsel, the following further opinions were obtained, and
were handed in by Lord Kenyon, at the same time.

CASE.

" The proposed Rules and Regulations of the Orange Institution, together with
" your former opinion thereon, are herewith again left for your perusal, for the
" purpose of considering the propriety of making such alterations in page 18, and
" in Rule 42, page 23, respecting the meeting of the Grand Lodge, which you
" have presumed to be composed of all the members of the Society. This Lodge
" has hitherto only been composed of the Dignitaries of the Institution, who are
" entrusted with the general superintendence and management of the affairs of the
" Society ; but all business transacted by the Grand Lodge is entered in the Books
" of the Society, and open to the inspection of all the members thereof, upon
" application for that purpose. It is therefore submitted, that in this respect it
" does not fall within the meaning of the second Section of the 39th of George the
" Third, chap. 79, relating to a division, branch, or part, acting separately ; but
" should the meeting of the Grand Lodge, so constituted, be considered as a
" division, or branch, acting separately, and thereby falling within the particular
" objections named in the Act, you are requested to advise whether the following
" alteration, proposed to be made in Rule 42, will be sufficient to obviate the
" difficulty. The proposed amendment is as follows :—*That all meetings of the*
" *Institution, are open of right to every Orangeman, upon producing his certificate,*
" *without which none shall be admitted, unless satisfactorily known by the President*
" *of the meeting to be an Orangeman ; but the right of voting in the Grand Lodge*
" *shall be confined to the Dignitaries of the Society at large.* And if this amend-
" ment be adopted, whether the Institution would then become strictly legal in
" this point. You are also requested more explicitly to state your opinion as to
" the legality of the secrecy of the signs used by the Institution, and if the adoption
" thereof merely for the purpose of preventing the intrusion of improper persons,
" will bring the Society within the meaning of the Statutes before referred to."

OPINION.

"I am of opinion, after referring more particularly to the formation of the
"Grand Lodge, the component parts of which are distinctly set forth and enumera-
"ted in the general Rules, No 3, and comparing that part of the Institution with
"the several descriptions of matters meant to be prohibited by the enactments of
"Section 2, of the 39th of George the Third, chap. 79, that this part of the Society
"is not liable to the objection of being deemed such a division, branch, or part, as
"is thereby meant to be prohibited I think the amendment proposed is unneces-
"sary, and would not cure the objection, if any such existed ; as the right of voting
"in the Grand Lodge, which is the material part of *acting separately or distinct,*
"*&c.,* is reserved to those members exclusively.

"It is for the *direction* of the affairs of the Society at large, that the Grand
"Lodge is declared to be assembled, and for *such direction* only, and not for any
"affairs of its own as a distinct division, branch or part. I still continue to think,
"that notwithstanding the large and comprehensive terms of the clause, this part
"of the Institution will not be deemed to fall within the scope of it.

"As to the use of secret signs and symbols, I retain the opinion which I before
"expressed, and have little to add to it. They are not within the prohibitory
"enactments, though mentioned in the Preamble But if the legality of any
"subsisting Society comes to be questioned, not with reference to these particular
"Statutes, but on the principles of the Common Law, the existence of such secret
"signs and symbols among the members would be urged in argument to excite
"suspicion and distrust its objects. The reason here given for its adoption, that
"is, to prevent the intrusion of improper persons, seems to me not entirely to
"remove the objections, as the same object may be otherwise provided for, and is
"already better secured by the 43rd Rule, by the production of the required
"certificate

"I think it would be advisable to omit this part of the Institution ; but, confining
"myself to the precise question as here proposed, I think it is not a violation of
"these statutable provisions, nor, simply considered, an offence at Common Law.

"JOHN LENS"

"Serjants' Inn, 16th Jan , 1822 "

Copy of Sir William Horne's opinion on the preceding case.

"I have perused the Acts of Parliament referred to, and the papers laid before
"me containing the Rules and Regulations of the Society in question, and upon
"the best consideration I have been able to give to the subject, I am of opinion
"that this Society is not, (due regard being had to the known principle of con-
"struction applied to Penal Acts of Parliament,) within any of the Acts referred
"to, so as to be a violation of the Acts, or so as to subject any of the Members
"individually to the penalties of them."

"WILLIAM HORNE."

"Lincoln's Inn 24th January, 1822."

Lord Kenyon was further asked by the Committee, in reference to those
opinions. as follow:

"*Question* 2619.—Were the new Rules intended *to be adopted, submitted to*
"Mr. Serjant Lens?—*Answer.* Yes, the manuscript was submitted at the same
"time those questions were asked.

"*Question* 2620.—Does your Lordship recollect whether those in manuscript
"were submitted with the first Case, as well as with the second?—*Answer.* I have
"no doubt of that. The first application to Serjant Lens was in December 1821;
"the second in January 1822; and the new print, the one which was corrected
"from the manuscript, was printed in 1822, after the time of the manuscript being
"so submitted.

"*Question* 2622.—This is stated to be the opinion of Sir William, then Mr.
"Horne?—*Answer.* Yes, that is a copy of his opinion.

"*Question* 2625.—When those opinions were obtained, were the opinions of any
"other Counsel taken?—*Answer.* Opinions were likewise asked from Mr. Baron
"Gurney, and from Mr. Adolphus: I cannot recollect any other name.

"*Question* 2626.—Has your Lordship any of those opinions?—*Answer.* I have
"not them by me, and do not know whether I can lay my hand upon them or not.

"*Question* 2629.—Does your Lordship recollect to what extent those opinions
"were more unfavourable; whether they selected any other particular points,
"than those which Serjant Lens, in his opinion, has noticed?—*Answer.* I should
"say certainly not.

"*Question* 2630.—After those opinions were obtained, were they submitted to
"the Grand Lodge?—*Answer.* Certainly.

"*Question* 2631.—Who was Grand Master at that time?—*Answer.* Nobody.

"*Question* 2632.—Who was the first Grand Master?—*Answer.* There was no
"Grand Master appointed after the resignation of the Duke of York, till the
"special application to the Duke of Cumberland.

"*Question* 2633.—When did the Duke of York become an Orangeman?—*Answer.*
"It does not exactly consist with my memory to state that, but I rather think it
"was about the beginning of the year 1819."

This evidence all goes to show the great care taken by Lord Kenyon,
and by the other Grand Officers of the English Grand Lodge, to remove
from the Society, (if indeed it was ever justly open to it,) the charge of illegality. Fortified by the opinions of such eminent counsel as Sir Robert
Gifford, (afterwards Lord Gifford, Chief Justice of England;) Mr. Gurney,
(afterwards Mr. Baron Gurney;) Mr. Horne, (afterwards Sir William
Horne;) Mr. Adolphus, (the great popular Whig pleader;) Mr. Serjant
Lens, (the eminent Whig barrister;) and Mr. Gazalee, they might well
indeed exclaim (as they do in the opening declaration then adopted;) how
loyalty can be prohibited with treason, or suppressed for sedition, many
honest men, not learned in the law, have wondered. The spirit of the
law can, by no ingenuity of perversion, be urged against the Orange
Institution, and argument might be heaped upon argument, to show that
Orangemen are beyond its purposes and its penalties.

It cannot be doubted however, that the charge of illegality, then urged against the English Grand Lodge, was the cause of serious injury to the Order, in that Kingdom. Not only did His Royal Highness the Duke of York withdraw from the Grand Mastership in consequence of the allegation: but several noble and influential members followed His Royal Highness' example　Lord Kenyon says, at page 124 of the Parliamentary Report, in reply to Questions :

Question 2643.—Did any other officer of the Institution resign his situation for "the same reason.—*Answer.* Lord Hartford and Lord Lowther　I do not recollect' "any other.

" *Question* 2644.—Lord Lowther was Secretary ?—*Answer*　He was."

CHAPTER XXXV

Lord Kenyon " the tender Friend and nursing Parent" of English Orangeism—Thanks to Sir Abraham Bradley King, and to Sir Robert Peel—Meeting of the Grand Lodge, 15th February 1827—Death of the Duke of York and Address of Condolence to the King—Letter from Sir John Eustace—Report of the Committee on the adoption of a new System—The Password then chosen—Evidence of Captain Staveley—Meeting of the Grand Lodge in June 1829—Appointment of His Royal Highness the Duke of Cumberland Lord Kenyon, the Duke of Gordon, the Bishop of Salisbury, the Marquis of Chandos, &c —Letter from the Duke of Cumberland to the Earl of Enniskillen—Appointment made by the Grand Master for the 17th of February 1831.

So great was the injury inflicted upon the whole Order, by the bare supposition that the Society was illegal, that it took five or six years to recover from the blow. From the period of the resignation of His Royal Highness the Duke of York, in 1821, to the appointment of His Royal Highness the Duke of Cumberland, in 1827, the office of Grand Master was vacant　During the whole of this lengthened period, the Deputy Grand Master, Lord Kenyon, (who might justly be termed " the tender Friend and the nursing Parent " of English Orangeism,) discharged the duties of Grand Master　His Lordship clearly saw that the Order was then in a transition state—that a terrible cloud had passed over its fair face, and had discharged upon that face, till then so lovely and so promising, all the venom of concentrated malice and envy on the one hand, and of cold-hearted neglect and abandonment on the other—that it would require time to recruit, and care to recover, the *prestige* it had lost, and that quiet action, rather than ostentatious show, was the truest policy. This course, the

Society, acting under his Lordship's immediate guidance, steadily pursued. From 1821 to 1827, English Orangeism was little obtruded upon the public gaze ; like the air, which gives life and vitality to the body, it was *felt* rather than *seen* ; its actions were quiet, but effective ; vigilant but unostentatious. At the meeting of the Grand Lodge in 1823 (16th of June,) thanks were publicly voted to Sir Abraham Bradley King, Bart. "for the gentlemanly, "firm and conscientious conduct he displayed at the bar of the House of " Commons, during his examination on the subject of Oaths and the Con- "stitution of the Orange Society, whereby we consider him to have com- "pletely established its entire coincidence with the true principles of our "glorious Constitution." At the same meeting the thanks of the Grand Lodge were also voted to Sir Robert Peel (at that period Mr. Secretary Peel,) "for his support of Protestant principles ;" and thanks were also voted to the Editor of the *John Bull* newspaper, "for his advocacy of Constitutional Orange principles."

In 1827, a sort of revival in English Orangeism seems to have commenced. The first meeting of the Grand Lodge in the year, took place at Lord Kenyon's, 9 Portman Square, London, on the 15th of February. His Lordship, as the Deputy Grand Master of Great Britain, presided. The following gentlemen were present.

The Rev. William Towne, D.D. Deputy Grand Chaplain.
The Rev. John Litton Crosbie. A.M. Deputy Grand Chaplain.
C. Eustace Chetwood, Esq. Deputy Grand Secretary.
Samuel Harman, Esq. Deputy Grand Treasurer.
John Simmons, Esq. Member of the Grand Com.
Thomas Thornley, Proxy for Oldham and Ashton under-Line.
John Eedes, M. 99.
C. S Masterman, M. 59.
Rev. George Montgomerey West, (late of Canada.)
John Gibson, D. G. M. Woolwich.
John Clark, Proxy for D. G. M. Holmes.
John Rayner, M. 100.
George Payne, Proxy for 209.
Amos Stoddart, of Lodge 154, Liverpool.
John Oldiss, } Grand Tylers.
John Evans, }

The opening prayers having been read by the Rev. Dr. Towne ; and the proceedings of the last Grand Lodge meeting, held on the 17th of October 1826, being also read : the Rev. John Litton Crosbie, in a most able and affecting speech, proposed an humble, dutiful and loyal address of condolence to His Most Gracious Majesty the King, on the ever-to-be-lamented death of His Royal Highness the Duke of York. This motion was unanimously adopted ; and the proposed address, as prepared by Brother Crosbie, being read paragraph by paragraph, and adopted, was ordered to be engrossed by the Deputy Grand Secretary   Lord Kenyon, Mr Crosbie, Mr. Simmons, Mr. Harman, Dr Towne, Mr. Eustace Chetwood, and Mr. Deakin, were appointed a committee (three to form a quorum,) to adopt measures for causing a medal to be framed, which might perpetuate in the recollection of all members of the Orange Institution, the name, the public virtues, and the exalted Protestant principles of our deceased Brother, the Illustrious Prince Frederick, Duke of York. A letter was read by Lord Kenyon, from Colonel Sir John Rowland Eustace, dated "Hanover, 29th November 1826," expressive of his attachment to the principles of the Orange Institution, his cordial approval of its Rules and Regulations, and his wish, and that of a gallant friend of his (Major Moultrie, of Aston, in Shropshire,) to become members of the Institution   Much routine business, and several matters of local importance only, having been disposed of, the Grand Lodge adjourned for a short time ; and having resumed its sitting, the Select Committee appointed to devise a NEW SYSTEM, made its report ; whereupon it was , *Resolved*,—That the said Committee be authorised to perfect the System now proposed, and to cause the same to be promulgated in the most regular and judicious manner.   The subject of the appointment of a GRAND MASTER was considered and discussed, and committed for the present to the consideration and managment of Lord Kenyon, who, with his usual urbanity towards the Brethren, and zeal for the Institution, most kindly undertook the mission. The Report of the Select Committee on the New System, as above referred to, it may be well to give in detail   It sets forth that the Committee having devised a new system, such as in their opinion, is best calculated, not only to protect the Institution from imposition, and from the intrusion of improper persons, but also to impress upon the brotherhood a due reverence for the Sacred Word of Truth, and a proper sense of the duties inculcated by the principles of the Society.   They express their earnest hope, that the System about to be promulgated, will have the beneficial effect of uniting the members more firmly to each other, and put an end to any irregularity that had hitherto prevailed.   The Committee strongly recommended, that the utmost attention be paid to the injunctions already issued by the Grand Lodge, prohibiting the reception of any Sign, Password, or Lecture, from any other than a duly authorised officer of the Institution   By an adherence to this course, regularity and uniformity could alone be preserved. For the purpose of meeting the convenience of the Country Brethren, the following arrangements were adopted for promulgating the System. The Deputy Grand Master, resident in London, with proper assistance, to communicate the System to the several Masters in the Metropolis ; and to the Deputy Grand Master at Cambridge, and to such other duly authorised persons as might apply previous to the next annual meeting of the Grand Lodge in June. The Deputy Grand Master at Cambridge to give the necessary information to the Deputy Grand Master at Norwich, and to the Brethren at Ipswich, should they require it. The Deputy Grand Master at Manchester, to obtain the System from London, and to communicate the same to the several Deputy Grand Masters in Lancashire and the adjoining Counties. The Deputy Grand Master at Newcastle-upon-Tyne, to receive the System from Manchester, and to communicate the same to the several Deputy Grand Masters in Scotland, &c. The Deputy Grand Master at Gloucester, to receive the System from London, and to communicate it to the Deputy Grand Master at Bristol and Carmarthen. These arrangements not to preclude any Deputy Grand Master, from attending personally at the Grand Lodge meeting, in June following, and there receive his instructions, should he think proper to give his attendance. This document is dated "London, 27th Feb. 1827." It is signed by

> John Simmons, Deputy Grand Master, London.
> John Litton Crosbie, Clerk.
> John Osmond Deakin, Clerk.
> Samuel Harman, Assistant Dy. G. Treasurer.
> Chetwood Eustace, Deputy Grand Secretary.

and in the left hand corner, it is marked, "*Approved*, KENYON, Deputy Grand Master of Great Britain." The promulgation of this System, was owing to the fact of the former Signs and Passwords, (which up to this period had been received from the Grand Orange Lodge of Ireland,) having been communicated by Colonel Verner, the Rev. Holt Waring, and other Dignitaries sent over from Ireland, to the Committee of the Parliament then sitting, and authorised to enquire into the nature of the Orange Society. The Password adopted at that time was "ELDON." It is given by J. F. Satveley, Esq., in his evidence before the Commons Committee, pages 86 and 87, questions 1768, 1769, 1770, 1771, 1772, 1773, 1774, 1775, 1776, and 1777 ; date, 18th August 1835. It seems also, that the signs and password at this time adopted by the English Grand Lodge, were subsequently introduced into Ireland, and became those in use in both countries. This is fully established in the evidence of Mr. Eustace Chetwood, the Deputy Grand Secretary of England, as an extract or two will show.

"*Question* 564.—The same Passwords and the same Signs were adopted by the "Grand Lodge in England and in Ireland?—*Answer*. The system of Signs and "Passwords adopted by the Orange Institution in Ireland, on its revival in 1828, "were framed by me, and in use in Great Britain.

"*Question* 565—Do you mean in 1832, when the new system was introduced? "—*Answer*. Yes.

"*Question* 566.—Do you mean to say, that the Grand Lodge of Great Britain "adopted Passwords and Signs, and that those were afterwards adopted by the "Orange Lodge of Ireland?—*Answer* It happened precisely so. In 1828 the "Act of Parliament passed, prohibiting political societies in Ireland, which was "thought by some persons to apply to all societies having that character. The "Orange Institution accordingly dissolved itself, in obedience to the Act. But "when the Act expired, the society was revived On the 15th of September "1828, I attended the general meeting held in Dublin, and on that occasion they "took our signs and passwords.

" *Question* 567.—Did your Lodge cease to act during the time the Lodge in "Ireland ceased to act?—*Answer*. No. The Law did not apply to Great Britain.

" *Question* 574 —The Password and Signs having been interchanged between "the two countries, the Orangemen of one County would readily recognize the "Orangemen of the other?—*Answer* Yes The same as the Masonic Order.

"*Question* 575.—In truth the two branches may be said to belong to the one "trunk?—*Answer* The English originated from the Irish

" *Question* 576.—And on the revival, the Irish originated again from the "English?—*Answer*. Yes; so far as adopting the Signs and Passwords, though "they managed their own general affairs separately "

At the meeting held on the 15th of February 1827, to the care and management of Lord Kenyon, was referred the choice of a Grand Master, who was to succeed the Duke of York in that high dignity. His Lordship it appears, was not idle in procuring a suitable successor for the Royal Duke then deceased, and in making other arrangements to promote the influence of the Order, in the highest quarters At the meeting of the Grand Lodge of England, held at Lord Kenyon's, Portman Square, on the 15th of June 1829, John Simmons, Esq, Deputy Grand Master, in the Chair, the following with other proceedings were had The Deputy Grand Secretary stated, that His Royal Highness the Duke of Cumberland intended to have honored the meeting by his presence, but was prevented by public business Letters of apology for their absence, were read from the Rev. J. L Crosby, the Honorable Thomas Kenyon, and other gentlemen The following Grand Officers were chosen

Grand Master —His Royal Highness, Prince Earnest Augustus, Duke of Cumberland and Teviotdale, Earl of Armagh in Ireland, Field Marshal in the Army; Chancellor of the University of Dublin, K.G and K of St P., D.C L. and F.S.A. &c &c. &c *Kew Palace, Middlesex.*

Deputy Grand Master of England and Wales —The Right Honorable George, Lord Kenyon, F S A and L L D &c &c &c *Portman Square, London,* and *Gredington Hall, Flintshire.*

Deputy Grand Master of Scotland.—His Grace the Duke of Gordon, F R S. &c. &c. &c. *Gordon Castle, Banffshire,* and *Strathbogy Castle, Aberdeenshire*

Grand Chaplain.—The Right Reverend Thomas, Lord Bishop of Salisbury, F.S.A. &c. &c. *Salisbury Palace, Wiltshire,* and *Salisbury Tower, Windsor Castle.*

Grand Secretary.—The Most Noble Richard Plantaganet Temple, Marquis of Chandos, M.P. and L.L.D. &c. &c. &c. *Stowe Park, Buckinghamshire,* and *Avington House, Hants.*

Grand Treasurer.—Colonel Fletcher, J. P. &c. &c. *Bolton,* near *Manchester, Lancashire.*

Deputy Grand Treasurer.—James Watkins, Esq. *London.*

Deputy Grand Secretary.—Chetwood Eustace Chetwood, Esq. *London.*

DEPUTY GRAND CHAPLAINS.

Rev. Henry Maxwell, A.M.	Rev. E. Booth, A.M.
Rev. Thomas Comber, A.M.	Rev. T. Lowe, A.M.
Rev. William Mann, A.M.	Rev. C. Cooper, A.M.
Rev. William Towne, D.D.	Rev. J. L. Crosbie, A.M.
Rev. John Wilkinson, A.M.	Rev. J. G. Deakin, A.M.
Rev. W. W. Wilcocks, A.M.	Rev. Thomas Wharton, A.M.
Rev. D. A. Williams, A.M.	

GRAND COMMITTEE.

The Hon. Thomas Kenyon.	G. J. Twiss.
Moses Jarvis.	Cornelius Backhouse.
Thomas Thornley.	W. E. Varcoe.
John Eedes.	Samuel Harman, Esquire.
J. W. Silvester.	The Hon Arthur Cole, M.P.
Josiah Towne.	Colonel Rochford, M.P.
Richard Rishworth.	John Fletcher.
Robert Holt.	John Langshaw.
W. A. Woodburne.	William Mason, Esquires.
John Simmons.	George Moore, Esq., M.P.
John Platt.	

The following letter from His Royal Highness the Duke of Cumberland, addressed to the Right Honorable the Earl of Enniskillen, was read.

"St. James' Palace, May 12, 1829.

" MY DEAR LORD.

" I was very sorry not to have seen you previous to your leaving London, " being anxious to convey through you, to our friends on the other side of the " water, my anxious hope that the spirit of Protestantism still continues, and will " continue to bear up manfully against the pressure of our recent misfortunes; and " at the same time to express my conviction, that caution and vigilance are, at " the present crisis, especially requisite for the prosperity and safety of our cause; " particulary in respect to our public Processions, which I think ought, by all " means, to be avoided. Judging from the temper of the times, I would say,

" that such Processions, leading probably, or at least being interpreted to lead,
" to an infraction of the law and a breach of the public peace, would draw with
" them the most mischievous consequences, and would probably be followed up
" by some Legislative measure, ruinous to the Orange Institution.

" I assure you I feel an intense anxiety on this subject, both from the respect I
" bear the Institution itself, and from a conviction that, upon its preservation and
" prosperity, depends the safety of the Protestants in Ireland

" If the Orangemen and other associated Protestants remain firm and united,
" and if that firmness and union be guided by prudence and tempered with caution,
" I still hope that our venerable Institutions will be preserved to us, and our
" sacred Religion sustained in that pre-eminence to which the purity of the
" Reformed Church so justly entitles her. Excuse this letter, which though
" hurried, is written with the truest attachment to our holy cause, and

" Believe me,

" To the Right Hon. the Earl of Enniskillen,   Very sincerely yours,
" Deputy Grand Master of the Orangemen in Ireland "   " EARNEST.

" Grand Master."

After the reading of this letter from His Royal Highness, and some
feeling and lucid remarks being made thereon, by several of the Brethren
present, it was *Resolved*—That the Grand Lodge fully concurs in the views
and feelings expressed by the Illustrious writer, and that the Brethren of
the Institution be entreated to pay the utmost attention to the injunctions
of our Royal Grand Master At this meeting it was further
resolved, that there be but two stated meetings of the Grand Lodge held
in each year, (previous to this the meetings had been held quarterly,) in
the months of May and November. If possible the latter to be held on
the 5th, but the appointment of the day to be left in the discretion of
the Grand Master, or the Deputy Grand Master The reason assigned
for this change, was the usual absence from the Metropolis in June, July,
August, and September, of many of the most distinguished friends and
supporters of the Institution, so that the Grand Lodge could not have the
advantage of their presence, if assembled in these months From this
period, (the 15th of June 1829,) there appears to have been no meeting
of the Grand Lodge of England, till the 4th of November, 1830. At the
meeting held on that day, at Portman Square, His Royal Highness the
Duke of Cumberland being absent, it was proposed by Lord Kenyon, and
unanimously agreed ; That to give every weight and respectability to the
Society, the meeting of the Grand Lodge be postponed, to obtain the
attendance of our Royal Grand Master and other distinguished Members.
This resolution having been communicated to His Royal Highness, he was
pleased to appoint the next meeting of the Grand Lodge, in the following
terms

" Having supposed that the meeting of the Grand Lodge, as proposed by myself,
" was postponed from pressure of public business : as I did not receive any

"further intimation, I did not attend, as I otherwise most undoubtedly would
"have done; fully impressed as I am, that at this moment it becomes highly
"necessary, for the preservation of the Protestant interest, that all true and honest
"Orangemen should remain firmly together; and for that, that it is highly advisa-
"ble another day be fixed for the purpose; and therefore I desire that the Grand
"Lodge shall assemble, *without fail*, on Thursday, the 17th of February 1831, at
"twelve, at No. 9, Portman Square."

"EARNEST.
Grand Master."

Having thus traced the Institution in England, from the formation of
a Grand Lodge in that Kingdom, down to the year 1830, inclusive, it is
proper that the reader's attention should be withdrawn from that portion
of the Empire, and carried back for some time to the "Emerald Isle."

CHAPTER XXXVI.

*Return to the history of the Order in Ireland.—Mr. Sampson's "Memoirs."—His
description of Orange Tests, Orange Secrets, and Orange Signs.—Forged
Rules of the Orangemen.—Reference to Parliamentary Papers.—Standing
Orders and Regulations of the Lurgan Yeomanry in 1809.—Colonel Auriol's
attempt to crush the Orange Yeomanry in the south of Ireland.—Captain
Gilman.—Lord Bandon.—Declaration of 600 of the Bandon Yeomanry.—
Colonel Auriol's official correspondence with the Government.—Captain Evanson's resignation.—Captain Connor insults Col. Auriol.—Colonel Auriol
removed, and the "Bandon Legion" restored.*

When the reader was drawn from the history of Irish Orangeism, the
progress of the Society in that Kingdom had been traced up to the year
1807, inclusive. At that period, most of the leading spirits of turmoil
and disaffection had left the Island; some had been transported to the
penal Colonies of the Empire, for their treasons; while others had
voluntarily withdrawn themselves to France, Spain, Austria, and other
Roman Catholic Countries of the European Continent. Some too had
sought refuge in the United States of America. Of this latter class was
a Doctor McNevin, and a Mr. Sampson, a Barrister. Those two men,
with a few others who had taken refuge in America, determined, that,
though their exile was a *coup de grace* to themselves; yet that their revolutionary doctrines, and the numerous false statements by which they were
supported should not be lost to their countrymen. In pursuance of this
determination, Mr. Sampson published in New York. those unfounded

accusations, under the title of "*Memoirs*," which he dare not publish in the land of his nativity. Any statements more utterly void of truth, than those contained in Mr. Sampson's work, are not to be found. A few samples are here given, so far as they relate to the Orange Society.

Extracts from Counsellor "SAMPSON'S MEMOIRS," *page* 419.

"Having promised some instances of the cruelty inflicted on the Irish, they " will naturally be expected. But what to select from such a mass of horrors is "a difficult question. If my professional occupation should leave me so much "leisure hereafter, I may probably employ it in the farther pursuit of a subject "so interesting to humanity, and so necessary to truth. For the present the "following extracts may suffice to authenticate all that has been asserted in the "correspondence. And it will readily appear to any candid mind, to which of "the contending parties in Ireland the imputation of treason is most deservedly "ascribable.

ORANGEMAN'S ORIGINAL TEST.

"I do hereby swear that I will be true to the King and Government, and that "I will EXTERMINATE as far as I am able the Catholics of Ireland.

SECRETS OF THE ORANGEMEN.

Q. "Where are you?

A. "At the House of Bondage.

Q. "Where are you going?

A. "To the Promised Land.

Q. "Stand fast yourself?

A. "Through the Red Sea.

Q. "What is your haste?

A. "I am afraid.

Q. "Don't be afraid, for the man who sought your life is dead?

Q. "Will you hold it or have it?

A. "I will hold it."

SIGNS OF THE ORANGEMEN.

"Take your right hand and put it into your right haunch, turn round, saying, "great is the man that sent me; then take your left hand and say, welcome brother "Prince of Orange."

It is scarcely necessary to say, that no statement could be penned, more utterly void of foundation, than the preceding. The evidence of Colonel Verner, of the Rev. Holt Waring, Dean of Down, and of several other gentlemen of undoubted veracity, all show that the allegations of Mr. Sampson, of Dr. McNevin, and of similar writers, rest upon no other foundation than sheer invention; the offspring of ignorance, united to "hatred, malice, and all uncharitableness." Mr. Sampson sets out on his journey after Orange iniquities, by reminding his readers, that he had promised to supply them with "some instances of the cruelties inflicted upon the Irish," by their Orange opponents. After a rather tedious ride, he pulls up to inform his audience, not of a single "cruelty inflicted," and promised to be stated, but to treat them to a mere "*mare's nest,*" under the guise of Orange mysteries, symbols, and passwords! Yet, 'tis with such trash as this, that Romish fancy was tickled, Romish hatred inflamed, and the public mind poisoned and misled.

But conduct like this was not new—slanderous inventions like Mr. Sampson's, was not the work of that period, or of his hand alone. So far back as the days of the Rebellion of 1798, similar slanders were fabricated, and the like calumnies circulated. This is abundantly evident, in the "*Report from the Committee of Secrecy*" laid before the Irish House of Commons, 21st of August, 1798, by Lord Viscount Castlereagh, and which is here copied. It may be found in the Appendix to the Report, No. XXVI, page 216. It is headed, "*Fabricated Rules and Regulations of the Orangemen,*" and is as follows.

"As an instance of the arts, used to make the Orange Association an occasion of "exciting in the breasts of the lower class of Catholics, the most malignant and "vindictive passions; the following series of fabricated Rules and Regulations, "intended to be considered as those of Orangemen, are here inserted. The copy "from which they are transcribed was found in the house of *Marlay* a Tailor, in "Hoey's Court; but similar copies were frequently found, both on the persons, "and in the houses of *United Irishmen.*

"*1st. Resolved unanimously,*—That each and every Member be furnished with "a case of Horse Pistols and a Sword; also that every Member shall have twelve "rounds of Ball Cartridge.

"*2nd. Resolved,*—That every Member shall be ready at a moment's warning.

"*3rd. Resolved,*—That no member is to introduce a Papist or Presbyterian, "Quaker, or Methodist, or any persuasion but a Protestant.

"*4th. Resolved,*—That no man wear Irish Manufacture, nor give employment "to any Papist.

"*5th. Resolved,*—That every man shall be ready at a moment's warning, to "burn all the Chapels and Meeting Houses in the City of Dublin.

"*6th. Resolved,*—That any man who will give any information of any House he "suspects to be a United Irishman's, will get the sum of £5, and his name kept "private.

"*7th. Resolved,*—That no Member will introduce any Man under the age of "nineteen, nor over the age of forty-six."

While Irish treason was resorting to such unjustifiable means as the circulation of slanders equally unfounded; while no effort was left untried to keep up agitation against English rule; to nurse Irish wrath and to keep it warm, for the first favourable opportunity to publicly display itself in a renewed attempt at insurrection; the Loyal Orange Association, were quietly enrolling their members in the Yeomanry Corps of the Kingdom, and adding their strength to the other resources of the Empire, to preserve its integrity and independence. Reference being had to the "*Parliamentary Papers,*" (Vol. 16.) as published by the British House of Commons in 1835, ample evidence will be found of the untiring zeal with which the Orangemen of Ireland clung to their allegiance at this period. Nearly all the Yeomanry Corps of the Island, were, at that period, members of the Orange Lodges. In truth, the Government could place no reliance whatever, in the fidelity of the Irish Roman Catholics, and it would, therefore, have been sheer treason to the State, to have placed arms in the hands of men, who would have turned them against their native country, the moment its soil was polluted by the presence of a Gallic force. To show the nature of the Obligations then taken by the Irish Yeomanry, and the rigid discipline to which they voluntarily subjected themselves, a few extracts are here taken from the evidence given before Parliament in 1835, as before alluded to. The Oath of the Yeoman of that day, was, as will be seen, a mere transcript of what had been already taken by each member, when initiated an Orangeman. The following is a copy of the "*Standing Orders and Regulations*" of the Lurgan Yeomanry, commanded by Charles Brownlow, Esq, M. P., (afterwards Lord Lurgan,) the 9th of March, 1809.

"Every officer, non-commissioned officer and private, on being admitted a mem-
"ber of the corps, to take the following oath; viz, '*I do sincerely promise and*
"*swear that I will be faithful and bear true allegiance to His Majesty King George*
"*the Third; and that I will faithfully support and maintain the laws and consti-*
"*tution of this Kingdom, and the succession to the throne in His Majesty's*
"*illustrious house. I furthermore do swear that I never was nor never will be a*
"*United Irishman, nor never took the oath of secrecy to that or any other treason-*
"*able society; and that I will use every means in my power to discover and bring*
"*to punishment all persons who would subvert our constitution and religion, as*
"*established among us by the great King William*' The corps being now formed
"into a battalion, consisting of one grenadier, one light infantry, and two battalion
"companies, each private on entering the corps to be attached to either of these
"companies, as the commanding officer may think proper; each non-commissioned
"officer and his private to fall in at their respective private parades on the first
"beating of the drummer's call or sound of the bugle, with their arms, accoutre-
"ments and clothing complete.

"Any man appearing duty or not properly dressed, agreeable to the orders of
"the corps, to be fined 1s. and forfeit his days pay, and on repetition of said
"offence to be expelled the corps.

"Each man's arms and accoutrements to be perfectly clean, bright, and in good
"order. Wooden snappers to be used at all times, unless ordered to the contrary,
"and when on parade, to fire blank or ball cartridge, flints to be put in with lead,
"which every man will receive for the purpose. Belt-slings and leathers of
"brushes and prickers to be of good white, pouch black and polished.

"The caps well put on, the tuft clean, band white, and the cap fronts clean and
"bright. The hair close cropped; every man will be provided with a military
"black stock; no black silk handkerchief or substitute for the stock will be
"allowed, and no appearance of shirt to be above the stock, such being unmilitary.

"Trousers and spats perfectly white, buttons clean; to be constantly worn on
"parade (except on inspection days or when ordered to the contrary). The regi-
"mental breeches and leggings to be kept clean and in good order, and worn only
"at inspections or when particularly ordered.

"No man will be entitled to pay who appears on parade without his arms,
"accoutrements and clothing complete. Any man wearing any part of his yeo-
"manry clothing, except upon the days of parade, will be fined for the first offence
"2s., and for the second expulsion. Should any damage have been received by
"being thus worn or used, he will be obliged to make it good.

"Any man talking in the ranks to have his pay stopped for that day. A fine
"of 3s. on any man absenting himself from inspection parades; all other parades
"6d., with the loss of his day's pay (sickness excepted). Any man being absent
"three successive days to be expelled the corps (sickness excepted). Any man
"leaving the ranks [after roll-call until regularly dismissed, whether on parade,
"on a march, or otherwise, without leave of the commanding officer, to be fined
"2s. 6d. Each orderly sergeant to call the roll on his private parade, and in
"the absence of his officers to inspect his company and report accordingly the
"state of said company to Captain McVeagh, or in his absence the officer
"commanding.

"Any sergeant giving in a false report of his division or company, on proper
"investigation, to be broke.

"The commanding officer is determined to assist and support in the most pe-
"remptory and effectual manner the officers and non-commissioned officers in the
"corps in their endeavours and exertions in having the foregoing rules and
"regulations enforced; and he expects the officers will attend parades as often
"as is in their power; and that the non-commissioned officers will by their cleanly
"and soldierlike appearance, show a proper example to the privates in their
"respective companies; and as an encouragement to discipline and correct conduct,
"such privates as are uniformly most attentive to their duty as a soldier, will meet
"a decided preference in being promoted.

GOD SAVE THE KING."

Regulations similar in their tendency, were adopted by most of the
yeomanry corps of the kingdom. In a few places in the south of Ireland,
an attempt was made by Lieut. Colonel Auriol, then acting as an Inspecting
Brigade Major, and whose sentiments were pro Romish, to crush the
Orange Yeomanry, and to supplant them, if possible, by the enrolment
of Roman Catholics. His Grace the Duke of Richmond was, at the time,
the Irish Viceroy, and Sir Edward Baker Littlehales, Bart., the Irish
Secretary. Major Auriol's first attempt was made at a place called Kilmeen, in the County of Cork. The yeomanry at this place were commanded
by a Captain Gilman, a weak-minded but well intentioned gentleman.
Captain Gilman was induced by Major Auriol, to apply for an augmentation of his corps, which, up to this period, had been Loyal and Protestant.
Through the interference of the Inspecting Field Officer, the augmentation

was granted; and Captain Gilman, in return for Major Auriol's kindness, enrolled the disaffected Roman Catholics in the neighbourhood of Kilmeen, in the augmentation granted to his corps. As many of the persons so enrolled, were openly disaffected to the Government, and had been violent partizans in the serious disturbances, the Loyal Yeomanry of Bandon, Bantry, Ballyaneen, Carrbery, Macroom, and other parts of the county, refused to serve with them. Though this course might be deemed indiscreet, it was certainly not surprising. At the present day, few persons would marvel, did the European Regiments now serving in India, refuse to act with the Sepoys engaged in the massacre of Delhi or Cawnpore, were those same Sepoys taken into British pay, and added as an augmentation to some British Battalion. Precisely analagous was the augmentation made by Major Anorial to the Kilmeen Yeomanry. This act of augmentation excited the liveliest feelings of indignation in the breasts of the Loyal Yeomanry of Cork, and in every part of that great county, the name of Auriol was held in reproach and detestation. Major Auriol having so far succeeded with Captain Gilman, next applied himself to the Earl of Bandon, the commandant of the "*Bandon Legion*," which included three corps. The idea of admitting the disaffected into their ranks, was, of course, out of the question; and all the gallant Major could do, was to induce their noble commandant, to recommend the "*Legion*" to dispense with the usual display, (an Orange lily,) which each man wore in his cap, at the annual parade on the 1st of July. This course, on the suggestion of the Inspecting Field Officer, Lord Bandon recommended. The result of this tampering with the feelings of the brave and high spirited men, enrolled in these corps, will be best told, by giving their own "Declaration" in their own words, and by adding to it, Major Auriol's equivocations and explanations, as conveyed in his official correspondence with the Irish Secretary.

"*Declaration of 600 of the Bandon Yeomanry, for the cause of laying down*
"*their Arms on the 6th day of July,* 1809.

" We, the members comprising the *Bandon Boyne, Boyne Union* and *True Blue* " corps of yeomanry, under the denomination of the ' *Loyal Bandon Legion,*' " having seen in a late publication a false and erroneous statement of our conduct " on a recent occasion, feel it our duty as well to satisfy the public mind as to " prevent a recurrence of similar evils, and vindicate our character, openly to " declare to our countrymen, the multitude of our brethren, and the world at " large, the sacred cause for which the Bandon Yeomanry laid down their arms. " On the 6th day of July, being the first parade after the anniversary of the " ever memorable FIRST OF JULY, we were ordered for inspection by Colonel " Auriol, our Brigade Major. The corps appeared on their respective parades, " wearing that simple, though grand characteristic of loyalty in their caps, an " ORANGE LILY. On all former occasions, Colonel Auriol, in common with his " predecessors bestowed the greatest praise on the Legion for its high state of

"discipline and military appearance, but he now entirely altered his tone, rep-
"resenting in the most insulting terms, and in the most degrading, reproachful,
"and mortifying language, the wearing of that lily ; telling us it was only a badge
"of cowardice, crying down the Revolution, under the degrading appellation of
"our forefathers having beaten a few unfortunate men, over an hundred years ago,
"accusing us of wanting to trample on them again, and declaring that although
"we wore that insignia in our caps, we may have the *United Irishman's Oath* in
"our pockets—that it was not safe to go into the field with such men. When he
"had thus given vent to every thing that had a tendency to inflame and irritate,
"he declared we must either take down that lily, or lay down our Arms—which
"latter command we instantly obeyed. Was this the treatment which our steady
"services called for? Were officers afraid to venture themselves with us when
"our offer of service was tendered and accepted to any part of the kingdom, in
"case of invasion or rebellion? Can such conduct be defended? To heap charges
"upon men who proudly defy both friends and enemies to select an instance,
"wherein not to say a rebel, but even a suspected person was ever found among
"our ranks—perhaps we have remained silent too long. Are not our feelings to
"be respected as well as others? Incapable of fear, but fully capable of loyal
"love, we openly declare our sentiments as *Protestants* and *Orangemen*, that we
"will faithfully support and defend His Majesty, King George the Third, his
"crown and dignity, the laws and constitution of these kingdoms, as delivered to
"us by our glorious Deliverer King William the Third of immortal memory ; and
"we further declare, that we will not serve as yeomen under any officer or
"officers, who are either afraid or ashamed to wear an ORANGE LILY on our grand
"festival, at the head of our true-hearted columns. And we defy any man, or
"numbers of men, to contradict our assertion of this our public declaration.

"Signed by order, and on behalf of the "*Bandon Legion*," July 24, 1809.

"F. M'DONALD,   *Bandon Boyne,*
"RICHARD BAYLEY,   *Bandon Union,*
"SIL. SULLIVAN,   *Bandon True Blues.*"

Such were the sentiments expressed by these noble-hearted men upon
that trying occasion. Here were men charged, with what? With the
treble crime of *cowardice, perjury,* and *treason!* And for what? For no
other crime, (if crime it must be called,) than that of placing an Orange
lily in their caps—a practice which they had followed up, without reproach
or remark, from their first enrolment.   The lily was expressly declared by
the Inspecting Major of Brigade, as "*a badge of cowardice* ;" the wearers
of it were told that "*although they wore the insignia in their caps, they
might have the United Irishman's Oath in their pockets,*" and that "*it was
not safe to go into the field with such men!*" And all this too, though every
man of the six hundred, had voluntarily sworn, *that he was not nor ever
would be, a member of the Society of United Irishmen, nor of any other
Society or body of men, that are enemies to His Majesty and our Glorious
Constitution.* Surely if ever a public servant of the crown, deserved dis-

missal, Colonel Auriol was that man.   But however bad his conduct, he must be allowed to speak for himself.   The following are copies of his correspondence with the Government in reference to this matter.

"From Brigade-Major Ancrial to Sir E. B. Littlehales, Bart., reporting the "misconduct of the Bandon Yeomanry.

"Bandon, July 8th, 1809.

"Sir,—It is with regret I have to request you will lay before His Grace the "Lord Lieutenant, the following unpleasant circumstance which has occurred "with the "*Bandon Loyal Legion.*" They had always made a parade business "with great rejoicing every 1st of July, which party distinction Lord Bandon as "well as myself, wished to have stopped, therefore I determined not to inspect "the corps on that day.   But the officer in command, Capt. Kingston, ordered a "parade for exercise, from which they were ordered to march to their separate "company parades and dismiss, instead of which they were marching up the town "in column to parade as usual, which the Earl of Bandon, who was himself in the "field, observing, immediately rode to the head of the column, ordered them to "halt, which they obeyed, and counter-march to their private parades, where they "were dismissed, when it was naturally hoped all was settled.   But in the middle "of the night some person fired a ball into one of Captain Kingston's upper "windows, which went through the bed where a lady of his family was sleeping. "Large rewards were offered in vain to discover the culprit, and on Thursday the "5th instant, as usual, I ordered the parade for inspection, when I was sorry to "find the whole "*legion,*" with few exceptions in the infantry, all in the most "disordered state.   Contrary to any former usage, they paraded with orange "lilies in their caps, and instead of promoting any attempt to discover who had "fired into the window, they meant the badge to insinuate they would oppose "inquiry.   The Earl of Bandon, who has ever felt interested in the good conduct "and credit of the corps, used all his eloquence to persuade them to be obedient "to their officers and to take out their lilies, but in vain.   It was great presump- "tion in me, when his Lordship had failed, to make any attempt ; however, I used "every argument I could command, to bring them to their senses, but they re- "fused to be commanded by any except Orangemen, and would sooner lay down "their arms than their lilies.   Finding all attempts to make them orderly in vain, "and to prevent anything more unpleasant happening, I recommended, with the "approbation of the Earl of Bandon, that they should give up their arms by the "roll of the corps.   I therefore requested Captain Bettsworth, who commanded "the artillery, to send his cars to receive their arms and lodge them in the "artillery stores, where they now are.   Some absentees have since sent in theirs, "and I now take the first post to acquaint you of this unpleasant event, and to "request you will let me know what his Grace the Lord Lieutenant would wish "me to do.   I am the more distressed at this misconduct, because I ever considered "this corps as far superior to any yeomen I had ever seen.   The cavalry alone "remain uncontaminated.

"I have, &c.

C. Ancrial, late B. M. Y

" *From Lord Bandon, respecting Captain Evanson's resignation.*

" Castle Bernard, July 29th, 1810.

" MY DEAR SIR,—To my great surprise, after I had sent my letter of this
" morning's date to you, through the Bandon post-office, I most unexpectedly
" received Mr. Evanson's resignation. My letter of this morning you will therefore
" have the goodness not to notice as far as respects him ; of course I request he
" may not be gazetted.

" I have, &c.

(Signed)   " BANDON.

" *From Lord Bandon, relative to Bandon Legion Officers.*

" Castle Bernard, Aug 14th, 1810.

" MY DEAR SIR,—I beg leave to send you the names of three officers to complete
" the number necessary for the Bandon Legion ; there are two new lieutenants of
" cavalry in consequence of the promotion of Robert Sealy and John Sivets,
" Esqrs., to the command of companies.

" I have &c.

(Signed)   " BANDON.

" Bandon Legion ; 2nd company (or Union.) John Sivets, Esq. to be Captain,
" from the Bandon Legion Cavalry.

Cavalry.

" John Beamish, Esq., to be 1st Lieutenant, vice Sealy promoted in the Infantry.

" James Allman, Esq.. to be 2nd Lieutenant, vice Swete, promoted in the
" Infantry.

" *From Brigade-Major Anorial to Sir E. B. Littlehales, Bart., relative to Capt.*
" *Connor's conduct towards him.*

" Bandon, Aug. 10th, 1809.

" On my return home from Bantry last inspection, the 12th ult., I stated to you
" the conduct of the Captain, &c. of the Ballyaneen corps ; not having any answer,
" I fear my letter may have miscarried, and as I wish to conduct myself on all
" occasions strictly according to the wishes of his Grace the Lord Lieutenant, I
" am induced once more to call your attention to the following circumstance, and
" to request you will be pleased to obtain me his Grace's orders how to conduct
" myself. Captain Connor, commanding the Ballyaneen Yeomanry is a most
" violent Orangeman, and had on the 1st of July marched his corps into Bandon
" to parade with the Bandon corps. I was absent from Bandon on that day ; on
" Monday the 10th I inspected the Ballyaneen, who were always in the habit of
" receiving me with presented arms, but this day paid me no more attention than
" if I had been a common traveller ; however I am perfectly indifferent about
" receiving any compliment. only as I bear His Majesty's commission as a lieu-
" tenant-colonel I feel I am bound to support the rank, therefore should wish to
" know his Grace the Lord Lieutenant's pleasure how I am to conduct myself ;
" and more particularly when he is informed, that notwithstanding Captain Connor
" knew the unpleasant circumstances which took place in Bandon on the 6th of
" July, yet me on the 10th not only paraded all his corps in orange lilies, but wore

" one himself; and again on the 12th he marched past me on my return from
" Bantry with lilies, &c., as before; and although I conceive it a great misfortune
" to keep alive all or any party distinction, yet I should be sorry to interfere
" without authority so to do; but I own I foresee great risk in unpleasant disputes
" between these yeomen who are Orangemen and those who are Catholics, par-
" ticularly when they meet in the same field for exercise; and indeed in the Kilmeen
" corps, some had lilies and some had not. The only cause Captain Connor has
" for taking this decided part is because he is inimical to Captain Gilman, of the
" Kilmeen, whose augmentation he used every argument with me to reject as
" rebels, so he calls them. I took infinite pains to learn all particulars, and knew
" I could well depend on the Rev. Mr. Kenny, who had once commanded that
" corps, and lives at Kilmeen; he convinced me of the prejudice of Captain
" Connor, who is on bad terms, I believe I may say, with every gentleman round
" him; his first objection to meet the other corps, you may remember, was because
" Mr. Spears was lieutenant in the East Carbery; on his resignation I proposed
" his joining the other three corps who meet at Ballyaneen, but on his coming into
" the field he began a long and endless argument about the Kilmeen augmentation,
" which to avoid I ordered the other corps to exercise as usual. It would be too
" tedious to give you all particulars, but I will be obliged to you to send me
" directions how I shall conduct myself, if to discourage or take no notice what-
" ever of the Orange distinction.

" I have, &c.

" C. ANORIAL, Lt.-Col. B. M. Y.

It is not necessary to say, that Colonel Anorial was not insulted or despised because he was the Inspecting Brigade Major of Yeomanry; that no offence was offered to him on account of his official rank or position, but simply the officers and men—for all, with two or three exceptions, joined—the independent Gentlemen and Yeomanry of the County, flung back in the face of their calumniator, the gratuitous insults he had offered them. The best answer to the calumnies of this man, is the fact, that upon official enquiry into all the circumstances, the Bandon Yeomanry were restored, and their Brigade Major removed. This however, was not effected, till after strong remonstrances from the Right Honorable the Grand Master, and other distinguished members of the Order.

CHAPTER XXXVII.

Special meeting of the Grand Lodge of Ireland, and admirable address of that
Body.—Orange difficulties in Belfast and Tyrone.—Second meeting and address
of the Grand Lodge.—Dying Legacy "of the Grand Master."—Death of
Mr. Ogle and eulogy to his memory.

The calumnies heaped upon the Society at this period, the injuries
inflicted upon many of its members, and the insults offered to all, induced
the Grand Master, the Right Honorable Mr. Ogle, M.P. to call a special
meeting of the Grand Lodge to consider these matters.   From this meeting
emanated the following admirable address, conveying sentiments of political wisdom and philosophy, which, even at this distant day, ought not to
be lost to Orangemen.   The views of the Grand Lodge are as eloquently
as ably expressed ; and the vigor and genius of Mr. Ogle's pen is clearly
traceable throughout the composition.

" The Grand Lodge, to the Orangemen of Ireland.

" BRETHREN,—Many communications have been lately made from different
" Districts, calling upon the Grand Orange Lodge for advice and direction, in
" consequence of transactions deeply involving as well the honor of the Orange
" Institution, as the tranquillity of the Country.

" The Grand Orange Lodge have, in many instances, addressed to the particular
" Districts from which these communications have been received, such advice
" and direction as appeared to them most likely to sustain those two great objects,
" the honour of the Institution and the tranquillity of Ireland.   But the demands
" upon their attention have at length become so numerous, that it is now thought
" expedient to combine in one general view the sentiments which they have
" hitherto, in particular cases, laboured to inculcate.

" In doing this, they wish in the first place to impress upon every brother the
" recollection of the first and leading principle under which we have voluntarily
" associated—the principle is, firm and unmixed loyalty to our Sovereign, and to
" the Constitution in Church and State, a loyalty not adapted for party purposes
" not shaped and moulded to the taste of one or other set of Ministers, not a
" loyalty of sale and barter for power or privilege, to be offered as a bribe or
" withdrawn in menace—but a steady, unchanged, and unchangeable sentiment,
" founded on the principles of the Constitution, as fixed at the glorious Revolution,
" and impressed still more deeply in our hearts by the personal virtues of our
" beloved Sovereign, the friend and father of his people.   Keeping this great
" sentiment steadily in our recollection, our conduct can never want a certain and
" unerring guide, and where it operates a dignified obedience to the laws of the

"land will ever distinguish Orangemen, and secure to them in return the support
"and protection of those laws.

"Whether it be owing to a preconcerted design, or be but the necessary result
"of the torrent of libels against our Institution, which even our patient contempt
"does not appear to have exhausted, or whether both may not have contributed,
"it is unnecessary to enquire, but it is obvious, that a very general attack has
"lately been directed, not merely against our principles, but against the persons
"of Orangemen, and their right of association. In one instance an ignorant
"magistrate has had the folly to menace our brethren with an abuse of his autho-
"rity, by an attempt to disturb their assemblies—in another instance, a perversion
"of military power deprived his Majesty of the service of six hundred Loyal
"Orangemen, by a combination of insult and absurdity, and the seditious news-
"papers having extolled these preliminary attacks, so consonant to the feelings
"and purposes of their editors; the worst passions of the ignorant or disaffected
"have been in consequence excited and encouraged to such acts of outrage as we
'must ever deplore, since they have deprived of life some of our most estimable
"brethren. In all these cases we have exhorted, and do still exhort Orangemen
"to look for redress *only* to the laws of the land—by these laws it will be always
"afforded, and it is by this demeanour that Orangemen will be honourably distin-
"guished from their misled and infatuated adversaries, whose object is the
"destruction of those laws and of the constitution, by which all his Majesty's
"subjects are equally protected.

"Of the persons who have committed the outrages to which we have alluded,
"we forbear to speak more particularly, they are already in the hands of the law
"and we seek not to raise a prejudice against them. But we cannot too deeply
"impress upon our brethren this truth, that the moment any Orangeman departs
"so far from the principles of our Association, as to infringe the tranquillity of
"his country, in that moment he reduces himself to the level of the lowest of his
"adversaries, with the additional disgrace of having deserted his principles. Of
"such conduct we trust that no brother will be guilty, but that however irritated
"he may feel by calumnies, however exposed to insult, he will respect even in
"the lowest officer of the crown the authority with which that officer is invested—
"any abuse of that authority will be subjected to legal punishment, but the
"authority must in the first instance be obeyed. In the selection of his servants
"our Sovereign may be deceived, they may be the tools of party or the agents
"of faction—the slaves of one, or the partisans of another administration; to us,
"as Orangemen, it will be indifferent by whom the power of the State is exercised,
"so it be employed to the service of the State. Those Governors who appear to
"act upon the first principles of the Constitution, shall receive our obedience,
"approbation and support; if, unhappily, men of a different description be placed
"in office, they would, while in office, receive as men put in authority by our
"Sovereign, the obedience which is due to those deputed by him. However we
"might regret an imposition upon his goodness, our loyalty would direct us to
"respect his servants.

"In no circumstance let this loyalty be forgotten, let no instances of official
"folly, no appearance of slight, no effusion of dummy affect this principle;

"let us, if called upon, (and when danger is at hand, we shall, as heretofore, be
"called upon) prove ourselves still unabated in our zeal, unaltered in our senti-
"ments, and let us hold ourselves ever ready to come forward, the cheerful and
"voluntary champions of that Constitution which placed the House of Hanover
"upon the Throne, and which was achieved by the genius and virtues of the
"immortal KING WILLIAM.

"By such conduct shall the calumnies thrown out against our Institution be
"retorted upon their inventors, and our principles, (which to be approved, only
"require to be known,) must receive, even from our enemies, the involuntary
"tribute of their respect.
                    "Signed by order of the Grand Lodge,
                                    "JOHN BROOKE,
                    "Secretary, Grand Orange Lodge, Ireland."

This admirable address was attended with the happiest effects. The
Orangemen throughout the kingdom, openly responded to the call to duty
and to honor, made upon them by the Grand Lodge. In the neighbourhood of Belfast only, were any symptons of disaffection openly evinced ;
and even there, and in Tyrone, (where the seeds of treason were reported
to have been scattered,) the rebelliously inclined chaff, was speedily sifted
from the wheat, and the grains of pure loyalty, one by one, deserted the
spurious weeds, by which they had well nigh been smothered, and sought
refuge again in the garden of British connexion. The reports from
Belfast and Tyrone, induced the Right Honourable the Grand Master to
call a special meeting of the Grand Lodge. The result of the deliberations
of this meeting was the adoption of the following address, which was an
emanation from the same pen that had traced the last preceding one.

"THE GRAND ORANGE LODGE OF IRELAND

" To the several Provincial, District, and County Lodges thereof.

"DEAR FRIENDS AND BELOVED BRETHREN,—WITH feelings of the most poignant
"sorrow and deep regret, but with hearts most truly affectionate, the GRAND
"ORANGE LODGE OF IRELAND addresses every individual of you. How different
"must this be from all our former Addresses ! Hitherto our delightful task has
"been, to advise and cheer you in the path of Loyalty and Honour ; or to applaud
"your faithful conduct in maintaining our happy Constitution, by setting a bright
"example of virtuous obedience to the Laws, and resisting every seditious attempt
"to infringe them.

"From our first institution to the present hour, you have been the firm pillar
"and strong support of the PROTESTANT CAUSE. No circumstance of danger—no
"artifice of sedition—no effusion of slander—has been able to shake your Loyalty,
"or to cause you to swerve from the Fidelity which you have sworn to your KING,
"or the Duty you owe your COUNTRY.—When a great part of Ireland was in
"rebellion—when it was invaded by foreign enemies—and when you yourselves
"were maligned, under the name of 'unlawful Associations'—still your principles
"remained unchanged ; still your conduct was so truly loyal, as to put to silence

" and to shame your adversaries.—When for two years the great and vital question
" of Union was under discussion, the Grand Lodge, vigilant and anxious for your
" safety and your honour, addressed you in circular letters, warning you of snares
" which crafty men were laying to entrap you into party; reminding you, that
" our GLORIOUS ORDER was no farther concerned in politics, than as bound by our
" engagements and our duty to support the Illustrious Family on the Throne, and
" the Constitution in Church and State, as settled by the immortal King WILLIAM,
" Prince of Orange : that, therefore, as ORANGEMEN, you had no right to interfere
" in the question then under discussion ; but as Freemen in Corporations, as
" Freeholders in Counties, and as individual Loyal Subjects of the KING, you had
" an unquestionable right to present your petitions, and to declare your sentiments,
" to every branch of the Legislature ; a right coeval with Liberty, and confirmed
" by the Bill of Rights—a law of our great Deliverer. Satisfied with this reason-
" ing, and acquiescing in the opinions of the Grand Lodge, the Members of the
" Order throughout all Ireland refused, as Orangemen, to make any declaration on
" the great question then before Parliament; but in their several capacities as
" Freemen, Freeholders, or Individuals, as they were lawfully warranted, they
" honestly declared their opinions.—How wise, how honourable, how constitutional
" was this conduct; but, alas! how different from that which some, whom we trust
" will be found impostors in the disguise of Orangemen, have been represented to
" us as having pursued, upon a very inferior occasion—conduct which, while we
" deplore, we blush to recite.

   " It has been represented to the Grand Lodge, that certain persons, pretending
" to be Orangemen, (or perhaps ignorant and unprincipled persons who had crept
" into our Order,) having joined the seditious rabble of Belfast, have broke out
" into most unbecoming conduct, and unwarrantable declarations, on the subject
" of the Corn Laws; that they have marched in procession towards that den of
" treason and of shame, at Cave Hill, where heretofore were celebrated, by the
" most abandoned traitors, the orgies of the French Rebellion; that, marching
" thither, they had entwined the sacred Emblem of our Liberty, the Orange
" Colours, with the Green Ensign of Rebellion; that there they had buried them
" together—thus pretending to bury all animosity, and joining Orangemen with
" United Irishmen in array against the Government.

   " To bury animosity is most desirable. Bless them that curse you, and pray
" for them that despitefully use you and persecute you, are truly Christian
" doctrines; but who are the wolves in sheep's clothing who pretend to teach
" them? and for what purpose? Are they not the very people who so lately
" insulted your Institution, and persecuted you for your lives? And is not their
" purpose, by enticing you into their snares, to delude you from your Fidelity—to
" expose you to the danger of the Law, to the ridicule of your enemies, and to
" the contempt of every Loyal Man? What will your betrayers say, if you swerve
" from your integrity?—*Orangemen, notwithstanding their high pretences, can be
" made Rebels; and, for a morsel of bread, they who swore to dedicate their lives
" and property to the support of the Constitution, may, in violation of the most
" solemn engagement, be set against the Government!* What malicious merriment

"will it afford to your hypocritical seducers to reflect, that all which arms, or
"slander, could not effect, may be produced by a little artifice!

"We call upon all Masters and Officers of Lodges, and upon every individual
"of our GLORIOUS ORDER: we adjure them, as they regard our Holy Religion, as
"they tender the sacred obligation of an Oath, as they love and honour our ven-
"erable SOVEREIGN, and as they prize our inestimable Constitution, to set their
"hearts and minds, their conduct and their countenance, against the disgraceful
"proceedings which have been represented to the Grand Lodge.

"We advise you Brethren, to assemble your different Lodges—to make strict
"enquiry whether the report which we have heard be founded in truth—whether
"they were not impostors who appeared as Orangemen with the seditious rabble
"of Belfast; and if it be found but too true, that any Orangeman has acted in a
"manner so unworthy, let that person be summoned before his Lodge: if it appear
"that he was deluded, let strict enquiry be made from whom the delusion pro-
"ceeded; if the Orangeman shew contrition, it will be for the Lodge to receive
"him again; but if it were possible that a whole Lodge be found corrupt, you
"will expel that Lodge, or any number of individuals who may be found seditious,
"and return the Numbers and Names to the Grand Lodge of Ireland, that they
"may be *for ever struck from the catalogue of the Loyal.*—A new prospect opens
"in Europe— we may again be called to the defence of our SOVEREIGN, our
"RELIGION, our CONSTITUTION, and all which we hold dear. Orangemen must not
"swerve from the principles on which they were formed; they must exist as
"faithful Loyalists, or they cannot exist at all.

"With our best wishes and most earnest prayers for your Honour and Prosperity,
"we subscribe ourselves, beloved Brethren and dear Friends,

"Your faithful Servants,

"GEORGE OGLE, Grand Master.
"JOHN GIFFARD, Deputy Grand Master.
"RICHARD MUSGRAVE, Grand Treasurer.
"WILLIAM TURNER, Acting Grand Secretary.
"L. LUTE, Secretary to the Grand Lodge of Ireland."

The preceding Address is supposed to have been the last paper written by
the Grand Master; and may therefore be taken as the "*dying LEGACY.*"
bequeathed by that Right Honourable and noble hearted Brother, to his
associates throughout the whole Order. Mr. Verner was the first Grand
Master of Ireland; Mr. Ogle the second. The first, full of years and of
honors, yet survives; but the other has long since been called to his final
account. The death of Mr. Ogle left a vacancy in the Grand Mastership
which it was found difficult to fill. The writer of these lines remembers
well, when yet a little boy, attending the funeral of that great and good
man, to the Family Tomb, at Ballycanow, in the County of Wexford—he
yet remembers the long line of carriages that filled the road-way upon
that mournful occasion—his memory is carried back to the thousands of
pedestrians who then crowded the grave-yard and lined the streets of the
little village of Ballycanow—but above all there is vividly impressed upon

his recollection, the craped bands, which were that day borne upon the scarlet-clad arms of the whole Yeomanry of the County, who upon that occasion attended to pay the last tribute of their respect to one whom they had so long loved and admired—whose able pen had defended them in the press—whose eloquent tongue had been their Parliamentary shield —whose generous heart was ever open to the complaints of the afflicted— whose purse-strings were never drawn against the claims of charity—who, through a lengthened career of public service, never betrayed his country to party—who disdained to barter his personal independence to faction— and who died poor in pelf, but rich in honor. This much, at least, is due by an Orange Historian, to the memory of his departed Chief.

CHAPTER XXXVIII.

Government discontinues the annual procession around the Statue of King William—meeting of the Grand Lodge in 1811, and Address from that Body- Orangeism defended by the Marquis of Huntley, Lords Yarmouth, Kirkwall and Lowther, and Mr. McNaughten—"Faulkner's Dublin Journal" in 1813— Declaration of the Orangemen of Down—Resolutions of the Orangemen of Cavan—proceedings of the Antrim Orangemen—ditto of Londonderry—changes in the Rules and Regulations.

From 1809 to 1813, a continued series of attacks upon Orangeism, appears to have been indulged in ; every receptacle of calumny seems to have been resorted to, to traduce them ; and the pro-Romish and Radical Press, was weekly stuffed with the bitterest tirades against the Society. The Government of Ireland, so far yielded to the outward pressure as to discontinue the annual procession, around the equestrian statue of King William, erected in College Green, in the City of Dublin. At the meeting of the Grand Lodge, held in June 1811, the subject was brought formally under the notice of that body, by the Grand Treasurer, Sir Richard Mus-grave, Bart., who concluded by moving the following Address to the Brethren. Mr. Giffard, Mr. Gowan, Mr. Cottingham, and other gentle-men, addressed the Grand Lodge in eloquent speeches, after which the address was adopted. It is as follows :

" DUBLIN, 27th June, 1811.

" *To the Orange Lodges of Ireland.*

" FRIENDS AND BROTHERS,—The Grand Lodge has heard with much anxiety and " regret, that a possibility exists of some commotion taking place in consequence

"of your annual celebrations. To men whose principles, whose honour, and
" whose oath, bind them to the strictest and purest loyalty, it were unnecessary to
" offer advice, had not the torrents of calumny which have been directed against
" our character and institution, naturally tended to excite irritations and resent-
" ment Those calumnies have spread from their source, the Popish Committee
" in Dublin, to the remotest corners of the British Isles, but we are happy to find
" they have had no other effect than to render their authors odious and contemptible.
" If we are calumniated, it is in common with the memory of our forefathers, and
" our great defender, King William, who established our happy Constitution—if
" we are calumniated, it is in common with the family of our revered and beloved
" Sovereign, with those who govern under him, with the amiable Duke of Rich-
" mond—in a word, with every loyal Protestant subject. Let us then, pitying
" and forgiving our maligners, who know not the Christian purity of our principles,
" act as the Government has done—with patience and good temper ; let no part
" of our conduct justify the reproaches which are daily cast upon us. The
" Government, in the spirit of conciliation, some time ago discontinued the annual
" procession round the Statue of our Deliverer—let us imitate so generous an
" example, let nothing insulting on our side appear, and above all, let the most
" implicit obedience be paid to those whom our Sovereign has put in authority
" over us. If thus acting we cannot avoid insult, let us not think of repelling
" force by force, but let us appeal to the laws of our country for redress.

" To such subjects as the Loyal Orangemen of Ireland, we have said, this Address
" is scarcely necessary ; but the anxiety of the Grand Lodge to preserve and
" perpetuate the high and honourable character which our Institution maintains
" and we trust will ever maintain amongst patriotic, good, and virtuous men, will
" apologize for the advice which we now give in the sincere spirit of friendship
" and brotherhood.

" Signed on behalf of the Grand Lodge now assembled,

" JOHN GIFFARD, Deputy Grand Master.
" RICHARD MUSGRAVE, Grand Treasurer,
" J. K MANNING, Secretary, Grand Lodge."

The incessant attacks indulged in against the Society in Ireland, for the
last few years, may be said to have culminated in 1813, in which year a
most violent assault was made upon the whole body, in Parliament. But
though deserted by many—and especially by Lord Castlereagh—who should
have been foremost in its defence, the Society was not left without able
and vigilant advocates. The Marquis of Huntley, the Earl of Yarmouth,
Lord Kirkwall, Lord Kenyon, Lord Lowther, the Honorable John O'Neill,
and Mr. McNaughten, came out boldly in its defence, and gave to the
Legislature a most ample vindication of the principles, the utility, and the
patriotism of the Institution. For the great energy and eloquence displayed by Mr. McNaughten upon that occasion, he received votes of thanks
from various Orange bodies ; amongst others, the following Address from
the Orangemen of Dunluce, in the County of Antrim, which is here
copied from " *Faulkner's Dublin Journal*," of the 14th of August, 1813.

"*To Edmd. Alex. McNaughten, Esq.*

"SIR,—Be so good as to accept our most sincere and heartfelt thanks, for your
" manly and spirited defence in Parliament of the Orangemen of Ireland.

"In this period of new opinions, when so many refuse to see the danger of a
" *Delegated Assembly*, endeavouring, by their speeches and resolutions, to spread
" disaffection, usurping the forms of Parliament, to vilify and traduce it, and
" soliciting foreign aid to enable them to establish in the state a permanent foreign
" influence—an influence that would possess an absolute control over a great
" proportion of the physical force of the nation ;—but are extremely jealous, and
" even afraid, lest any portion of His Majesty's subjects, confiding in each other,
" and in the justice of their cause, the support of His Majesty's Throne, and the
" ancient and venerable Constitution of their country, should associate for securing
" these important objects :—When the consequences of such a perverted order of
" things threaten us, we cannot but be sensible of the value and importance of
" having men like you in Parliament and in high situations.

" We do not, however, despond : the principles which have guided your Parlia-
" mentary conduct are rapidly gaining ground, and will at length prevail and re-
" establish the peace and security of the nation. The day is not far distant when
" the Government, if it scorn to chastise those who publicly celebrate the
" anniversary of the *French Revolution*, the parent of more and of greater crimes
" and cruelties than ever sprung from any other event in the annals of the world,
" will also not refuse protection to those meeting to commemorate with loyal hearts,
" that glorious character, William III., under whose auspices our liberties and
" independence have been fixed, on a basis which, we trust, time can never shake.

" With every sentiment of the highest respect and regard, we have the honour
" to be, Sir, your greatly obliged, and faithful servants, for ourselves and our
" respective Lodges, in the district of Upper and Lower Dunluce.

" ROBERT COLVIN, M. 1187.	GEO. DAVIDSON, M. 749.
" JAMES TWADEL, M. 1196.	J. CUNNINGHAM, M. Disp.
" SAMUEL NICKEL, M. 1197.	ALEX. WILSON, M. 914.
" JOHN M'CURDY, M. Disp.	JAMES ROBINSON, M. 1072.
" CHAS. M'KENZIE, M. Disp.	ALEX. M'ALESTER, M.
" ALEX. M'CONAGHY, M. 528.	

" *Answer.*

" Beardeville, Aug. 7th, 1813.

" GENTLEMEN.—I beg to return you my very sincere thanks for the honour you
" have done me, in noticing my late conduct in the House of Commons, when the
" Orangemen of Ireland were the subject of debate there. I felt it to be nothing
" more than my duty, to bear testimony, to the loyalty of so respectable a body
" of His Majesty's subjects, many of whom are among my late constituents. I
" have the honour to remain, Gentlemen, your very faithful humble servant.

" EDMD. ALEX. McNAUGHTEN."

In various parts of the Kingdom, the Orangemen of Ireland found it
necessary, to step forward and vindicate their principles, against the
torrents of systematic abuse and misrepresentation, to which, they were at

that time exposed. The following admirable *exposé* of Orange principles, is selected from the numerous resolutions and addresses, at that time adopted by many of the Lodges.

" *Declaration of the Orangemen of the County of Down.*

" We, the Orangemen of the County of Down, feel it a duty to our country and " ourselves at the present crisis, to make this public avowal of the causes that led " to, and the principles which actuated our Association.

" In the years immediately preceding the Rebellion of 1798, when numerous " and active conspirators were organizing treason, the danger of our country " aroused those principles of our forefathers, which had slumbered in our breasts " since the Revolution ; and the loyal Protestants of the North, resolved to support " the laws, and to defend with all their power, the Government and Religion their " ancestors had bled to establish. And in order the more effectually to resist the " machinations of *combined* traitors, to expose their designs, and to protect the " wavering, or the weak, from their arts and intimidations, they formed an *Asso-* " *ciation*, secured from the intrusion of the disaffected by precautionary signs, and " bound by solemn obligations, to loyalty and to mutual assistance in the active " maintenance of the Constitution of their country, as established at the glorious " Revolution, under the happy auspices of King William the Third, Prince of " Orange.

" The well-affected hailed the Institution with joy, and pressed forward in " great numbers to join its standard, becoming throughout the kingdom the watch- " ful sentinels of Government, and the active assistants of the laws. And when " Rebellion was (through the blessing of Divine Providence) subdued, we feel an " honest pride in the conviction, that the Orangemen, by their humble, yet zealous " exertions, aided the Government in no slight degree, towards its speedy extinction.

" About that period, when, as at present, we were assailed by every species of " calumny that the malice of *disappointed treason* could invent and disseminate, " we unanimously adopted and published the following declaration. ' We " solemnly declare in the presence of Almighty God, that the idea of injuring any " man on account of his religion never entered our heads, we regard every loyal " subject as our friend, be his religion what it may ; *we have no enemies but the* " *enemies of our country.*' To this declaration we now once more solemnly subscribe. " Our principles are unalterably the same, and deeply do we deplore the attempts " now so conspicuously made, to raise the cry of religious war in this land. How- " ever, when we know that treason is once more organizing in this kingdom— " when we behold the seditious poison daily issuing from the press—the State " and its venerable Religion reviled and condemned by *self-constituted inquisitors* " —when we mark the *pardoned conspirators* of the *late* Rebellion, fanning the " torch of discord into *fresh* flame—when the Government is braved—the laws " and their venerable guardians traduced, and our loyal Association attacked, " we cannot allow an ill-timed and false idea of liberality to suppress the expression " of our feelings, and prevent us from making this declaration of our confirmed " veneration for the glorious Constitution of this realm as established in Church " and State, and our determination, by a dutiful and active co-operation with the

CPSIA information can be obtained at www.ICGtesting.com
Printed in the USA
LVOW11s2048051113

360112LV00028B/1674/P